EK LOAN

DATA MINING
METHODS AND
MODELS

DATA MINING METHODS AND MODELS

DANIEL T. LAROSE
Department of Mathematical Sciences
Central Connecticut State University

WILEY-INTERSCIENCE

A JOHN WILEY & SONS, INC PUBLICATION

Published by John Wiley & Sons, Inc., Hoboken, New Jersey.
Published simultaneously in Canada.

For general information on our other products and services please contact our Customer Care Department
within the U.S. at 877-762-2974, outside the U.S. at 317-572-3993 or fax 317-572-4002.

Wiley also publishes its books in a variety of electronic formats. Some content that appears in print,
however, may not be available in electronic format. For more information about Wiley products, visit our
web site at www.wiley.com

Library of Congress Cataloging-in-Publication Data:

Larose, Daniel T.
    Data mining methods and models / Daniel T. Larose.
      p.   cm.
    Includes bibliographical references.
    ISBN-13 978-0-471-66656-1
    ISBN-10 0-471-66656-4 (cloth)
    1. Data mining.   I. Title.
    QA76.9.D343L378 2005
    005.74–dc22

                         2005010801

Printed in the United States of America

10 9 8 7 6 5 4 3 2 1

DEDICATION

To those who have gone before,
including my parents, Ernest Larose (1920–1981)
and Irene Larose (1924–2005),
and my daughter, Ellyriane Soleil Larose (1997–1997);

For those who come after,
including my daughters, Chantal Danielle Larose (1988)
and Ravel Renaissance Larose (1999),
and my son, Tristan Spring Larose (1999).

© Chantal Larose

CONTENTS

PREFACE

WHAT IS DATA MINING?

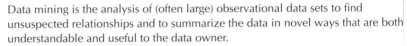

> Data mining is the analysis of (often large) observational data sets to find unsuspected relationships and to summarize the data in novel ways that are both understandable and useful to the data owner.
>
> —David Hand, Heikki Mannila, and Padhraic Smyth, *Principles of Data Mining*, MIT Press, Cambridge, MA, 2001

Data mining is predicted to be "one of the most revolutionary developments of the next decade," according to the online technology magazine *ZDNET News* (February 8, 2001). In fact, the *MIT Technology Review* chose data mining as one of 10 emerging technologies that will change the world.

Because data mining represents such an important field, Wiley-Interscience and I have teamed up to publish a new series on data mining, initially consisting of three volumes. The first volume in this series, *Discovering Knowledge in Data: An Introduction to Data Mining*, appeared in 2005 and introduced the reader to this rapidly growing field. The second volume in the series, *Data Mining Methods and Models*, explores the process of data mining from the point of view of *model building:* the development of complex and powerful predictive models that can deliver actionable results for a wide range of business and research problems.

WHY IS THIS BOOK NEEDED?

Data Mining Methods and Models continues the thrust of *Discovering Knowledge in Data*, providing the reader with:

- Models and techniques to uncover hidden nuggets of information
- Insight into how the data mining algorithms really work
- Experience of actually performing data mining on large data sets

"WHITE-BOX" APPROACH: UNDERSTANDING THE UNDERLYING ALGORITHMIC AND MODEL STRUCTURES

The best way to avoid costly errors stemming from a blind black-box approach to data mining is to instead apply a "white-box" methodology, which emphasizes an understanding of the algorithmic and statistical model structures underlying the software.

Data Mining Methods and Models applies the white-box approach by:

- Walking the reader through the various algorithms
- Providing examples of the operation of the algorithm on actual large data sets
- Testing the reader's level of understanding of the concepts and algorithms
- Providing an opportunity for the reader to do some real data mining on large data sets

Algorithm Walk-Throughs

Data Mining Methods and Models walks the reader through the operations and nuances of the various algorithms, using small sample data sets, so that the reader gets a true appreciation of what is really going on inside the algorithm. For example, in Chapter 2 we observe how a single new data value can seriously alter the model results. Also, in Chapter 6 we proceed step by step to find the optimal solution using the selection, crossover, and mutation operators.

Applications of the Algorithms and Models to Large Data Sets

Data Mining Methods and Models provides examples of the application of the various algorithms and models on actual large data sets. For example, in Chapter 3 we analytically unlock the relationship between nutrition rating and cereal content using a real-world data set. In Chapter 1 we apply principal components analysis to real-world census data about California. All data sets are available from the book series Web site: www.dataminingconsultant.com.

Chapter Exercises: Checking to Make Sure That You Understand It

Data Mining Methods and Models includes over 110 chapter exercises, which allow readers to assess their depth of understanding of the material, as well as having a little fun playing with numbers and data. These include Clarifying the Concept exercises, which help to clarify some of the more challenging concepts in data mining, and Working with the Data exercises, which challenge the reader to apply the particular data mining algorithm to a small data set and, step by step, to arrive at a computationally sound solution. For example, in Chapter 5 readers are asked to find the maximum a posteriori classification for the data set and network provided in the chapter.

Hands-on Analysis: Learn Data Mining by Doing Data Mining

Chapters 1 to 6 provide the reader with *hands-on analysis problems*, representing an opportunity for the reader to apply his or her newly acquired data mining expertise to solving real problems using large data sets. Many people learn by doing. *Data Mining Methods and Models* provides a framework by which the reader can learn data mining by doing data mining. For example, in Chapter 4 readers are challenged to approach a real-world credit approval classification data set, and construct their best possible logistic regression model using the methods learned in this chapter to provide strong interpretive support for the model, including explanations of derived and indicator variables.

Case Study: Bringing It All Together

Data Mining Methods and Models culminates in a detailed case study, Modeling Response to Direct Mail Marketing. Here the reader has the opportunity to see how everything that he or she has learned is brought all together to create actionable and profitable solutions. The case study includes over 50 pages of graphical, exploratory data analysis, predictive modeling, and customer profiling, and offers different solutions, depending on the requisites of the client. The models are evaluated using a custom-built cost/benefit table, reflecting the true costs of classification errors rather than the usual methods, such as overall error rate. Thus, the analyst can compare models using the estimated profit per customer contacted, and can predict how much money the models will earn based on the number of customers contacted.

DATA MINING AS A PROCESS

Data Mining Methods and Models continues the coverage of data mining as a process. The particular standard process used is the CRISP–DM framework: the Cross-Industry Standard Process for Data Mining. CRISP–DM demands that data mining be seen as an entire process, from communication of the business problem, through data collection and management, data preprocessing, model building, model evaluation, and finally, model deployment. Therefore, this book is not only for analysts and managers but also for data management professionals, database analysts, and decision makers.

SOFTWARE

The software used in this book includes the following:

- Clementine data mining software suite
- SPSS statistical software
- Minitab statistical software
- WEKA open-source data mining software

Clementine (`http://www.spss.com/clementine/`), one of the most widely used data mining software suites, is distributed by SPSS, whose base software is also used in this book. SPSS is available for download on a trial basis from their

Web site at www.spss.com. Minitab is an easy-to-use statistical software package, available for download on a trial basis from their Web site at www.minitab.com.

WEKA: Open-Source Alternative

The WEKA (Waikato Environment for Knowledge Analysis) machine learning workbench is open-source software issued under the GNU General Public License, which includes a collection of tools for completing many data mining tasks. *Data Mining Methods and Models* presents several hands-on, step-by-step tutorial examples using WEKA 3.4, along with input files available from the book's companion Web site www.dataminingconsultant.com. The reader is shown how to carry out the following types of analysis, using WEKA: logistic regression (Chapter 4), naive Bayes classification (Chapter 5), Bayesian networks classification (Chapter 5), and genetic algorithms (Chapter 6). For more information regarding Weka, see http://www.cs.waikato.ac.nz/~ml/. The author is deeply grateful to James Steck for providing these WEKA examples and exercises. James Steck (james_steck@comcast.net) served as graduate assistant to the author during the 2004–2005 academic year. He was one of the first students to complete the master of science in data mining from Central Connecticut State University in 2005 (GPA 4.0) and received the first data mining Graduate Academic Award. James lives with his wife and son in Issaquah, Washington.

COMPANION WEB SITE:
www.dataminingconsultant.com

The reader will find supporting materials for this book and for my other data mining books written for Wiley-Interscience, at the companion Web site, www.dataminingconsultant.com. There one may download the many data sets used in the book, so that the reader may develop a hands-on feeling for the analytic methods and models encountered throughout the book. Errata are also available, as is a comprehensive set of data mining resources, including links to data sets, data mining groups, and research papers.

However, the real power of the companion Web site is available to faculty adopters of the textbook, who have access to the following resources:

- Solutions to all the exercises, including the hands-on analyses
- Powerpoint presentations of each chapter, ready for deployment in the classroom
- Sample data mining course projects, written by the author for use in his own courses and ready to be adapted for your course
- Real-world data sets, to be used with the course projects
- Multiple-choice chapter quizzes
- Chapter-by-chapter Web resources

DATA MINING METHODS AND MODELS AS A TEXTBOOK

Data Mining Methods and Models naturally fits the role of textbook for an introductory course in data mining. Instructors will appreciate the following:

- The presentation of data mining as a *process*
- The white-box approach, emphasizing an understanding of the underlying algorithmic structures:

  Algorithm walk-throughs

  Application of the algorithms to large data sets

  Chapter exercises

  Hands-on analysis
- The logical presentation, flowing naturally from the CRISP–DM standard process and the set of data mining tasks
- The detailed case study, bringing together many of the lessons learned from both *Data Mining Methods and Models* and *Discovering Knowledge in Data*
- The companion Web site, providing the array of resources for adopters detailed above

Data Mining Methods and Models is appropriate for advanced undergraduate- or graduate-level courses. Some calculus is assumed in a few of the chapters, but the gist of the development can be understood without it. An introductory statistics course would be nice but is not required. No computer programming or database expertise is required.

ACKNOWLEDGMENTS

I wish to thank all the folks at Wiley, especially my editor, Val Moliere, for your guidance and support. A heartfelt thanks to James Steck for contributing the WEKA material to this volume.

I also wish to thank Dr. Chun Jin, Dr. Daniel S. Miller, Dr. Roger Bilisoly, and Dr. Darius Dziuda, my colleagues in the master of science in data mining program at Central Connecticut State University, Dr. Timothy Craine, chair of the Department of Mathematical Sciences, Dr. Dipak K. Dey, chair of the Department of Statistics at the University of Connecticut, and Dr. John Judge, chair of the Department of Mathematics at Westfield State College. Without you, this book would have remained a dream.

Thanks to my mom, Irene R. Larose, who passed away this year, and to my dad, Ernest L. Larose, who made all this possible. Thanks to my daughter Chantal for her lovely artwork and boundless joy. Thanks to my twin children, Tristan and Ravel, for sharing the computer and for sharing their true perspective. Not least, I would like to express my eternal gratitude to my dear wife, Debra J. Larose, for her patience and love and "for everlasting bond of fellowship."

> Live hand in hand,
> and together we'll stand,
> on the threshold of a dream. . . .
> —The Moody Blues

Daniel T. Larose, Ph.D.
Director, Data Mining@CCSU
www.math.ccsu.edu/larose

CHAPTER 1

DIMENSION REDUCTION METHODS

NEED FOR DIMENSION REDUCTION IN DATA MINING

PRINCIPAL COMPONENTS ANALYSIS

FACTOR ANALYSIS

USER-DEFINED COMPOSITES

NEED FOR DIMENSION REDUCTION IN DATA MINING

The databases typically used in data mining may have millions of records and thousands of variables. It is unlikely that all of the variables are independent, with no correlation structure among them. As mentioned in *Discovering Knowledge in Data: An Introduction to Data Mining* [1], data analysts need to guard against *multicollinearity*, a condition where some of the predictor variables are correlated with each other. Multicollinearity leads to instability in the solution space, leading to possible incoherent results, such as in multiple regression, where a multicollinear set of predictors can result in a regression that is significant overall, even when none of the individual variables are significant. Even if such instability is avoided, inclusion of variables that are highly correlated tends to overemphasize a particular component of the model, since the component is essentially being double counted.

Bellman [2] noted that the sample size needed to fit a multivariate function grows exponentially with the number of variables. In other words, higher-dimension spaces are inherently sparse. For example, the empirical rule tells us that in one dimension, about 68% of normally distributed variates lie between 1 and -1, whereas for a 10-dimensional multivariate normal distribution, only 0.02% of the data lie within the analogous hypersphere.

The use of too many predictor variables to model a relationship with a response variable can unnecessarily complicate the interpretation of the analysis and violates the principle of parsimony: that one should consider keeping the number of predictors to a size that could easily be interpreted. Also, retaining too many variables may lead to overfitting, in which the generality of the findings is hindered because the new data do not behave the same as the training data for all the variables.

Further, analysis solely at the variable level might miss the fundamental underlying relationships among predictors. For example, several predictors might fall naturally into a single group (a *factor* or a *component*) that addresses a single aspect of the data. For example, the variables savings account balance, checking account-balance, home equity, stock portfolio value, and 401K balance might all fall together under the single component, *assets*.

In some applications, such as image analysis, retaining full dimensionality would make most problems intractable. For example, a face classification system based on 256×256 pixel images could potentially require vectors of dimension 65,536. Humans are endowed innately with visual pattern recognition abilities, which enable us in an intuitive manner to discern patterns in graphic images at a glance, patterns that might elude us if presented algebraically or textually. However, even the most advanced data visualization techniques do not go much beyond five dimensions. How, then, can we hope to visualize the relationship among the hundreds of variables in our massive data sets?

Dimension reduction methods have the goal of using the correlation structure among the predictor variables to accomplish the following:

- To reduce the number of predictor components
- To help ensure that these components are independent
- To provide a framework for interpretability of the results

In this chapter we examine the following dimension reduction methods:

- Principal components analysis
- Factor analysis
- User-defined composites

This chapter calls upon knowledge of matrix algebra. For those of you whose matrix algebra may be rusty, see the book series Web site for review resources. We shall apply all of the following terminology and notation in terms of a concrete example, using real-world data.

PRINCIPAL COMPONENTS ANALYSIS

Principal components analysis (PCA) seeks to explain the correlation structure of a set of predictor variables using a smaller set of linear combinations of these variables. These linear combinations are called *components*. The total variability of a data set produced by the complete set of m variables can often be accounted for primarily by a smaller set of k linear combinations of these variables, which would mean that there is almost as much information in the k components as there is in the original m variables. If desired, the analyst can then replace the original m variables with the $k < m$

components, so that the working data set now consists of n records on k components rather than n records on m variables.

Suppose that the original variables $X_1, X_2, \ldots, X_m$ form a coordinate system in m-dimensional space. The principal components represent a new coordinate system, found by rotating the original system along the directions of maximum variability. When preparing to perform data reduction, the analyst should first standardize the data so that the mean for each variable is zero and the standard deviation is 1. Let each variable X_i represent an $n \times 1$ vector, where n is the number of records. Then represent the standardized variable as the $n \times 1$ vector Z_i, where $Z_i = (X_i - \mu_i)/\sigma_{ii}$, μ_i is the mean of X_i, and σ_{ii} is the standard deviation of X_i. In matrix notation, this standardization is expressed as $\mathbf{Z} = \left(\mathbf{V}^{1/2}\right)^{-1}(\mathbf{X} - \boldsymbol{\mu})$, where the "−1" exponent refers to the matrix inverse, and $\mathbf{V}^{1/2}$ is a diagonal matrix (nonzero entries only on the diagonal), the $m \times m$ *standard deviation matrix*:

$$
\mathbf{V}^{1/2} = \begin{bmatrix} \sigma_{11} & 0 & \cdots & 0 \\ 0 & \sigma_{22} & \cdots & 0 \\ \vdots & \vdots & \ddots & \vdots \\ 0 & 0 & \cdots & \sigma_{pp} \end{bmatrix}
$$

Let Σ refer to the symmetric *covariance matrix*:

$$
\Sigma = \begin{bmatrix} \sigma_{11}^2 & \sigma_{12}^2 & \cdots & \sigma_{1m}^2 \\ \sigma_{12}^2 & \sigma_{22}^2 & \cdots & \sigma_{2m}^2 \\ \vdots & \vdots & \ddots & \vdots \\ \sigma_{1m}^2 & \sigma_{2m}^2 & \cdots & \sigma_{mm}^2 \end{bmatrix}
$$

where σ_{ij}^2, $i \neq j$ refers to the *covariance* between X_i and X_j:

$$
\sigma_{ij}^2 = \frac{\sum_{k=1}^n (x_{ki} - \mu_i)(x_{kj} - \mu_j)}{n}
$$

The covariance is a measure of the degree to which two variables vary together. Positive covariance indicates that when one variable increases, the other tends to increase. Negative covariance indicates that when one variable increases, the other tends to decrease. The notation σ_{ij}^2 is used to denote the variance of X_i. If X_i and X_j are independent, $\sigma_{ij}^2 = 0$, but $\sigma_{ij}^2 = 0$ does not imply that X_i and X_j are independent. Note that the covariance measure is not scaled, so that changing the units of measure would change the value of the covariance.

The *correlation coefficient* r_{ij} avoids this difficulty by scaling the covariance by each of the standard deviations:

$$
r_{ij} = \frac{\sigma_{ij}^2}{\sigma_{ii}\sigma_{jj}}
$$

Then the *correlation matrix* is denoted as ρ (*rho*, the Greek letter for *r*):

$$\rho = \begin{bmatrix} \dfrac{\sigma_{11}^2}{\sigma_{11}\sigma_{11}} & \dfrac{\sigma_{12}^2}{\sigma_{11}\sigma_{22}} & \cdots & \dfrac{\sigma_{1m}^2}{\sigma_{11}\sigma_{mm}} \\[2ex] \dfrac{\sigma_{12}^2}{\sigma_{11}\sigma_{22}} & \dfrac{\sigma_{22}^2}{\sigma_{22}\sigma_{22}} & \cdots & \dfrac{\sigma_{2m}^2}{\sigma_{22}\sigma_{mm}} \\[2ex] \vdots & \vdots & \ddots & \vdots \\[2ex] \dfrac{\sigma_{1m}^2}{\sigma_{11}\sigma_{mm}} & \dfrac{\sigma_{2m}^2}{\sigma_{22}\sigma_{mm}} & \cdots & \dfrac{\sigma_{mm}^2}{\sigma_{mm}\sigma_{mm}} \end{bmatrix}$$

Consider again the standardized data matrix $\mathbf{Z} = \left(\mathbf{V}^{1/2}\right)^{-1}(\mathbf{X} - \boldsymbol{\mu})$. Then since each variable has been standardized, we have $E(\mathbf{Z}) = \mathbf{0}$, where $\mathbf{0}$ denotes an $n \times 1$ vector of zeros and $\mathbf{Z}$ has covariance matrix $\text{Cov}(\mathbf{Z}) = \left(\mathbf{V}^{1/2}\right)^{-1} \Sigma \left(\mathbf{V}^{1/2}\right)^{-1} = \rho$. Thus, for the standardized data set, the covariance matrix and the correlation matrix are the same.

The *i*th *principal component* of the standardized data matrix $\mathbf{Z} = [Z_1, Z_2, \ldots, Z_m]$ is given by $Y_i = \mathbf{e}_i'\mathbf{Z}$, where $\mathbf{e}_i$ refers to the *i*th *eigenvector* (discussed below) and $\mathbf{e}_i'$ refers to the transpose of $\mathbf{e}_i$. The principal components are linear combinations $Y_1, Y_2, \ldots, Y_k$ of the standardized variables in $\mathbf{Z}$ such that (1) the variances of the Y_i are as large as possible, and (2) the Y_i are uncorrelated.

The first principal component is the linear combination

$$Y_1 = \mathbf{e}_1'Z = e_{11}Z_1 + e_{12}Z_2 + \cdots + e_{1m}Z_m$$

which has greater variability than any other possible linear combination of the Z variables. Thus:

- The first principal component is the linear combination $Y_1 = \mathbf{e}_1'\mathbf{Z}$, which maximizes $\text{Var}(Y_1) = \mathbf{e}_1'\rho\,\mathbf{e}_1$.
- The second principal component is the linear combination $Y_2 = \mathbf{e}_2'\mathbf{Z}$, which *is independent of* Y_1 and maximizes $\text{Var}(Y_2) = \mathbf{e}_2'\rho\,\mathbf{e}_2$.
- The *i*th principal component is the linear combination $Y_i = \mathbf{e}_i'\mathbf{X}$, which *is independent of all the other principal components* Y_j, $j < i$, and maximizes $\text{Var}(Y_i) = \mathbf{e}_i'\rho\,\mathbf{e}_i$.

We have the following definitions:

- *Eigenvalues.* Let $\mathbf{B}$ be an $m \times m$ matrix, and let $\mathbf{I}$ be the $m \times m$ identity matrix (diagonal matrix with 1's on the diagonal). Then the scalars (numbers of dimension 1×1) $\lambda_1, \lambda_1, \ldots, \lambda_m$ are said to be the *eigenvalues* of $\mathbf{B}$ if they satisfy $|\mathbf{B} - \lambda\mathbf{I}| = 0$.
- *Eigenvectors.* Let $\mathbf{B}$ be an $m \times m$ matrix, and let λ be an eigenvalue of $\mathbf{B}$. Then nonzero $m \times 1$ vector $\mathbf{e}$ is said to be an *eigenvector* of $\mathbf{B}$ if $\mathbf{Be} = \lambda\mathbf{e}$.

The following results are very important for our PCA analysis.

- *Result 1.* The total variability in the standardized data set equals the sum of the variances for each Z-vector, which equals the sum of the variances for each component, which equals the sum of the eigenvalues, which equals the number of variables. That is,

$$\sum_{i=1}^{m} \text{Var}(Y_i) = \sum_{i=1}^{m} \text{Var}(Z_i) = \sum_{i=1}^{m} \lambda_i = m$$

- *Result 2.* The partial correlation between a given component and a given variable is a function of an eigenvector and an eigenvalue. Specifically, Corr(Y_i, Z_j) = $e_{ij} \sqrt{\lambda_i}$, $i, j = 1, 2, \ldots, m$, where $(\lambda_1, \mathbf{e}_1), (\lambda_2, \mathbf{e}_2), \ldots, (\lambda_m, \mathbf{e}_m)$ are the eigenvalue–eigenvector pairs for the correlation matrix $\boldsymbol{\rho}$, and we note that $\lambda_1 \geq \lambda_2 \geq \cdots \geq \lambda_m$. A *partial correlation coefficient* is a correlation coefficient that takes into account the effect of all the other variables.

- *Result 3.* The proportion of the total variability in **Z** that is explained by the *i*th principal component is the ratio of the *i*th eigenvalue to the number of variables, that is, the ratio λ_i / m.

Next, to illustrate how to apply principal components analysis on real data, we turn to an example.

Applying Principal Components Analysis to the *Houses* Data Set

We turn to the *houses* data set [3], which provides census information from all the block groups from the 1990 California census. For this data set, a block group has an average of 1425.5 people living in an area that is geographically compact. Block groups that contained zero entries for any of the variables were excluded. *Median house value* is the response variable; the predictor variables are:

- *Median income*
- *Housing median age*
- *Total rooms*
- *Total bedrooms*

- *Population*
- *Households*
- *Latitude*
- *Longitude*

The original data set had 20,640 records, of which 18,540 were selected randomly for a training data set, and 2100 held out for a test data set. A quick look at the variables is provided in Figure 1.1. ("Range" is Clementine's type label for continuous variables.) *Median house value* appears to be in dollars, but *median income* has been scaled to a continuous scale from 0 to 15. Note that *longitude* is expressed in negative terms, meaning west of Greenwich. Larger absolute values for longitude indicate geographic locations farther west.

Relating this data set to our earlier notation, we have X_1 = *median income*, X_2 = *housing median age*, ..., X_8 = *longitude*, so that $m = 8$ and $n = 18,540$. A glimpse of the first 20 records in the data set looks like Figure 1.2. So, for example, for the first block group, the *median house value* is \$452,600, the *median income* is 8.325 (on the census scale), the *housing median age* is 41, the *total rooms* is 880, the *total bedrooms* is 129, the *population* is 322, the *number of households* is 126, the *latitude* is 37.88 North and the *longitude* is 122.23 West. Clearly, this is a smallish block group with very high median house value. A map search reveals that this block group

Field	Sample Graph	Type	Min	Max	Mean	Std. Dev
median_house_value	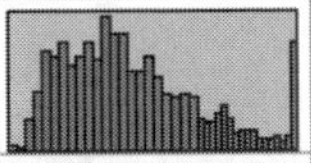	Range	14999	500001	206918.067	115485.040
median_income	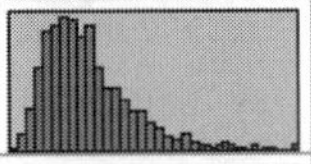	Range	0.500	15.000	3.873	1.906
housing_median_age	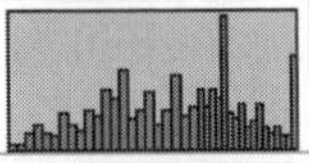	Range	1	52	28.656	12.582
total_rooms	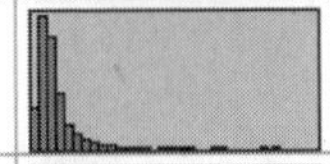	Range	2	37937	2621.653	2131.644
total_bedrooms		Range	1	6445	535.096	413.541
population		Range	3	35682	1418.971	1122.534
households		Range	1	6082	497.332	377.378
latitude	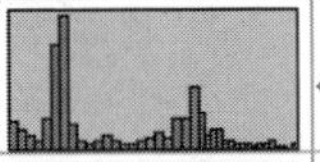	Range	32.540	41.950	35.630	2.137
longitude	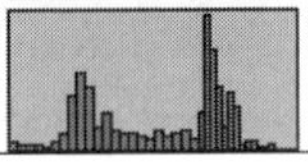	Range	-124.350	-114.310	-119.567	2.003

Figure 1.1 *Houses* data set (Clementine data audit node).

is centered between the University of California at Berkeley and Tilden Regional Park.

Note from Figure 1.1 the great disparity in variability among the variables. *Median income* has a standard deviation less than 2, while *total rooms* has a standard deviation over 2100. If we proceeded to apply principal components analysis without first standardizing the variables, *total rooms* would dominate *median income*'s influence,

	median_house_value	median_income	housing_median_age	total_rooms	total_bedrooms	population	households	latitude	longitude
1	452600	8.325	41	880	129	322	126	37.880	-122.230
2	358500	8.301	21	7099	1106	2401	1138	37.860	-122.220
3	352100	7.257	52	1467	190	496	177	37.850	-122.240
4	342200	3.846	52	1627	280	565	259	37.850	-122.250
5	299200	3.659	52	2535	489	1094	514	37.840	-122.250
6	241400	3.120	52	3104	687	1157	647	37.840	-122.250
7	226700	2.080	42	2555	665	1206	595	37.840	-122.260
8	261100	3.691	52	3549	707	1551	714	37.840	-122.250
9	241800	3.270	52	3503	752	1504	734	37.850	-122.260
10	191300	2.674	52	696	191	345	174	37.840	-122.260
11	159200	1.917	52	2643	626	1212	620	37.850	-122.260
12	140000	2.125	50	1120	283	697	264	37.850	-122.260
13	152500	2.775	52	1966	347	793	331	37.850	-122.270
14	155500	2.120	52	1228	293	648	303	37.850	-122.270
15	158700	1.991	50	2239	455	990	419	37.840	-122.260
16	147500	1.358	40	751	184	409	166	37.850	-122.270
17	159800	1.714	42	1639	367	929	366	37.850	-122.270
18	99700	2.181	52	1688	337	853	325	37.840	-122.270
19	132600	2.600	52	2224	437	1006	422	37.850	-122.270
20	107500	2.404	41	535	123	317	119	37.850	-122.280

Figure 1.2 First 20 records in the *houses* data set.

and similarly across the spectrum of variabilities. Therefore, standardization is called for. The variables were standardized and the Z-vectors found, $Z_i = (X_i - \mu_i)/\sigma_{ii}$, using the means and standard deviations from Figure 1.1.

Note that normality of the data is not strictly required to perform noninferential PCA [4] but that departures from normality may diminish the correlations observed [5]. Since we do not plan to perform inference based on our PCA, we will not worry about normality at this time. In Chapters 2 and 3 we discuss methods for transforming nonnormal data.

Next, we examine the matrix plot of the predictors in Figure 1.3 to explore whether correlations exist. Diagonally from left to right, we have the standardized variables *minc-z* (median income), *hage-z* (housing median age), *rooms-z* (total rooms), *bedrms-z* (total bedrooms), *popn-z* (population), *hhlds-z* (number of households), *lat-z* (latitude), and *long-z* (longitude). What does the matrix plot tell us about the correlation among the variables? Rooms, bedrooms, population, and households all appear to be positively correlated. Latitude and longitude appear to be negatively correlated. (What does the plot of latitude versus longitude look like? Did you say the state of California?) Which variable appears to be correlated the least with the other predictors? Probably *housing median age*. Table 1.1 shows the correlation matrix ρ for the predictors. Note that the matrix is symmetrical and that the diagonal elements all equal 1. A matrix plot and the correlation matrix are two ways of looking at the

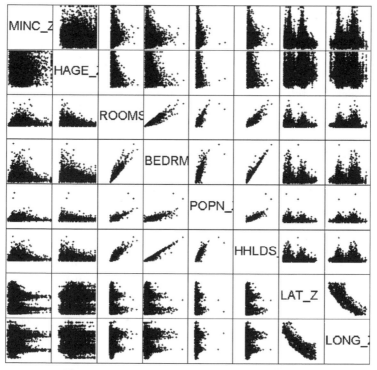

Figure 1.3   Matrix plot of the predictor variables.

TABLE 1.1 Correlation Matrix ρ

	minc-z	hage-z	rooms-z	bedrms-z	popn-z	hhlds-z	lat-z	long-z
minc-z	1.000	−0.117	0.199	−0.012	0.002	0.010	−0.083	−0.012
hage-z	−0.117	1.000	−0.360	−0.318	−0.292	−0.300	0.011	−0.107
rooms-z	0.199	−0.360	1.000	0.928	0.856	0.919	−0.035	0.041
bedrms-z	−0.012	−0.318	0.928	1.000	0.878	0.981	−0.064	0.064
popn-z	0.002	−0.292	0.856	0.878	1.000	0.907	−0.107	0.097
hhlds-z	0.010	−0.300	0.919	0.981	0.907	1.000	−0.069	0.051
lat-z	−0.083	0.011	−0.035	−0.064	−0.107	−0.069	1.000	−0.925
long-z	−0.012	−0.107	0.041	0.064	0.097	0.051	−0.925	1.000

same thing: the correlation structure among the predictor variables. Note that the cells for the correlation matrix ρ line up one to one with the graphs in the matrix plot.

What would happen if we performed, say, a multiple regression analysis of *median housing value* on the predictors, despite the strong evidence for multicollinearity in the data set? The regression results would become quite unstable, with (among other things) tiny shifts in the predictors leading to large changes in the regression coefficients. In short, we could not use the regression results for profiling. That is where PCA comes in. Principal components analysis can sift through this correlation structure and identify the components underlying the correlated variables. Then the principal components can be used for further analysis downstream, such as in regression analysis, classification, and so on.

Principal components analysis was carried out on the eight predictors in the *houses* data set. The *component matrix* is shown in Table 1.2. Each of the columns in Table 1.2 represents one of the components $Y_i = \mathbf{e}_i' \mathbf{Z}$. The cell entries, called the *component weights*, represent the partial correlation between the variable and the component. *Result 2* tells us that these component weights therefore equal $\mathrm{Corr}(Y_i, Z_j) = e_{ij}\sqrt{\lambda_i}$, a product involving the ith eigenvector and eigenvalue. Since the component weights are correlations, they range between 1 and −1.

In general, the first principal component may be viewed as the single best summary of the correlations among the predictors. Specifically, this particular linear

TABLE 1.2 Component Matrix[a]

	Component							
	1	2	3	4	5	6	7	8
minc-z	0.086	−0.058	0.922	0.370	−0.02	−0.018	0.037	−0.004
hage-z	−0.429	0.025	−0.407	0.806	0.014	0.026	0.009	−0.001
rooms-z	0.956	0.100	0.102	0.104	0.120	0.162	−0.119	0.015
bedrms-z	0.970	0.083	−0.121	0.056	0.144	−0.068	0.051	−0.083
popn-z	0.933	0.034	−0.121	0.076	−0.327	0.034	0.006	−0.015
hhlds-z	0.972	0.086	−0.113	0.087	0.058	−0.112	0.061	0.083
lat-z	−0.140	0.970	0.017	−0.088	0.017	0.132	0.113	0.005
long-z	0.144	−0.969	−0.062	−0.063	0.037	0.136	0.109	0.007

[a] Extraction method: principal component analysis; eight components extracted.

TABLE 1.3   Eigenvalues and Proportion of Variance Explained by Component

Component	Total	% of Variance	Cumulative %
		Initial Eigenvalues	
1	3.901	48.767	48.767
2	1.910	23.881	72.648
3	1.073	13.409	86.057
4	0.825	10.311	96.368
5	0.148	1.847	98.215
6	0.082	1.020	99.235
7	0.047	0.586	99.821
8	0.014	0.179	100.000

combination of the variables accounts for more variability than that of any other conceivable linear combination. It has maximized the variance $\text{Var}(Y_1) = \mathbf{e}'_1 \boldsymbol{\rho} \mathbf{e}_1$. As we suspected from the matrix plot and the correlation matrix, there is evidence that *total rooms*, *total bedrooms*, *population*, and *households* vary together. Here, they all have very high (and very similar) component weights, indicating that all four variables are highly correlated with the first principal component.

Let's examine Table 1.3, which shows the eigenvalues for each component along with the percentage of the total variance explained by that component. Recall that *result 3* showed us that the proportion of the total variability in $\mathbf{Z}$ that is explained by the ith principal component is λ_i / m, the ratio of the ith eigenvalue to the number of variables. Here we see that the first eigenvalue is 3.901, and since there are eight predictor variables, this first component explains $3.901/8 = 48.767\%$ of the variance, as shown in Table 1.3 (allowing for rounding). So a single component accounts for nearly half of the variability in the set of eight predictor variables, meaning that this single component by itself carries about half of the information in all eight predictors. Notice also that the eigenvalues decrease in magnitude, $\lambda_1 \geq \lambda_2 \geq \cdots \geq \lambda_m, \lambda_1 \geq \lambda_2 \geq \cdots \geq \lambda_8$, as we noted in *result 2*.

The second principal component Y_2 is the second-best linear combination of the variables, on the condition that it is *orthogonal* to the first principal component. Two vectors are *orthogonal* if they are mathematically independent, have no correlation, and are at right angles to each other. The second component is derived from the variability that is left over once the first component has been accounted for. The third component is the third-best linear combination of the variables, on the condition that it is orthogonal to the first two components. The third component is derived from the variance remaining after the first two components have been extracted. The remaining components are defined similarly.

How Many Components Should We Extract?

Next, recall that one of the motivations for principal components analysis was to reduce the number of distinct explanatory elements. The question arises: How do we determine how many components to extract? For example, should we retain only the first principal component, since it explains nearly half the variability? Or should we retain all eight components, since they explain 100% of the variability? Well, clearly, retaining all eight components does not help us to reduce the number of distinct explanatory elements. As usual, the answer lies somewhere between these two extremes. Note from Table 1.3 that the eigenvalues for several of the components are rather low, explaining less than 2% of the variability in the Z-variables. Perhaps these would be the components we should consider not retaining in our analysis? The criteria used for deciding how many components to extract are (1) the eigenvalue criterion, (2) the proportion of variance explained criterion, (3) the minimum communality criterion, and (4) the scree plot criterion.

Eigenvalue Criterion

Recall from result 1 that the sum of the eigenvalues represents the number of variables entered into the PCA. An eigenvalue of 1 would then mean that the component would explain about "one variable's worth" of the variability. The rationale for using the eigenvalue criterion is that each component should explain at least one variable's worth of the variability, and therefore the eigenvalue criterion states that only components with eigenvalues greater than 1 should be retained. Note that if there are fewer than 20 variables, the eigenvalue criterion tends to recommend extracting too few components, while if there are more than 50 variables, this criterion may recommend extracting too many. From Table 1.3 we see that three components have eigenvalues greater than 1 and are therefore retained. Component 4 has an eigenvalue of 0.825, which is not too far from 1, so that if other criteria support such a decision, we may decide to consider retaining this component as well, especially in view of the tendency of this criterion to recommend extracting too few components.

Proportion of Variance Explained Criterion

First, the analyst specifies how much of the total variability he or she would like the principal components to account for. Then the analyst simply selects the components one by one until the desired proportion of variability explained is attained. For example, suppose that we would like our components to explain 85% of the variability in the variables. Then, from Table 1.3, we would choose components 1 to 3, which together explain 86.057% of the variability. On the other hand, if we wanted our components to explain 90% or 95% of the variability, we would need to include component 4 with components 1 to 3, which together would explain 96.368% of the variability. Again, as with the eigenvalue criterion, how large a proportion is enough?

This question is akin to asking how large a value of r^2 (coefficient of determination) is enough in the realm of linear regression. The answer depends in part on the field of study. Social scientists may be content for their components to explain only 60% or so of the variability, since human response factors are so unpredictable, whereas natural scientists might expect their components to explain 90 to 95% of the variability, since their measurements are intrinsically less variable. Other factors also affect how large a proportion is needed. For example, if the principal components are being used for descriptive purposes only, such as customer profiling, the proportion of variability explained may be a shade lower than otherwise. On the other hand, if the principal components are to be used as replacements for the original (standardized) data set and used for further inference in models downstream, the proportion of variability explained should be as much as can conveniently be achieved given the constraints of the other criteria.

Minimum Communality Criterion

We postpone discussion of this criterion until we introduce the concept of *communality* below.

Scree Plot Criterion

A scree plot is a graphical plot of the eigenvalues against the component number. Scree plots are useful for finding an upper bound (maximum) for the number of components that should be retained. See Figure 1.4 for the scree plot for this example. Most scree plots look broadly similar in shape, starting high on the left, falling rather quickly, and then flattening out at some point. This is because the first component usually explains much of the variability, the next few components explain a moderate amount, and the latter components explain only a small amount of the variability. The scree plot criterion is this: The maximum number of components that should be extracted is *just prior to* where the plot first begins to straighten out into a horizontal line. For example, in Figure 1.4, the plot straightens out horizontally starting at component 5.

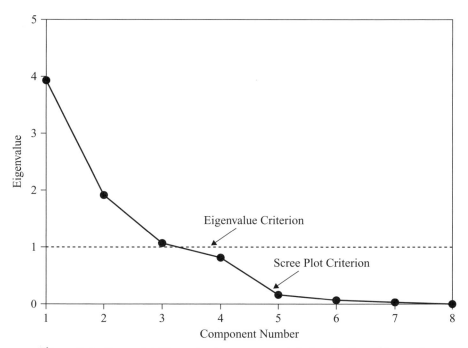

Figure 1.4   Scree plot. Stop extracting components before the line flattens out.

The line is nearly horizontal because the components all explain approximately the same amount of variance, which is not much. Therefore, the scree plot criterion would indicate that the maximum number of components we should extract is four, since the fourth component occurs just prior to where the line first begins to straighten out.

To summarize, the recommendations of our criteria are as follows:

- *Eigenvalue criterion.* Retain components 1 to 3, but don't throw component 4 away yet.
- *Proportion of variance explained criterion.* Components 1 to 3 account for a solid 86% of the variability, and adding component 4 gives us a superb 96% of the variability.
- *Scree plot criterion.* Don't extract more than four components.

So we will extract at least three but no more than four components. Which is it to be, three or four? As in much of data analysis, there is no absolute answer in this case to the question of how many components to extract. This is what makes data mining an art as well as a science, and this is another reason why data mining requires human direction. The data miner or data analyst must weigh all the factors involved in a decision and apply his or her judgment, tempered by experience.

In a case like this, where there is no clear-cut best solution, why not try it both ways and see what happens? Consider Table 1.4, which compares the component matrixes when three and four components are extracted, respectively. Component weights smaller than 0.15 are suppressed to ease component interpretation. Note that the first three components are each exactly the same in both cases, and each is the same as when we extracted all eight components, as shown in Table 1.2 (after suppressing the small weights). This is because each component extracts its portion of the variability sequentially, so that later component extractions do not affect the earlier ones.

TABLE 1.4 Component Matrixes for Extracting Three and Four Components[a]

	Component			Component			
	1	2	3	1	2	3	4
minc-z			0.922			0.922	0.370
hage-z	−0.429		−0.407	−0.429		−0.407	0.806
rooms-z	0.956			0.956			
bedrms-z	0.970			0.970			
popn-z	0.933			0.933			
hhlds-z	0.972			0.972			
lat-z		0.970			0.970		
long-z		−0.969			−0.969		

[a] Extraction method: principal components analysis.

Profiling the Principal Components

The analyst is usually interested in profiling the principal components. Let us now examine the salient characteristics of each principal component.

- *Principal component 1*, as we saw earlier, is composed largely of the "block group size" variables *total rooms*, *total bedrooms*, *population*, and *households*, which are all either large or small together. That is, large block groups have a strong tendency to have large values for all four variables, whereas small block groups tend to have small values for all four variables. *Median housing age* is a smaller, lonely counterweight to these four variables, tending to be low (recently built housing) for large block groups, and high (older, established housing) for smaller block groups.

- *Principal component 2* is a "geographical" component, composed solely of the *latitude* and *longitude* variables, which are strongly negatively correlated, as we can tell by the opposite signs of their component weights. This supports our earlier EDA regarding these two variables in Figure 1.3 and Table 1.1. The negative correlation is because of the way that latitude and longitude are signed by definition, and because California is broadly situated from northwest to southeast. If California were situated from northeast to southwest, latitude and longitude would be positively correlated.

- *Principal component 3* refers chiefly to the *median income* of the block group, with a smaller effect due to the *housing median age* of the block group. That is, in the data set, high median income is associated with recently built housing, whereas lower median income is associated with older, established housing.

- *Principal component 4* is of interest, because it is the one that we have not decided whether or not to retain. Again, it focuses on the combination of *housing median age* and *median income*. Here, we see that *once the negative correlation between these two variables has been accounted for*, there is left over a positive relationship between these variables. That is, once the association between, for example, high incomes and recent housing has been extracted, there is left over some further association between high incomes and older housing.

To further investigate the relationship between *principal components 3* and *4* and their constituent variables, we next consider factor scores. *Factor scores* are estimated values of the factors for each observation, and are based on *factor analysis*, discussed in the next section. For the derivation of factor scores, see Johnson and Wichern [4].

Consider Figure 1.5, which provides two matrix plots. The matrix plot in Figure 1.5*a* displays the relationships among *median income*, *housing median age*, and the factor scores for *component 3*; the matrix plot in Figure 1.5*b* displays the relationships among *median income*, *housing median age*, and the factor scores for *component 4*. Table 1.4 showed that *components 3* and *4* both included each of these variables as constituents. However, there seemed to be a large difference in the absolute

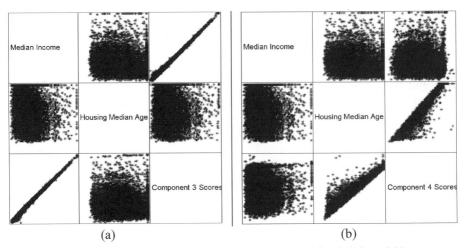

(a)   (b)

Figure 1.5   Correlations between *components 3* and *4* and their variables.

component weights, as, for example, 0.922 having a greater amplitude than −0.407 for the *component 3* component weights. Is this difference in magnitude reflected in the matrix plots?

Consider Figure 1.5*a*. The strong positive correlation between *component 3* and *median income* is strikingly evident, reflecting the 0.922 positive correlation. But the relationship between *component 3* and *housing median age* is rather amorphous. It would be difficult with only the scatter plot to guide us to estimate the correlation between *component 3* and *housing median age* as being −0.407. Similarly, for Figure 1.5*b*, the relationship between *component 4* and *housing median age* is crystal clear, reflecting the 0.806 positive correlation, while the relationship between *component 3* and *median income* is not entirely clear, reflecting its lower positive correlation of 0.370. We conclude, therefore, that the component weight of −0.407 for *housing median age* in *component 3* is not of practical significance, and similarly for the component weight for *median income* in *component 4*.

This discussion leads us to the following criterion for assessing the component weights. For a component weight to be considered of practical significance, it should exceed ±0.50 in magnitude. Note that the component weight represents the correlation between the component and the variable; thus, the squared component weight represents the amount of the variable's total variability that is explained by the component. Thus, this threshold value of ±0.50 requires that at least 25% of the variable's variance be explained by a particular component. Table 1.5 therefore presents the component matrix from Table 1.4, this time suppressing the component weights below ±0.50 in magnitude. The component profiles should now be clear and uncluttered:

- *Principal component 1* represents the "block group size" component and consists of four variables: *total rooms*, *total bedrooms*, *population*, and *households*.

TABLE 1.5 Matrix of Component Weights, Suppressing Magnitudes Below ±0.50[a]

	Component			
	1	2	3	4
minc-z			0.922	
hage-z				0.806
rooms-z	0.956			
bedrms-z	0.970			
popn-z	0.933			
hhlds-z	0.972			
lat-z		0.970		
long-z		−0.969		

[a] Extraction method: principal component analysis; four components extracted.

- *Principal component 2* represents the "geographical" component and consists of two variables, *latitude* and *longitude*.
- *Principal component 3* represents the "income" component and consists of only one variable, *median income*.
- *Principal component 4* represents the "housing age" component and consists of only one variable, *housing median age*.

Note that the partition of the variables among the four components is *mutually exclusive*, meaning that no variable is shared (after suppression) by any two components, and *exhaustive*, meaning that all eight variables are contained in the four components. Further, support for this 4–2–1–1 partition of the variables among the first four components is found in the similar relationship identified among the first four eigenvalues: 3.901–1.910–1.073–0.825 (see Table 1.3).

A note about positive and negative loadings is in order. Consider *component 2*, which has a strong positive loading for *latitude* and a strong negative loading for *longitude*. It is possible that a replication study would find that the signs for these loadings would be reversed, so that *latitude* had a negative loading and *longitude* had a positive loading. If so, the interpretation is exactly the same, because we interpret the relationship between the variables rather than the signs per se.

Communalities

We are moving toward a decision regarding how many components to retain. One more piece of the puzzle needs to be set in place: *communality*. PCA does not extract all the variance from the variables, only that proportion of the variance that is shared by several variables. Communality represents the proportion of variance of a particular variable that is shared with other variables.

The communalities represent the overall importance of each variable in the PCA as a whole. For example, a variable with a communality much smaller than the other variables indicates that this variable shares much less of the common variability among the variables and contributes less to the PCA solution. Communalities that are very low for a particular variable should be an indication to the analyst that the particular variable might not participate in the PCA solution (i.e., might not be a member of any of the principal components). Overall, large communality values indicate that the principal components have successfully extracted a large proportion of the variability in the original variables; small communality values show that there is still much variation in the data set that has not been accounted for by the principal components.

Communality values are calculated as the sum of squared component weights for a given variable. We are trying to determine whether to retain *component 4*, the "housing age" component. Thus, we calculate the commonality value for the variable *housing median age*, using the component weights for this variable (*hage-z*) from Table 1.2. Two communality values for *housing median age* are calculated, one for retaining three components and the other for retaining four components.

- Communality (*housing median age*, three components):

$$(-0.429)^2 + (0.025)^2 + (-0.407)^2 = 0.350315$$

- Communality (*housing median age*, four components):

$$(-0.429)^2 + (0.025)^2 + (-0.407)^2 + (0.806)^2 = 0.999951$$

Communalities less than 0.5 can be considered to be too low, since this would mean that the variable shares less than half of its variability in common with the other variables. Now, suppose that for some reason we wanted or needed to keep the variable *housing median age* as an active part of the analysis. Then, extracting only three components would not be adequate, since *housing median age* shares only 35% of its variance with the other variables. If we wanted to keep this variable in the analysis, we would need to extract the fourth component, which lifts the communality for *housing median age* over the 50% threshold. This leads us to the statement of the *minimum communality criterion* for component selection, which we alluded to earlier.

Minimum Communality Criterion

Suppose that it is required to keep a certain set of variables in the analysis. Then enough components should be extracted so that the communalities for each of these variables exceeds a certain threshold (e.g., 50%).

Hence, we are finally ready to decide how many components to retain. We have decided to retain four components, for the following reasons:

- The eigenvalue criterion recommended three components but did not absolutely reject the fourth component. Also, for small numbers of variables, this criterion can underestimate the best number of components to extract.

- The proportion of variance explained criterion stated that we needed to use four components if we wanted to account for that superb 96% of the variability. *Since our ultimate goal is to substitute these components for the original data and use them in further modeling downstream*, being able to explain so much of the variability in the original data is very attractive.

- The scree plot criterion said not to exceed four components. We have not.
- The minimum communality criterion stated that if we wanted to keep *housing median age* in the analysis, we had to extract the fourth component. Since we intend to substitute the components for the original data, we need to keep this variable, and therefore we need to extract the fourth component.

Validation of the Principal Components

Recall that the original data set was divided into a training data set and a test data set. All of the analysis above has been carried out on the training data set. To validate the principal components uncovered here, we now perform PCA on the standardized variables for the test data set. The resulting component matrix is shown in Table 1.6, with component weights smaller than ± 0.50 suppressed. Although the component weights do not exactly equal those of the training set, the same four components were extracted, with a one-to-one correspondence in terms of which variables are associated with which component. This may be considered validation of the principal components analysis performed. Therefore, we shall substitute these principal components for the standardized variables in our later analysis on this data set. Specifically, we investigate whether the components are useful for estimating the *median house value*.

If the split-sample method described here does not successfully provide validation, the analyst should take this as an indication that the results (for the data set as a whole) are not generalizable, and the results should not be reported as valid. If the lack of validation stems from a subset of the variables, the analyst may consider omitting these variables and performing the principal components analysis again. An example of the use of principal component analysis in multiple regression is provided in Chapter 3.

TABLE 1.6   Validating the PCA: Matrix of Component Weights for the Test Set[a]

Variables	Component			
	1	2	3	4
minc-z			0.920	
hage-z				0.785
rooms-z	0.957			
bedrms-z	0.967			
popn-z	0.935			
hhlds-z	0.968			
lat-z		0.962		
long-z		−0.961		

[a] Extraction method: principal components analysis; four components extracted.

FACTOR ANALYSIS

Factor analysis is related to principal components, but the two methods have different goals. Principal components seeks to identify orthogonal linear combinations of the variables, to be used either for descriptive purposes or to substitute a smaller number of uncorrelated components for the original variables. In contrast, factor analysis represents a *model* for the data, and as such is more elaborate.

The *factor analysis model* hypothesizes that the response vector $X_1, X_2, \ldots,$ X_m can be modeled as linear combinations of a smaller set of k unobserved, "latent" random variables $F_1, F_2, \ldots, F_k$, called *common factors*, along with an error term $\varepsilon = \varepsilon_1, \varepsilon_2, \ldots, \varepsilon_k$. Specifically, the factor analysis model is

$$\underset{m \times 1}{\mathbf{X} - \boldsymbol{\mu}} = \underset{m \times k}{\mathbf{L}} \underset{k \times 1}{\mathbf{F}} + \underset{m \times 1}{\boldsymbol{\varepsilon}}$$

where $\underset{m \times 1}{\mathbf{X} - \boldsymbol{\mu}}$ is the response vector, centered by the mean vector; $\underset{m \times k}{\mathbf{L}}$ is the matrix of *factor loadings*, with l_{ij} representing the factor loading of the ith variable on the jth factor; $\underset{k \times 1}{\mathbf{F}}$ represents the vector of unobservable common factors and $\underset{m \times 1}{\boldsymbol{\varepsilon}}$ the error vector. The factor analysis model differs from other models, such as the linear regression model, in that the *predictor variables* $F_1, F_2, \ldots, F_k$ *are unobservable*. Because so many terms are unobserved, further assumptions must be made before we may uncover the factors from the observed responses alone. These assumptions are that $E(\mathbf{F}) = \mathbf{0}$, $\mathrm{Cov}(\mathbf{F}) = \mathbf{I}$, $E(\boldsymbol{\varepsilon}) = \mathbf{0}$, and $\mathrm{Cov}(\boldsymbol{\varepsilon})$ is a diagonal matrix. See Johnson and Wichern [4] for further elucidation of the factor analysis model.

Unfortunately, the factor solutions provided by factor analysis are not invariant to transformations. Two models, $\mathbf{X} - \boldsymbol{\mu} = \mathbf{L}\,\mathbf{F} + \boldsymbol{\varepsilon}$ and $\mathbf{X} - \boldsymbol{\mu} = (\mathbf{LT})(\mathbf{TF}) + \boldsymbol{\varepsilon}$, where $\mathbf{T}$ represents an orthogonal transformations matrix, will both provide the same results. Hence, the factors uncovered by the model are in essence nonunique, without further constraints. This indistinctness provides the motivation for factor rotation, which we will examine shortly.

Applying Factor Analysis to the *Adult* Data Set

Recall the *Adult* data set [6] we worked with in *Discovering Knowledge in Data: An Introduction to Data Mining* [1]. The data set was extracted from data provided by the U.S. Census Bureau. The intended task is to find the set of demographic characteristics that can best predict whether or not a person has an income of over $50,000 per year. For this example, we use only the following variables for the purpose of our factor analysis: *age*, *demogweight* (a measure of the socioeconomic status of the person's district), *education-num*, *hours-per-week*, and *capnet* (= capital gain – capital loss). The training data set contains 25,000 records, and the test data set contains 7561 records. The variables were standardized and the Z-vectors found, $Z_i = (X_i - \mu_i)/\sigma_{ii}$. The correlation matrix is shown in Table 1.7. Note that the correlations, although statistically significant in several cases, are overall much weaker than the correlations from the *houses* data set above. A weaker correlation structure should pose more of a challenge for the dimension reduction method.

TABLE 1.7   Correlation Matrix for the Factor Analysis Example

	age-z	dem-z	educ-z	capnet-z	hours-z
age-z	1.000	−0.076**	0.033**	0.070**	0.069**
dem-z	−0.076**	1.000	−0.044**	0.005	−0.015*
educ-z	0.033**	−0.044**	1.000	0.116**	0.146**
capnet-z	0.070**	0.005	0.116**	1.000	0.077**
hours-z	0.069**	−0.015*	0.146**	0.077**	1.000

** Correlation is significant at the 0.01 level (two-tailed).
 * Correlation is significant at the 0.05 level (two-tailed).

To function appropriately, factor analysis requires a certain level of correlation. Tests have been developed to ascertain whether there exists sufficiently high correlation to perform factor analysis.

- The proportion of variability within the standardized predictor variables which is shared in common, and therefore might be caused by underlying factors, is measured by the *Kaiser–Meyer–Olkin measure of sampling adequacy*. Values of the KMO statistic less than 0.50 indicate that factor analysis may not be appropriate.

- *Bartlett's test of sphericity* tests the null hypothesis that the correlation matrix is an identity matrix, that is, that the variables are really uncorrelated. The statistic reported is the p-value, so that very small values would indicate evidence against the null hypothesis (i.e., the variables really are correlated). For p-values much larger than 0.10, there is insufficient evidence that the variables are not uncorrelated, so factor analysis may not be suitable.

Table 1.8 provides the results of these statistical tests. The KMO statistic has a value of 0.549, which is not less than 0.5, meaning that this test does not find the level of correlation to be too low for factor analysis. The p-value for Bartlett's test of sphericity rounds to zero, so that the null hypothesis that no correlation exists among the variables is rejected. We therefore proceed with the factor analysis.

To allow us to view the results using a scatter plot, we decide a priori to extract only two factors. The following factor analysis is performed using the *principal axis factoring* option. In principal axis factoring, an iterative procedure is used to estimate the communalities and the factor solution. This particular analysis required 152 such iterations before reaching convergence. The eigenvalues and the proportions of the variance explained by each factor are shown in Table 1.9. Note that the first two factors

TABLE 1.8   Is There Sufficiently High Correlation to Run Factor Analysis?

Kaiser–Meyer–Olkin measure of sampling adequacy	0.549
Bartlett's test of sphericity	
Approx. chi-square	1397.824
degrees of freedom (df)	10
p-value	0.000

TABLE 1.9 Eigenvalues and Proportions of Variance Explained: Factor Analysis[a]

Factor	Initial Eigenvalues		
	Total	% of Variance	Cumulative %
1	1.277	25.533	25.533
2	1.036	20.715	46.248
3	0.951	19.028	65.276
4	0.912	18.241	83.517
5	0.824	16.483	100.000

[a] Extraction method: principal axis factoring.

extract less than half of the total variability in the variables, as contrasted with the *houses* data set, where the first two components extracted over 72% of the variability. This is due to the weaker correlation structure inherent in the original data.

The *factor loadings* $\mathbf{L}_{m \times k}$ are shown in Table 1.10. Factor loadings are analogous to the component weights in principal components analysis and represent the correlation between the ith variable and the jth factor. Notice that the factor loadings are much weaker than the previous *houses* example, again due to the weaker correlations among the standardized variables. The communalities are also much weaker than the *houses* example, as shown in Table 1.11. The low communality values reflect the fact that there is not much shared correlation among the variables. Note that the factor extraction increases the shared correlation.

Factor Rotation

To assist in the interpretation of the factors, *factor rotation* may be performed. Factor rotation corresponds to a transformation (usually, orthogonal) of the coordinate axes, leading to a different set of factor loadings. We may look upon factor rotation as analogous to a scientist attempting to elicit greater contrast and detail by adjusting the focus of a microscope.

The sharpest focus occurs when each variable has high factor loadings on a single factor, with low to moderate loadings on the other factors. For the *houses* example, this sharp focus already occurred on the unrotated factor loadings (e.g.,

TABLE 1.10 Factor Loadings[a]

	Factor	
	1	2
age-z	0.590	−0.329
educ-z	0.295	0.424
capnet-z	0.193	0.142
hours-z	0.224	0.193
dem-z	−0.115	0.013

[a] Extraction method: principal axis factoring; two factors extracted, 152 iterations required. Factor loadings are much weaker than for the preceding example.

TABLE 1.11 Communalities[a]

	Initial	Extraction
age-z	0.015	0.457
educ-z	0.034	0.267
capnet-z	0.021	0.058
hours-z	0.029	0.087
dem-z	0.008	0.013

[a] Extraction method: principal axis factoring. Communalities are low, reflecting not much shared correlation.

Table 1.5), so rotation was not necessary. However, Table 1.10 shows that we should perhaps try factor rotation for the *adult* data set, to help improve our interpretation of the two factors. Figure 1.6 shows the graphical view of the vectors of factors of loadings for each variable from Table 1.10. Note that most vectors do not closely follow the coordinate axes, which means that there is poor "contrast" among the variables for each factor, thereby reducing interpretability.

Next, a *varimax* rotation (discussed shortly) was applied to the matrix of factor loadings, resulting in the new set of factor loadings in Table 1.12. Note that the contrast has been increased for most variables, which is perhaps made clearer by Figure 1.7, the graphical view of the rotated vectors of factor loadings. The figure shows that the factor loadings have been rotated along the axes of maximum variability, represented by *factors 1* and *2*. Often, the first factor extracted represents a "general factor" and accounts for much of the total variability. The effect of factor rotation is to redistribute the variability explained among the second, third, and subsequent factors.

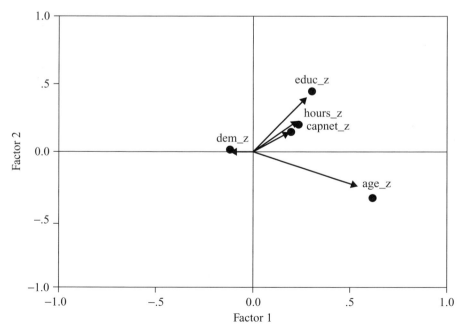

Figure 1.6   Unrotated vectors of factor loadings do not follow the coordinate axes.

TABLE 1.12   Factor Loadings After Varimax Rotation[a]

	Factor	
	1	2
age-z	0.675	0.041
educ-z	0.020	0.516
capnet-z	0.086	0.224
hours-z	0.084	0.283
dem-z	−0.104	−0.051

[a] Extraction method: principal axis factoring; rotation method: varimax with kaiser normalization; rotation converged in three iterations.

For example, consider Table 1.13, which shows the percent of variance explained by *factors 1* and *2*, for the initial unrotated extraction (left side) and the rotated version (right side).

The sums of squared loadings for *factor 1* for the unrotated case is (using Table 1.10 and allowing for rounding, as always) $0.590^2 + 0.295^2 + 0.193^2 + 0.224^2 + -0.115^2 = 0.536$. This represents 10.7% of the total variability and about 61% of the variance explained by the first two factors. For the rotated case, *factor 1*'s influence has been partially redistributed to *factor 2* in this simplified example, now accounting for 9.6% of the total variability and about 55% of the variance explained by the first two factors.

Next we describe three methods for *orthogonal rotation*, in which the axes are rigidly maintained at 90°. When rotating the matrix of factor loadings, the goal is to

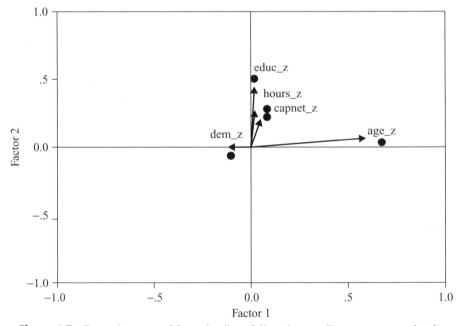

Figure 1.7   Rotated vectors of factor loadings follow the coordinate axes more closely.

TABLE 1.13   Factor Rotation Redistributes the Percentage of Variance Explained[a]

	Extraction Sums of Squared Loadings			Rotation Sums of Squared Loadings		
Factor	Total	% of Variance	Cumulative %	Total	% of Variance	Cumulative %
1	0.536	10.722	10.722	0.481	9.616	9.616
2	0.346	6.912	17.635	0.401	8.019	17.635

[a] Extraction method: principal axis factoring.

ease interpretability by simplifying the rows and columns of the column matrix. In the following discussion we assume that the columns in a matrix of factor loadings represent the factors and that the rows represent the variables, just as in Table 1.10, for example. Simplifying the rows of this matrix would entail maximizing the loading of a particular variable on one particular factor and keeping the loadings for this variable on the other factors as low as possible (ideal: row of zeros and ones). Similarly, simplifying the columns of this matrix would entail maximizing the loading of a particular factor on one particular variable and keeping the loadings for this factor on the other variables as low as possible (ideal: column of zeros and ones).

- *Quartimax rotation* seeks to simplify the rows of a matrix of factor loadings. Quartimax rotation tends to rotate the axes so that the variables have high loadings for the first factor and low loadings thereafter. The difficulty is that it can generate a strong "general" first factor, in which almost every variable has high loadings.

- *Varimax rotation* prefers to simplify the column of the factor loading matrix. Varimax rotation maximizes the variability in the loadings for the factors, with a goal of working toward the ideal column of zeros and ones for each variable. The rationale for varimax rotation is that we can best interpret the factors when they are strongly associated with some variable and strongly not associated with other variables. Kaiser [7,8] showed that the varimax rotation is more invariant than the quartimax rotation.

- *Equimax rotation* seeks to compromise between simplifying the columns and the rows.

The researcher may prefer to avoid the requirement that the rotated factors remain orthogonal (independent). In this case, *oblique rotation* methods are available in which the factors may be correlated with each other. This rotation method is called oblique because the axes are no longer required to be at 90°, but may form an oblique angle. For more on oblique rotation methods, see Harmon [9].

USER-DEFINED COMPOSITES

Factor analysis continues to be controversial, in part due to the lack of invariance under transformation and the consequent nonuniqueness of the factor solutions. Analysts may prefer a much more straightforward alternative: *user-defined composites*. A user-defined composite is simply a linear combination of the variables which combines several variables into a single composite measure. In the behavior science literature, user-defined composites are known as *summated scales* (e.g., Robinson et al. [10]).

User-defined composites take the form

$$W = \mathbf{a}'Z = a_1 Z_1 + a_2 Z_2 + \cdots + a_k Z_k$$

where $\sum_{i=1}^{k} a_i = 1, k \leq m$, and the Z_i are the standardized variables. Whichever form the linear combination takes, however, the variables should be standardized first so that one variable with high dispersion does not overwhelm the others. The simplest user-defined composite is simply the mean of the variables. In this case, $a_i = 1/k, i = 1, 2, \ldots, k$. However, if the analyst has prior information or expert knowledge available to indicate that the variables should not all be weighted equally, each coefficient a_i can be chosen to reflect the relative weight of that variable, with more important variables receiving higher weights.

What are the benefits of utilizing user-defined composites? When compared to the use of individual variables, user-defined composites provide a way to diminish the effect of measurement error. *Measurement error* refers to the disparity between the variable values observed, and the "true" variable value. Such disparity can be due to a variety of reasons, including mistranscription and instrument failure. Measurement error contributes to the background error noise, interfering with the ability of models to accurately process the signal provided by the data, with the result that truly significant relationships may be missed. User-defined composites reduce measurement error by combining multiple variables into a single measure.

Appropriately constructed user-defined composites allow the analyst to represent the manifold aspects of a particular concept using a single measure. Thus, user-defined composites enable the analyst to embrace the range of model characteristics while retaining the benefits of a parsimonious model. Analysts should ensure that the conceptual definition for their user-defined composites lies grounded in prior research or established practice. The conceptual definition of a composite refers to the theoretical foundations for the composite. For example, have other researchers used the same composite, or does this composite follow from best practices in one's field of business? If the analyst is aware of no such precedent for his or her user-defined composite, a solid rationale should be provided to support the conceptual definition of the composite.

The variables comprising the user-defined composite should be highly correlated with each other and uncorrelated with other variables used in the analysis. This unidimensionality should be confirmed empirically, perhaps through the use of principal components analysis, with the variables having high loadings on a single component and low-to-moderate loadings on the other components.

Example of a User-Defined Composite

Consider again the *houses* data set. Suppose that the analyst had reason to believe that the four variables *total rooms*, *total bedrooms*, *population*, and *households* were highly correlated with each other and not with other variables. The analyst could then construct the following user-defined composite:

$$W = \mathbf{a}'Z = \frac{a_1(\textit{total rooms}) + a_2(\textit{total bedrooms}) + a_3(\textit{population}) + a_2(\textit{households})}{4},$$

with $a_i = 1/4, i = 1, \ldots, 4$, so that *composite W* represented the mean of the four (standardized) variables.

The conceptual definition of *composite W* is "block group size," a natural and straightforward concept. It is unlikely that all block groups have exactly the same size and therefore that, differences in block group size may account for part of the variability in the other variables. We might expect large block groups tending to have large values for all four variables, and small block groups tending to have small values for all four variables.

The analyst should seek out support in the research or business literature for the conceptual definition of the composite. The evidence for the existence and relevance of the user-defined composite should be clear and convincing. For example, for *composite W*, the analyst may cite the study from the National Academy of Sciences by Hope et al. [11], which states that block groups in urban areas average 5.3 square kilometers in size, whereas block groups outside urban areas averaged 168 square kilometers in size. Since we may not presume that block groups inside and outside urban areas have exactly similar characteristics, this may mean that block group size could conceivably be associated with differences in block group characteristics, including *median housing value*, the response variable. Further, the analyst could cite the U.S. Census Bureau's notice in the *Federal Register* [12] that population density was much lower for block groups whose size was greater than 2 square miles. Hence, block group size may be considered a "real" and relevant concept to be used in further analysis downstream.

SUMMARY

Dimension reduction methods have the goal of using the correlation structure among the predictor variables to accomplish the following:

- To reduce the number of predictor components
- To help ensure that these components are independent
- To provide a framework for interpretability of the results

In this chapter we examined the following dimension reduction methods:

- Principal components analysis
- Factor analysis
- User-defined composites

Principal components analysis (PCA) seeks to explain the correlation structure of a set of predictor variables using a smaller set of linear combinations of these variables. These linear combinations are called *components*. The total variability of a data set produced by the complete set of m variables can often be accounted for primarily by a smaller set of k linear combinations of these variables, which would mean that there is almost as much information in the k components as there is in the original m variables. Principal components analysis can sift through the correlation structure of the predictor variables and identify the components underlying the correlated variables. Then the principal components can be used for further analysis downstream, such as in regression analysis, classification, and so on.

The first principal component may be viewed in general as the single best summary of the correlations among the predictors. Specifically, this particular linear combination of the variables accounts for more variability than any other conceivable linear combination. The second principal component, Y_2, is the second-best linear combination of the variables, on the condition that it is orthogonal to the first principal component. Two vectors are *orthogonal* if they are mathematically independent, have no correlation, and are at right angles to each other. The second component is derived from the variability that is left over once the first component has been accounted for. The third component is the third-best linear combination of the variables, on the condition that it is orthogonal to the first two components. The third component is derived from the variance remaining after the first two components have been extracted. The remaining components are defined similarly.

The criteria used for deciding how many components to extract are the following:

- Eigenvalue criterion
- Proportion of variance explained criterion
- Minimum communality criterion
- Scree plot criterion

The eigenvalue criterion states that each component should explain at least one variable's worth of the variability, and therefore the eigenvalue criterion states that only components with eigenvalues greater than 1 should be retained. For the proportion of variance explained criterion, the analyst simply selects the components one by one until the desired proportion of variability explained is attained. The minimum communality criterion states that enough components should be extracted so that the communalities for each of these variables exceeds a certain threshold (e.g., 50%). The scree plot criterion is this: The maximum number of components that should be extracted is *just prior to* where the plot begins to straighten out into a horizontal line.

Part of the PCA output takes the form of a component matrix, with cell entries called the *component weights*. These component weights represent the partial correlation between a particular variable and a given component. For a component weight to be considered of practical significance, it should exceed ±0.50 in magnitude. Note that the component weight represents the correlation between the component and the variable; thus, the squared component weight represents the amount of the variable's total variability that is explained by the component. Thus, this threshold value of ±0.50 requires that at least 25% of the variable's variance be explained by a particular component.

PCA does not extract all the variance from the variables, only that proportion of the variance that is shared by several variables. *Communality* represents the proportion of variance of a particular variable that is shared with other variables. The communalities represent the overall importance of each of the variables in the PCA as a whole. Communality values are calculated as the sum of squared component weights for a given variable. Communalities less than 0.5 can be considered to be too low, since this would mean that the variable shares less than half of its variability in common with the other variables.

Factor analysis is related to principal components, but the two methods have different goals. Principal components seeks to identify orthogonal linear combinations of the variables, to be used either for descriptive purposes or to substitute a smaller number of uncorrelated components for the original variables. In contrast, factor analysis represents a *model* for the data, and as such is more elaborate.

Unfortunately, the factor solutions provided by factor analysis are not invariant to transformations. Hence, the factors uncovered by the model are in essence nonunique, without further constraints. The Kaiser–Meyer–Olkin measure of sampling adequacy and Bartlett's test of sphericity are used to determine whether a sufficient level of correlation exists among the predictor variables to apply factor analysis.

Factor loadings are analogous to the component weights in principal components analysis and represent the correlation between the ith variable and the jth factor. To assist in the interpretation of the factors, *factor rotation* may be performed. Factor rotation corresponds to a transformation (usually, orthogonal) of the coordinate axes, leading to a different set of factor loadings. Often, the first factor extracted represents a "general factor" and accounts for much of the total variability. The effect of factor rotation is to redistribute the variability explained among the second, third, and subsequent factors.

Three methods for orthogonal rotation are quartimax rotation, varimax rotation, and equimax rotation. Quartimax rotation tends to rotate the axes so that the variables have high loadings for the first factor and low loadings thereafter. Varimax rotation maximizes the variability in the loadings for the factors, with a goal of working toward the ideal column of zeros and ones for each variable. Equimax seeks to compromise between the previous two methods. Oblique rotation methods are also available in which the factors may be correlated with each other.

A user-defined composite is simply a linear combination of the variables, which combines several variables together into a single composite measure. User-defined composites provide a way to diminish the effect of measurement error by combining multiple variables into a single measure. User-defined composites enable the analyst to embrace the range of model characteristics while retaining the benefits of a parsimonious model. Analysts should ensure that the conceptual definition for their user-defined composites lies grounded in prior research or established practice. The variables comprising the user-defined composite should be highly correlated with each other and uncorrelated with other variables used in the analysis.

REFERENCES

1. Daniel Larose, *Discovering Knowledge in Data: An Introduction to Data Mining*, Wiley, Hoboken, NJ, 2005.
2. R. Bellman, *Adaptive Control Processes: A Guided Tour*, Princeton University Press, Princeton, NJ, 1961.
3. R. Kelley Pace and Ronald Berry, Sparse spatial autoregressions, *Statistics and Probability Letters*, Vol. 33, No. 3, pp. 291–297. May 5, 1997. Data set available from StatLib: `http://lib.stat.cmu.edu/datasets/houses.zip`. Also available at the book series Web site.
4. Richard A. Johnson and Dean Wichern, *Applied Multivariate Statistical Analysis*, Prentice Hall, Upper Saddle River, NJ, 1998.
5. Joseph Hair, Rolph Anderson, Ronald Tatham, and William Black, *Multivariate Data Analysis*, 4th ed., Prentice Hall, Upper Saddle River, NJ, 1995.
6. Adult data set, in C. L. Blake and C. J. Merz, UCI Repository of Machine Learning Databases, `http://www.ics.uci.edu/~mlearn/MLRepository.html`, University of California, Department of Information and Computer Science, Irvine, CA, *Adult* data set compiled by Ron Kohavi. Also available at the book series Web site.
7. H. F. Kaiser, A second-generation Little Jiffy, *Psychometrika*, Vol. 35, pp. 401–15, 1970.
8. H. F. Kaiser, Little Jiffy, Mark IV, *Educational and Psychological Measurement*, Vol. 34, pp. 111–117, 1974.
9. H. H. Harmon, *Modern Factor Analysis*, 2nd ed., University of Chicago Press, Chicago.
10. J. P. Robinson, P. R. Shaver, and L. S. Wrightsman, Criteria for scale selection and evaluation, in J. P. Robinson, P. R. Shaver, and L. S. Wrightsman, eds. *Measures of Personality and Social Psychological Attitudes*, Academic Press, San Diego, CA, 1991.
11. Diane Hope, Corinna Gries, Weixung Zhu, William F. Fagan, Charles L. Redman, Nancy B. Grimm, Amy L. Nelson, Chris Martin, and Ann Kinzig, Socioeconomics drive urban plant diversity, *Proceedings of the National Academy of Sciences*, Vol. 100, No. 15, pp. 8788–8792, July 22, 2003.
12. U.S. Census, Bureau, Urban area criteria for census 2000, *Federal Register*, Vol, 67, No. 51, March 15, 2002; `http://www.census.gov/geo/www/ua/uafedreg031502.pdf`.
13. Churn data set, in C. L. Blake and C. J. Merz, UCI Repository of Machine Learning Databases, `http://www.ics.uci.edu/~mlearn/MLRepository.html`, University of California, Department of Information and Computer Science, Irvine, CA, 1998. Also available at the book series Web site.

EXERCISES

Clarifying the Concepts

1.1. Determine whether the following statements are true or false. If a statement is false, explain why and suggest how one might alter the statement to make it true.

(a) Positive correlation indicates that as one variable increases, the other variable increases as well.

(b) Changing the scale of measurement for the covariance matrix (e.g., from meters to kilometers) will change the value of the covariance.

(c) The total variability in the data set equals the number of records.

(d) The value of the ith principal component equals the ith eigenvalue divided by the number of variables.

(e) The second principal component represents any linear combination of the variables that accounts for the most variability in the data once the first principal component has been extracted.

(f) For a component weight to be considered of practical significance, it should exceed ±0.50 in magnitude.

(g) The principal components are always mutually exclusive and exhaustive of the variables.

(h) When validating the principal components, we would expect the component weights from the training and test data sets to have the same signs.

(i) For factor analysis to function properly, the predictor variables should not be highly correlated.

1.2. For what type of data are the covariance and correlation matrices identical? In this case, what is Σ?

1.3. What is special about the first principal component in terms of variability?

1.4. Describe the four criteria for choosing how many components to extract. Explain the rationale for each.

1.5. Explain the concept of communality, so that someone new to the field could understand it.

1.6. Explain the difference between principal components analysis and factor analysis. What is a drawback of factor analysis?

1.7. Describe two tests for determining whether there exists sufficient correlation within a data set for factor analysis to proceed. Which results from these tests would allow us to proceed?

1.8. Explain why we perform factor rotation. Describe three different methods for factor rotation.

1.9. What is a user-defined-composite, and what is the benefit of using it in place of individual variables?

Working with the Data

The following computer output explores the application of principal components analysis to the *churn* data set [13].

1.10 Based on the information given in Table E1.10, does there exist an adequate amount of correlation among the predictors to pursue principal components analysis? Explain how you know this, and how we may be getting mixed signals.

TABLE E1.10

Kaiser–Meyer–Olkin measure of sampling adequacy	0.512
Bartlett's test of sphericity	
Approx. chi-square	34.908
df	55
Significance	0.984

1.11 Suppose that we go ahead and perform the PCA, in this case using seven components. Considering the communalities given in Table E1.11, which variable or variables might we be well advised to omit from the PCA, and why? If we really need all these variables in the analysis, what should we do?

TABLE E1.11[a]

	Initial	Extraction
Zacctlen	1.000	0.606
Zvmailme	1.000	0.836
Zdaycall	1.000	0.528
Zdaychar	1.000	0.954
Zevecall	1.000	0.704
Zevechar	1.000	0.621
Znitecal	1.000	0.543
Znitecha	1.000	0.637
Zintcall	1.000	0.439
Zintchar	1.000	0.588
Zcsc	1.000	0.710

[a] Extraction method: principal component analysis.

1.12 Based on the information given in Table E1.12, how many components should be extracted using (a) the eigenvalue criterion, and (b) the proportion of variance explained criterion?

TABLE E1.12

	Initial Eigenvalues		
Component	Total	% of Variance	Cumulative %
1	1.088	9.890	9.890
2	1.056	9.596	19.486
3	1.040	9.454	28.939
4	1.023	9.296	38.236
5	1.000	9.094	47.329
6	0.989	8.987	56.317
7	0.972	8.834	65.151
8	0.969	8.811	73.961
9	0.963	8.754	82.715
10	0.962	8.747	91.462
11	0.939	8.538	100.000

1.13 Based on the scree plot shown in Figure E1.13, how many components should be extracted using the scree plot criterion? Now, based on the three criteria, work toward a decision on the number of components to extract.

1.14 (a) Based on the following rotated component matrix; provide a quick profile of the first four components.

(b) If we extracted an sixth component, describe how the first component would change.

(c) What is your considered opinion as to the usefulness of applying PCA on this data set?

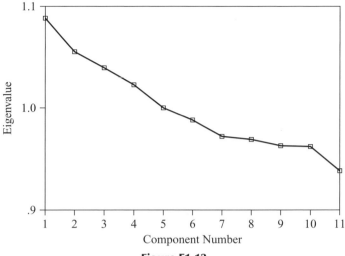

Figure E1.13

TABLE E1.14   Rotated Component Matrix[a]

	Component				
	1	2	3	4	5
Zacctlen	0.652				
Zvmailme				0.521	
Zdaycall	0.623				
Zevecall			0.508		
Znitecal			0.551		
Zintcall		0.601			
Zcsc				−0.592	
Zdaychar			0.617		
Zevechar				0.429	−0.572
Znitechar					0.697
Zintchar		0.657			

[a] Rotation converged in 8 iterations.
Extraction method: principal component analysis.
Rotation method: Varimax with Kaiser normalization.

Hands-on Analysis

For the following exercises, work with the *baseball* data set, available from the book series Web site.

1.15 Filter out all batters with fewer than 100 at bats. Standardize all the numerical variables using z-scores.

1.16 Suppose that we are interested in estimating the number of home runs based on the other numerical variables in the data set. So all the other numeric variables will be our predictors. Investigate whether sufficient variability exists among the predictors to perform PCA.

1.17 How many components should be extracted according to:

    (a) The eigenvalue criterion?

    (b) The proportion of variance explained criterion?

    (c) The scree plot criterion?

    (d) The communality criterion?

1.18 Based on the information from Exercise 1.17, make a decision about how many components you should extract.

1.19 Apply PCA using varimax rotation with your chosen number of components. Write up a short profile of the first few components extracted.

1.20 Construct a useful user-defined composite using the predictors. Describe situations where the composite would be more appropriate or useful than the principal components, and vice versa.

CHAPTER 2

REGRESSION MODELING

Regression modeling represents a powerful and elegant method for estimating the value of a continuous target variable. In this chapter we introduce regression modeling through simple linear regression, where a straight line is used to approximate the relationship between a single continuous predictor variable and a single continuous response variable. Later, in Chapter 3, we turn to multiple regression, where several predictor variables are used to estimate a single response. We introduced regression analysis in Chapter 4 of *Discovering Knowledge in Data: An Introduction to Data Mining* [1]. Here, we explore the many aspects of simple linear regression in greater detail.

Data Mining Methods and Models By Daniel T. Larose
Copyright © 2006 John Wiley & Sons, Inc.

EXAMPLE OF SIMPLE LINEAR REGRESSION

To develop the simple linear regression model, consider the *cereals* data set, an excerpt of which is presented in Table 2.1. The *cereals* data set (Data and Story Library[2]) contains nutritional information for 77 breakfast cereals and includes the following variables:

- Cereal name
- Cereal manufacturer
- Type (hot or cold)
- Calories per serving
- Grams of protein
- Grams of fat
- Milligrams of sodium
- Grams of fiber
- Grams of carbohydrates
- Grams of sugar
- Milligrams of potassium
- Percentage of recommended daily allowance of vitamins (0%, 25%, or 100%)
- Weight of one serving
- Number of cups per serving
- Shelf location (1, bottom; 2, middle; 3, top)
- Nutritional rating, as calculated by *Consumer Reports*

TABLE 2.1 Excerpt from the *Cereals* Data Set: Eight Fields, First 16 Cereals

Cereal Name	Manuf.	Sugars	Calories	Protein	Fat	Sodium	Rating
100% Bran	N	6	70	4	1	130	68.4030
100% Natural Bran	Q	8	120	3	5	15	33.9837
All-Bran	K	5	70	4	1	260	59.4255
All-Bran Extra Fiber	K	0	50	4	0	140	93.7049
Almond Delight	R	8	110	2	2	200	34.3848
Apple Cinnamon Cheerios	G	10	110	2	2	180	29.5095
Apple Jacks	K	14	110	2	0	125	33.1741
Basic 4	G	8	130	3	2	210	37.0386
Bran Chex	R	6	90	2	1	200	49.1203
Bran Flakes	P	5	90	3	0	210	53.3138
Cap'n crunch	Q	12	120	1	2	220	18.0429
Cheerios	G	1	110	6	2	290	50.7650
Cinnamon Toast Crunch	G	9	120	1	3	210	19.8236
Clusters	G	7	110	3	2	140	40.4002
Cocoa Puffs	G	13	110	1	1	180	22.7364

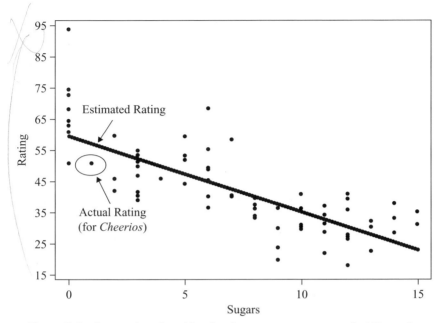

Figure 2.1   Scatter plot of nutritional rating versus sugar content for 77 cereals.

Suppose that we are interested in estimating the nutritional *rating* of a cereal given its *sugar* content. Figure 2.1 presents a scatter plot of the nutritional rating versus the sugar content for the 77 cereals, along with the least-squares regression line. The regression line is written in the form $\hat{y} = b_0 + b_1 x$, called the regression equation or *estimated regression equation* (ERE), where:

- $\hat{y}$ is the estimated value of the response variable.
- b_0 is the *y-intercept* of the regression line.
- b_1 is the *slope* of the regression line.
- b_0 and b_1, together, are called the *regression coefficients*.

In this case, the ERE is given as $\hat{y} = 59.4 - 2.42(sugars)$, so that $b_0 = 59.4$ and $b_1 = -2.42$. Below we demonstrate how this equation is calculated. This estimated regression equation can then be interpreted as: The estimated cereal rating equals 59.4 minus 2.42 times the sugar content in grams. The regression line, and the ERE, is used as a *linear approximation* of the relationship between the x (predictor) and y (response) variables, that is, between sugar content and nutritional rating. We can use the regression line or the ERE to make estimates or predictions. For example, suppose that we are interested in estimating the nutritional rating for a new cereal (not in the original data) that contains $x = 1$ gram of sugar. Using the ERE, we find the estimated nutritional rating for a cereal with 1 gram of sugar to be $\hat{y} = 59.4 - 2.42(2.1) = 56.98$. Note that this estimated value for the nutritional rating lies directly on the regression line, at the location ($x = 1$, $\hat{y} = 56.98$), as shown in Figure 2.1. In fact, for any given value of x (sugar content), the estimated value for $\hat{y}$ (nutritional rating) lies precisely on the regression line.

Now there is one cereal in our data set that does have a sugar content of 1 gram—Cheerios. Its nutritional rating, however, is 50.765, not 56.98 as we estimated above for the new cereal with 1 gram of sugar. Cheerios' point in the scatter plot is located at ($x = 1$, $y = 50.765$), within the oval in Figure 2.1. Now, the upper arrow in Figure 2.1 is pointing to a location on the regression line directly above the Cheerios point. This is where the regression equation predicted the nutrition rating to be for a cereal with a sugar content of 1 gram. The prediction was too high by $56.98 - 50.765 = 6.215$ rating points, which represents the vertical distance from the Cheerios data point to the regression line. This vertical distance of 6.215 rating points, in general $y - \hat{y}$, is known variously as the *prediction error*, *estimation error*, or *residual*.

We of course seek to minimize the overall size of our prediction errors. *Least-squares regression* works by choosing the unique regression line that minimizes the sum of squared residuals over all the data points. There are alternative methods of choosing the line that best approximates the linear relationship between the variables, such as median regression, although least squares remains the most common method.

LEAST-SQUARES ESTIMATES

Now suppose that our data set contained a sample of 77 cereals different from the sample in our *cereals* data set. Would we expect that the relationship between nutritional rating and sugar content to be exactly the same as that found above, $\hat{y} = 59.4 - 2.42(sugars)$? Probably not. Here, b_0 and b_1 are *statistics*, whose values differs from sample to sample. Like other statistics, b_0 and b_1 are used to estimate population parameters, in this case β_0 and β_1, the y-intercept, and the slope of the true regression line. That is,

$$y = \beta_0 + \beta_1 x + \varepsilon \tag{2.1}$$

represents the true linear relationship between nutritional rating and sugar content for *all* cereals, not just those in our sample. The *error term* ε is needed to account for the indeterminacy in the model, since two cereals may have the same sugar content but different nutritional ratings. The residuals ($y_i - \hat{y}$) are estimates of the error terms, ε_i, $i = 1, \ldots, n$. Equation (2.1) is called the regression equation or *true population regression equation*; it is associated with the true or population regression line.

Earlier, we found the estimated regression equation for estimating the nutritional rating from sugar content to be $\hat{y} = 59.4 - 2.42(sugars)$. Where did these values for b_0 and b_1 come from? Let us now derive the formulas for estimating the y-intercept and slope of the estimated regression line given the data. Suppose that we have n observations from the model in equation (2.1); that is, we have

$$y_i = \beta_0 + \beta_1 x_i + \varepsilon_i \qquad i = 1, \ldots, n$$

The least-squares line is that line which minimizes the population sum of squared errors, $\text{SSE}_p = \sum_{i=1}^{n} \varepsilon_i^2$. First, we reexpress the population sum of squared errors as

$$\text{SSE}_p = \sum_{i=1}^{n} \varepsilon_i^2 = \sum_{i=1}^{n} (y_i - \beta_0 - \beta_1 x_i)^2 \tag{2.2}$$

Then, recalling our differential calculus, we may find the values of β_0 and β_1 that minimize $\sum_{i=1}^{n} \varepsilon_i^2$ by differentiating equation (2.2) with respect to β_0 and β_1 and setting the results equal to zero. The partial derivatives of equation (2.2) with respect to β_0 and β_1 are, respectively,

$$\frac{\partial \text{SSE}_p}{\partial \beta_0} = -2 \sum_{i=1}^{n} (y_i - \beta_0 - \beta_1 x_i)$$

$$\frac{\partial \text{SSE}_p}{\partial \beta_1} = -2 \sum_{i=1}^{n} x_i (y_i - \beta_0 - \beta_1 x_i)$$

(2.3)

We are interested in the values for the estimates b_0 and b_1, so setting equations (2.3) equal to zero, we have

$$\sum_{i=1}^{n} (y_i - b_0 - b_1 x_i) = 0$$

$$\sum_{i=1}^{n} x_i (y_i - b_0 - b_1 x_i) = 0$$

Distributing the summation gives us

$$\sum_{i=1}^{n} y_i - n b_0 - b_1 \sum_{i=1}^{n} x_i = 0$$

$$\sum_{i=1}^{n} x_i y_i - b_0 \sum_{i=1}^{n} x_i - b_1 \sum_{i=1}^{n} x_i^2 = 0$$

which is reexpressed as

$$b_0 n + b_1 \sum_{i=1}^{n} x_i = \sum_{i=1}^{n} y_i$$

(2.4)

$$b_0 \sum_{i=1}^{n} x_i + b_1 \sum_{i=1}^{n} x_i^2 = \sum_{i=1}^{n} x_i y_i$$

Solving equations (2.4) for b_1 and b_0, we have

$$b_1 = \frac{\sum x_i y_i - \left[\left(\sum x_i \right) \left(\sum y_i \right) \right] / n}{\sum x_i^2 - \left(\sum x_i \right)^2 / n}$$

(2.5)

$$b_0 = \bar{y} - b_1 \bar{x}$$

(2.6)

where n is the total number of observations, $\bar{x}$ the mean value for the predictor variable, $\bar{y}$ the mean value for the response variable, and the summations are $i = 1$ to n. Equations (2.5) and (2.6) are therefore the least-squares estimates for β_0 and β_1, the values that minimize the sum of squared errors.

We now illustrate how we may find the values $b_0 = 59.4$ and $b_1 = -2.42$, using equations (2.5) and (2.6) and the summary statistics from Table 2.2, which shows the values for x_i, y_i, $x_i y_i$, and x_i^2 for the cereals in the data set (note that only 16 of the 77 cereals are shown). It turns out that for this data set, $\sum x_i = 534$, $\sum y_i = 3285.26$, $\sum x_i y_i = 19,186.7$, and $\sum x_i^2 = 5190$. Plugging into formulas (2.5) and (2.6), we

TABLE 2.2 Summary Statistics for Finding b_0 and b_1

Cereal Name	Sugars, x	Rating, y	xy	x^2
100% Bran	6	68.4030	410.418	36
100% Natural Bran	8	33.9837	271.870	64
All-Bran	5	59.4255	297.128	25
All-Bran Extra Fiber	0	93.7049	0.000	0
Almond Delight	8	34.3848	275.078	64
Apple Cinnamon Cheerios	10	29.5095	295.095	100
Apple Jacks	14	33.1741	464.437	196
Basic 4	8	37.0386	296.309	64
Bran Chex	6	49.1203	294.722	36
Bran Flakes	5	53.3138	266.569	25
Cap'n Crunch	12	18.0429	216.515	144
Cheerios	1	50.7650	50.765	1
Cinnamon Toast Crunch	9	19.8236	178.412	81
Clusters	7	40.4002	282.801	49
Cocoa Puffs	13	22.7364	295.573	169
$\vdots$	$\vdots$	$\vdots$		
Wheaties Honey Gold	8	36.1876	289.501	64

$$\sum x_i = 534 \qquad \sum y_i = 3285.26$$
$$\bar{x} = 534/77 \qquad \bar{y} = 3285.26/77 \qquad \sum x_i y_i \qquad \sum x_i^2$$
$$= 6.935 \qquad = 42.6657 \qquad = 19,186.7 \qquad = 5190$$

find that

$$b_1 = \frac{\sum x_i y_i - \left[\left(\sum x_i\right)\left(\sum y_i\right)\right]/n}{\sum x_i^2 - \left(\sum x_i\right)^2/n} = \frac{19,186.7 - (534)(3285.26)/77}{5190 - (534)^2/77}$$

$$= \frac{-3596.791429}{1486.675325} = -2.42$$

$$b_0 = \bar{y} - b_1 \bar{x} = 42.6657 - 2.42(6.935) = 59.4$$

These values for the slope and y-intercept provide us with the estimated regression line indicated in Figure 2.1.

The y-intercept b_0 is the location on the y-axis where the regression line intercepts the y-axis, that is, the estimated value for the response variable when the predictor variable equals zero. Now, in many regression situations, a value of zero for the predictor variable would not make sense. For example, suppose that we were trying to predict elementary school students' weight (y) based on the students' height (x). The meaning of *height* $= 0$ is unclear, so that the denotative meaning of the y-intercept would not make interpretive sense in this case.

However, for our data set, a value of zero for the sugar content does make sense, as several cereals contain zero grams of sugar. Therefore, for our data set, the y-intercept $b_0 = 59.4$ simply represents the estimated nutritional rating for cereals with zero sugar content. Note that none of the cereals containing zero grams of sugar have this estimated nutritional rating of exactly 59.4. The actual ratings, along with the prediction errors, are shown in Table 2.2. Note that all the predicted ratings are the same, since all these cereals had identical values for the predictor variable ($x = 0$).

The slope of the regression line indicates the estimated change in y per unit increase in x. We interpret $b_1 = -2.42$ to mean the following: For each increase of 1 gram in sugar content, the estimated nutritional rating decreases by 2.42 rating points. For example, cereal A with 5 more grams of sugar than cereal B would have an estimated nutritional rating $5(2.42) = 12.1$ ratings points lower than cereal B.

COEFFICIENT OF DETERMINATION

Of course, a least-squares regression line could be found to approximate the relationship between any two continuous variables; but this does not guarantee that the regression will be useful. The question therefore arises as to how we may determine whether a particular estimated regression equation is useful for making predictions. We shall work toward developing a statistic, r^2, for measuring the goodness of fit of the regression. That is, r^2, known as the *coefficient of determination*, measures how well the linear approximation produced by the least-squares regression line actually fits the data observed. Recall that $\hat{y}$ represents the estimated value of the response variable and that $y - \hat{y}$ represents the *prediction error* or *residual*.

Consider the data set in Table 2.3, which shows the distance in kilometers traveled by a sample of 10 orienteering competitors, along with the elapsed time in hours. For example, the first competitor traveled 10 kilometers in 2 hours. Based on these 10 competitors, the estimated regression takes the form $\hat{y} = 6 + 2x$, so that the estimated distance traveled equals 6 kilometers plus two times the number of hours. You should verify that you can calculate this estimated regression equation, using either software or equations (2.5) and (2.6).

This estimated regression equation can be used to make predictions about the distance traveled for a given number of hours. These estimated values of y are given as

TABLE 2.3 SSE for the Orienteering Example

Subject	Time, x (hours)	Distance, y (km)	Score Predicted, $\hat{y} = 6 + 2x$	Error in Prediction, $y - \hat{y}$	(Error in Prediction)^2, $(y - \hat{y})^2$
1	2	10	10	0	0
2	2	11	10	1	1
3	3	12	12	0	0
4	4	13	14	−1	1
5	4	14	14	0	0
6	5	15	16	−1	1
7	6	20	18	2	4
8	7	18	20	−2	4
9	8	22	22	0	0
10	9	25	24	1	1
				$\text{SSE} = \sum (y - \hat{y})^2 = 12$	

the predicted score in Table 2.3. The prediction error and squared prediction error may then be calculated. The sum of the squared prediction errors, or the *sum of squares error*, SSE $= \sum (y - \hat{y})^2$, represents an overall measure of the error in prediction resulting from the use of the estimated regression equation. Here we have SSE $= 12$. Is this value large? We are unable to state whether this value SSE $= 12$ is large, since at this point we have no other measure to which to compare it.

Now imagine for a moment that we were interested in estimating the distance traveled *without knowledge of the number of hours*. That is, suppose that we did not have access to the x-variable information for use in estimating the y-variable. Clearly, our estimates of the distance traveled would be degraded, on the whole, since less information usually results in less accurate estimates.

Because we lack access to the predictor information, our best estimate for y is simply $\bar{y}$, the sample mean of the number of hours traveled. We would be forced to use $\bar{y} = 16$ to estimate the number of kilometers traveled for every competitor, regardless of the number of hours that person had traveled. Consider Figure 2.2. The estimates for distance traveled when ignoring the time information is shown by the horizontal line $\bar{y} = 16$. Disregarding the time information entails predicting $\bar{y} = 16$ kilometers for the distance traveled, for orienteering competitors who have been hiking only 2 or 3 hours, as well as for those who have been out all day (8 or 9 hours). This is clearly not optimal.

The data points in Figure 2.2 seem to "cluster" tighter around the estimated regression line than around the line $\bar{y} = 16$, which suggests that overall, the prediction errors are smaller when we use the x-information than otherwise. For example, consider competitor 10, who hiked $y = 25$ kilometers in $x = 9$ hours. If we ignore the x-information, the estimation error would be $y - \bar{y} = 25 - 16 = 9$ kilometers. This prediction error is indicated as the vertical line between the data point for this competitor and the horizontal line, that is, the vertical distance between the y observed and the $\bar{y} = 16$ predicted.

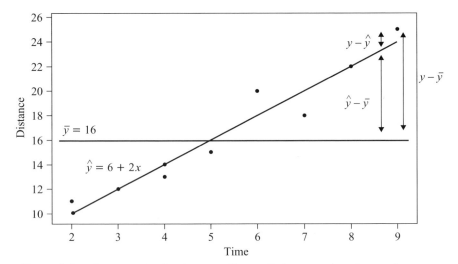

Figure 2.2 The regression line has a smaller prediction error than the sample mean.

Suppose that we proceeded to find $y - \bar{y}$ for every record in the data set and then found the sum of squares of these measures, just as we did for $y - \hat{y}$ when we calculated the sum of squares error. This would lead us to SST, the *sum of squares total*:

$$\text{SST} = \sum_{i=1}^{n} (y - \bar{y})^2$$

SST, also known as the total sum of squares, is a measure of the total variability in the values of the response variable alone, without reference to the predictor. Note that SST is a function of the *variance* of y, where the variance is the square of the standard deviation of y:

$$\text{SST} = \sum_{i=1}^{n} (y - \bar{y})^2 = (n - 1) \, \text{Var}(y) = (n - 1) \, [\text{SD}(y)]^2$$

Thus, all three of these measures, SST, variance, and standard deviation, are univariate measures of the variability in y alone (although, of course, we could find the variance and standard deviation of the predictor as well).

Would we expect SST to be larger or smaller than SSE? Using the calculations shown in Table 2.4, we have SST $= 228$, which is much larger than SSE $= 12$. We now have something to compare SSE against. Since SSE is so much smaller than SST, this indicates that using the predictor information in the regression results in much tighter estimates overall than ignoring the predictor information. These sums of squares measure errors in prediction, so that smaller is better. In other words, using the regression improves our estimates of the distance traveled.

Next, what we would like is a measure of how much the estimated regression equation improves the estimates. Once again examine Figure 2.2. For hiker 10, the estimation error when using the regression is $y - \hat{y} = 25 - 24 = 1$, and the estimation error when ignoring the time information is $y - \bar{y} = 25 - 16 = 9$. Therefore, the amount of *improvement* (reduction in estimation error) is $\hat{y} - \bar{y} = 24 - 16 = 8$.

Once again, we may proceed to construct a sum of squares statistic based on $\hat{y} - \bar{y}$. Such a statistic is known as SSR, the *sum of squares regression*, a measure of

TABLE 2.4   SST for the Orienteering Example

Student	Time, x	Score, y	$\bar{y}$	$y - \bar{y}$	$(y - \bar{y})^2$
1	2	10	16	-6	36
2	2	11	16	-5	25
3	3	12	16	-4	16
4	4	13	16	-3	9
5	4	14	16	-2	4
6	5	15	16	-1	1
7	6	20	16	4	16
8	7	18	16	2	4
9	8	22	16	6	36
10	9	25	16	9	81
					SST $= \sum (y - \bar{y})^2 = 228$

the overall improvement in prediction accuracy when using the regression as opposed to ignoring the predictor information.

$$SSR = \sum_{i=1}^{n} (\hat{y} - \bar{y})^2$$

Observe from Figure 2.2 that the vertical distance $y - \bar{y}$ may be partitioned into two "pieces," $\hat{y} - \bar{y}$ and $y - \hat{y}$. This follows from the following identity:

$$y - \bar{y} = (\hat{y} - \bar{y}) + (y - \hat{y}) \tag{2.7}$$

Now, suppose that we square each side and take the summation. We then obtain

$$\sum (y_i - \bar{y})^2 = \sum (\hat{y}_i - \bar{y})^2 + \sum (y_i - \hat{y}_i)^2 \tag{2.8}$$

[The cross-product term $2 \sum (\hat{y}_i - \bar{y})(y_i - \hat{y}_i)$ cancels out; see Draper and Smith [3] for details.]

We recognize from equation (2.8) the three sums of squares we have been developing and can therefore express the relationship among them as follows:

$$SST = SSR + SSE \tag{2.9}$$

We have seen that SST measures the total variability in the response variable. We may then think of SSR as the amount of variability in the response variable that is "explained" by the regression. In other words, SSR measures that portion of the variability in the response variable that is accounted for by the linear relationship between the response and the predictor.

However, since not all the data points lie precisely on the regression line, this means that there remains some variability in the y-variable that is not accounted for by the regression. SSE can be thought of as measuring all the variability in y from all sources, including random error, after the linear relationship between x and y has been accounted for by the regression. Earlier we found that SST = 228 and SSE = 12. Then, using equation (2.9), we can find SSR to be SSR = SST − SSE = 228 − 12 = 216. Of course, these sums of squares must always be nonnegative.

We are now ready to introduce the *coefficient of determination*, r^2, which measures the goodness of fit of the regression as an approximation of the linear relationship between the predictor and response variables.

$$r^2 = \frac{SSR}{SST}$$

Since r^2 takes the form of a ratio of SSR to SST, we may interpret r^2 to represent the proportion of the variability in the y-variable that is explained by the regression, that is, by the linear relationship between the predictor and response variables.

What is the maximum value that r^2 can take? The maximum value for r^2 would occur when the regression is a perfect fit to the data set, which takes place when each of the data points lies precisely on the estimated regression line. In this optimal situation, there would be no estimation errors from using the regression, meaning that each of the residuals would equal zero, which in turn would mean that SSE would equal zero. From equation (2.9) we have that SST = SSR + SSE. If SSE = 0, then

SST = SSR, so that r^2 would equal SSR/SST = 1. Thus, the maximum value for r^2 is 1, which occurs when the regression is a perfect fit.

What is the minimum value that r^2 can take? Suppose that the regression showed no improvement at all; that is, suppose that the regression explained none of the variability in y. This would result in SSR equaling zero, and consequently, r^2 would equal zero as well. Thus, r^2 is bounded between zero and 1, inclusive. How are we to interpret the value that r^2 takes? Essentially, the higher the value of r^2, the better the fit of the regression to the data set. Values of r^2 near 1 denote an extremely good fit of the regression to the data; values near zero denote an extremely poor fit.

A very rough rule of thumb for the interpretation of r^2 might be to imagine it as a grade received on a very difficult exam. One might be quite pleased to get higher than 90%, happy with higher than 80%, somewhat satisfied with better than 70%, but disappointed with less than 50%. This heuristic must be applied carefully, however, since the interpretation of r^2 varies from field to field. In the physical sciences, for example, one encounters relationships that elicit very high values of r^2, whereas in the social sciences one may need to be content with lower values of r^2, because of person-to-person variability. As usual, the analyst's judgment should be tempered with the domain expert's experience.

STANDARD ERROR OF THE ESTIMATE

We have seen how the r^2 statistic measures the goodness of fit of the regression to the data set. Next, the s statistic, known as the *standard error of the estimate*, is a measure of the accuracy of the estimates produced by the regression. Clearly, s is one of the most important statistics to consider when performing a regression analysis. To find the value of s, we first find the *mean squared error*:

$$\text{MSE} = \frac{\text{SSE}}{n - m - 1}$$

where m indicates the number of predictor variables, which is 1 for the simple linear regression case and greater than 1 for the multiple regression case. Like SSE, MSE represents a measure of the variability in the response variable left unexplained by the regression.

Then the standard error of the estimate is given by

$$s = \sqrt{\text{MSE}} = \sqrt{\frac{\text{SSE}}{n - m - 1}}$$

The value of s provides an estimate of the "typical" residual, much as the value of the standard deviation in univariate analysis provides an estimate of the typical deviation. In other words, s is a measure of the typical error in estimation, the typical difference between the response value predicted and the actual response value. In this way, the standard error of the estimate s represents the precision of the predictions generated by the regression equation estimated. Smaller values of s are better.

For the orienteering example, we have

$$s = \sqrt{\text{MSE}} = \sqrt{\frac{12}{10 - 1 - 1}} = 1.2$$

Thus, the typical estimation error when using the regression model to predict distance is 1.2 kilometers. That is, if we are told how long a hiker has been traveling, our estimate of the distance covered will typically differ from the actual distance by about 1.2 kilometers. Note from Table 2.3 that all of the residuals lie between zero and 2 in absolute value, so that 1.2 may be considered a reasonable estimate of the typical residual. (Other measures, such as the mean absolute deviation of the residuals, may also be considered but are not widely reported in commercial software packages.)

We may compare $s = 1.2$ kilometers against the typical estimation error obtained from ignoring the predictor data, obtained from the standard deviation of the response,

$$\text{SD}_y = \sqrt{\frac{\sum_{i=1}^{n} (y - \bar{y})^2}{n - 1}} = 5.0$$

The typical prediction error when ignoring the time data is 5 kilometers. Using the regression has reduced the typical prediction error from 5 kilometers to 1.2 kilometers.

In the absence of software, one may use the following computational formulas for calculating the values of SST and SSR. The formula for SSR is exactly the same as for the slope b_1 except that the numerator is squared.

$$\text{SST} = \sum y^2 - \left(\sum y\right)^2 / n$$

$$\text{SSR} = \frac{\left[\sum xy - \left(\sum x\right)\left(\sum y\right)/n\right]^2}{\sum x^2 - \left(\sum x\right)^2 / n}$$

Let us use these formulas to find the values of SST and SSR for the orienteering example. You should verify that we have $\sum x = 50$, $\sum y = 160$, $\sum xy = 908$, $\sum x^2 = 304$, and $\sum y^2 = 2788$. Then

$$\text{SST} = \sum y^2 - \left(\sum y\right)^2 / n = 2788 - (160)^2/10 = 2478 - 2560 = 228$$

and

$$\text{SSR} = \frac{\left[\sum xy - \left(\sum x\right)\left(\sum y\right)/n\right]^2}{\sum x^2 - \left(\sum x\right)^2 / n} = \frac{[908 - (50)(160)/10]^2}{304 - (50)^2/10} = \frac{108^2}{54} = 216$$

Of course these are the same values that we found earlier using the more onerous tabular method. Finally, we calculate the value of the coefficient of determination r^2 to be

$$r^2 = \frac{\text{SSR}}{\text{SST}} = \frac{216}{228} = 0.9474$$

In other words, the linear relationship between time and distance accounts for 94.74% of the variability in the distances traveled. The regression model fits the data very nicely.

CORRELATION COEFFICIENT

A common measure used to quantify the linear relationship between two quantitative variables is the *correlation coefficient*. The correlation coefficient r (also known as the *Pearson product moment correlation coefficient*) is an indication of the strength of the linear relationship between two quantitative variables and is defined as follows:

$$ r = \frac{\sum (x - \overline{x})(y - \overline{y})}{(n - 1)s_x s_y} $$

where s_x and s_y represent the sample standard deviations of the x and y data values, respectively. The correlation coefficient r always takes on values between 1 and -1, inclusive. Following are some standard interpretations for the value of the correlation coefficient.

INTERPRETING THE CORRELATION COEFFICIENT r

- Values of r close to 1 indicate variables that are *positively correlated*.
  - As the value of x increases, the value of y tends to increase as well.
- Values of r close to -1 indicate variables that are *negatively correlated*.
  - An increase in the x variable is associated with a decrease in the y variable.
  - As the value of x increases, the value of y tends to decrease.
- Other values of r indicate variables that are *uncorrelated*.
  - As the value of x increases, the value of y tends to remain unaffected.

The question is: How close is close? We offer a rough rule of thumb for ascertaining the presence of correlation, while again noting that the analyst needs to temper these heuristics with specialist domain knowledge, applicable to the particular field of study. The analyst should beware of black-and-white verdicts concerning the presence or absence of correlation, since the degree of correlation ranges continuously from -1 to 1, including areas in shades of gray. This rule of thumb should not take the place of more rigorous tests for determining the association between variables.

ROUGH RULE OF THUMB: ASCERTAINING THE PRESENCE OF CORRELATION

If the value of the correlation coefficient r is:

- Greater than 0.7, the variables are positively correlated.
- Between 0.33 and 0.7, the variables are mildly positively correlated.
- Between -0.33 and 0.33, the variables are not correlated.
- Between -0.7 and -0.33, the variables are mildly negatively correlated.
- Less than -0.7, the variables are negatively correlated.

The definition formula for the correlation coefficient above may be tedious, since the numerator would require the calculation of the deviations for both the x and y data. We therefore have recourse, in the absence of software, to the following computational formula for r:

$$r = \frac{\sum xy - (\sum x)(\sum y)/n}{\sqrt{\sum x^2 - (\sum x)^2/n}\ \sqrt{\sum y^2 - (\sum y)^2/n}}$$

For the orienteering example, we have:

$$r = \frac{\sum xy - (\sum x)(\sum y)/n}{\sqrt{\sum x^2 - (\sum x)^2/n}\ \sqrt{\sum y^2 - (\sum y)^2/n}}$$
$$= \frac{908 - (50)(160)/10}{\sqrt{304 - (50)^2/10}\ \sqrt{2788 - (160)^2/10}}$$
$$= \frac{108}{\sqrt{54}\sqrt{228}} = 0.9733$$

We would say that the time spent traveling and the distance traveled are strongly positively correlated. As the time spent hiking increases, the distance traveled tends to increase. However, it is more convenient to express the correlation coefficient r as $r = \pm\sqrt{r^2}$. When the slope b_1 of the estimated regression line is positive, the correlation coefficient is also positive, $r = \sqrt{r^2}$; when the slope is negative, the correlation coefficient is also negative, $r = -\sqrt{r^2}$. In the orienteering example, we have $b_1 = 2$. This is positive, which means that the correlation coefficient will also be positive, $r = \sqrt{r^2} = \sqrt{0.9474} = 0.9733$.

ANOVA TABLE

Regression statistics may be presented succinctly in an ANOVA table, the general form of which is shown in Table 2.5. Here m represents the number of predictor variables, so that for simple linear regression, $m = 1$. The ANOVA table conveniently displays the relationships among several statistics, showing for example that the sums of squares add up to SST. The *mean squares* are presented as the ratios of the items to their left, and for inference, the test statistic F is represented as the ratio of the mean squares. Tables 2.6 and 2.7 show the Minitab regression results, including the ANOVA tables, for the orienteering and cereal examples, respectively.

TABLE 2.5 ANOVA Table for Simple Linear Regression

Source of Variation	Sum of Squares	df	Mean Square	F
Regression	SSR	m	$MSR = \dfrac{SSR}{m}$	$F = \dfrac{MSR}{MSE}$
Error (or residual)	SSE	$n - m - 1$	$MSE = \dfrac{SSE}{n - m - 1}$	
Total	$SST = SSR + SSE$	$n - 1$		

TABLE 2.6   Results of Regression of *Distance* on *Time*

```
The regression equation is
distance = 6.00 + 2.00 time

Predictor    Coef   SE Coef      T      P
Constant   6.0000    0.9189   6.53  0.000
time       2.0000    0.1667  12.00  0.000


S = 1.2247   R-Sq = 94.7%   R-Sq(adj) = 94.1%


Analysis of Variance

Source           DF       SS      MS       F      P
Regression        1   216.00  216.00  144.00  0.000
Residual Error    8    12.00    1.50
Total             9   228.00
```

TABLE 2.7   Results of Regression of *Nutritional Rating* on *Sugar Content*

```
The regression equation is
Rating = 59.4 - 2.42 Sugars

Predictor     Coef   SE Coef       T      P
Constant    59.444     1.951   30.47  0.000
Sugars     -2.4193    0.2376  -10.18  0.000

S = 9.16160 R-Sq = 58.0% R-Sq(adj) = 57.5%

Analysis of Variance

Source           DF        SS      MS       F      P
Regression        1    8701.7  8701.7  103.67  0.000
Residual Error   75    6295.1    83.9
Total            76   14996.8

Unusual Observations

Obs  Sugars  Rating    Fit  SE Fit  Residual  St Resid
  1     6.0   68.40  44.93    1.07     23.48     2.58R
  4     0.0   93.70  59.44    1.95     34.26     3.83R
R denotes an observation with a large standardized residual.
```

OUTLIERS, HIGH LEVERAGE POINTS, AND INFLUENTIAL OBSERVATIONS

Next, we discuss the role of three types of observations that may or may not exert undue influence on the regression results: (1) outliers, (2) high leverage points, and (3) influential observations. An *outlier* is an observation that has a very large standardized residual in absolute value. Consider the scatter plot of nutritional rating against sugars in Figure 2.3. The two observations with the largest absolute residuals are identified as All-Bran Extra Fiber and 100% Bran. Note that the vertical distance away from the regression line (indicated by the vertical arrows) is greater for these two observations than for any other cereals, indicating the largest residuals. For example, the nutritional rating for All-Bran Extra Fiber (93.7) is much higher than predicted (59.44) based on its sugar content alone (0 grams). Similarly, the nutritional rating for 100% Bran (68.4) is much higher than would have been estimated (44.93) based on its sugar content alone (6 grams).

Residuals may have different variances, so that it is preferable to use the standardized residuals in order to identify outliers. Standardized residuals are residuals divided by their standard error, so that they are all on the same scale. Let $s_{i,\,\text{resid}}$ denote the standard error of the ith residual. Then

$$s_{i,\,\text{resid}} = s\sqrt{1 - h_i}$$

where h_i refers to the *leverage* of the ith observation (see below). The standardized residual,

$$\text{residual}_{i,\,\text{standardized}} = \frac{y_i - \hat{y}_i}{s_{i,\,\text{resid}}}$$

A rough rule of thumb is to flag observations whose standardized residuals exceed 2 in absolute value as being outliers. For example, note from Table 2.7 that Minitab identifies observations 1 and 4 as outliers based on their large standardized

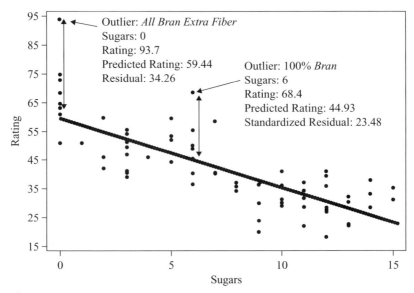

Figure 2.3 Identifying the outliers in regression of *nutritional rating* on *sugars*.

residuals; these are All-Bran Extra Fiber and 100% Bran. In general, if the residual is *positive*, we may say that the y-value observed is *higher* than the regression estimated given the x-value. If the residual is *negative*, we may say that the y-value observed is *lower* than the regression estimated given the x-value.

A *high leverage point* is an observation that is extreme in the predictor space. In other words, a high leverage point takes on extreme values for the x-variable(s), without reference to the y-variable. That is, leverage takes into account only the x-variables and ignores the y-variable. The term *leverage* is derived from the physics concept of the lever, which Archimedes asserted could move the Earth itself if only it were long enough. The leverage h_i for the ith observation may be denoted as follows:

$$ h_i = \frac{1}{n} + \frac{(x_i - \bar{x})^2}{\sum (x_i - \bar{x})^2} $$

For a given data set, the quantities $1/n$ and $\sum (x_i - \bar{x})^2$ may be considered to be constants, so that the leverage for the ith observation depends solely on $(x_i - \bar{x})^2$, the squared distance between the value of the predictor and the mean value of the predictor. The farther the observation differs from the mean of the observations in the x-space, the greater the leverage. The lower bound on leverage values is $1/n$, and the upper bound is 1.0. An observation with leverage greater than about $2(m + 1)/n$ or $3(m + 1)/n$ may be considered to have high leverage (where m indicates the number of predictors).

For example, in the orienteering example, suppose that there was a new observation, a real hard-core orienteering competitor, who hiked for 16 hours and traveled 39 kilometers. Figure 2.4 shows the scatter plot, updated with this eleventh hiker. Note from Figure 2.4 that the time traveled by the new hiker (16 hours) is extreme in the x-space, as indicated by the horizontal arrows. This is sufficient to identify this observation as a high leverage point without reference to how many kilometers he or she actually traveled. Examine Table 2.8, which shows the updated regression results for the 11 hikers. Note that Minitab points out correctly that this is an unusual observation. It is unusual because it is a high leverage point. However, Minitab is not,

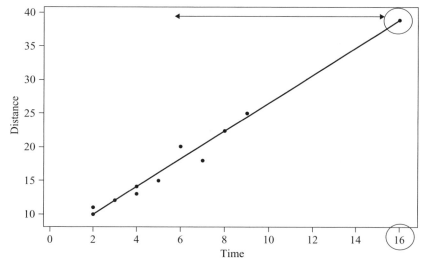

Figure 2.4 Scatter plot of distance versus time, with new competitor who hiked for 16 hours.

TABLE 2.8 Updated Regression Results Including the 16-Hour Hiker

```
The regression equation is
distance = 5.73 + 2.06 time

Predictor     Coef  SE Coef       T      P
Constant    5.7251   0.6513    8.79  0.000
time       2.06098  0.09128   22.58  0.000

S = 1.16901 R-Sq = 98.3% R-Sq(adj) = 98.1%

Analysis of Variance

Source           DF      SS      MS       F      P
Regression        1  696.61  696.61  509.74  0.000
Residual Error    9   12.30    1.37
Total            10  708.91

Unusual Observations

Obs  time  distance     Fit  SE Fit  Residual  St Resid
 11  16.0    39.000  38.701   0.979     0.299     0.47 X

X denotes an observation whose X value gives it large influence.
```

The hard-core orienteering competitor is a high-leverage point. (Courtesy: Chantal Larose).

strictly speaking, correct to call it an observation with large influence. To see what we mean by this, let's next discuss what it means to be an influential observation.

In the context of history, what does it mean to be an influential person? A person is influential if his or her presence or absence changes the history of the world significantly. In the context of Bedford Falls (*It's a Wonderful Life*), George Bailey discovers that he really was influential when an angel shows him how different (and

TABLE 2.9   Regression Results Including the Person Who Hiked 20 Kilometers in 5 Hours

```
The regression equation is
distance = 6.36 + 2.00 time

Predictor     Coef  SE Coef     T      P
Constant     6.364    1.278  4.98  0.001
time        2.0000   0.2337  8.56  0.000

S = 1.71741 R-Sq = 89.1% R-Sq(adj) = 87.8%

Analysis of Variance

Source            DF      SS      MS      F      P
Regression         1  216.00  216.00  73.23  0.000
Residual Error     9   26.55    2.95
Total             10  242.55

Unusual Observations

Obs  time  distance     Fit  SE Fit  Residual  St Resid
 11  5.00    20.000  16.364   0.518     3.636     2.22R
R denotes an observation with a large standardized residual.
```

poorer) the world would have been had he never been born. Similarly, in regression, an observation is *influential* if the regression parameters alter significantly based on the presence or absence of the observation in the data set.

An outlier may or may not be influential. Similarly, a high leverage point may or may not be influential. Usually, influential observations combine the characteristics of a large residual and high leverage. It is possible for an observation to be not quite flagged as an outlier and not quite flagged as a high leverage point, but still be influential through the combination of the two characteristics.

First, let's consider an example of an observation that is an outlier but is not influential. Suppose that we replace our eleventh observation (no more hard-core guy) with someone who hiked 20 kilometers in 5 hours. Examine Table 2.9, which presents the regression results for these 11 hikers. Note from Table 2.9 that the new observation is flagged as an outlier (unusual observation with large standardized residual). This is because the distance traveled (20 kilometers) is higher than the regression predicted (16.364 kilometers) given the time (5 hours). Now would we consider this observation to be influential? Overall, probably not. Compare Tables 2.9 and 2.6 to assess the effect the presence of this new observation has on the regression coefficients. The y-intercept changes from $b_0 = 6.00$ to $b_0 = 6.36$, but the slope does not change at all, remaining at $b_1 = 2.00$ regardless of the presence of the new hiker.

Figure 2.5 shows the relatively mild effect that this outlier has on the estimated regression line, shifting it vertically a small amount without affecting the slope at all. Although it is an outlier, this observation is not influential because it has very low leverage, being situated exactly on the mean of the x-values, so that it has the minimum possible leverage for a data set of size $n = 11$. We can calculate the leverage for this observation ($x = 5$, $y = 20$) as follows. Since $\bar{x} = 5$, we have

$$\sum (x_i - \bar{x})^2 = (2 - 5)^2 + (2 - 5)^2 + (3 - 5)^2 + \cdots + (9 - 5)^2 + (5 - 5)^2 = 54$$

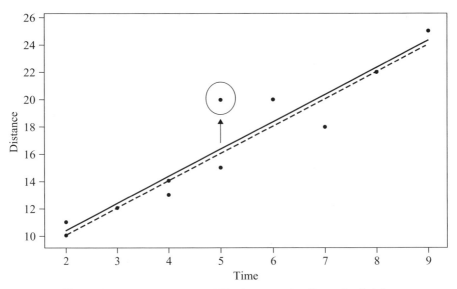

Figure 2.5   The mild outlier shifts the regression line only slightly.

Then

$$h_{(5,20)} = \frac{1}{11} + \frac{(5-5)^2}{54} = 0.0909$$

Now that we have the leverage for this observation, we may also find the standardized residual, as follows. First, we have the standard error of the residual:

$$s_{(5,20),\text{ resid}} = 1.71741 \sqrt{1 - 0.0909} = 1.6375$$

so that the standardized residual,

$$\text{residual}_{(5,20),\text{ standardized}} = \frac{y_i - \hat{y}_i}{s_{(5,20),\text{ resid}}} = \frac{20 - 16.364}{1.6375} = 2.22$$

as shown in Table 2.9.

Cook's distance measures the level of influence of an observation by taking into account both the size of the residual and the amount of leverage for that observation. Cook's distance takes the following form for the ith observation:

$$D_i = \frac{(y_i - \hat{y}_i)^2}{(m+1)s^2} \frac{h_i}{(1 - h_i)^2}$$

where $y_i - \hat{y}_i$ represents the ith residual, m the number of predictors, s the standard error of the estimate, and h_i the leverage of the ith observation. The left-hand ratio in the formula for Cook's distance contains an element representing the residual, and the right-hand ratio contains functions of the leverage. Thus, Cook's distance combines the two concepts of outlier and leverage into a single measure of influence. The value of the Cook's distance measure for the hiker who traveled 20 kilometers in 5 hours is as follows:

$$D_i = \frac{(20 - 16.364)^2}{(1+1)\,1.71741^2} \left[\frac{0.0909}{(1 - 0.0909)^2} \right] = 0.2465$$

A rough rule of thumb for determining whether an observation is influential is if its Cook's distance exceeds 1.0. More accurately, one may also compare the Cook's distance against the percentiles of the F-distribution with $(m, n - m)$ degrees of freedom. If the observed value lies within the first quartile of this distribution (lower than the 25th percentile), the observation has little influence on the regression; however, if the Cook's distance is greater than the median of this distribution, the observation is influential. For this observation, the Cook's distance of 0.2465 lies within the 37th percentile of the $F_{1, 10}$ distribution, indicating that while the influence of the observation is not negligible, neither is the observation particularly influential.

What about the hard-core hiker we encountered earlier? Was that observation influential? Recall that this hiker traveled 39 kilometers in 16 hours, providing the eleventh observation in the results reported in Table 2.8. First, let's find the leverage. We have $n = 11$ and $m = 1$, so that observations having $h_i > 2(m + 1)/n = 0.36$ or $h_i > 3(m + 1)/n = 0.55$ may be considered to have high leverage. This observation has $h_i = 0.7007$, which indicates that this durable hiker does indeed have high leverage, as mentioned with reference to Figure 2.4. This figure seems to indicate that this hiker ($x = 16$, $y = 39$) is not, however, an outlier, since the observation lies near the regression line. The standardized residual supports this, having a value of 0.46801. The reader will be asked to verify these values for leverage and standardized residual in the exercises.

Finally, the Cook's distance for this observation is 0.2564, which is about the same as our previous example, indicating that the observation is not particularly influential, although not completely without influence on the regression coefficients. Figure 2.6 shows the slight change in the regression with (solid line) and without (dashed line) this observation. So we have seen that an observation that is an outlier with low influence, or an observation that is a high leverage point with a small residual, may not be particularly influential. We next illustrate how a data point that has a moderately high residual and moderately high leverage may indeed be influential.

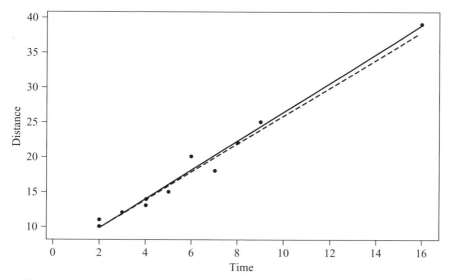

Figure 2.6 Slight change in the regression line when the hard-core hiker is added.

TABLE 2.10 **Regression Results from a New Observation with *Time* = 10, *Distance* = 23**

```
The regression equation is
distance = 6.70 + 1.82 time

Predictor    Coef  SE Coef       T      P
Constant   6.6967   0.9718    6.89  0.000
time       1.8223   0.1604   11.36  0.000

S = 1.40469 R-Sq = 93.5% R-Sq(adj) = 92.8%

Analysis of Variance

Source            DF      SS      MS       F      P
Regression         1  254.79  254.79  129.13  0.000
Residual Error     9   17.76    1.97
Total             10  272.55
```

Suppose that our eleventh hiker had instead hiked for 10 hours and traveled 23 kilometers. The regression analysis for the 11 hikers is given in Table 2.10. Note that Minitab does not identify the new observation as either an outlier or a high leverage point. This is because, as the reader is asked to verify in the exercises, the leverage of this new hiker is $h_i = 0.36019$ and the standardized residual equals -1.70831. However, despite lacking either a particularly large leverage or a large residual, this observation is nevertheless influential, as measured by its Cook's distance of $D_i = 0.821457$, which is in line with the 62nd percentile of the $F_{1, 10}$ distribution. The influence of this observation stems from the combination of its moderately large

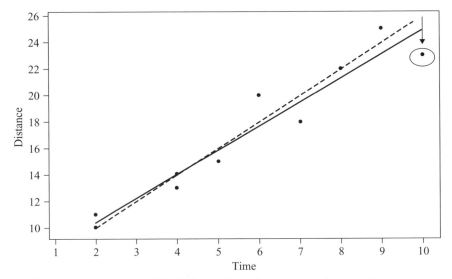

Figure 2.7 Moderate residual plus moderate leverage = influential observation.

residual with its moderately large leverage. Figure 2.7 shows the influence this single hiker has on the regression line, pulling down on the right side to decrease the slope (from 2.00 to 1.82) and thereby increase the y-intercept (from 6.00 to 6.70).

REGRESSION MODEL

Least-squares regression is a powerful and elegant methodology. However, if the assumptions of the regression model are not validated, the resulting inference and model building are undermined. Deploying a model whose results are based on unverified assumptions may lead to expensive failures later. The simple linear regression model is given as follows. We have a set of n bivariate observations, with response value y_i related to predictor value x_i through the linear relationship that follows.

REGRESSION MODEL

$$y = \beta_0 + \beta_1 x + \varepsilon$$

where

- β_0 and β_1 represent the model parameters for the y-intercept and slope, respectively. These are constants, whose true value remains unknown and which are estimated from the data using least-squares estimates.

- ε represents the error term. Since most predictor–response relationships are not deterministic, a certain amount of error will be introduced by any linear approximation of the actual relationship. Therefore, an error term, modeled by a random variable, is needed.

Assumptions About the Error Term

1. *Zero-mean assumption.* The error term ε is a random variable, with mean or expected value equal to zero. In other words, $E(\varepsilon) = 0$.

2. *Constant-variance assumption.* The variance of ε, denoted by σ^2, is constant regardless of the value of x.

3. *Independence assumption.* The values of ε are independent.

4. *Normality assumption.* The error term ε is a normally distributed random variable.

In other words, the values of the error term ε_i are independent normal random variables, with mean 0 and variance σ^2.

Based on these four assumptions, we can derive four implications for the behavior of the response variable, y, as follows.

Figure 2.8 illustrates graphically the normality of the y_i, with mean $\beta_0 + \beta_1 x$ and constant variance σ^2. Suppose that we have a data set which includes predictor values at $x = 5$, 10, and 15, among other values. Then, at each of these values of x, the regression assumptions assert that observed values of y are samples from a normally

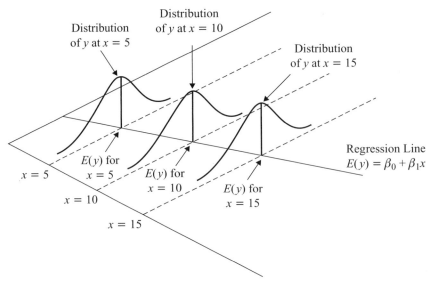

Figure 2.8 For each value of x, the y_i are normally distributed, with mean on the regression line and constant variance.

distributed population with a mean on the regression line $[E(y) = \beta_0 + \beta_1 x]$ and constant standard deviation σ^2. Note from Figure 2.8 that each of the normal curves has precisely the same shape, which indicates that the variance is constant for each value of x.

If one is interested in using regression analysis in a strictly descriptive manner, with no inference and no model building, one need not worry quite so much about

---

IMPLICATIONS OF THE ASSUMPTIONS FOR THE BEHAVIOR OF THE RESPONSE VARIABLE y

1. Based on the zero-mean assumption, we have

$$E(y) = E(\beta_0 + \beta_1 x + \varepsilon) = E(\beta_0) + E(\beta_1 x) + E(\varepsilon) = \beta_0 + \beta_1 x$$

That is, for each value of x, the mean of the y's lies on the regression line.

2. Based on the constant-variance assumption, we have the variance of y, $\mathrm{Var}(y)$, given as

$$\mathrm{Var}(y) = \mathrm{Var}(\beta_0 + \beta_1 x + \varepsilon) = \mathrm{Var}(\varepsilon) = \sigma^2$$

That is, regardless of which value is taken by the predictor x, the variance of the y's is always constant.

3. Based on the independence assumption, it follows that for any particular value of x, the values of y are independent as well.

4. Based on the normality assumption, it follows that y is also a normally distributed random variable.

In other words, the values of the response variable y_i are independent normal random variables, with mean $\beta_0 + \beta_1 x$ and variance σ^2.

assumption validation. This is because the assumptions are about the error term. If the error term is not involved, the assumptions are not needed. However, if one wishes to do inference or model building, the assumptions must be verified.

INFERENCE IN REGRESSION

Consider the regression results given in Table 2.11. We have a predictor X and a response Y, and assume that we are unfamiliar with this type of data, except that each variable ranges from about -4 to 4. We are interested in using X to predict Y. Now the coefficient of determination takes on the value $r^2 = 0.3\%$, which would tend to indicate that the model is not at all useful. We are tempted to conclude that there is no linear relationship between x and y.

However, are we sure that there is no linear relationship between the variables? It is possible that such a relationship could exist even though r^2 is small. The question is: Does there exist some systematic approach for determining whether a linear relationship exists between two variables? The answer, of course, is yes: Inference in regression offers a systematic framework for assessing the significance of linear association between two variables.

We shall examine four inferential methods in this chapter:

1. The t-test for the relationship between the response variable and the predictor variable
2. The confidence interval for the slope, β_1
3. The confidence interval for the mean of the response variable given a particular value of the predictor
4. The prediction interval for a random value of the response variable given a particular value of the predictor

In Chapter 3 we also investigate the F-test for the significance of the regression as a whole. However, for simple linear regression, the t-test and the F-test are equivalent.

How do we go about performing inference in regression? Take a moment to consider the form of the regression equation:

$$y = \beta_0 + \beta_1 x + \varepsilon$$

TABLE 2.11   Regression That Is Not Very Useful, or Is It?

```
The regression equation is
Y = 0.783 + 0.0559 X

Predictor     Coef   SE Coef      T      P
Constant   0.78262  0.03791  20.64  0.000
Y          0.05594  0.03056   1.83  0.067

S = 0.983986 R-Sq = 0.3% R-Sq(adj) = 0.2%
```

This equation asserts that there is a linear relationship between y on the one hand and some function of x on the other. Now, β_1 is a model parameter, so that it is a constant whose value is unknown. Is there some value that β_1 could take such that if β_1 took that value, there would no longer exist a linear relationship between x and y?

Consider what would happen if β_1 were zero. Then the regression equation would be

$$y = \beta_0 + (0)x + \varepsilon$$

In other words, when $\beta_1 = 0$, the regression equation becomes

$$y = \beta_0 + \varepsilon$$

That is, a linear relationship between x and y no longer exists. On the other hand, if β_1 takes on any conceivable value other than zero, a linear relationship of some kind exists between the response and the predictor. Much of our regression inference in this chapter is based on this key idea: that the linear relationship between x and y depends on the value of β_1.

t-Test for the Relationship Between *x* and *y*

The least-squares estimate of the slope, b_1, is a statistic. Like all statistics, it has a sampling distribution with a particular mean and standard error. The sampling distribution of b_1 has as its mean the (unknown) value of the true slope β_1 and has as its standard error the following:

$$\sigma_{b_1} = \frac{\sigma}{\sqrt{\sum x^2 - \left(\sum x\right)^2 / n}}$$

Just as one-sample inference about the mean is based on the sampling distribution of $\bar{x}$, so regression inference about the slope β_1 is based on this sampling distribution of b_1.

The point estimate of σ_{b_1} is s_{b_1}, given by

$$s_{b_1} = \frac{s}{\sqrt{\sum x^2 - \left(\sum x\right)^2 / n}}$$

where s is the standard error of the estimate, reported in the regression results. The s_{b_1} statistic is to be interpreted as a measure of the variability of the slope. Large values of s_{b_1} indicate that the estimate of the slope b_1 is unstable, while small values of s_{b_1} indicate that the estimate of the slope b_1 is precise.

The t-test is based on the distribution of $t = (\beta_1 - \beta_1)/s_{b_1}$, which follows a t-distribution with $n - 2$ degrees of freedom. When the null hypothesis is true, the test statistic $t = b_1/s_{b_1}$ follows a t-distribution with $n - 2$ degrees of freedom.

To illustrate, we shall carry out the t-test using the results from Table 2.7, the regression of nutritional rating on sugar content. For convenience, part of Table 2.7 is reproduced here as Table 2.12. Consider the row in Table 2.12, labeled "Sugars."

TABLE 2.12 Results of Regression of Nutritional Rating on Sugar Content

```
The regression equation is
Rating = 59.4 - 2.42 Sugars


Predictor     Coef  SE Coef        T      P
Constant    59.444    1.951    30.47  0.000
Sugars     -2.4193   0.2376   -10.18  0.000


S = 9.16160 R-Sq = 98.0% R-Sq(adj) = 57.5%


Analysis of Variance


Source           DF       SS      MS       F      P
Regression        1   8701.7  8701.7  103.67  0.000
Residual Error   75   6295.1    83.9
Total            76  14996.8
```

- Under "Coef" is found the value of b_1, -2.4193.
- Under "SE Coef" is found the value of s_{b_1}, the standard error of the slope. Here $s_{b_1} = 0.2376$.
- Under "T" is found the value of the t-statistic, that is, the test statistic for the t-test, $t = b_1/s_{b_1} = -2.4193/0.2376 = -10.18$.
- Under "P" is found the p-value of the t-statistic. Since this is a two-tailed test, this p-value takes the following form: p-value $= P(|t| > t_{obs})$, where t_{obs} represent the observed value of the t-statistic from the regression results. Here p-value $= P(|t| > t_{obs}) = P(|t| > -10.18) \approx 0.000$, although, of course, no continuous p-value ever equals precisely zero.

The null hypothesis asserts that no linear relationship exists between the variables, while the alternative hypothesis states that such a relationship does indeed exist.

- H_0: $\beta_1 = 0$ (There is no linear relationship between sugar content and nutritional rating.)
- H_a: $\beta_1 \neq 0$ (Yes, there is a linear relationship between sugar content and nutritional rating.)

We shall carry out the hypothesis test using the p-value method, where the null hypothesis is rejected when the p-value of the test statistic is small. What determines how small is small depends on the field of study, the analyst, and domain experts although many analysts routinely use 0.05 as a threshold. Here, we have p-value ≈ 0.00, which is surely smaller than any reasonable threshold of significance. We therefore reject the null hypothesis and conclude that a linear relationship exists between sugar content and nutritional rating.

Confidence Interval for the Slope of the Regression Line

Researchers may consider that hypothesis tests are too black and white in their conclusions, and prefer to estimate the slope of the regression line β_1 using a confidence interval. The interval used is a *t-interval*, based on the sampling distribution for b_1 above. The form of the confidence interval is as follows.

100$(1 - \alpha)$% CONFIDENCE INTERVAL FOR THE TRUE SLOPE β_1 OF THE REGRESSION LINE

We can be $100(1 - \alpha)$% confident that the true slope β_1 of the regression line lies between

$$b_1 \pm (t_{n-2})(S_{b_1})$$

where t_{n-2} is based on $n - 2$ degrees of freedom.

For example, let us construct a 95% confidence interval for the true slope of the regression line, β_1. We have the point estimate given as $b_1 = -2.4193$. The *t*-critical value for 95% confidence and $n - 2 = 75$ degrees of freedom is $t_{75,95\%} = 2.0$. From Table 2.12 we have $s_{b_1} = 0.2376$. Thus, our confidence interval is as follows:

$$b_1 - (t_{n-2})(s_{b_1}) = -2.4193 - (2.0)\,(0.2376) = -2.8945$$
$$b_1 + (t_{n-2})(s_{b_1}) = -2.4193 + (2.0)\,(0.2376) = -1.9441$$

We are 95% confident that the true slope of the regression line lies between -2.89 and -1.94. That is, for every additional gram of sugar, the nutritional rating will decrease between 1.94 and 2.89 points. Since the point $\beta_1 = 0$ is not contained within this interval, we can be sure of the significance of the relationship between the variables with 95% confidence.

Confidence Interval for the Mean Value of *y* Given *x*

Point estimates for values of the response variable for a given value of the predictor value may be obtained using the estimated regression equation $\hat{y} = b_0 + b_1 x$. Unfortunately, these kinds of point estimates do not provide a probability statement regarding their accuracy. The analyst is therefore advised to provide the user with two

---

CONFIDENCE INTERVAL FOR THE MEAN VALUE OF *y* FOR A GIVEN VALUE OF *x*

$$\hat{y}_p \pm t_{n-2}(s) \sqrt{\frac{1}{n} + \frac{\left(x_p - \bar{x}\right)^2}{\sum \left(x_i - \bar{x}\right)^2}}$$

where $\hat{y}_p$ is the point estimate of y for a particular value of x, t_{n-2} a multiplier associated with the sample size and confidence level, s the standard error of the estimate, and x_p the particular value of x for which the prediction is being made.

---

types of intervals: (1) a confidence interval for the mean value of y given x, and (2) a prediction interval for the value of a randomly chosen y given x.

Before we look at an example of this type of confidence interval, we are first introduced to a new type of interval, the prediction interval.

Prediction Interval for a Randomly Chosen Value of *y* Given *x*

Baseball buffs, which is easier to predict: the mean batting average for an entire team or the batting average of a randomly chosen player? You may have noticed while perusing weekly batting average statistics that team batting averages (which each represent the mean batting average of all the players on a particular team) are more tightly bunched together than are the batting averages of the individual players. This would indicate that an estimate of the team batting average would be more precise than an estimate of a randomly chosen baseball player given the same confidence level. Thus, in general, it is easier to predict the mean value of a variable than to predict a randomly chosen value of that variable.

For another example of this phenomenon, consider exam scores. We would not think that it unusual for a randomly chosen student's grade to exceed 98, but it would be quite remarkable for the class mean to exceed 98. Recall from elementary statistics that the variability associated with the mean of a variable is smaller than the variability associated with an individual observation of that variable. For example, the standard deviation of the univariate random variable x is σ, whereas the standard deviation of the sampling distribution of the sample mean $\bar{x}$ is σ/n. Hence, predicting the class average on an exam is an easier task than predicting the grade of a randomly selected student.

In many situations, analysts are more interested in predicting an individual value than the mean of all the values, given x. For example, an analyst may be more interested in predicting the credit score for a particular credit applicant rather than predicting the mean credit score of all similar applicants. Or a geneticist may be interested in the expression of a particular gene rather than the mean expression of all similar genes.

Prediction intervals are used to estimate the value of a randomly chosen value of y given x. Clearly, this is a more difficult task than estimating the mean, resulting in intervals of greater width (lower precision) than confidence intervals for the mean with the same confidence level.

PREDICTION INTERVAL FOR A RANDOMLY CHOSEN VALUE OF *y* FOR A GIVEN VALUE OF *x*

$$\hat{y}_p \pm t_{n-2}(s)\sqrt{1 + \frac{1}{n} + \frac{(x_p - \bar{x})^2}{\sum(x_i - \bar{x})^2}}$$

Note that this formula is precisely the same as the formula for the confidence interval for the mean value of y, given x, except for the presence of the "1+" inside the square root. This reflects the greater variability associated with estimating a single value of y rather than the mean; it also ensures that the prediction interval is always wider than the analogous confidence interval.

Recall the orienteering example, where the time and distance traveled was observed for 10 hikers. Suppose that we are interested in estimating the distance traveled for a hiker traveling for $y_p = 5x = 5$ hours. The point estimate is obtained easily using the estimated regression equation from Table 2.6: $\hat{y} = 6 + 2x = 6 + 2(2.5) = 16$. That is, the estimated distance traveled for a hiker walking for 5 hours is 16 kilometers. Note from Figure 2.2 that this prediction ($x = 5$, $y = 16$) falls directly on the regression line, as do all such predictions.

However, we must ask the question: How sure are we about the accuracy of our point estimate? That is, are we certain that this hiker will walk precisely 16 kilometers, not 15.9 or 16.1 kilometers? As usual with point estimates, there is no measure of confidence associated with it, which limits the applicability and usefulness of the point estimate. We would therefore like to construct a confidence interval. Recall that the regression model assumes that at each of the x-values, the observed values of y are samples from a normally distributed population with a mean on the regression line $E(y) = \beta_0 + \beta_1 x$ and constant variance σ^2, as illustrated in Figure 2.8. The point estimate represents the mean of this population, as estimated by the data.

Now, in this case, of course, we have only observed a single observation with the value $x = 5$ hours. Nevertheless, the regression model assumes the existence of an entire normally distributed population of possible hikers with this value for *time*. Of all possible hikers in this distribution, 95% will travel within a certain bounded distance (the margin of error) from the point estimate of 16 kilometers. We may therefore obtain a 95% confidence interval (or whatever confidence level is desired) for the mean distance traveled by all possible hikers who walked for 5 hours. We use the formula provided above:

$$\hat{y}_p \pm t_{n-2}(s)\sqrt{\frac{1}{n} + \frac{(x_p - \bar{x})^2}{\sum (x_i - \bar{x})^2}}$$

with

- $\hat{y}_p = 16$, the point estimate
- $t_{n-2,\alpha} = t_{8,95\%} = 2.306$
- $s = 1.22474$, from Table 2.6

- $n = 10$
- $x_p = 5$
- $\bar{x} = 5$

We have

$$\sum (x_i - \bar{x})^2 = (2 - 5)^2 + (2 - 5)^2 + (3 - 5)^2 + \cdots + (9 - 5)^2 = 54$$

and we therefore calculate the 95% confidence interval as follows:

$$\hat{y}_p \pm t_{n-2}(s)\sqrt{\frac{1}{n} + \frac{(x_p - \bar{x})^2}{\sum (x_i - \bar{x})^2}} = 16 \pm (2.306)(1.22474)\sqrt{\frac{1}{10} + \frac{(5 - 5)^2}{54}}$$

$$= 16 \pm 0.893 = (15.107, \ 16.893)$$

We are 95% confident that the mean distance traveled by all possible 5-hour hikers lies between 15.107 and 16.893 kilometers.

However, are we sure that this mean of all possible 5-hour hikers is the quantity that we really want to estimate? Wouldn't it be more useful to estimate the distance traveled by a particular randomly selected hiker? Many analysts would agree and would therefore prefer a prediction interval for a single hiker rather than the confidence interval for the mean of the hikers. The calculation of the prediction interval is quite similar to the confidence interval above, but the interpretation is quite different. We have

$$\hat{y}_p \ \pm \ t_{n-2}(s)\sqrt{1 + \frac{1}{n} + \frac{(x_p - \bar{x})^2}{\sum (x_i - \bar{x})^2}} = 16$$

$$\pm \ (2.306)\,(1.22474)\sqrt{1 + \frac{1}{10} + \frac{(5-5)^2}{54}}$$

$$= 16 \ \pm \ 2.962 = (13.038, \ 18.962)$$

In other words, we are 95% confident that the distance traveled by a randomly chosen hiker who had walked for 5 hours lies between 13.038 and 18.962 kilometers. Note that as mentioned earlier, the prediction interval is wider than the confidence interval, since estimating a single response is more difficult than estimating the mean response. However, also note that the interpretation of the prediction interval is probably more useful for the data miner.

We verify our calculations by providing in Table 2.13 the Minitab results for the regression of distance on time, with the confidence interval and prediction interval indicated at the bottom ("Predicted Values for New Observations"). The *fit* of 16 is the point estimate, the standard error of the fit equals

$$(s)\sqrt{\frac{1}{n} + \frac{(x_p - \bar{x})^2}{\sum (x_i - \bar{x})^2}}$$

the 95% CI indicates the confidence interval for the mean distance of all 5-hour hikers, and the 95% PI indicates the prediction interval for the distance traveled by a randomly chosen 5-hour hiker.

VERIFYING THE REGRESSION ASSUMPTIONS

All of the inferential methods just described depend on the adherence of the data to the regression assumptions outlined earlier. So how does one go about verifying the regression assumptions? The two main graphical methods used to verify regression assumptions are (1) a normal probability plot of the residuals, and (2) a plot of the standardized residuals against the fitted (predicted) values.

A *normal probability plot* is a quantile–quantile plot of the quantiles of a particular distribution against the quantiles of the standard normal distribution, used to

TABLE 2.13 Results of Regression of Distance on Time

```
The regression equation is
distance = 6.00 + 2.00 time

Predictor     Coef  SE Coef      T      P
Constant    6.0000   0.9189   6.53  0.000
time        2.0000   0.1667  12.00  0.000


S = 1.22474   R-Sq = 94.7%   R-Sq(adj) = 94.1%


Analysis of Variance

Source          DF       SS      MS       F      P
Regression       1   216.00  216.00  144.00  0.000
Residual Error   8    12.00    1.50
Total            9   228.00

Predicted Values for New Observations

New
Obs     Fit  SE Fit       95% CI              95% PI
  1  16.000   0.387  (15.107, 16.893)  (13.038, 18.962)
```

determine whether the specified distribution deviates from normality. (Similar to a percentile, a *quantile* of a distribution is a value x_p such that $p\%$ of the distribution values are less than or equal to x_p.) In a normality plot, the values observed for the distribution of interest are compared against the same number of values that would be expected from the normal distribution. If the distribution is normal, the bulk of the points in the plot should fall on a straight line; systematic deviations from linearity in this plot indicate nonnormality.

To illustrate the behavior of the normal probability plot for different kinds of data distributions, we provide three examples. Figures 2.9, 2.10, and 2.11 contain the normal probability plots for a uniform (0, 1) distribution, a chi-square (5) distribution, and a normal (0, 1) distribution, respectively. Note in Figure 2.9 that the bulk of the data do not line up on the straight line, and that a clear pattern (reverse S curve) emerges, indicating systematic deviation from normality. The uniform distribution is a rectangular distribution whose tails are much heavier than those for the normal distribution. Thus, Figure 2.9 is an example of a probability plot for a distribution with heavier tails than those for the normal distribution.

Figure 2.10 also contains a clear curved pattern, indicating systematic deviation from normality. The chi-square (5) distribution is right-skewed, so that the curve pattern apparent in Figure 2.10 may be considered typical of the pattern made by right-skewed distributions in a normal probability plot.

In Figure 2.11 the points line up nicely on a straight line, indicating normality, which is not surprising since the data are drawn from a normal (0, 1) distribution. It

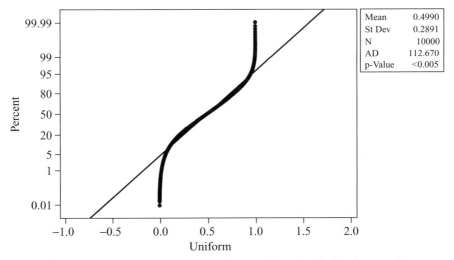

Figure 2.9 Normal probability plot for a uniform distribution: heavy tails.

should be remarked that we should not expect real-world data to behave this nicely. The presence of sampling error and other sources of noise will usually render our decisions about normality less clear-cut than this.

Note the AD statistic and p-value reported by Minitab in each of Figures 2.9 to 2.11. This refers to the *Anderson–Darling test for normality*. Smaller values of the AD statistic indicate that the normal distribution is a better fit for the data. The null hypothesis is that the normal distribution fits, so that small p-values will indicate lack of fit. Note that for the uniform and chi-square examples, the p-value for the AD test is

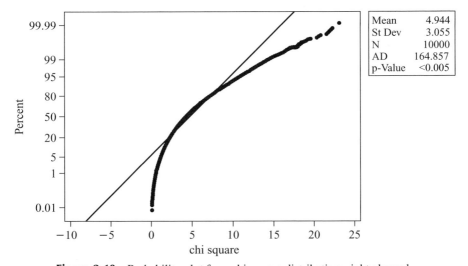

Figure 2.10 Probability plot for a chi-square distribution: right-skewed.

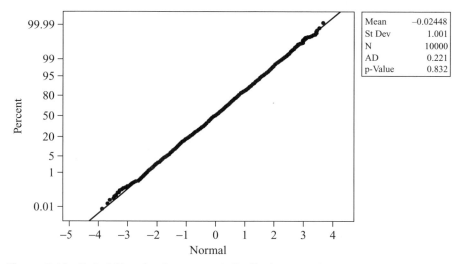

Figure 2.11 Probability plot for a normal distribution. (Don't expect real-world data to behave this nicely.)

less than 0.005, indicating strong evidence for lack of fit with the normal distribution. On the other hand, the p-value for the normal example is 0.832, indicating no evidence against the null hypothesis that the distribution is normal.

The second graphical method used to assess the validity of the regression assumptions is a plot of the standardized residuals against the fits (predicted values). An example of this type of graph is given in Figure 2.12, for the regression of *distance* versus *time* for the original 10 observations in the orienteering example. Note the close relationship between this graph and the original scatter plot in Figure 2.2.

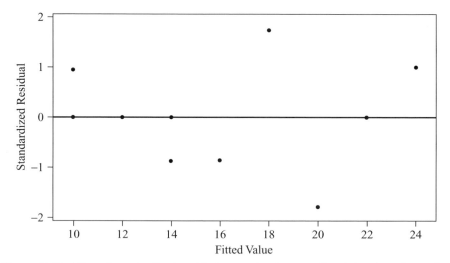

Figure 2.12 Plot of standardized residuals versus values predicted for the orienteering example.

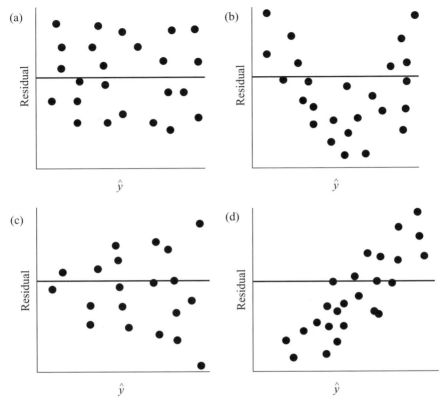

Figure 2.13 Four possible patterns in the plot of residuals versus fits.

The regression line from Figure 2.2 is now the horizontal zero line in Figure 2.12. Points that were either above/below/on the regression line in Figure 2.2 now lie either above/below/on the horizontal zero line in Figure 2.12.

We evaluate the validity of the regression assumptions by observing whether certain patterns exist in the plot of the residuals versus fits, in which case one of the assumptions has been violated, or whether no such discernible patterns exists, in which case the assumptions remain intact. The 10 data points in Figure 2.12 are really too few to try to determine whether any patterns exist. In data mining applications, of course, paucity of data is rarely the issue.

Let us see what types of patterns we should watch out for. Figure 2.13 shows four pattern "archetypes" that may be observed in residual-fit plots. Plot (*a*) shows a "healthy" plot, where no noticeable patterns are observed and the points display an essentially rectangular shape from left to right. Plot (*b*) exhibits curvature, which violates the independence assumption. Plot (*c*) displays a "funnel" pattern, which violates the constant-variance assumption. Finally, plot (*d*) exhibits a pattern that increases from left to right, which violates the zero-mean assumption.

Why does plot (*b*) violate the independence assumption? Because the errors are assumed to be independent, the residuals (which estimate the errors) should exhibit independent behavior as well. However, if the residuals form a curved pattern, then, for a given residual, we may predict where its neighbors to the left and right will fall, within a certain margin of error. If the residuals were truly independent, such a prediction would not be possible.

Why does plot (c) violate the constant-variance assumption? Note from plot (a) that the variability in the residuals, as shown by the vertical distance, is fairly constant regardless of the value of x. On the other hand, in plot (c), the variability of the residuals is smaller for smaller values of x and larger for larger values of x. Therefore, the variability is nonconstant, which violates the constant-variance assumption.

Why does plot (d) violate the zero-mean assumption? The zero-mean assumption states that the mean of the error term is zero regardless of the value of x. However, plot (d) shows that for small values of x, the mean of the residuals is less than zero, whereas for large values of x, the mean of the residuals is greater than zero. This is a violation of the zero-mean assumption as well as a violation of the independence assumption.

Apart from these graphical methods, there are several diagnostic hypothesis tests that may be carried out to assess the validity of the regression assumptions. As mentioned above, the Anderson–Darling test may be used to indicate the fit of residuals to a normal distribution. For assessing whether the constant variance assumption has been violated, either Bartlett's or Levene's test may be used. For determining whether the independence assumption has been violated, either the Durban–Watson or runs test may be used. Information about all these diagnostic tests may be found in Draper and Smith [3].

If the normal probability plot shows no systematic deviations from linearity, and the residuals–fits plot shows no discernible patterns, we may conclude that there is no graphical evidence for the violation of the regression assumptions, and we may then proceed with the regression analysis. However, *what do we do if these graphs indicate violations of the assumptions?* For example, suppose that our normal probability plot of the residuals looked something like plot (c) in Figure 2.13, indicating nonconstant variance? Then we may apply a transformation to the response variable y, such as the *ln* (natural log, log to the base e) transformation.

EXAMPLE: *BASEBALL* DATA SET

To illustrate the use of transformations, we turn to the *baseball* data set, a collection of batting statistics for 331 baseball players who played in the American League in 2002. In this case we are interested in whether there is a relationship between batting average and the number of home runs that a player hits. Some fans might argue, for example, that those who hit lots of home runs also tend to make a lot of strikeouts, so that their batting average is lower. Let's check it out using a regression of the number of home runs against the player's batting average (hits divided by at bats).

Because baseball batting averages tend to be highly variable for low numbers of at bats, we restrict our data set to those players who had at least 100 at bats for the 2002 season. This leaves us with 209 players. A scatter plot of *home runs* versus *batting average* is shown in Figure 2.14. The scatter plot indicates that there may be a positive

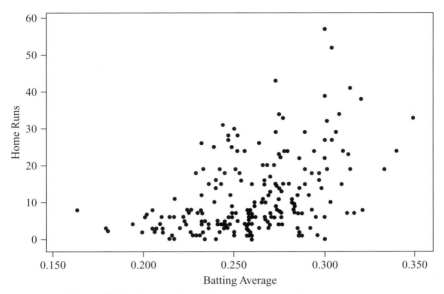

Figure 2.14 Scatter plot of *home runs* versus *batting average*.

linear relationship between home runs and batting average, but that the variability of the number of home runs is greater for those with higher batting averages. This may presage problems with the constant-variance assumption.

We therefore examine whether the regression assumptions are valid, using the graphical methods introduced above. A regression of home runs on batting average produced the normal probability plot of the standardized residuals given in Figure 2.15. The normal probability plot resembles that of Figure 2.10, where the distribution was right-skewed and not normal. This indicates that the normality assumption has been violated. Next, we turn to a plot of the standardized residuals versus the fitted (predicted) values given in Figure 2.16. This plot exhibits a fairly classic funnel pattern, similar to plot (*c*) in Figure 2.13, which is an indication of nonconstant variance.

The results for the regression of *home runs* on *batting average* are given in Table 2.14. The estimated regression equation is as follows: The estimated number of home runs is given as −28.1 plus 154 times the player's batting average. For example, a player with a 0.300 batting average would have an estimated (−28.1) + (154)(0.300) = 18.1 home runs. Unfortunately, because the normality and constant-variance assumptions have been violated, we cannot use these regression results for inference or model building. Since model building is a primary goal of data mining, we should seek to remedy these violations, using transformations.

It should be emphasized any inference or model building based on the regression results in Table 2.14 should be viewed with extreme caution. Deploying such a model, built upon erroneous assumptions, is not recommended. The underlying statistical and mathematical foundation of the regression model is faulty, and like a cracked foundation for a house, may cause expensive reconstruction in the future. To bring our data in line with the regression model assumptions, we therefore apply the natural

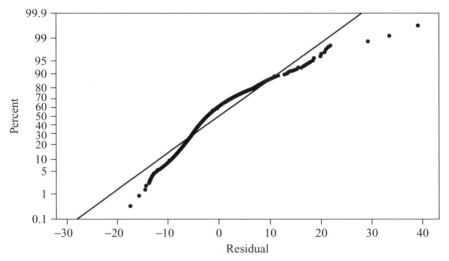

Figure 2.15 Normal probability plot of standardized residuals. Violation of the normality assumption is indicated.

log (*ln*) transformation to the response, *home runs*, giving us the transformed response, *ln home runs*. We then investigate the graphical evidence regarding the validity of model assumptions for the regression of *ln home runs* on *batting average*.

Figure 2.17 provides the normal probability plot of the standardized residuals for this model. Note that most of the data line up nicely along the straight line, indicating that the bulk of the data set follows a normal distribution. The normality assumption tends to break down somewhat in the tails, where there are fewer data points; however, no real-world data set will ever follow a perfectly normal distribution,

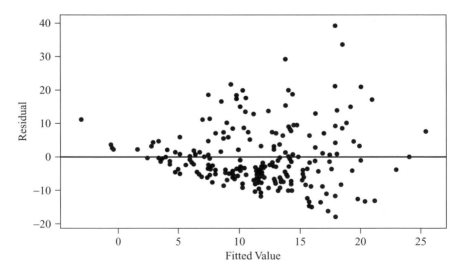

Figure 2.16 Plot of standardized residuals versus fits. Violation of the constant-variance assumption is indicated.

TABLE 2.14   Results of Regression of *Home Runs* on *Batting Average*[a]

```
The regression equation is
home runs = -28.1 + 154 bat ave

Predictor     Coef  SE Coef      T      P
Constant   -28.149    5.083  -5.54  0.000
bat ave     153.55    19.50   7.87  0.000


S = 9.14046 R-Sq = 23.0% R-Sq(adj) = 22.7%


Analysis of Variance

Source          DF       SS      MS      F      P
Regression       1   5179.0  5179.0  61.99  0.000
Residual Error 207  17294.5    83.5
Total          208  22473.5
```

[a] Not valid for inference or model building.

and we conclude that there is insufficient evidence to reject the normality assumption for this model.

Figure 2.18 provides a plot of the standardized residuals versus the fitted values for the regression of *ln home runs* on *batting average*. The plot shows no strong evidence that the constant-variance assumption has been violated. When examining plots for patterns, beware of the "Rorschach effect" of seeing patterns in randomness. The null hypothesis when examining these plots is that the assumptions are intact; only systematic and clearly identifiable patterns in the residuals plots offer evidence to the contrary. We therefore conclude that the regression assumptions are validated

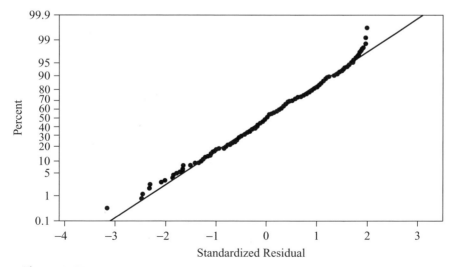

Figure 2.17   Normal probability plot after *ln* transformation: acceptable normality.

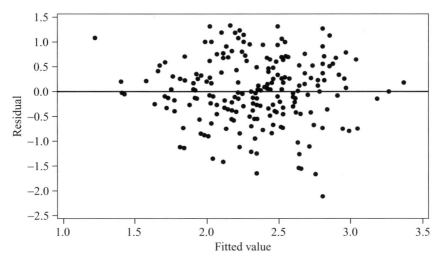

Figure 2.18 Residuals versus fits plot: no strong evidence of assumption violations.

for the model:

$$ln\ home\ runs = \beta_0 + \beta_1\ batting\ average + \varepsilon$$

The results from the regression of *ln home runs* on *batting average* are provided in Table 2.15. Using the more precisely reported results, the estimated regression equation is as follows: The estimated *ln home runs* equals –0.6608 plus 11.555 times *batting average*. To provide a point estimate example, a player with a 0.300 batting average would have an estimated *ln home runs* of $(-0.6608) + (11.555)(0.300) = 2.8057$, giving him an estimated $e^{2.8057} = 16.54$ home runs. (This is compared to the 18.1 home runs estimated earlier under the unvalidated model.)

The standard error of the estimate is $s = 0.673186$, which is expressed in the same units as the response variable, *ln home runs*. This means that our typical error in predicting the number of home runs, based on the player's batting average, is $e^{0.673186} = 1.96$ home runs, which seems to indicate fairly precise estimation.

The coefficient of determination is $r^2 = 23.8\%$, which tells us that the batting average accounts for 23.8% of the variability in (the *ln* of) the number of home runs a player hits. Of course, many other factors should affect a person's ability to hit home runs, such as size, strength, number of at bats, and other factors. However, batting average alone accounts for nearly one-fourth of the variability in the response.

Turning to inference, is there evidence that *batting average* and *ln home runs* are linearly related? The null hypothesis is that there is no linear relationship between the variables. We are provided with the following statistics from Table 2.15:

- The slope estimate is $b_1 = 11.555$.
- The standard error of the slope estimate is $s_{b_1} = 1.436$, which together with the slope estimate, gives us
- The *t*-statistic, $t = 11.555/1.436 = 8.05$, which is also reported (note the slight rounding differences). Finally, we have
- The *p*-value, $P(|t| > t_{obs}) = P(|t| > 8.05) \approx 0.000$.

TABLE 2.15   Results of Regression of *ln Home Runs* on *Batting Average*

```
The regression equation is
ln home runs = - 0.661 + 11.6 bat ave

Predictor      Coef  SE Coef      T      P
Constant    -0.6608   0.3744  -1.77  0.079
bat ave      11.555    1.436   8.04  0.000


S = 0.673186 R-Sq = 23.8% R-Sq(adj) = 23.4%


Analysis of Variance

Source             DF       SS       MS       F      P
Regression          1   29.327   29.327   64.71  0.000
Residual Error    207   93.808    0.453
Total             208  123.135

Predicted Values for New Observations

New
Obs     Fit  SE Fit        95% CI              95% PI
  1  2.8056  0.0755  (2.6567, 2.9545)  1.4701, 4.1411
```

Since the *p*-value is smaller than any reasonable threshold of significance, we therefore reject the null hypothesis and conclude that *batting average* and *ln home runs* are linearly related. A 95% confidence interval for the unknown true slope of the regression between these two variables is given by

$$b_1 \pm (t_{n-2})(s_{b_1}) = b_1 \pm (t_{207,\,95\%})(s_{b_1})$$
$$= 11.555 \pm (1.97)(1.436)$$
$$= (8.73, 14.38)$$

Since the confidence interval does not include zero, we can conclude with 95% confidence that *batting average* and *ln home runs* are linear related.

The correlation coefficient between the variables is $r = \sqrt{r^2} = \sqrt{0.238} = 0.4879$. Note that this is lower than the threshold in our earlier rule of thumb, which would have led us to believe that the variables are uncorrelated. However, as mentioned earlier, rules of thumb must give way to more rigorous tests of association, including the *t*-test and confidence interval performed here. *Batting average* and *ln home runs* are clearly mildly positively correlated. As batting average increases, there is a mild tendency for the number of home runs to increase.

The 95% confidence interval for the mean number of home runs for all players who had a batting average of 0.300 is given by $\left(e^{2.6567}, e^{2.9545}\right) = (14.25, 19.19)$. The 95% prediction interval for the number of home runs by a randomly selected player with a 0.300 batting average is given by $\left(e^{1.4701}, e^{4.1411}\right) = (4.35, 62.87)$. This prediction interval is much too wide to be useful.

TABLE 2.16   Outliers for the *Baseball* Data Set

Obs.	Player	Team	Batting Ave.	HR	St. Res.	Given His Batting Average, His Number of Home Runs Is:
2	Josh Paul	Chicago White Sox	0.240	2	−2.11	Low
4	Jose Macias	Detroit Tigers	0.234	2	−2.01	Low
5	D'Ange Jimenez	Chicago White Sox	0.287	3	−2.32	Low
53	Gabe Kapler	Texas Rangers	0.260	2	−2.46	Low
55	Rusty Greer	Texas Rangers	0.296	3	−2.48	Low
76	Orland Palmeiro	Anaheim Angels	0.300	2	−3.16	Low
110	Rey Sanchez	Boston Red Sox	0.286	3	−2.30	Low

With respect to the unusual observations, the outliers are given in Table 2.16 and the high leverage points are given in Table 2.17. The outliers are all on the low side, meaning that the number of home runs hit by the outliers was all less than expected given the player's batting average. The high leverage points includes those players with the highest and lowest batting averages in the American League in 2002. No data points were deemed to be influential, with the highest value for Cook's distance belonging to Greg Vaughn ($D = 0.066$) of the Tampa Bay Devil Rays, who had a relatively high number of home runs ($e^{2.3026} = 10$) for his low batting average (0.163). The next most influential point was Orland Palmeiro ($D = 0.064$), who had a relatively low number of home runs ($e^{0.6931} = 2$) for his high batting average (0.300). However, none of the Cook's distances exceeded the 20th percentile of the $F_{1,208}$ distribution, so none of the data points is influential according to that criterion.

EXAMPLE: *CALIFORNIA* DATA SET

Let us examine the *California* data set [4] (available from the book series Web site), which consists of some census information for 858 towns and cities in California. This example will give us a chance to investigate handling outliers and high leverage

TABLE 2.17   High Leverage Points for the *Baseball* Data Set

Obs.	Player	Team	Batting Ave.	HR	His Batting Average Is:
3	Enrique Wilson	New York Yankees	0.181	4	Low
12	DeWayne Wise	Toronto Blue Jays	0.179	5	Low
32	Joe Lawrence	Toronto Blue Jays	0.180	4	Low
70	Greg Vaughn	Tampa Bay Devil Rays	0.163	10	Low
132	Manny Ramirez	Boston Red Sox	0.349	35	High
148	Mike Sweeney	Kansas City Royals	0.340	26	High
196	Bernie Williams	New York Yankees	0.333	21	High

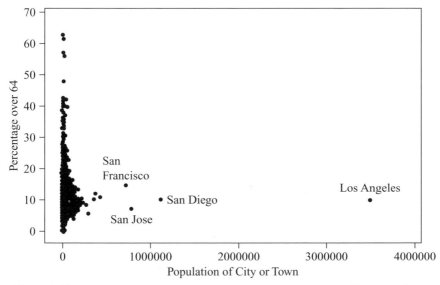

Figure 2.19   Scatter plot of *percentage over 64* versus *population* (effect of outliers).

points as well as transformations of both the predictor and response. We are interested in approximating the relationship, if any, between the percentage of townspeople who are citizens and the total population of the town. That is, do the towns with higher proportions of senior citizens (over 64 years of age) tend to be larger towns or smaller towns?

We begin, as any simple linear regression should begin, with a scatter plot of the response variable against the predictor (Figure 2.19). Most of the data points are squished up against the left axis, due to the presence of several outliers, including Los Angeles, San Diego, San Jose, and San Francisco. Thus, we do not have a solid feel for the nature of the relationship between the two variables. The problem is that the distribution of the total population variable is extremely right-skewed, since there are many towns of small and moderate size, and fewer cities of large size. One way of handling such skewness is to apply a transformation to the variable, such as the square-root transformation or the *ln* transformation. Here we apply the *ln* transformation to the predictor, giving us the transformed predictor variable *ln popn*, the natural log of the total population. Note that the application of this transformation is to the predictor, not the response, and is due solely to the skewness inherent in the variable itself and is not the result of the regression diagnostics above.

We then examine a scatter plot of the relationship between the *percentage over 64* and *ln popn* (Figure 2.20). This scatter plot is much better behaved than Figure 2.19, and provides some indication of a possible relationship between the two variables. For example, none of the communities with very high percentages of senior citizens tend to be very large. We therefore perform a regression of *percentage over 64* versus *ln popn*, with the results shown in Table 2.18. We see from the table that the regression results are significant (*p*-value of the *F*-test very small) and that the estimated percentage of senior citizens is 22.8 minus 1.15 times the natural log of the

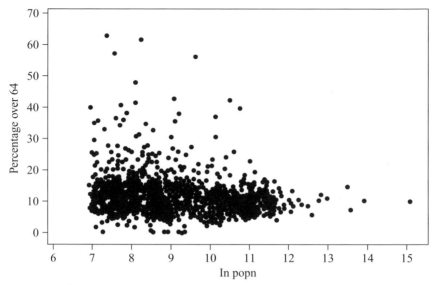

Figure 2.20 Scatter plot of *percentage over 64* versus *ln popn.*

population. However, how much faith can we have that these results are not built on a house of sand? That is, we have not yet checked whether the regression assumptions have been verified.

We therefore produce a normal probability plot of the standardized residuals, which is shown in Figure 2.21. Comparing Figure 2.21 to the plots in Figures 2.9 to 2.11, we find that it most resembles the plot in Figure 2.10, which indicated that the distribution, in this case the distribution of the residuals, was right-skewed. Also, the p-value for the Anderson–Darling test is very small, which rejects the hypothesis that

TABLE 2.18   Results of Regression of *Percentage over 64* on *ln popn*

```
The regression equation is
pct > 64 = 22.8 - 1.15 ln popn

Predictor      Coef   SE Coef      T      P
Constant     22.807     1.657  13.77  0.000
ln popn     -1.1486    0.1780  -6.45  0.000

S = 7.25519 R-Sq = 4.6% R-Sq(adj) = 4.5%

Analysis of Variance

Source           DF       SS       MS      F      P
Regression        1   2191.3 2191.327  41.63  0.000
Residual Error  856  45058.0     52.6
Total           857  47249.3
```

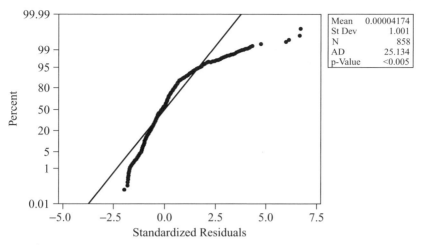

Figure 2.21   Normal probability plot shows right-skewness of residuals.

the standardized residuals are normally distributed. Of course, the residuals should generally be normally distributed, to reflect the assumption that the error terms ε_i are distributed normally. We therefore conclude that the normality assumption is violated for this regression.

We also examine the plot of the standardized residuals versus the fitted values for this regression, shown in Figure 2.22. Again, the funnel pattern emerges, indicating problems with the constant-variance assumption. The variability is smaller for towns and cities with smaller predicted percentages of senior citizens than for those towns and cities with larger predicted percentages. However, the regression model

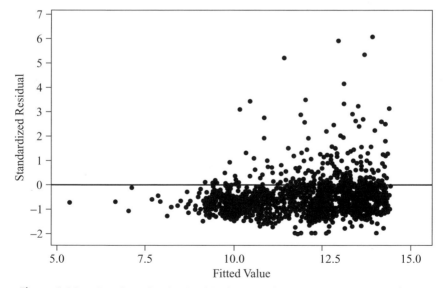

Figure 2.22   Plot of standardized residuals versus fits shows nonconstant variance.

assumes that the variability in the response should be constant regardless of the town or city. Therefore, the assumption of constant variance is violated for this regression.

As mentioned earlier, we can often alleviate violations of the regression assumptions by applying a transformation to the response variable. We therefore apply the natural log transformation to the response variable, *percentage over 64*, giving us the transformed response variable *ln pct*. The regression of *ln pct* on *ln popn* is then performed, and the plot of the standardized residuals versus fits is obtained (Figure 2.23). Note the set of outliers in the lower right, which have an extremely low proportion of senior citizens (indicated by their strong negative standardized residuals) given their population. These outliers are as follows:

- Camp Pendleton Marine Corps Base, South
- Camp Pendleton Marine Corps Base, North
- Vandenberg Air Force Base
- Edwards Air Force Base
- Beale Air Force Base
- El Toro Marine Corps Station
- George Air Force Base
- Mather Air Force Base
- Nebo Center

All but one of these outliers represent military installations, the exception being Nebo Center, a desert town with high unemployment and low housing values 112 miles east of Los Angeles. It is not surprising that the proportion of seniors citizens living in these places is very low. The analyst may therefore decide to set aside this group of observations and proceed with analysis of the remaining 848 records. We continue with the analysis of the *California* data set in the exercises.

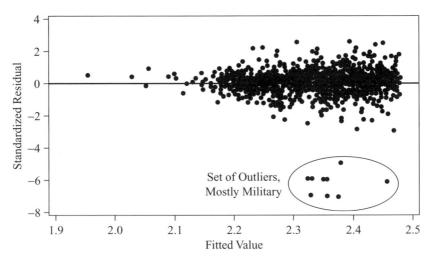

Figure 2.23 Plot of residuals versus fits for regression of *ln pct* on *ln popn*.

TRANSFORMATIONS TO ACHIEVE LINEARITY

Have you ever played the game of Scrabble? Scrabble is a game in which the players randomly select letters from a pool of letter tiles and build crosswords. Each letter tile has a certain number of points associated with it. For instance, the letter "E" is worth one point, the letter "Q" is worth 10 points. The point value of a letter tile is related roughly to its letter frequency, the number of times the letter appears in the pool. Table 2.19 contains the frequency and point value of each letter in the game. Suppose that we were interested in approximating the relationship between frequency and point value, using linear regression. As always when performing simple linear regression, the first thing an analyst should do is to construct a scatter plot of the response versus the predictor to see if the relationship between the two variables is indeed linear. Figure 2.24 presents a scatter plot of the point value versus the frequency. Note that each dot may represent more than one letter.

Perusal of the scatter plot indicates clearly that there is a relationship between point value and letter frequency. However, the relationship is not linear but *curvi*linear, in this case quadratic. It would not be appropriate to model the relationship between point value and letter frequency using a linear approximation such as simple linear regression. Such a model would lead to erroneous estimates and incorrect inference. Instead, the analyst has a couple of choices about how to proceed. He or she may apply multinomial regression, which we will learn about in Chapter 3, or the analyst may apply a transformation to achieve linearity in the relationship.

Mosteller and Tukey, in their book *Data Analysis and Regression* [5], suggest the *bulging rule* for finding transformations to achieve linearity. To understand the bulging rule for quadratic curves, consider Figure 2.25. Compare the curve seen in our scatter plot (Figure 2.24) to the curves shown in Figure 2.25. It is most similar to the curve in the lower left quadrant, the one labeled "*x* down, *y* down." Mosteller and Tukey propose a "ladder of re-expressions," which are essentially a set of power transformations, with one exception, $\ln(t)$.

LADDER OF RE-EXPRESSIONS (MOSTELLER AND TUKEY)
The ladder of re-expressions consists of the following ordered set of transformations for any continuous variable t. $$t^{-3} \quad t^{-2} \quad t^{-1} \quad t^{-1/2} \quad \ln(t) \quad \sqrt{t} \quad t^{1} \quad t^{2} \quad t^{3}$$

For our curve, the heuristic from the bulging rule is: "*x* down, *y* down." This means that we should transform the variable *x* by going down one or more spots from *x*'s present position on the ladder. Similarly, the same transformation is made for *y*. The present position for all untransformed variables is t^{1}. Thus, the bulging rule suggests that we apply either the square-root transformation or the natural log transformation to both letter tile frequency and point value to achieve a linear relationship between the two variables. Thus, we apply the square-root transformation to both *frequency* and *points* and consider the scatter plot of *sqrt points* versus *sqrt frequency*

TABLE 2.19 Frequencies and Point Values in Scrabble

Letter	Frequency	Point Value	Letter	Frequency	Point Value
A	9	1	N	6	1
B	2	3	O	8	1
C	2	3	P	2	3
D	4	2	Q	1	10
E	12	1	R	6	1
F	2	4	S	4	1
G	3	2	T	6	1
H	2	4	U	4	1
I	9	1	V	2	4
J	1	8	W	2	4
K	1	5	X	1	8
L	4	1	Y	2	4
M	2	3	Z	1	10

(Figure 2.26). Unfortunately, the graph indicates that the relationship between sqrt points and sqrt frequency is still not linear, so that it would still be inappropriate to apply linear regression. Evidently, the square-root transformation was too mild to effect linearity in this case.

We therefore move one more notch down the ladder of re-expressions and apply the natural log transformation to each of frequency and point value, generating the transformed variables ln points and ln frequency. The scatter plot of *ln points* versus *ln frequency* is shown in Figure 2.26. This scatter plot exhibits acceptable linearity, although, as with any real-world scatter plot, the linearity is imperfect. We may therefore proceed with the regression analysis for *ln points* and *ln frequency*.

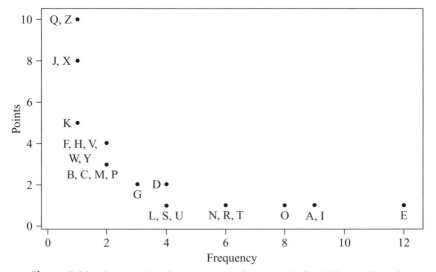

Figure 2.24 Scatter plot of *points* versus *frequency* in Scrabble: nonlinear!

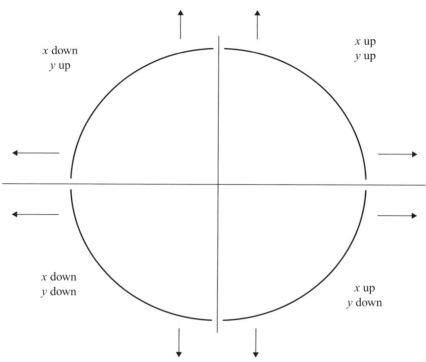

Figure 2.25   Bulging rule: heuristic for variable transformation to achieve linearity. (After Ref. 5.)

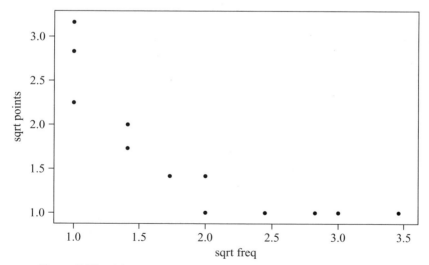

Figure 2.26   After applying square-root transformation, still not linear.

TABLE 2.20 Results of Regression of *ln points* on *ln frequency*

```
The regression equation is
ln points = 1.94 - 1.01 ln freq

Predictor       Coef  SE Coef        T      P
Constant     1.94031  0.09916    19.57  0.000
ln freq     -1.00537  0.07710   -13.04  0.000


S = 0.293745 R-Sq = 87.6% R-Sq(adj) = 87.1%

Analysis of Variance

Source          DF      SS      MS       F      P
Regression       1  14.671  14.671  170.03  0.000
Residual Error  24   2.071   0.086
Total           25  16.742

Unusual Observations

Obs  ln freq  ln points      Fit  SE Fit  Residual  St Resid
  5     2.48     0.0000  -0.5579  0.1250    0.5579     2.10R

R denotes an observation with a large standardized residual.
```

Table 2.20 presents the results from the regression of *ln points* on *ln frequency*. Let's compare these results with the results from the inappropriate regression of points on frequency, with neither variable transformed, shown in Table 2.21. The coefficient of determination for the untransformed case is only 45.5%, compared to 87.6% for the transformed case, meaning that the transformed predictor accounts for nearly twice as much of the variability in the transformed response as do the untransformed variables. Not only is the use of untransformed variables inappropriate in this case, it also leads to degradation in model performance. Comparing the standard errors of the estimate, we find that the typical error in predicting point value using the appropriate regression is $e^s = e^{0.293745} = 1.34$ points, compared to the typical prediction error from the inappropriate regression, $s = 2.1$ points.

TABLE 2.21 Results of *Inappropriate* Regression of *Points* on *Frequency*, Untransformed

```
The regression equation is
Points = 5.73 - 0.633 Frequency

Predictor       Coef  SE Coef        T      P
Constant      5.7322   0.6743     8.50  0.000
Frequency    -0.6330   0.1413    -4.48  0.000


S = 2.10827 R-Sq = 45.5% R-Sq(adj) = 43.3%
```

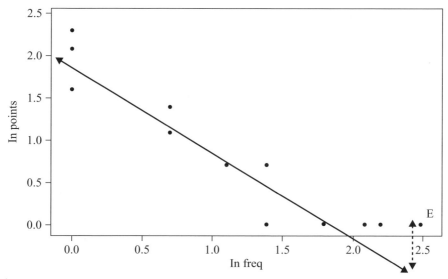

Figure 2.27 The natural log transformation has achieved acceptable linearity (single outlier, *E*, indicated).

We can also compare the point value predicted for a given frequency, say frequency = 4 tiles. For the proper regression, the estimated *ln points* equals $1.94 - 1.01(ln\ freq) = 1.94 - 1.01(1.386) = 0.5401$, giving us an estimated $e^{0.5398} = 1.72e^{0.5401} = 1.72$ points for a letter with frequency 4. Since the actual point values for letters with this frequency are all either one or two points, this estimate makes sense. However, using the untransformed variables, the estimated point value for a letter with frequency 4 is $5.73 - 0.633(\text{frequency}) = 5.73 - 0.633(2.4) = 3.198$, which is much larger than any of the actual point values for a letter with frequency 4. This exemplifies the danger of applying predictions from inappropriate models.

In Table 2.20 there is a single outlier, the letter *E*. Since the standardized residual is positive, this indicates that the point value for *E* is higher than expected, given its frequency, which is the highest in the bunch, 12. The residual of 0.5579 is indicated by the dashed vertical line in Figure 2.27. The letter *E* is also the only "influential" observation, with a Cook's distance of 0.5081 (not shown), which just exceeds the 50th percentile of the $F_{1,\ 25}$ distribution.

Box–Cox Transformations

Generalizing from the idea of a ladder of transformations, to admit powers of any continuous value we may apply a *Box–Cox transformation* [6]. A Box–Cox transformation is of the form

$$W = \begin{cases} \dfrac{y^{\lambda} - 1}{\lambda} & \text{for } \lambda \neq 0 \\ \ln y & \text{for } \lambda = 0 \end{cases}$$

For example, we could have $\lambda = 0.75$, giving us the following transformation, $W = \left(y^{0.75} - 1\right)/0.75$. Draper and Smith [3] provide a method of using maximum likelihood to choose the optimal value of λ. This method involves first choosing a set of candidate values for λ and finding SSE for regressions performed using each value of λ. Then, plotting SSE_λ versus λ, find the lowest point of a curve through the points in the plot. This represents the maximum likelihood estimate of λ.

SUMMARY

In simple linear regression, a straight line is used to approximate the relationship between a single continuous predictor and a single continuous response. The regression line is written in the form $\hat{y} = b_0 + b_1 x$, called the regression equation or *estimated regression equation* (ERE), where $\hat{y}$ is the estimated value of the response variable, b_0 the *y-intercept* of the regression line, b_1 the *slope* of the regression line, and b_0 and b_1 together are called *regression coefficients*. We can use the regression line or the ERE to make estimates or predictions.

The vertical distance between the actual response and the estimated response, $y - \hat{y}$, is known as the *prediction error, estimation error*, or *residual*. We seek to minimize the overall size of our prediction errors. *Least-squares regression* works by choosing the unique regression line that minimizes the sum of squared residuals over all the data points.

The observed coefficients b_0 and b_1 are sample statistics used to estimate the population parameters β_0 and β_1, the y-intercept and the slope of the true regression line. That is, the equation $y = \beta_0 + \beta_1 x + \varepsilon$ represents the true linear relationship between the response and predictor variables for the entire population, not just the sample. Because the sample represents only a subset of the population, the *error term ε* is needed to account for the indeterminacy in the model.

The sum of squares error (SSE) represents an overall measure of the error in prediction resulting from use of the estimated regression equation. The total sum of squares (SST) is a measure of the total variability in the values of the response variable alone, without reference to the predictor. The sum of squares regression (SSR) is a measure of the overall improvement in prediction accuracy when using the regression as opposed to ignoring the predictor information. The relationship among these sums of squares is $\text{SST} = \text{SSR} + \text{SSE}$.

The statistic, r^2, known as the *coefficient of determination*, measures how well the linear approximation produced by the least-squares regression line actually fits the observed data. Since r^2 takes the form of a ratio of SSR to SST, we may interpret r^2 to represent the proportion of the variability in the y-variable that is explained by the linear relationship between the predictor and response variables. Its value ranges from 0 to 1.

The s statistic, known as the *standard error of the estimate* and given by $s = \sqrt{\text{MSE}} = \sqrt{\text{SSE}/(n - m - 1)}$ is a measure of the accuracy of the estimates produced by the regression. The value of s is a measure of the typical error in estimation, the typical difference between the predicted and actual response values. In this way, the standard error of the estimate s represents the precision of the predictions generated by the estimated regression equation. Smaller values of s are better.

The correlation coefficient r (also known as the *Pearson product moment correlation coefficient*) is an indication of the strength of the linear relationship between two quantitative variables. The correlation coefficient r always takes on values between 1 and -1 inclusive. Values of r close to 1 indicate variables that are *positively correlated*; values of r close to -1 indicate variables that are *negatively correlated*. It is convenient to express the correlation coefficient as $r = \pm\sqrt{r^2}$. When the slope b_1 of the estimated regression line is positive, the correlation coefficient is also positive, $r = \sqrt{r^2}$; when the slope is negative, the correlation coefficient is also negative, $r = -\sqrt{r^2}$.

An *outlier* is an observation that has a very large standardized residual in absolute value. In general, if the residual is *positive*, we may say that the y-value observed is *higher* than the regression estimated given the x-value. If the residual is *negative*, we may say that the observed y-value is *lower* than the regression estimated given the x-value. A *high leverage point* is an observation that is extreme in the predictor space. In other words, a high leverage point takes on extreme values for the x-variable(s), without reference to the y-variable.

An observation is *influential* if the regression parameters alter significantly based on the presence or absence of the observation in the data set. An outlier may or may not be influential. Similarly, a high leverage point may or may not be influential. Usually, influential observations combine both large residual and high leverage characteristics. *Cook's distance* measures the level of influence of an observation by taking into account both the size of the residual and the amount of leverage for that observation.

If the assumptions of the regression model are not validated, the resulting inference and model building are undermined. In the regression model, $y = \beta_0 + \beta_1 x + \varepsilon$, ε represents the error term, which is a random variable with the following assumptions:

1. The error term ε is a random variable with mean or expected value equal to zero. In other words, $E(\varepsilon) = 0$.

2. The variance of ε, denoted by σ^2, is constant regardless of the value of x.

3. The values of ε are independent.

4. The error term ε is a normally distributed random variable. In other words, the values of the error term ε_i are independent normal random variables with mean zero and variance σ^2.

In the regression model, when $\beta_1 = 0$, the regression equation becomes $y = \beta_0 + \varepsilon$, so there no longer exists a linear relationship between x and y. On the other hand, if β_1 takes on any conceivable value other than zero, a linear relationship of some kind exists between the response and the predictor. We may use this key idea to apply regression-based inference. For example, the t-test tests directly whether $\beta_1 = 0$, with the null hypothesis representing the claim that no linear relationship exists. We may also construct a confidence interval for the true slope of the regression line. If the confidence interval includes zero, this is evidence that no linear relationship exists.

Point estimates for values of the response variable for a given value of the predictor value may be obtained by an application of the estimated regression equation $\hat{y} = b_0 + b_1 x$. Unfortunately, these kinds of point estimates do not provide a probability statement regarding their accuracy. We may therefore construct two types of intervals: (1) a confidence interval for the mean value of y given x, and (2) a prediction interval for the value of a randomly chosen y given x. The prediction interval is always wider, since its task is more difficult.

All of the inferential methods just described depend on the adherence of the data to the regression assumptions outlined earlier. The two main graphical methods used to verify regression assumptions are (1) a normal probability plot of the residuals, and (2) a plot of the standardized residuals against the fitted (predicted) values. A *normal probability plot* is a quantile–quantile plot of the quantiles of a particular distribution against the quantiles of the standard normal distribution, for the purposes of determining whether the specified distribution deviates from normality. In a normality plot, the values observed for the distribution of interest are compared against the same number of values which would be expected from the normal distribution. If the distribution is normal, the bulk of the points in the plot should fall on a straight line; systematic deviations from linearity in this plot indicate nonnormality. We evaluate the validity of the regression assumptions by observing whether certain patterns exist in the plot of the residuals versus fits, in which case one of the assumptions has been violated, or whether no such discernible patterns exists, in which case the assumptions remain intact.

If these graphs indicate violations of the assumptions, we may apply a transformation to the response variable y, such as the *ln* (natural log, log to the base e) transformation. Transformations may also be called for if the relationship between the predictor and the response variables is not linear. We may use either Mosteller and Tukey's ladder of re-expressions or a Box–Cox transformation.

REFERENCES

1. Daniel Larose, *Discovering Knowledge in Data: An Introduction to Data Mining*, Wiley, Hoboken, N. J. 2005.
2. Cereals data set, in Data and Story Library, http://lib.stat.cmu.edu/DASL/. Also available at the book series Web site.
3. Norman Draper and Harry Smith, *Applied Regression Analysis*, Wiley, New York, 1998.
4. California data set, U.S. Census Bureau, http://www.census.gov/. Also available at the book series Web site.
5. Frederick Mosteller and John Tukey, *Data Analysis and Regression*, Addison-Wesley, Reading, MA, 1977.
6. G. E. P. Box and D. R. Cox, An analysis of transformations, *Journal of the Royal Statistical Society, Series B*, Vol. 26, pp. 211–243, 1964.

EXERCISES

Clarifying the Concepts

2.1. Determine whether the following statements are true or false. If a statement is false, explain why and suggest how one might alter the statement to make it true.

(a) The least-squares line is that line which minimizes the sum of the residuals.

(b) If all the residuals equal zero, SST = SSR.

(c) If the value of the correlation coefficient is negative, this indicates that the variables are negatively correlated.

(d) The value of the correlation coefficient can be calculated given the value of r^2 alone.

(e) Outliers are influential observations.

(f) If the residual for an outlier is positive, we may say that the observed y-value is higher than the regression estimated, given the x-value.

(g) An observation may be influential even though it is neither an outlier nor a high leverage point.

(h) The best way of determining whether an observation is influential is to see whether its Cook's distance exceeds 1.0.

(i) If one is interested in using regression analysis in a strictly descriptive manner, with no inference and no model building, one need not worry quite so much about assumption validation.

(j) In a normality plot, if the distribution is normal, the bulk of the points should fall on a straight line.

(k) The chi-square distribution is left-skewed.

(l) Small p-values for the Anderson–Darling test statistic indicate that the data are right-skewed.

(m) A funnel pattern in the plot of residuals versus fits indicates a violation of the independence assumption.

2.2. Describe the difference between the estimated regression line and the true regression line.

2.3. Calculate the estimated regression equation for the orienteering example using the data in Table 2.3. Use either the formulas or software of your choice.

2.4. Where would a data point be situated which has the smallest possible leverage?

2.5. Calculate the values for leverage, standardized residual, and Cook's distance for the hard-core hiker example in the text.

2.6. Calculate the values for leverage, standardized residual, and Cook's distance for the eleventh hiker who had hiked for 10 hours and traveled 23 kilometers. Show that although it is neither an outlier nor of high leverage, it is nevertheless influential.

2.7. Match each of the following regression terms with its definition.

Term		Definition
(a)	Influential observation	Measures the typical difference between the predicted and actual response values.
(b)	SSE	Represents the total variability in the values of the response variable alone, without reference to the predictor.

	Term	Definition
(c)	r^2	An observation that has a very large standardized residual in absolute value.
(d)	Residual	Measures the strength of the linear relationship between two quantitative variables, with values ranging from −1 to 1.
(e)	s	An observation that alters the regression parameters significantly based on its presence or absence in the data set.
(f)	High leverage point	Measures the level of influence of an observation by taking into account both the size of the residual and the amount of leverage for that observation.
(g)	r	Represents an overall measure of the error in prediction resulting from the use of the estimated regression equation.
(h)	SST	An observation that is extreme in the predictor space, without reference to the response variable.
(i)	Outlier	Measures the overall improvement in prediction accuracy when using the regression as opposed to ignoring the predictor information.
(j)	SSR	The vertical distance between the response predicted and the actual response.
(k)	Cook's distance	The proportion of the variability in the response that is explained by the linear relationship between the predictor and response variables.

2.8. Explain in your own words the implications of the regression assumptions for the behavior of the response variable y.

2.9. Explain what statistics from Table 2.11 indicate to us that there may indeed be a linear relationship between x and y in this example, even though the value for r^2 is less than 1%.

2.10. Which values of the slope parameter indicate that no linear relationship exists between the predictor and response variables? Explain how this works.

2.11. Explain what information is conveyed by the value of the standard error of the slope estimate.

2.12. Describe the criterion for rejecting the null hypothesis when using the p-value method for hypothesis testing. Who chooses the value of the level of significance, α? Make up a situation (one p-value and two different values of α) where the very same data could lead to two different conclusions of the hypothesis test. Comment.

2.13. (a) Explain why an analyst may prefer a confidence interval to a hypothesis test.

(b) Describe how a confidence interval may be used to assess significance.

2.14. Explain the difference between a confidence interval and a prediction interval. Which interval is always wider? Why? Which interval is probably, depending on the situation, more useful to a data miner? Why?

2.15. Clearly explain the correspondence between an original scatter plot of the data and a plot of the residuals versus fitted values.

2.16. What recourse do we have if the residual analysis indicates that the regression assumptions have been violated? Describe three different rules, heuristics, or family of functions that will help us.

2.17. A colleague would like to use linear regression to predict whether or not customers will make a purchase based on some predictor variable. What would you explain to your colleague?

Working with the Data

2.18. Based on the scatter plot of attendance at football games versus winning percentage of the home team shown in Figure E2.18, answer the following questions.

(a) Describe any correlation between the variables, and estimate the value of the correlation coefficient r.

(b) Estimate as best you can the values of the regression coefficients b_0 and b_1.

(c) Will the p-value for the hypothesis test for the existence of a linear relationship between the variables be small or large? Explain.

(d) Will the confidence interval for the slope parameter include zero? Explain.

(e) Will the value of s be closer to 10, 100, 1000, or 10,000? Why?

(f) Is there an observation that may look as though it is an outlier?

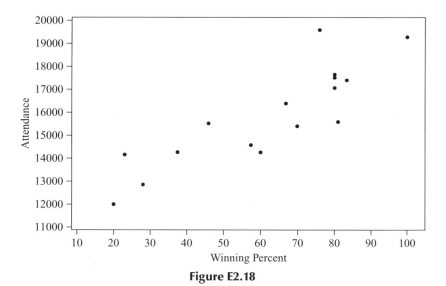

Figure E2.18

2.19. Use the regression output (shown in Table E2.19) to verify your responses from Exercise 2.18.

TABLE E2.19

```
The regeression equation is
Attendance = 11067 + 77.2 Winning Percent

Predictor              Coef  SE Coef      T      P
Constant            11066.8    793.3  13.95  0.000
Winning Percent       77.22    12.00   6.44  0.000

S = 1127.51    R-Sq = 74.7%    R-Sq(adj) = 72.9%

Analysis of Variance

Source            DF        SS        MS      F      P
Regression         1  52675342  52675342  41.43  0.000
Residual Error    14  17797913   1271280
Total             15  70473255

Unusual Observations

      Winning
Obs   Percent  Attendance    Fit  SE Fit  Residual  St Resid
 10        76       19593  16936     329      2657     2.46R

R denotes an observation with a large standardized residual.
```

2.20. Based on the scatter plot shown in Figure E2.20, answer the following questions.

   (a) Is it appropriate to perform linear regression? Why or why not?

   (b) What type of transformation or transformations are called for? Use the bulging rule.

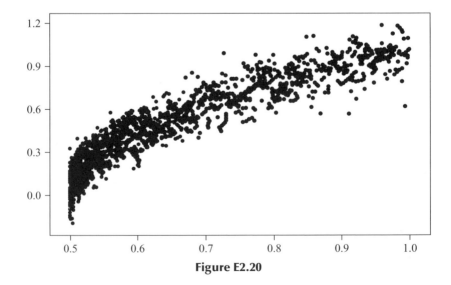

Figure E2.20

2.21. Based on the regression output shown in Table E2.21 (from the *churn* data set), answer the following questions.

(a) Is there evidence of a linear relationship between *z vmail messages* (z-scores of the number of voice mail messages) and *z day calls* (z-scores of the number of day calls made)? Explain.

(b) Since it has been standardized, the response *z vmail messages* has a standard deviation of 1.0. What would be the typical error in predicting *z vmail messages* if we simply used the sample mean response and no information about day calls? Now, from the printout, what is the typical error in predicting *z vmail messages* given *z day calls*? Comment.

TABLE E2.21

```
The regression equation is
z vmail messages = 0.0000 - 0.0095 z day calls

Predictor         Coef  SE Coef       T      P
Constant       0.00000  0.01732    0.00  1.000
z day calls   -0.00955  0.01733   -0.55  0.582

S = 1.00010    R-Sq = 0.0%    R-Sq(adj) = 0.0%

Analysis of Variance

Source               DF        SS      MS      F      P
Regression            1     0.304   0.304   0.30  0.582
Residual Error     3331  3331.693   1.000
Total              3332  3331.997
```

Hands-on Analysis

2.22. Open the *baseball* data set, which is available at the book series Web site. Subset the data so that we are working with batters who have at least 100 at bats.

(a) We are interested in investigating whether there is a linear relationship between the number of times a player has been caught stealing and the number of stolen bases the player has. Construct a scatter plot with *caught* as the response. Is there evidence of a linear relationship?

(b) Based on the scatter plot, is a transformation to linearity called for? Why or why not?

(c) Perform the regression of the number of times a player has been caught stealing versus the number of stolen bases the player has.

(d) Find and interpret the statistic which tells you how well the data fit the model.

(e) What is the typical error in predicting the number of times a player is caught stealing given his number of stolen bases?

(f) Interpret the *y*-intercept. Does this make sense? Why or why not?

(g) Inferentially, is there a significant relationship between the two variables? What tells you this?

(h) Calculate and interpret the correlation coefficient.

(i) Clearly interpret the meaning of the slope coefficient.

(j) Suppose someone said that knowing the number of stolen bases a player has explains most of the variability in the number of times the player gets caught stealing. What would you say?

2.23. Open the *cereals* data set, which is available at the book series Web site.

(a) We are interested in predicting nutrition rating based on sodium content. Construct the appropriate scatter plot.

(b) Based on the scatter plot, is there strong evidence of a linear relationship between the variables? Discuss. Characterize their relationship, if any.

(c) Perform the appropriate regression.

(d) Which cereal is an outlier? Explain why this cereal is an outlier.

(e) What is the typical error in predicting rating based on sodium content?

(f) Interpret the *y*-intercept. Does this make any sense? Why or why not?

(g) Inferentially, is there a significant relationship between the two variables? What tells you this?

(h) Calculate and interpret the correlation coefficient.

(i) Clearly interpret the meaning of the slope coefficient.

(j) Construct and interpret a 95% confidence interval for the true nutrition rating for all cereals with a sodium content of 100.

(k) Construct and interpret a 95% confidence interval for the nutrition rating for a randomly chosen cereal with sodium content of 100.

2.24. Open the *California* data set, which is available at the book series Web site.

(a) Recapitulate the analysis performed within the chapter.

(b) Set aside the military outliers and proceed with the analysis with the remaining 848 records. Apply whatever data transformations are necessary to construct your best regression model.

CHAPTER 3

MULTIPLE REGRESSION AND MODEL BUILDING

EXAMPLE OF MULTIPLE REGRESSION

In Chapter 2 we examined regression modeling for the simple linear regression case of a single predictor and a single response. Clearly, however, data miners are usually interested in the relationship between the target variable and a set of (more than one) predictor variables. Most data mining applications enjoy a wealth of data, with some data sets including hundreds or thousands of variables, many of which may have a linear relationship with the target (response) variable. *Multiple regression modeling* provides an elegant method of describing such relationships. Compared to simple linear regression, multiple regression models provide improved precision for estimation and prediction, analogous to the improved precision of regression estimates over univariate estimates.

A *multiple regression model* uses a linear surface such as a plane or hyperplane to approximate the relationship between a continuous response (target) variable and

Data Mining Methods and Models By Daniel T. Larose
Copyright © 2006 John Wiley & Sons, Inc.

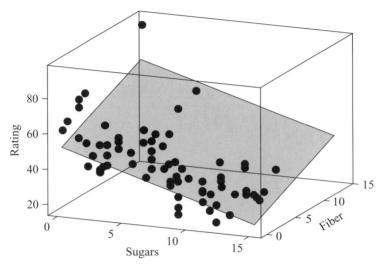

Figure 3.1 A plane approximates the linear relationship between one response and two continuous predictors.

a set of predictor variables. Although the predictor variables are typically continuous, categorical predictor variables may be included as well, through the use of indicator (dummy) variables. In simple linear regression, we used a straight line (of dimension 1) to approximate the relationship between the response and one predictor. Now, suppose that we would like to approximate the relationship between a response and two continuous predictors. In this case, we would need a plane to approximate such a relationship, since a plane is linear in two dimensions.

For example, returning to the *cereals* data set [1], suppose that we are interested in trying to estimate the value of the target variable, *nutritional rating*, but this time using two variables, *sugars* and *fiber*, rather than sugars alone as in Chapter 2. The three-dimensional scatter plot of the data is shown in Figure 3.1. High fiber levels seem to be associated with high nutritional rating, and high sugar levels seem to be associated with low nutritional rating. These relationships are approximated by the plane that is shown in Figure 3.1, in a manner analogous to the straight-line approximation for simple linear regression. The plane tilts downward to the right (for high sugar levels) and toward the front (for low fiber levels).

Now suppose that we performed a multiple regression of nutritional rating on both predictor variables, *sugars* and *fiber*. The results are provided in Table 3.1; let us examine these results. The estimated regression equation for multiple regression with two predictor variables takes the form

$$\hat{y} = b_0 + b_1 x_1 + b_2 x_2$$

For a multiple regression with m variables, the estimated regression equation takes the form

$$\hat{y} = b_0 + b_1 x_1 + b_2 x_2 + \cdots + b_m x_m$$

TABLE 3.1 Results of Regression of Nutritional *Rating* on *Sugars* and *Fiber*

```
The regression equation is
Rating = 51.8 - 2.21 Sugars + 2.84 Fiber


Predictor        Coef    SE Coef        T       P
Constant       51.787      1.559    33.21   0.000
Sugars        -2.2090      0.1633  -13.53   0.000
Fiber          2.8408      0.3032    9.37   0.000


S = 6.23743   R-Sq = 80.8%  R-Sq(adj) = 80.3%


Analysis of Variance

Source            DF        SS      MS       F       P
Regression         2   12117.8  6058.9  155.73   0.000
Residual Error    74    2879.0    38.9
Total             76   14996.8

Source            DF    Seq SS
Sugars             1    8701.7
Fiber              1    3416.1


Unusual Observations

Obs   Sugars  Rating     Fit  SE Fit  Residual  St Resid
2        0.0  93.705  91.558   3.676     2.147     0.43 X
8        0.0  72.802  60.309   1.331    12.493     2.05R
27       5.0  59.426  66.309   2.168    -6.884    -1.18 X
32       6.0  68.403  66.941   2.459     1.462     0.26 X
41       7.0  58.345  44.847   0.753    13.499     2.18R
76      15.0  35.252  18.653   1.561    16.600     2.75R

R denotes an observation with a large standardized residual.
X denotes an observation whose X value gives it large influence.


Predicted Values for New Observations

New
Obs     Fit  SE Fit       95% CI              95% PI
  1  54.946   1.123  (52.709, 57.183)  (42.318, 67.574)


Values of Predictors for New Observations

New
Obs  Sugars  Fiber
  1    5.00   5.00
```

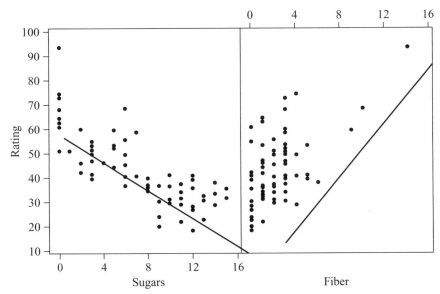

Figure 3.2 Individual variable scatter plots of *rating* versus *sugars* and *fiber*.

Here, we have $b_0 = 51.787$, $b_1 = -2.2090$, $b_2 = 2.8408$, $x_1 = sugars$, and $x_2 = fiber$. Thus, the estimated regression equation for this example is

$$\hat{y} = 51.787 - 2.2090\,sugars + 2.8408\,fiber$$

That is, the estimated nutritional rating equals 51.787 minus 2.2090 times the grams of sugar plus 2.8408 times the grams of fiber. Note that the coefficient for *sugars* is negative, indicating a negative relationship between *sugars* and *rating*, whereas the coefficient for *fiber* is positive, indicating a positive relationship. These results concur with the characteristics of the plane shown in Figure 3.1. In case the three-dimensional plot is not clear enough for exploratory purposes, we may examine individual scatter plots of the response against each of the predictors, as shown in Figure 3.2. The straight lines shown in Figure 3.2 represent the value of the slope coefficients for each variable: – 2.2090 for *sugars* and 2.8408 for *fiber*.

The interpretations of the slope coefficients b_1 and b_2 are slightly different than for the simple linear regression case. For example, to interpret $b_1 = -2.2090$, we say that "the estimated decrease in nutritional rating for a unit increase in sugar content is 2.2090 points *when the fiber content is held constant*." Similarly, we interpret $b_2 = 2.8408$ as follows: The estimated increase in nutritional rating for a unit increase in fiber content is 2.8408 points *when the sugar content is held constant*. In general, for a multiple regression with *m* predictor variables, we would interpret coefficient b_i as follows: The estimated change in the response variable for a unit increase in variable x_i is b_i *when all other variables are held constant*.

Recall that errors in prediction are measured by the *residual*, $y - \hat{y}$. In simple linear regression, this residual represented the vertical distance between the actual data point and the regression line. In multiple regression, the residual is represented by the vertical distance between the data point and the regression plane or hyperplane.

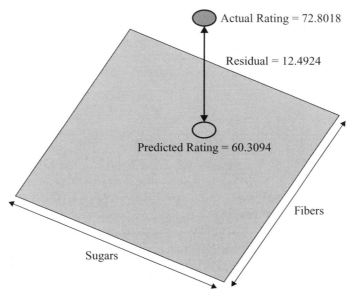

Figure 3.3 Estimation error is the vertical distance between the actual data point and the regression plane or hyperplane.

For example, Spoon Size Shredded Wheat has $x_1 = 0$ grams of sugar, $x_2 = 3$ grams of fiber, and a nutritional rating of 72.8018. The estimated regression equation would predict, however, that the nutritional rating for this cereal would be

$$\hat{y} = 51.787 - 2.2090(0) + 2.8408(3) = 60.3094$$

Therefore, we have a residual for Spoon Size Shredded Wheat of $y - \hat{y} = 72.8018 - 60.3094 = 12.4924$, illustrated in Figure 3.3.

Each observation has its own residual, which, taken together, leads to the calculation of the sum of squares error as an overall measure of the estimation errors. Just as for the simple linear regression case, we may again calculate the three sums of squares as follows:

$$SSE = \sum (y - \hat{y})^2$$
$$SSR = \sum (\hat{y} - \bar{y})^2$$
$$SST = \sum (y - \bar{y})^2$$

We may again present the regression statistics succinctly in a convenient ANOVA table, shown here in Table 3.2, where m represents the number of predictor variables. Finally, for multiple regression, we have the *multiple coefficient of determination*, which is simply

$$R^2 = \frac{SSR}{SST}$$

For multiple regression, R^2 is interpreted as the proportion of the variability in the target variable that is accounted for by its linear relationship with the set of predictor variables.

TABLE 3.2   ANOVA Table for Multiple Regression

Source of Variation	Sum of Squares	df	Mean Square	F
Regression	SSR	m	$\text{MSR} = \dfrac{\text{SSR}}{m}$	
Error (or residual)	SSE	$n - m - 1$	$\text{MSE} = \dfrac{\text{SSE}}{n - m - 1}$	$F = \dfrac{\text{MSR}}{\text{MSE}}$
Total	$\text{SST} = \text{SSR} + \text{SSE}$	$n - 1$		

From Table 3.1 we can see that the value of R^2 is 80.8%, which means that 80.8% of the variability in nutritional rating is accounted for by the linear relationship (the plane) between rating and the set of predictors, sugar content and fiber content. Would we expect R^2 to be greater than the value for the coefficient of determination we got from the simple linear regression of nutritional rating on sugars alone? The answer is yes. Whenever a new predictor variable is added to the model, the value of R^2 always goes up. If the new variable is useful, the value of R^2 will increase significantly; if the new variable is not useful, the value of R^2 may barely increase at all.

Table 2.7 provides us with the coefficient of determination for the simple linear regression case, $r^2 = 58\%$. Thus, by adding the new predictor, fiber content, to the model, we can account for an additional $80.8\% - 58\% = 22.8\%$ of the variability in the nutritional rating. This seems like a significant increase, but we shall defer this determination until later.

The typical error in estimation is provided by the standard error of the estimate, s. The value of s here is about 6.24 rating points. Therefore, our estimation of the nutritional rating of the cereals, based on sugar and fiber content, is typically in error by about 6.24 points. Would we expect this error to be greater or less than the value for s obtained by the simple linear regression of nutritional rating on sugars alone? In general, the answer depends on the usefulness of the new predictor. If the new variable is useful, s will decrease; but if the new variable is not useful for predicting the target variable, s may in fact increase. This type of behavior makes s, the standard error of the estimate, a more attractive indicator than R^2 of whether a new variable should be added to the model, since R^2 always increases when a new variable is added, regardless of its usefulness. Table 2.7 shows that the value for s from the regression of rating on sugars alone was 9.16. Thus, the addition of fiber content as a predictor decreased the typical error in estimating nutritional content from 9.16 points to 6.24 points, a decrease of 2.92 points.

With respect to outliers, Table 3.1 shows that there are three outliers in this data set, as indicated by "R" in the list of unusual observations:

- *Observation 8:* Spoon Size Shredded Wheat
- *Observation 41:* Frosted Mini-Wheats
- *Observation 76:* Golden Crisp

Since the residuals associated with these observations are all positive, we say that the observed nutritional rating is higher than the regression estimate given the sugar content and fiber content of the cereal. This may be due to other factors not yet included in the model, such as sodium content.

Three observations are flagged by Minitab as having high leverage:

- *Observation 2:* All-Bran Extra Fiber (with 14 grams of fiber)
- *Observation 27:* All-Bran (with 9 grams of fiber)
- *Observation 32:* 100% Bran (with 10 grams of fiber)

High leverage points are defined as data points that are extreme in the x-space. The three high-leverage points show up in Figure 3.2b as the three isolated data points on the right, since no other cereal contains more than 6 grams of fiber. This extremeness with respect to fiber content is enough in this instance for these observations to be labeled high leverage points.

The most influential observation is Golden Crisp, with a Cook's distance of 0.168 (not shown), which lies within the 16th percentile of the $F_{2,76}$-distribution. Since this is less than the 20th percentile, we may conclude that there are no observations in this data set which are particularly influential. Before we turn to inference in multiple regression, we examine the details of the multiple regression model.

MULTIPLE REGRESSION MODEL

We have seen that for simple linear regression, the regression model takes the form

$$y = \beta_0 + \beta_1 x + \varepsilon \tag{3.1}$$

with β_0 and β_1 as the unknown values of the true regression coefficients, and ε the error term, with its associated assumption, discussed in Chapter 2. The multiple regression model is a straightforward extension of the simple linear regression model (3.1), as follows.

MULTIPLE REGRESSION MODEL

$$y = \beta_0 + \beta_1 x_1 + \beta_2 x_2 + \cdots + \beta_m x_m + \varepsilon$$

where

- $\beta_0, \beta_1, \ldots, \beta_m$ represent the model parameters. These are constants, whose true value remains unknown, which are estimated from the data using the least-squares estimates.
- ε represents the error term.

Assumptions About the Error Term

1. *Zero-mean assumption.* The error term ε is a random variable with mean or expected value equal to zero. In other words, $E(\varepsilon) = 0$.
2. *Constant-variance assumption.* The variance of ε, denoted by σ^2, is constant, regardless of the value of $x_1, x_2 \ldots, x_m$.
3. *Independence assumption.* The values of ε are independent.
4. *Normality assumption.* The error term ε is a normally distributed random variable.

In other words, the values of the error term ε_i are independent normal random variables with mean 0 and variance σ^2.

Just as we did for the simple linear regression case, we can derive four implications for the behavior of the response variable, y, as follows.

IMPLICATIONS OF THE ASSUMPTIONS FOR THE BEHAVIOR OF THE RESPONSE VARIABLE y

1. Based on the zero-mean assumption, we have

$$E(y) = E\left(\beta_0 + \beta_1 x_1 + \beta_2 x_2 + \cdots + \beta_m x_m + \varepsilon\right)$$
$$= E\left(\beta_0\right) + E\left(\beta_1 x_1\right) + \cdots + E(\beta_m x_m) + E\left(\varepsilon\right)$$
$$= \beta_0 + \beta_1 x_1 + \beta_2 x_2 + \cdots + \beta_m x_m$$

   That is, for each set of values for $x_1, x_2, \cdots, x_m$, the mean of the y's lies on the regression line.

2. Based on the constant-variance assumption, we have the variance of y, $\text{Var}(y)$, given as

$$\text{Var}(y) = \text{Var}\left(\beta_0 + \beta_1 x_1 + \beta_2 x_2 + \cdots + \beta_m x_m + \varepsilon\right) = \text{Var}\left(\varepsilon\right) = \sigma^2$$

   That is, regardless of which value is taken by the predictors $x_1, x_2, \ldots, x_m$, the variance of the y's is always constant.

3. Based on the independence assumption, it follows that for any particular set of values for $x_1, x_2, \ldots, x_m$, the values of y are independent as well.

4. Based on the normality assumption, it follows that y is also a normally distributed random variable.

   In other words, the values of the response variable y_i are independent normal random variables with mean $\beta_0 + \beta_1 x_1 + \beta_2 x_2 + \cdots + \beta_m x_m$ and variance σ^2.

INFERENCE IN MULTIPLE REGRESSION

We examine five inferential methods in this chapter:

1. The t-test for the relationship between the response variable y and a particular predictor variable x_i, in the presence of the other predictor variables, $x_{(i)}$, where $x_{(i)} = x_1, x_2, \ldots, x_{i-1}, x_{i+1}, \ldots x_m$ denotes the set of all predictors not including x_i.

2. The F-test for the significance of the regression as a whole.

3. The confidence interval, β_i, for the slope of the ith predictor variable.

4. The confidence interval for the mean of the response variable y given a set of particular values for the predictor variables $x_1, x_2, \ldots, x_m$.

5. The prediction interval for a random value of the response variable y given a set of particular values for the predictor variables $x_1, x_2, \ldots, x_m$.

t-Test for the Relationship Between *y* and x_i

The hypotheses for a t-test between y and x_i are given by

- H_0: $\beta_i = 0$
- H_a: $\beta_i \neq 0$

The models implied by these hypotheses are given by:

- Under H_0: $y = \beta_0 + \beta_1 x_1 + \cdots + \beta_{i-1} x_{i-1} + \beta_i x_i + \beta_{i+1} x_{i+1} + \cdots$
  $+\beta_m x_m + \varepsilon$

- Under H_a: $y = \beta_0 + \beta_1 x_1 + \cdots + \beta_{i-1} x_{i-1} + \beta_{i+1} x_{i+1} + \cdots$
  $+\beta_m x_m + \varepsilon$

Note that the only difference between the two models is the presence or absence of the ith term. All other terms are the same in both models. Therefore, interpretations of the results for this t-test must include some reference to the other predictor variables being held constant.

Under the null hypothesis, the test statistic $t = b_i/s_{b_i}$ follows a t-distribution with $n - m - 1$ degrees of freedom, where s_{b_i} refers to the standard error of the slope for the ith predictor variable. We proceed to perform the t-test for each of the predictor variables in turn, using the results displayed in Table 3.1.

t-*Test for the Relationship Between Nutritional* Rating *and* Sugars

- H_0: $\beta_1 = 0$; model: $y = \beta_0 + \beta_2(fiber) + \varepsilon$.
- H_a: $\beta_1 \neq 0$; model: $y = \beta_0 + \beta_1(sugars) + \beta_2(fiber) + \varepsilon$.
- In Table 3.1, under "Coef" in the "Sugars" row is found the value of b_1, -2.2090.
- Under "SE Coef" in the "Sugars" row is found the value of s_{b_1}, the standard error of the slope for sugar content. Here $s_{b_1} = 0.1633$.
- Under "T" is found the value of the t-statistic, that is, the test statistic for the t-test,

$$t = \frac{b_1}{s_{b_1}} = \frac{-2.2090}{0.1633} = -13.53$$

- Under "P" is found the p-value of the t-statistic. Since this is a two-tailed test, this p-value takes the form $p\text{-value} = P(|t| > t_{\text{obs}})$, where t_{obs} represents the value of the t-statistic observed from the regression results. Here $p\text{-value} = P(|t| > t_{\text{obs}}) = P(|t| > -13.53) \approx 0.000$, although of course no continuous p-value ever equals precisely zero.

The p-value method is used, whereby the null hypothesis is rejected when the p-value of the test statistic is small. Here we have $p\text{-value} \approx 0.00$, which is smaller than any reasonable threshold of significance. Our conclusion is therefore to reject the null hypothesis. The interpretation of this conclusion is that there is evidence for a linear relationship between nutritional rating and sugar content in the presence of fiber content.

t-Test for the Relationship Between Nutritional Rating and Fiber Content

- H_0: $\beta_2 = 0$; model: $y = \beta_0 + \beta_1(sugars) + \varepsilon$.
- H_a: $\beta_2 \neq 0$; model: $y = \beta_0 + \beta_1(sugars) + \beta_2(fiber) + \varepsilon$.
- In Table 3.1, under "Coef" in the "Fiber" row is found $b_2 = 2.8408$.
- Under "SE Coef" in the "Fiber" row is found the standard error of the slope for fiber content, $s_{b_2} = 0.3032$.
- Under "T" is found the test statistic for the t-test,

$$t = \frac{b_2}{s_{b_2}} = \frac{2.8408}{0.3032} = 9.37$$

- Under "P" is found the p-value of the t-statistic. Again, p-value ≈ 0.000.

Thus, our conclusion is again to reject the null hypothesis. We interpret this to mean that there is evidence for a linear relationship between nutritional rating and fiber content in the presence of sugar content.

F-Test for the Significance of the Overall Regression Model

Next we introduce the F-test for the significance of the overall regression model. Figure 3.4 illustrates the difference between the t-test and the F-test. One may apply a separate t-test for each predictor x_1, x_2, or x_3, examining whether a linear relationship

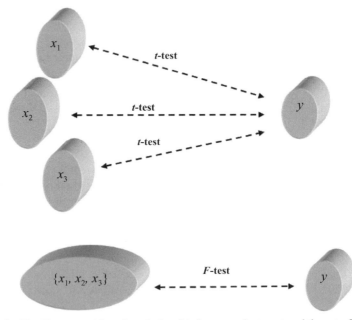

Figure 3.4 The F-test considers the relationship between the target and the set of predictors, taken as a whole.

exists between the target variable y and that particular predictor. On the other hand, the F-test considers the linear relationship between the target variable y and the *set of predictors* (e.g., $\{x_1, x_2, x_3\}$) taken as a whole.

The hypotheses for the F-test are given by

- H_0: $\beta_1 = \beta_2 = \cdots = \beta_m = 0$.
- H_a: At least one of the β_i does not equal 0.

The null hypothesis asserts that there is no linear relationship between the target variable y and the set of predictors, $x_1, x_2, \ldots, x_m$. Thus, the null hypothesis states that the coefficient β_i for each predictor x_i exactly equals zero, leaving the null model to be

- Model under H_0: $y = \beta_0 + \varepsilon$

The alternative hypothesis does not assert that the regression coefficients all differ from zero. For the alternative hypothesis to be true, it is sufficient for a single, unspecified regression coefficient to differ from zero. Hence, the alternative hypothesis for the F-test does not specify a particular model, since it would be true if any, some, or all of the coefficients differed from zero.

As shown in Table 3.2, the F-statistic consists of a ratio of two mean squares: the mean square regression (MSR) and the mean square error (MSE). A *mean square* represents a sum of squares divided by the degrees of freedom associated with that sum of squares statistic. Since the sums of squares are always nonnegative, so are the mean squares. To understand how the F-test works, we should consider the following.

The MSE is always a good estimate of the overall variance (see model assumption 2) σ^2, regardless of whether or not the null hypothesis is true. (In fact, recall that we use the standard error of the estimate, $s = \sqrt{\text{MSE}}$, as a measure of the usefulness of the regression, without reference to an inferential model.) Now, the MSR is also a good estimate of σ^2, but only on the condition that the null hypothesis is true. If the null hypothesis is false, MSR overestimates σ^2.

So consider the value of $F = \text{MSR}/\text{MSE}$ with respect to the null hypothesis. Suppose that MSR and MSE are close to each other, so that the value of F is small (near 1.0). Since MSE is always a good estimate of σ^2, and MSR is only a good estimate of σ^2 when the null hypothesis is true, the circumstance that MSR and MSE are close to each other will occur only when the null hypothesis is true. Therefore, when the value of F is small, this is evidence that the null hypothesis is true.

However, suppose that MSR is much greater than MSE, so that the value of F is large. MSR is large (overestimates σ^2) when the null hypothesis is false. Therefore, when the value of F is large, this is evidence that the null hypothesis is false. Therefore, for the F test, we shall reject the null hypothesis when the value of the test statistic F is large.

The F-statistic observed, $F = F_{\text{obs}} = \text{MSR}/\text{MSE}$, follows an $F_{m,\,n-m-1}$ distribution. Since all F-values are nonnegative, the F-test is a right-tailed test. Thus, we will reject the null hypothesis when the p-value is small, where the p-value is the area in the tail to the right of the observed F-statistic. That is, p-value $= P(F_{m,\,n-m-1} > F_{\text{obs}})$, and we reject the null hypothesis when $P(F_{m,\,n-m-1} > F_{\text{obs}})$ is small.

F-*Test for the Relationship Between Nutritional Rating and {Sugar and Fiber} Taken Together*

- H_0: $\beta_1 = \beta_2 = 0$; model: $y = \beta_0 + \varepsilon$.
- H_a: At least one of β_1 and β_2 does not equal zero.
- The model implied by H_a is not specified, and may be any one of the following:

$$y = \beta_0 + \beta_1(sugars) + \varepsilon$$
$$y = \beta_0 + \beta_2(fiber) + \varepsilon$$
$$y = \beta_0 + \beta_1(sugars) + \beta_2(fiber) + \varepsilon$$

- In Table 3.1, under "MS" in the "Regression" row of the "Analysis of Variance" table, is found the value of MSR, the mean square regression, MSR = 6058.9.
- Under "MS" in the "Residual Error" row of the "Analysis of Variance" table is found the value of MSE, the mean-squared error, MSE = 38.9.
- Under "F" in the "Regression," row of the "Analysis of Variance" table is found the value of the test statistic,

$$F = \frac{\text{MSR}}{\text{MSE}} = \frac{6058.9}{38.9} = 155.73$$

- The degrees of freedom for the F-statistic are given in the column marked "DF," so that we have $m = 2$, and $n - m - 1 = 74$.
- Under "P" in the "Regression" row of the "Analysis of Variance" table is found the p-value of the F-statistic. Here, the p-value is $P(F_{m,n-m-1} > F_{\text{obs}}) = P(F_{2,74} > 155.73) \approx 0.000$, although again no continuous p-value ever equals precisely zero.

This p-value of approximately zero is less than any reasonable threshold of significance. Our conclusion is therefore to reject the null hypothesis. The interpretation of this conclusion is the following. There is evidence for a linear relationship between nutritional rating on the one hand, and the set of predictors, sugar content and fiber content, on the other. More succinctly, we may simply say that the overall regression model is significant.

Confidence Interval for a Particular Coefficient

Just as for simple linear regression, we may construct a $100(1 - \alpha)\%$ confidence interval for a particular coefficient, β_i, as follows. We can be $100(1 - \alpha)\%$ confident that the true value of a particular coefficient β_i lies within the following interval:

$$b_i \pm (t_{n-m-1})(s_{b_i})$$

where t_{n-m-1} is based on $n - m - 1$ degrees of freedom, and s_{b_i} represents the standard error of the ith coefficient estimate. For example, let us construct a 95% confidence interval for the true value of the coefficient β_1 for x_1, sugar content. From Table 3.1, the point estimate is given as $b_1 = -2.2090$. The t-critical value for 95% confidence and $n - m - 1 = 74$ degrees of freedom is $t_{n-m-1} = 2.0$. The standard error of the coefficient estimate is $s_{b_1} = 0.1633$. Thus, our confidence interval is as follows:

$$b_1 \pm (t_{n-m-1})(s_{b_1}) = -2.2090 \pm 2.00(0.1633)$$
$$= (-2.54, -1.88)$$

We are 95% confident that the value for the coefficient β_1 lies between -2.54 and -1.88. In other words, for every additional gram of sugar, the nutritional rating will decrease by between 1.88 and 2.54 points *when fiber content is held constant*. For example, suppose a nutrition researcher claimed that nutritional rating would fall two points for every additional gram of sugar when fiber is held constant. Since 2.0 lies within the 95% confidence interval, we would not reject this hypothesis, with 95% confidence.

Confidence Interval for the Mean Value of y Given
$x_1, x_2, \ldots, x_m$

We may find confidence intervals for the mean value of the target variable y given a particular set of values for the predictors $x_1, x_2, \ldots, x_m$. The formula is a multivariate extension of the analogous formula from Chapter 2, requires matrix multiplication, and may be found in Draper and Smith [2]. For example, the bottom of Table 3.1 ("Values of Predictors for New Observations") shows that we are interested in finding the confidence interval for the mean of the distribution of all nutritional ratings when the cereal contains 5.00 grams of sugar and 5.00 grams of fiber. The resulting 95% confidence interval is given under "Predicted Values for New Observations" as "95% CI" $= (52,709, 57.183)$. That is, we can be 95% confident that the mean nutritional rating of all cereals with 5.00 grams of sugar and 5.00 grams of fiber lies between 52.709 and 57.183 points.

Prediction Interval for a Randomly Chosen Value of y
Given $x_1, x_2, \ldots, x_m$

Similarly, we may find a prediction interval for a randomly selected value of the target variable given a particular set of values for the predictors $x_1, x_2, \ldots, x_m$. We refer to Table 3.1 for our example of interest: 5.00 grams of sugar and 5.00 grams of fiber. Under "95% PI" we find the prediction interval to be $(42.318, 67.574)$. In other words, we can be 95% confident that the nutritional rating for a randomly chosen cereal with 5.00 grams of sugar and 5.00 grams of fiber lies between 42.318 and 67.574 points. Again, note that the prediction interval is wider than the confidence interval, as expected.

REGRESSION WITH CATEGORICAL PREDICTORS

Thus far, our predictors have all been continuous. However, categorical predictor variables may also be used as inputs to regression models, through the use of indicator variables (dummy variables). For example, in the *cereals* data set, consider the variable

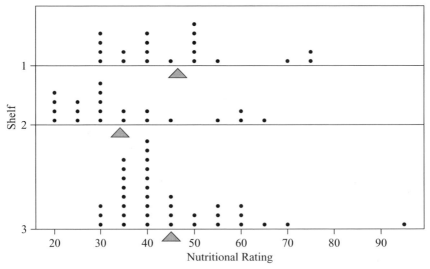

Figure 3.5 Is there evidence that shelf location affects nutritional rating?

shelf, which indicates which supermarket shelf the particular cereal was located on. Of the 77 cereals, 20 were located on shelf 1, 21 were located on shelf 2, and 36 were located on shelf 3.

A dot plot of the nutritional rating for the cereals on each shelf is provided in Figure 3.5, with the shelf means indicated by the triangles. Now, if we were to use only the categorical variables (such as shelf, manufacturer, and so on) as predictors, we could apply a type of analysis known as *analysis of variance*. (For more on analysis of variance, see any good introductory statistics textbook, such as *Introduction to the Practice of Statistics* by Moore and McCabe [3].) However, we are interested in using the categorical variable *shelf* along with continuous variables such as sugar and fiber content. Therefore, we shall use multiple regression analysis with indicator variables.

Based on the comparison dot plot in Figure 3.5, does there seem to be evidence that shelf location affects nutritional rating? It would seem that shelf 2 cereals, with their average nutritional rating of 34.97, seem to lag somewhat behind the cereals on shelves 1 and 3, with their respective average nutritional ratings of 46.15 and 45.22. However, it is not clear whether this difference is significant. Further, this dot plot does not take into account the other variables, such as sugar content and fiber content; it is unclear how any "shelf effect" would manifest itself in the presence of these other variables.

For use in regression, a categorical variable with k categories must be transformed into a set of $k - 1$ indicator variables. An *indicator variable*, also known as a *dummy variable*, is a binary 0/1 variable, which takes the value 1 if the observation belongs to the given category, and takes the value 0 otherwise. For the present example, we define the following indicator variables:

$$Shelf\ 1 = \begin{cases} 1 & \text{if cereal located on shelf 1} \\ 0 & \text{otherwise} \end{cases}$$

$$Shelf\ 2 = \begin{cases} 1 & \text{if cereal located on shelf 2} \\ 0 & \text{otherwise} \end{cases}$$

TABLE 3.3   Values Taken by the Indicator Variables for Cereals
Located on Shelves 1, 2, and 3, Respectively

Cereal Location	Value of Variable *Shelf 1*	Value of Variable *Shelf 2*
Shelf 1	1	0
Shelf 2	0	1
Shelf 3	0	0

Table 3.3 indicates the values taken by these indicator variables, for cereals located on shelves 1, 2, and 3, respectively. Note that it is not necessary to define a third indicator variable *shelf 3*, since cereals located on shelf 3 will have zero values for each of the *shelf 1* and *shelf 2* indicator variables, and this is sufficient to distinguish them. In fact, one should not define this third dummy variable because the resulting covariate matrix will be singular, and the regression will not work.

The category that is not assigned an indicator variable is denoted the *reference category*. Here, shelf 3 is the reference category. Later we measure the effect of the location of a given cereal (e.g., on shelf 1) on nutritional rating, with respect to (i.e., with reference to) shelf 3, the reference category.

We therefore proceed to perform multiple regression for the linear relationship between nutritional rating and sugar content, fiber content, and shelf location, using the two dummy variables from Table 3.3. The general model looks like the following:

$$y = \beta_0 + \beta_1(sugars) + \beta_2(fiber) + \beta_3(shelf\,1) + \beta_4(shelf\,2) + \varepsilon$$

with its estimated regression equation given as

$$\hat{y} = b_0 + b_1(sugars) + b_2(fiber) + b_3(shelf\,1) + b_4(shelf\,2)$$

For cereals located on shelf 1, the model and the estimated regression equation look as follows:

$$
\begin{aligned}
\text{Model:} \quad y &= \beta_0 + \beta_1(sugars) + \beta_2(fiber) + \beta_3(3.1) + \beta_4(0) + \varepsilon \\
&= (\beta_0 + \beta_3) + \beta_1(sugars) + \beta_2(fiber) + \varepsilon \\
\text{ERE:} \quad \hat{y} &= b_0 + b_1(sugars) + b_2(fiber) + b_3(3.1) + b_4(0) \\
&= (b_0 + b_3) + b_1(sugars) + b_2(fiber)
\end{aligned}
$$

For cereals located on shelf 2, the model and the estimated regression equation are as follows:

$$
\begin{aligned}
\text{Model:} \quad y &= \beta_0 + \beta_1(sugars) + \beta_2(fiber) + \beta_3(0) + \beta_4(3.1) + \varepsilon \\
&= (\beta_0 + \beta_4) + \beta_1(sugars) + \beta_2(fiber) + \varepsilon \\
\text{ERE:} \quad \hat{y} &= b_0 + b_1(sugars) + b_2(fiber) + b_3(0) + b_4(1) \\
&= (b_0 + b_4) + b_1(sugars) + b_2(fiber)
\end{aligned}
$$

Finally, for cereals located on shelf 3, the model and the estimated regression equation are given as follows:

$$
\begin{aligned}
\text{Model:} \quad y &= \beta_0 + \beta_1(sugars) + \beta_2(fiber) + \beta_3(0) + \beta_4(0) + \varepsilon \\
&= \beta_0 + \beta_1(sugars) + \beta_2(fiber) \\
\text{ERE:} \quad \hat{y} &= b_0 + b_1(sugars) + b_2(fiber) + b_3(0) + b_4(0) \\
&= b_0 + b_1(sugars) + b_2(fiber)
\end{aligned}
$$

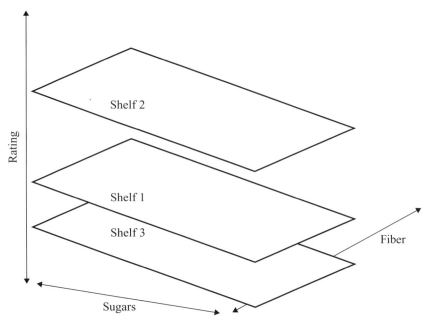

Figure 3.6 The use of indicator variables in multiple regression leads to a set of parallel planes (or hyperplanes).

Note the relationship of the model equations to each other. The three models represent parallel planes, as illustrated in Figure 3.6. (Note that the planes do not, of course, directly represent the shelves themselves but rather, the fit of the regression model to the nutritional rating for the cereals on the various shelves.)

The results for the regression of nutritional rating on sugar content, fiber content, and shelf location are provided in Table 3.4. The general form of the estimated regression equation looks like

$$\hat{y} = 50.433 - 2.2954(sugars) + 3.0856(fiber) + 1.446(shelf\ 1) + 3.828(shelf\ 2)$$

Thus, the estimated regression equation for cereals located on the various shelves are given as follows:

Shelf 1: $\hat{y} = 50.433 - 2.2954(sugars) + 3.0856(fiber) + 1.446(1)$
$= 51.879 - 2.2954(sugars) + 3.0856(fiber)$

Shelf 2: $\hat{y} = 50.433 - 2.2954(sugars) + 3.0856(fiber) + 3.828(1)$
$= 54.261 - 2.2954(sugars) + 3.0856(fiber)$

Shelf 3: $\hat{y} = 50.433 - 2.2954(sugars) + 3.0856(fiber)$

Note that these estimated regression equations are exactly the same except for the y-intercept. This means that cereals on each shelf are modeled as following exactly the same slope in the sugars dimension (-2.2954) and exactly the same slope in the fiber dimension (3.0856), which gives us the three parallel planes shown in Figure 3.6. The only difference lies in the value of the y-intercept for the cereals on the three shelves. The reference category in this case is shelf 3. What is the vertical distance

TABLE 3.4   Results of Regression of Nutritional Rating on Sugar Content, Fiber Content, and Shelf Location

```
The regression equation is
Rating = 50.4 - 2.30 Sugars + 3.09 Fiber + 1.45 shelf 1+ 3.83
         shelf 2


Predictor      Coef  SE Coef       T       P
Constant     50.433    1.888   26.71   0.000
Sugars      -2.2954    0.1749 -13.12   0.000
Fiber        3.0856    0.3256   9.48   0.000
shelf 1       1.446    1.806    0.80   0.426
shelf 2       3.828    1.908    2.01   0.049


S = 6.15345 R-Sq = 81.8% R-Sq(adj) = 80.8%


Analysis of Variance


Source             DF        SS      MS       F       P
Regression          4   12270.5  3067.6   81.01   0.000
Residual Error     72    2726.3    37.9
Total              76   14996.8

Source    DF   Seq SS
Sugars     1   8701. 7
Fiber      1   3416.1
shelf 1    1      0.3
shelf 2    1    152.4
```

between the shelf 3 plane and, for example, the shelf 1 plane? Note from the derivations above that the estimated regression equation for the cereals on shelf 1 is given as

$$\hat{y} = (b_0 + b_3) + b_1(sugars) + b_2(fiber)$$

so that the y-intercept is $b_0 + b_3$. We also have the estimated regression equation for the cereals on shelf 3 to be

$$\hat{y} = b_0 + b_1(sugars) + b_2(fiber)$$

Thus, the difference between the y-intercepts is $(b_0 + b_3) - b_0 = b_3$. We can verify this by noting that $(b_0 + b_3) - b_0 = 51.879 - 50.433 = 1.446$, which is the value of b_3 reported in Table 3.4. The vertical distance between the planes representing shelves 1 and 3 is everywhere 1.446 rating points, as shown in Figure 3.7.

Of particular importance is the interpretation of this value for b_3. The y-intercept represents the estimated nutritional rating when sugars and fiber both equal zero. However, since the planes are parallel, the difference in the y-intercepts among the shelves remains constant throughout the range of sugar and fiber values. Thus, the vertical distance between the parallel planes, as measured by the coefficient for the indicator variable, represents the estimated effect of the particular indicator variable on the target variable with respect to the reference category.

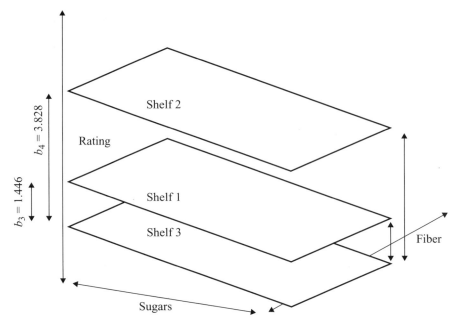

Figure 3.7 The indicator variables' coefficients estimate the difference in the response value compared to the reference category.

In this example, $b_3 = 1.446$ represents the estimated difference in nutritional rating for cereals located on shelf 1 compared to the cereals on shelf 3. Since b_3 is positive, this indicates that the estimated nutritional rating for shelf 1 cereals is higher. We thus interpret b_3 as follows: The estimated increase in nutritional rating for cereals located on shelf 1, as compared to cereals located on shelf 3, is $b_3 = 1.446$ points when sugars and fiber content are held constant.

Similarly for the cereals on shelf 2: We have the estimated regression equation for these cereals as

$$\hat{y} = (b_0 + b_4) + b_1(sugars) + b_2(fiber)$$

so that the difference between the y-intercepts for the planes representing shelves 2 and 3 is $(b_0 + b_4) - b_0 = b_4$. We thus have $(b_0 + b_4) - b_0 = 54.261 - 50.433 = 3.828$, which is the value for b_4 reported in Table 3.4. That is, the vertical distance between the planes representing shelves 2 and 3 is everywhere 3.828 rating points, as shown in Figure 3.7. Therefore, the estimated increase in nutritional rating for cereals located on shelf 2, compared to cereals located on shelf 3, is $b_4 = 3.828$ points when sugars and fiber content are held constant.

We may then infer the estimated difference in nutritional rating between shelves 2 and 1. This is given as $(b_0 + b_4) - (b_0 + b_3) = b_4 - b_3 = 3.828 - 1.446 = 2.382$ points. The estimated increase in nutritional rating for cereals located on shelf 2 compared to cereals located on shelf 1 is 2.382 points when sugars and fiber content are held constant.

TABLE 3.5   Using Sugars and Fiber Only, the Regression Model Underestimates the Nutritional Rating of Shelf 2 Cereals

Shelf	Mean Sugars	Mean Fiber	Mean Rating	Mean Estimated Rating[a]	Mean Error
1	4.85	1.75	46.15	46.04	−0.11
2	9.62	0.92	34.97	33.11	−1.86
3	6.53	3.17	45.22	46.36	+1.14

[a] Rating estimated using sugars and fiber only, not shelf location.

Now recall Figure 3.5, where we encountered evidence that shelf 2 cereals had the lowest nutritional rating, with an average of about 35, compared to average ratings of 46 and 45 for the cereals on the other shelves. How can this knowledge be reconciled with the dummy variable results, which seem to show the highest rating for shelf 2? The answer is that our indicator variable results are accounting for the presence of the other variables, sugar content and fiber content. It is true that the cereals on shelf 2 have the lowest nutritional rating; however, as shown in Table 3.5, these cereals also have the highest sugar content (average 9.62 grams compared to 4.85 and 6.53 grams for shelves 1 and 3) and the lowest fiber content (average 0.92 gram compared to 1.75 and 3.17 grams for shelves 1 and 3). Because of the negative correlation between sugar and rating, and the positive correlation between fiber and rating, the shelf 2 cereals already have a relatively low estimated nutritional rating based on these two predictors alone.

Table 3.5 shows the mean fitted values (estimated ratings) for the cereals on the various shelves when sugar and fiber content are included in the model but shelf location is not included as a predictor. Note that, on average, the nutritional rating of the shelf 2 cereals is underestimated by 1.86 points. On the other hand, the nutritional rating of the shelf 3 cereals is overestimated by 1.14 points. Therefore, when shelf location is introduced into the model, these over- and underestimates can be compensated for. Note from Table 3.5 that the *relative* estimation error difference between shelves 2 and 3 is $1.14 + 1.86 = 3.00$. Thus, we would expect that if shelf location were going to compensate for the underestimate of shelf 2 cereals relative to shelf 3 cereals, it would add a factor in the neighborhood of 3.00 rating points. Recall from Table 3.4 that $b_4 = 3.828$, which is in the ballpark of 3.00. Also note that the relative estimation error difference between shelves 1 and 3 is $1.14 + 0.11 = 1.25$. We would expect that the shelf indicator variable compensating for this estimation error would be not far from 1.25, and indeed, we have the relevant coefficient as $b_3 = 1.446$.

This example illustrates the flavor of working with multiple regression, in that the relationship of the *set* of predictors with the target variable is not necessarily dictated by the individual bivariate relationships the target variable has with each of the predictors. For example, Figure 3.5 would have led us to believe that shelf 2 cereals would have had an indicator variable adjusting the estimated nutritional rating downward. But the actual multiple regression model, which included sugars, fiber, and shelf location, had an indicator variable adjusting the estimated nutritional rating upward, because of the effects of the other predictors.

TABLE 3.6 Results of Regression of Nutritional Rating on Shelf Location Only

```
The regression equation is
Rating = 45.2 + 0.93 shelf 1 - 10.2 shelf 2

Predictor      Coef  SE Coef      T      P
Constant     45.220    2.232  20.26  0.000
shelf 1       0.925    3.736   0.25  0.805
shelf 2     -10.247    3.678  -2.79  0.007


S = 13.3947   R-Sq = 11.5%   R-Sq(adj) = 9.1%


Analysis of Variance

Source              DF        SS      MS      F      P
Regression           2    1719.8   859.9   4.79  0.011
Residual Error      74   13276.9   179.4
Total               76   14996.8

Source   DF  Seq SS
shelf 1   1    327.1
shelf 2   1   1392.7
```

On the other hand, what would have happened had sugars and fiber not been in the model? That is, suppose that we had the following model:

$$y = \beta_0 + \beta_3(shelf\ 1) + \beta_4(shelf\ 2) + \varepsilon$$

with its associated estimated regression equation:

$$\hat{y} = b_0 + b_3(shelf\ 1) + b_4(shelf\ 2)$$

What would the character of our indicator variables have been in this case? Well, based on Figure 3.5, we might expect that b_4 would be negative, adjusting the estimated rating downward for shelf 2 cereals compared to shelf 3 cereals. We might also expect b_3 to be essentially negligible but slightly positive, reflecting a slight upward adjustment for shelf 1 cereals compared with shelf 3 cereals.

Table 3.6 contains the results of the regression of nutritional rating on shelf location only. Note that the coefficient for the shelf 2 dummy variable is -10.247, which is equal (after rounding) to the signed difference in the mean nutritional ratings between cereals on shelves 2 and 3 (see Table 3.5). Similarly, the coefficient for the shelf 1 dummy variable is 0.925, which equals the signed difference in the mean ratings between cereals on shelves 1 and 3. Thus, in a one-dimensional sense, when no other predictors are in the model, the dummy variable behavior is quite predictable based on one-dimensional summary measures and graphs. However, in multiple regression, in the presence of other variables, it is difficult to predict how the variables will interact.

Consider again Table 3.4, where the regression results from our "full" model (all predictors included) are given. Note that the p-values for the sugar coefficient and the fiber coefficient are both quite small (near zero), so that we may include both of these predictors in the model. However, the p-value for the shelf 1 coefficient is

TABLE 3.7   Results of Regression of Nutritional Rating on Sugars, Fiber, and the Shelf 2 Indicator Variable

```
The regression equation is
Rating = 51.3 - 2.32 Sugars + 3.02 Fiber + 3.28 shelf 2

Predictor      Coef  SE Coef       T      P
Constant     51.281    1.559   32.90  0.000
Sugars      -2.3204   0.1717  -13.52  0.000
Fiber        3.0164   0.3131    9.63  0.000
shelf 2       3.282    1.778    1.85  0.069

S = 6.13829   R-Sq = 81.7%   R-Sq(adj) = 80.9%

Analysis of Variance

Source            DF       SS      MS       F      P
Regression         3  12246.2  4082.1  108.34  0.000
Residual Error    73   2750.5    37.7
Total             76  14996.8

Source   DF  Seq SS
Sugars    1  8701.7
Fiber     1  3416.1
shelf 2   1   128.5
```

large (0.426), indicating that the relationship between this variable is not statistically significant. In other words, in the presence of sugar and fiber content, the difference in nutritional rating between shelf 1 and shelf 3 cereals is not significant. We may therefore consider eliminating the shelf 1 indicator variable from the model. Note also that the p-value (0.049) for the shelf 2 coefficient is of only borderline significance.

Suppose that because of its large p-value, we go ahead and eliminate the shelf 1 indicator variable from the model but retain the shelf 2 indicator variable. The results from the regression of nutritional rating on sugar content, fiber content, and shelf 2 (compared to shelf 3) location are given in Table 3.7. Note from the table that the p-value for the shelf 2 dummy variable has increased from 0.049 to 0.069, indicating that its significance is slightly lower than previously. However, analysts should not automatically omit variables whose p-values are higher than 0.05. There is nothing magical about the 0.05 threshold level apart from its widespread use. Rather, the analyst should perhaps include these types of variables, especially in interim analyses, until the model takes more concrete form downstream. The analyst needs to balance the demands of parsimony and an easily explained model against the higher predictive power of a well-parametrized model.

Adjusting R^2: Penalizing Models for Including Predictors That Are Not Useful

Recall that adding a variable to the model will increase the value of the coefficient of determination R^2, regardless of the usefulness of the variable. This is not a particularly attractive feature of this measure, since it may lead us to prefer models with marginally larger values for R^2, simply because they have more variables, not because the extra variables are useful.

Therefore, in the interests of parsimony, we should find some way to penalize the R^2 measure for models that include predictors that are not useful. Fortunately, such a penalized form for R^2 does exist and is known as the *adjusted R^2*. The formula for adjusted R^2 is

$$R^2_{adj} = 1 - (1 - R^2)\frac{n-1}{n-m-1}$$

If R^2_{adj} is much less than R^2, this is an indication that at least one variable in the model may be extraneous and that the analyst should consider omitting that variable from the model.

As an example of calculating R^2_{adj}, consider Table 3.4, where we have $R^2 = 0.818$, $R^2_{adj} = 0.808$, $n = 77$, and $m = 4$. Then

$$R^2_{adj} = 1 - (1 - R^2)\frac{n-1}{n-m-1} = 1 - (1 - 0.818)\frac{76}{72} = 0.808$$

Let us now compare Tables 3.4 and 3.7, where the regression model was run with and without the shelf 1 indicator variable, respectively. The shelf 1 indicator variable was found not to be useful for estimating nutritional rating. How did this affect R^2, R^2_{adj}, and s? The statistics are provided in Table 3.8. The value of R^2 is higher for the model with more variables in it, even though the extra variable is not useful. This reflects the fact that R^2 never decreases when extra variables are added into the model, but always increases, if even by a tiny amount. On the other hand, the penalized measure, R^2_{adj}, is smaller for the model with the extra, unuseful variable in it. This reflects how R^2_{adj} adjusts the value of R^2 downward when extraneous variables are entered into the model. Finally, note how s is smaller for the model without the extraneous variable, reflecting the fact that a more precise model for estimating nutritional rating can be obtained by ignoring shelf 1 variable. Hence, when one is building models in multiple regression, one should use R^2_{adj} and s rather than the raw R^2.

TABLE 3.8 Comparison of R^2, R^2_{adj}, and s for Models Including and Excluding a Variable That Is Not Useful

Model	R^2	R^2_{adj}	s
Table 3.4: $y = \beta_0 + \beta_1(sugars) + \beta_2(fiber) + \beta_3(shelf\,1) + \beta_4(shelf\,2) + \varepsilon$	0.818	0.808	6.153
Table 3.7: $y = \beta_0 + \beta_1(sugars) + \beta_2(fiber) + \beta_4(shelf\,2) + \varepsilon$	0.817	0.809	6.138

Sequential Sums of Squares

Some analysts use the information provided in the sequential sums of squares, provided by many software packages, to help them get a better idea of which variables to include in the model. The sequential sums of squares represent a partitioning of SSR, the regression sum of squares. Recall that SSR represents the proportion of the variability in the target variable that is explained by the linear relationship of the target variable with the set of predictor variables.

The *sequential sums of squares* partitions the SSR into the unique portions of the SSR that are explained by the particular predictors given any earlier predictors. Thus, the values of the sequential sums of squares depends on the *order* in which the variables are entered into the model. For example, the sequential sums of squares for the model,

$$y = \beta_0 + \beta_1(sugars) + \beta_2(fiber) + \beta_3(shelf\,1) + \beta_4(shelf\,2) + \varepsilon$$

are given in Table 3.4 and repeated in Table 3.9. The sequential sum of squares shown for sugars, 8701.7 represents the variability in nutritional rating that is explained by the linear relationship between rating and sugar content. In other words, this first sequential sum of squares is exactly the value for SSR from the simple linear regression of nutritional rating on sugar content.

The second sequential sum of squares from Table 3.9, for fiber content, equals 3416.1. This represents the amount of unique additional variability in nutritional rating that is explained by the linear relationship of rating with fiber content given that the variability explained by sugars has already been extracted. The third sequential sum of squares, for shelf 1, is 0.3. This represents the amount of unique additional variability in nutritional rating that is accounted for by location on shelf 1 (compared to the reference class shelf 3) given that the variability accounted for by sugars and fiber has already been separated out. This tiny value for the sequential sum of squares for shelf 1 indicates that the variable is probably not useful for estimating nutritional rating. Finally, the sequential sum of squares for shelf 2 is a moderate 152.4, supporting our earlier finding that this variable is of borderline significance. (The determination of statistical significance can be made by the partial F-test discussed later).

Now, suppose that we changed the ordering of the variables into the regression model. This would change the values of the sequential sums of squares. For example, suppose that we perform an analysis based on the following model:

$$y = \beta_0 + \beta_1(shelf\,1) + \beta_2(shelf\,2) + \beta_3(sugars) + \beta_4(fiber) + \varepsilon$$

TABLE 3.9   Sequential Sums of Squares for the Model
$y = \beta_0 + \beta_1(sugars) + \beta_2(fiber) + \beta_3(shelf\,1) + \beta_4(shelf\,2) + \varepsilon$

Source	DF	Seq SS
Sugars	1	8701.7
Fiber	1	3416.1
shelf 1	1	0.3
shelf 2	1	152.4

TABLE 3.10 Changing the Ordering of the Variables into the Model Changes Nothing Except the Sequential Sums of Squares

```
The regression equation is
Rating = 50.4 + 1.45 shelf 1 + 3.83 shelf 2
           + 3.09 Fiber - 2.30 Sugars


Predictor      Coef  SE Coef       T      P
Constant     50.433    1.888   26.71  0.000
shelf 1       1.446    1.806    0.80  0.426
shelf 2       3.828    1.908    2.01  0.049
Fiber        3.0856   0.3256    9.48  0.000
Sugars      -2.2954   0.1749  -13.12  0.000


S = 6.15345 R-Sq = 81.8% R-Sq(adj) = 80.8%


Analysis of Variance

Source             DF       SS      MS      F      P
Regression          4  12270.5  3067.6  81.01  0.000
Residual Error     72   2726.3    37.9
Total              76  14996.8

Source   DF   Seq SS
shelf 1   1    327.1
shelf 2   1   1392.7
Fiber     1   4029.8
Sugar     1   6520.9
```

The results for this regression are provided in Table 3.10. Note that all the results in Table 3.10 except the values of the sequential sums of squares are exactly the same as in Table 3.4 (apart from ordering). This time, the indicator variables are able to "claim" their unique portions of the variability before the other variables are entered, thus giving them larger values for their sequential sums of squares. See Neter et al. [4] for more information on applying sequential sums of squares for variable selection. We use the sequential sums of squares, in the context of a partial F-test, later in this chapter to perform variable selection.

MULTICOLLINEARITY

Suppose that we are now interested in adding the predictor *potassium* to the model, so that our new multiple regression model looks as follows:

$$y = \beta_0 + \beta_1(sugars) + \beta_2(fiber) + \beta_3(shelf\ 1) + \beta_4(potassium) + \varepsilon$$

with the associated estimated regression equation

$$\hat{y} = b_0 + b_1(sugars) + b_2(fiber) + b_3(shelf\ 1) + b_4(potassium)$$

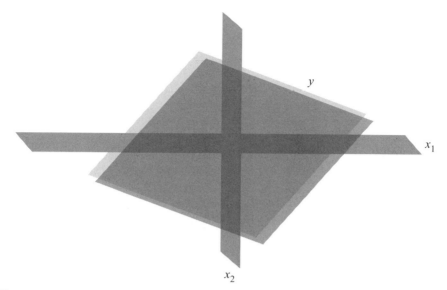

Figure 3.8 When the predictors x_1 and x_2 are uncorrelated, the response surface y rests on a solid basis, providing stable coefficient estimates.

Data miners need to guard against *multicollinearity*, a condition where some of the predictor variables are correlated with each other. Multicollinearity leads to instability in the solution space, leading to possible incoherent results. For example, in a data set with severe multicollinearity, it is possible for the F-test for the overall regression to be significant, whereas none of the t-tests for the individual predictors are significant. This situation is analogous to enjoying the whole pizza while not enjoying any of the slices.

Consider Figures 3.8 and 3.9. Figure 3.8 illustrates a situation where the predictors x_1 and x_2 are not correlated with each other; that is, they are orthogonal, or independent. In such a case, the predictors form a solid basis upon which the response surface y may rest sturdily, thereby providing stable coefficient estimates b_1 and b_2, each with small variability s_{b_1} and s_{b_2}. On the other hand, Figure 3.9 illustrates a multicollinear situation where the predictors x_1 and x_2 are correlated with each other, so that as one of them increases, so does the other. In this case, the predictors no longer form a solid basis upon which the response surface may firmly rest. Instead, when the predictors are correlated, the response surface is unstable, providing highly variable coefficient estimates b_1 and b_2, with inflated values for s_{b_1} and s_{b_2}.

The high variability associated with the estimates means that *different samples may produce coefficient estimates with widely different values.* For example, one sample may produce a positive coefficient estimate for x_1, where as a second sample may produce a negative coefficient estimate. This situation is unacceptable when the analytic task calls for an explanation of the relationship between the response and the predictors individually. Even if such instability is avoided, inclusion of variables that are highly correlated tends to overemphasize a particular component of the model, since the component is essentially being double counted.

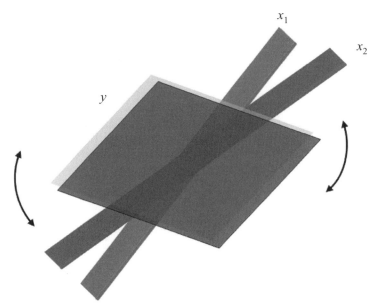

Figure 3.9 Multicollinearity: When the predictors are correlated, the response surface is unstable, resulting in dubious and highly variable coefficient estimates.

To avoid multicollinearity, the analyst should investigate the correlation structure among the predictor variables (ignoring the target variable for the moment). Table 3.11 provides the correlation coefficients among the predictors for our present model. For example, the correlation coefficient between sugars and fiber is -0.137, and the correlation coefficient between sugars and potassium is 0.022. Unfortunately, there is one pair of variables that are strongly correlated: fiber and potassium, with $r = 0.905$. Another method of assessing whether the predictors are correlated is to construct a matrix plot of the predictors, such as Figure 3.10. The matrix plot supports the finding that fiber and potassium are positively correlated.

However, suppose that we did not check for the presence of correlation among our predictors, but went ahead and performed the regression anyway. Is there some way that the regression results can warn us of the presence of multicollinearity? The answer is yes: We may ask for the *variance inflation factors* (VIFs) to be reported. What are variance inflation factors? First, recall that s_{b_i} represents the variability associated with the coefficient b_i for the ith predictor variable x_i. We may express s_{b_i} as a product of s, the standard error of the estimate, and c_i, which is a constant whose value depends on the predictor values observed. That is, $s_{b_i} = sc_i$. Now, s is fairly

TABLE 3.11 Correlation Coefficients Among the Predictor Variables: We Have a Problem

	Sugars	Fiber	Shelf 2
Fiber	-0.137		
Shelf 2	0.374	-0.330	
Potass	0.022	**0.905**	-0.331

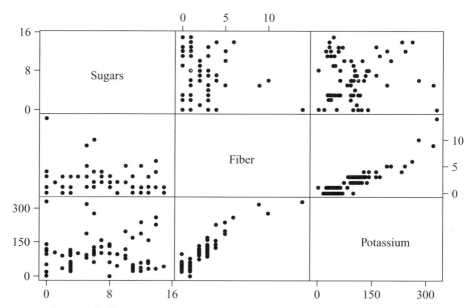

Figure 3.10 Matrix plot of the predictor variables shows correlation between fiber and potassium.

robust with respect to the inclusion of correlated variables in the model, as we shall verify in the exercises. So in the presence of correlated predictors, we would look to c_i to help explain large changes in s_{b_i}.

We may express c_i as

$$c_i = \sqrt{\frac{1}{(n-1)\,s_i^2}\,\frac{1}{1-R_i^2}}$$

where s_i^2 represents the sample variance of the observed values of the ith predictor, x_i, and R_i^2 represents the R^2 value obtained by regressing x_i on the other predictor variables. Note that R_i^2 will be large when x_i is highly correlated with the other predictors. Note that of the two terms in c_i, the first factor, $1/((n-1)s_i^2)$, measures only the intrinsic variability within the of ith predictor, x_i. It is the second factor, $1/(1-R_i^2)$ that measures the correlation between the ith predictor x_i and the remaining predictor variables. For this reason, this second factor is denoted as the *variance inflation factor* (VIF) for x_i:

$$\text{VIF}_i = \frac{1}{1-R_i^2}$$

Can we describe the behavior of the VIF? Suppose that x_i is completely uncorrelated with the remaining predictors, so that $R_i^2 = 0$. Then we will have $\text{VIF}_i = 1/(1-0) = 1$. That is, the minimum value for VIF is 1, which is reached when x_i is completely uncorrelated with the remaining predictors. However, as the degree of correlation between x_i and the other predictors increases, R_i^2 will also increase. In that case, $\text{VIF}_i = 1/(1-R_i^2)$ will increase without bound as R_i^2 approaches 1. Thus, there is no upper limit to the value that VIF_i can take.

What effect do these changes in VIF_i have on s_{b_i}, the variability of the ith coefficient? We have

$$s_{b_i} = sc_i = s\sqrt{\frac{1}{(n-1)\ s_i^2}\ \frac{1}{1-R_i^2}} = s\sqrt{\frac{VIF_i}{(n-1)\ s_i^2}}$$

If x_i is uncorrelated with the other predictors, $VIF_i = 1$, and the standard error of the coefficient s_{b_i} will not be inflated. However, if x_i is correlated with the other predictors, the large VIF_i value will produce an overinflation of the standard error of the coefficient s_{b_i}. As you know, inflating the variance estimates will result in a degradation in the precision of the estimation.

A rough rule of thumb for interpreting the value of the VIF is to consider $VIF_i \geq 5$ to be an indicator of moderate multicollinearity and to consider $VIF_i \geq 10$ to be an indicator of severe multicollinearity. A variance inflation factor of 5 corresponds to $R_i^2 = 0.80$, and $VIF_i = 10$ corresponds to $R_i^2 = 0.90$.

Getting back to our example, suppose that we went ahead with the regression of nutritional rating on sugars, fiber, the shelf 2 indicator, and the new variable, potassium, which is correlated with fiber. The results, including the observed variance inflation factors, are shown in Table 3.12. The estimated regression equation for this model is

$$\hat{y} = 52.184 - 2.1953(sugars) + 4.1449(fiber)$$
$$+ 2.588(shelf) - 0.04208(potassium)$$

The p-value for potassium is not very small (0.099), so at first glance the variable may or may not be included in the model. Also, the p-value for the shelf 2 indicator variable (0.156) has increased to such an extent that we should perhaps not include it in the model. However, we should probably not put too much credence into any of these results, since the VIFs observed seem to indicate the presence of a multicollinearity problem. We need to resolve the evident multicollinearity *before* moving forward with this model.

The VIF for fiber is 6.5 and the VIF for potassium is 6.7, with both values indicating moderate-to-strong multicollinearity. At least the problem is localized with these two variables only, as the other VIFs are reported at acceptably low values. How shall we deal with this problem? Some texts suggest choosing one of the variables and eliminating it from the model. However, this should be viewed only as a last resort, since the variable omitted may have something to teach us. As we saw in Chapter 1, principal components can be a powerful method for using the correlation structure in a large group of predictors to produce a smaller set of independent components. However, the multicollinearity problem in this example is strictly localized to two variables, so the application of principal components analysis in this instance might be considered overkill. Instead, we may prefer to construct a user-defined composite, as discussed in Chapter 1. Here, our user-defined composite will be as simple as possible, the mean of $fiber_z$ and $potassium_z$, where the z-subscript notation indicates that the variables have been standardized. Thus, our composite W is defined as $W = (fiber_z + potassium_z)/2$.

TABLE 3.12   Regression Results, with Variance Inflation Factors Indicating a Multicollinearity Problem

```
The regression equation is
Rating = 52.2 - 2.20 Sugars + 4.14 Fiber + 2.59 shelf 2
             - 0.0421 Potass


Predictor        Coef  SE Coef       T      P  VIF
Constant       52.184    1.632   31.97  0.000
Sugars        -2.1953   0.1854  -11.84  0.000  1.4
Fiber          4.1449   0.7433    5.58  0.000  6.5
shelf 2         2.588    1.805    1.43  0.156  1.4
Potass       -0.04208  0.02520   -1.67  0.099  6.7


S = 6.06446 R-Sq = 82.3% R-Sq(adj) = 81.4%


Analysis of Variance


Source           DF       SS      MS      F      P
Regression        4  12348.8  3087.2  83.94  0.000
Residual Error   72   2648.0    36.8
Total            76  14996.8

Source   DF  Seq SS
Sugars    1  8701.7
Fiber     1  3416.1
shelf 2   1   128.5
Potass    1   102.5
```

Note that we need to standardize the variables involved in the composite, to avoid the possibility that the greater variability of one of the variables will overwhelm that of the other variable. For example, the standard deviation of fiber among all cereals is 2.38 grams, and the standard deviation of potassium is 71.29 milligrams. (The grams/milligrams scale difference is not at issue here. What is relevant is the difference in variability, even on their respective scales.) Figure 3.11 illustrates the difference in variability.

We therefore proceed to perform the regression of nutritional rating on the variables $sugars_z$ and $shelf\,2$, and $W = (fiber_z + potassium_z)/2$. The results are provided in Table 3.13.

Note first that the multicollinearity problem seems to have been resolved, with the VIF values all near 1. Note also, however, that the regression results are rather disappointing, with the values of R^2, R^2_{adj}, and s all underperforming the model results found in Table 3.7, from the model $y = \beta_0 + \beta_1(sugars) + \beta_2(fiber) + \beta_4(shelf\,2) + \varepsilon$, which did not even include the potassium variable.

What is going on here? The problem stems from the fact that the fiber variable is a very good predictor of nutritional rating, especially when coupled with sugar content, as we shall see later when we perform best subsets regression. Therefore,

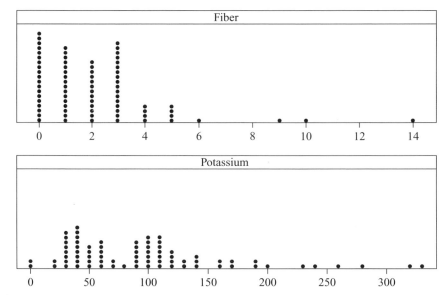

Figure 3.11 Fiber and potassium have different variabilities, requiring standardization prior to construction of a user-defined composite.

using the fiber variable to form a composite with a variable that has weaker correlation with rating dilutes the strength of fiber's strong association with rating and so degrades the efficacy of the model.

Thus, reluctantly, we put aside the model $y = \beta_0 + \beta_1(sugars_z) + \beta_4$ $(shelf\ 2) + \beta_5(W) + \varepsilon$. One possible alternative is to change the weights in the composite, to increase the weight of fiber with respect to potassium. For example,

TABLE 3.13 Results of Regression of Rating on *Sugars, Shelf 2,* and the *Fiber/Potassium* Composite

```
The regression equation is
Rating = 41.7 - 10.9 sugars z + 3.67 shelf 2 + 6.97 fiber_potass

Predictor          Coef  SE Coef        T      P VIF
Constant        41.6642   0.9149    45.54  0.000
sugars z       -10.9149   0.8149   -13.39  0.000 1.2
shelf 2           3.672    1.929     1.90  0.061 1.3
fiber_potass     6.9722   0.8230     8.47  0.000 1.1


S = 6.56878 R-Sq = 79.0% R-Sq(adj) = 78.1%


Analysis of Variance

Source           DF       SS       MS      F      P
Regression        3  11846.9   3949.0  91.52  0.000
Residual Error   73   3149.9     43.1
Total            76  14996.8
```

we could use $W_2 = (0.9 \times fiber_z + 0.1 \times potassium_z)$. However, the model performance would still be slightly below that of using fiber alone. Other alternatives include performing principal components analysis or simply omitting the variable potassium.

Now, depending on the task confronting the analyst, multicollinearity may not in fact present a fatal defect. Weiss [5] notes that multicollinearity "does not adversely affect the ability of the sample regression equation to predict the response variable." He adds that multicollinearity does not significantly affect point estimates of the target variable, confidence intervals for the mean response value, or prediction intervals for a randomly selected response value. However, the data miner must therefore strictly limit the use of a multicollinear model to estimation and prediction of the target variable. Interpretation of the model would not be appropriate, since the individual coefficients may not make sense in the presence of multicollinearity.

VARIABLE SELECTION METHODS

To assist the data analyst in determining which variables should be included in a multiple regression model, several different *variable selection methods* have been developed, including (1) forward selection, (2) backward elimination, (3) stepwise selection, and (4) best subsets. These variable selection methods are essentially algorithms to help construct the model with the optimal set of predictors.

Partial *F*-Test

To discuss variable selection methods, we first need to learn about the *partial F-test*. Suppose that we already have p variables in the model, $x_1, x_2, \ldots, x_p$ and we are interested in whether or not one extra variable x^* should be included in the model. Recall our earlier discussion of the sequential sums of squares. Here we would calculate the extra (sequential) sum of squares from adding x^* to the model given that $x_1, x_2, \ldots, x_p$ are already in the model. Denote this quantity by $SS_{extra} = SS(x^*|x_1, x_2, \ldots, x_p)$. Now, this extra sum of squares is computed by finding the regression sum of squares for the full model (including $x_1, x_2, \ldots, x_p$ and x^*), denoted $SS_{full} = SS(x_1, x_2, \ldots, x_p, x^*)$, and subtracting the regression sum of squares from the reduced model (including only $x_1, x_2, \ldots, x_p$), denoted $SS_{reduced} = SS(x_1, x_2, \ldots, x_p)$. In other words,

$$SS_{extra} = SS_{full} - SS_{reduced}$$

that is,

$$SS(x^*|x_1, x_2, \ldots, x_p) = SS(x_1, x_2, \ldots, x_p, x^*) - SS(x_1, x_2, \ldots, x_p)$$

The null hypothesis for the partial *F*-test is as follows:

- H_0: No, the SS_{extra} associated with x^* does not contribute significantly to the regression sum of squares for a model already containing $x_1, x_2, \ldots, x_p$. Therefore, do not include x^* in the model.

The alternative hypothesis is:

- H_a: Yes, the SS_{extra} associated with x^* does contribute significantly to the regression sum of squares for a model already containing $x_1, x_2, \ldots, x_p$. Therefore, do include x^* in the model.

The test statistic for the partial F-test is

$$F(x^* | x_1, x_2, \ldots, x_p) = \frac{SS_{extra}}{MSE_{full}}$$

where MSE_{full} denotes the mean-squared error term from the full model, including $x_1, x_2, \ldots, x_p$ and x^*. This is known as the *partial F-statistic* for x^*. When the null hypothesis is true, this test statistic follows an $F_{1, n-p-2}$-distribution. We would therefore reject the null hypothesis when $F(x^* | x_1, x_2, \ldots, x_p)$ is large or when its associated p-value is small.

An alternative to the partial F-test is the t-test. Now an F-test with 1 and $n - p - 2$ degrees of freedom is equivalent to a t-test with $n - p - 2$ degrees of freedom. This is due to the distributional relationship that $F_{1, n-p-2} = (t_{n-p-2})^2$. Thus, either the F-test or the t-test may be performed. Similar to our treatment of the t-test earlier in the chapter, the hypotheses are given by

- H_0: $\beta^* = 0$
- H_a: $\beta^* \neq 0$

The associated models are:

- Under H_0: $y = \beta_0 + \beta_1 x_1 + \cdots + \beta_p x_p + \varepsilon$
- Under H_a: $y = \beta_0 + \beta_1 x_1 + \cdots + \beta_p x_p + \beta^* x^* + \varepsilon$

Under the null hypothesis, the test statistic $t = b^*/s_{b^*}$ follows a t-distribution with $n - p - 2$ degrees of freedom. Reject the null hypothesis when the two-tailed p-value, $P(|t| > t_{obs})$, is small.

Finally, we need to discuss the difference between sequential sums of squares and partial sums of squares. The sequential sums of squares are as described earlier in the chapter. As each variable is entered into the model, the sequential sum of squares represents the additional unique variability in the response explained by that variable, after the variability accounted for by variables entered earlier in the model has been extracted. That is, the *ordering* of the entry of the variables into the model is germane to the sequential sums of squares.

On the other hand, ordering is not relevant to the partial sums of squares. For a particular variable, the partial sum of squares represents the additional unique variability in the response explained by that variable after the variability accounted for by all the other variables in the model has been extracted. Table 3.14 shows the difference between sequential and partial sums of squares, for a model with four predictors, x_1, x_2, x_3, x_4.

TABLE 3.14   Difference Between Sequential and Partial SS

Variable	Sequential SS	Partial SS
x_1	SS (x_1)	SS $(x_1|x_2, x_3, x_4)$
x_2	SS$(x_2|x_1)$	SS$(x_2|x_1, x_3, x_4)$
x_3	SS$(x_3|x_1, x_2)$	SS$(x_3|x_1, x_2, x_4)$
x_4	SS$(x_4|x_1, x_2, x_3)$	SS$(x_4|x_1, x_2, x_3)$

Forward Selection Procedure

The forward selection procedure starts with no variables in the model.

1. For the first variable to enter the model, select the predictor most highly correlated with the target. (Without loss of generality, denote this variable x_1.) If the resulting model is not significant, stop and report that no variables are important predictors; otherwise proceed to step 2.

2. For each remaining variable, compute the sequential F-statistic for that variable given the variables already in the model. For example, in this first pass through the algorithm, these sequential F-statistics would be $F(x_2|x_1)$, $F(x_3|x_1)$, and $F(x_4|x_1)$. On the second pass through the algorithm, these might be $F(x_3|x_1, x_2)$ and $F(x_4|x_1, x_2)$. Select the variable with the largest sequential F-statistic.

3. For the variable selected in step 2, test for the significance of the sequential F-statistic. If the resulting model is not significant, stop, and report the current model without adding the variable from step 2. Otherwise, add the variable from step 2 into the model and return to step 2.

Backward Elimination Procedure

The backward elimination procedure begins with all the variables, or all of a user-specified set of variables, in the model.

1. Perform the regression on the full model, that is, using all available variables. For example, perhaps the full model has four variables, x_1, x_2, x_3, x_4.

2. For each variable in the current model, compute the partial F-statistic. In the first pass through the algorithm, these would be $F(x_1|x_2, x_3, x_4)$, $F(x_2|x_1, x_3, x_4)$, $F(x_3|x_1, x_2, x_4)$, and $F(x_4|x_1, x_2, x_3)$. Select the variable with the smallest partial F-statistic. Denote this value F_{min}.

3. Test for the significance of F_{min}. If F_{min} is not significant, remove the variable associated with F_{min} from the model, and return to step 2. If F_{min} is significant, stop the algorithm and report the current model. If this is the first pass through the algorithm, the current model is the full model. If this is not the first pass, the current model has been reduced by one or more variables from the full model.

Stepwise Procedure

The stepwise procedure represents a modification of the forward selection procedure. A variable that has been entered into the model early in the forward selection process may turn out to be nonsignificant once other variables have been entered into the model. The stepwise procedure checks on this possibility by performing at each step a partial F-test using the partial sum of squares for each variable currently in the model. If there is a variable in the model that is no longer significant, the variable with the smallest partial F-statistic is removed from the model. The procedure terminates when no further variables can be entered or removed.

Best Subsets Procedure

For data sets where the number of predictors is not too large, the best subsets procedure represents an attractive variable selection method. However, if there are more than 30 or so predictors, the best subsets method encounters a combinatorial explosion and becomes intractably slow. The best subsets procedure works as follows.

1. The analyst specifies how many (k) models of each size that he or she would like reported, as well as the maximum number of predictors (p) the analyst wants in the model.
2. All models of one predictor are built: for example, $y = \beta_0 + \beta_1 (sugars) + \varepsilon$, $y = \beta_0 + \beta_2(fiber) + \varepsilon$, and so on. Their R^2, R^2_{adj}, Mallows' C_p (see below), and s values are calculated. The best k models are reported based on these measures.
3. Then all models of two predictors are built: for example, $y = \beta_0 + \beta_1 (sugars) + \beta_2(fiber) + \varepsilon$, $y = \beta_0 + \beta_1 (sugars) + \beta_4(shelf2) + \varepsilon$, and so on etc. Their R^2, R^2_{adj}, Mallows' C_p, and s values are calculated, and the best k models are reported.

The procedure continues in this way until the maximum number of predictors (p) is reached. The analyst then has a listing of the best models of each size $1, 2, \ldots, p$ to assist in selection of the best overall model.

All-Possible-Subsets Procedure

The four methods of model selection we have discussed are essentially optimization algorithms over a large sample space. Because of that, there is no guarantee that the globally optimal model will be found; that is, there is no guarantee that these variable selection algorithms will uncover the model with the lowest s, the highest R^2_{adj}, and so on [2,6]. The only way to ensure that the absolute best model has been found is simply to perform all the possible regressions. Unfortunately, in data mining applications, there are usually so many candidate predictor variables available that this method is simply not practicable. Not counting the null model $y = \beta_0 + \varepsilon$, there are $2^p - 1$ possible models to be built using p predictors.

For small numbers of predictors, it is not a problem to construct all possible regressions. For example, for $p = 5$ predictors, there are $2^5 - 1 = 31$ possible models. However, as the number of predictors starts to grow, the search space grows exponentially. For instance, for $p = 10$ predictors, there are $2^{10} - 1 = 1023$ possible models; and for $p = 20$ predictors, there are $2^{20} - 1 = 1,048,575$ possible models.

Thus, for most data mining applications, in which there may be hundreds of predictors, the all-possible-regressions procedure is not applicable. Therefore, the data miner may be inclined to turn to one of the four variable selection procedures discussed above. Even though there is no guarantee that the globally best model is found, these methods usually provide a useful set of models, which can provide positive results. The analyst can then adopt these models as starting points and apply tweaks and modifications to coax the best available performance out of them.

APPLICATION OF THE VARIABLE SELECTION METHODS

Suppose that we are interested in building a multiple regression model for estimating nutritional rating based on the following set of candidate predictors. We would like the most parsimonious model that does not leave out any significant predictors.

- *Calories*
- *Protein*
- *Fat*
- *Sodium*
- *Fiber*
- *Carbohydrates*
- *Sugars*
- *Potassium*
- *Vitamins*
- *Shelf 2 indicator variable*
- *Cups*
- *Weight*

The variables *cups* and *weight* do not really belong in the set of predictors as such, for reasons that we verify in the exercises. However, we include them here as examples of variables that will not be selected for inclusion in the model. We apply the four variable selection methods described above and compare the models suggested by each procedure.

Forward Selection Procedure Applied to the *Cereals* Data Set

In the forward selection procedure, we begin with no variables in the model. Then the variable most strongly correlated with nutritional rating is selected and, if significant, entered into the model. This variable is *sugars*, which has the highest correlation coefficient ($r = 0.762$) with rating among the predictors. Then the sequential F-tests are performed, such as $F(fiber|sugars)$, $F(sodium|sugars)$, and so on. It turns out that the highest sequential F-statistic is given by the significance test of $F(fiber|sugars)$, so that the variable *fiber* becomes the second variable entered into the model. Once again, the sequential F-tests are performed, such as $F(sodium|sugars, fiber)$ and $F(fat|sugars, fiber)$. The highest sequential F-statistic is associated with *sodium*, which becomes the third variable entered into the model.

The procedure continues in this manner, adding the following variables in order: *fat*, *protein*, *carbohydrates*, *calories*, *vitamins*, and *potassium*. The procedure then does not find any other significant variables to enter into the model and so terminates, reporting the following multiple regression model for nutritional rating:

$$y = \beta_0 + \beta_1(sugars) + \beta_2(fiber) + \beta_3(sodium)$$
$$+ \beta_4(fat) + \beta_5(protein) + \beta_6(carbohydrates)$$
$$+ \beta_7(calories) + \beta_8(vitamins) + \beta_9(potassium) + \varepsilon$$

Denote this model as model A. Note that the forward selection procedure did not include the following variables in the model: *cups, weight,* and the *shelf 2* indicator variable. Table 3.15 shows the summaries for the models as variables were entered (from *Clementine* software). Note that, as variables are entered into the model, R^2_{adj} increases, and the standard error s decreases, both of which indicate that the newly entered variables are useful.

We may use the results in Table 3.16 to calculate the sequential F-statistics. The table contains the ANOVA tables for the first four models selected by the forward selection procedure. Model 1 represents the model with *sugars* as the only predictor. Model 2 represents the model with both *sugars* and *fiber* entered as predictors. Since $SS_{extra} = SS_{full} - SS_{reduced}$, we have

$$SS_{fiber \mid sugars} = SS_{sugars, fiber} - SS_{sugars}$$

From Table 3.16 we have $SS_{sugars, fiber} = 12,117.782$ and $SS_{sugars} = 8701.675$, giving us

$$SS_{fiber \mid sugars} = SS_{sugars, fiber} - SS_{sugars} = 12,117.782 - 8701.675 = 3416.107$$

The test statistic for the partial (or, in this case, sequential) F-test is the following:

$$F(fiber \mid sugars) = \frac{SS_{fiber \mid sugars}}{MSE_{sugars, fiber}}$$

TABLE 3.15   Model Summaries from the Forward Selection Procedure

Model	R	R^2	Adjusted R^2	Std. Error of the Estimate
1	0.762[a]	0.580	0.575	9.16160
2	0.899[b]	0.808	0.803	6.23743
3	0.948[c]	0.899	0.895	4.54638
4	0.981[d]	0.962	0.960	2.82604
5	0.985[e]	0.970	0.968	2.50543
6	0.987[f]	0.975	0.973	2.31269
7	0.995[g]	0.990	0.989	1.47893
8	0.998[h]	0.995	0.995	1.01477
9	0.999[i]	0.999	0.999	0.52216

[a] Predictors: (constant), *sugars.*
[b] Predictors: (constant), *sugars, fiber.*
[c] Predictors: (constant), *sugars, fiber, sodium.*
[d] Predictors: (constant), *sugars, fiber, sodium, fat.*
[e] Predictors: (constant), *sugars, fiber, sodium, fat, protein.*
[f] Predictors: (constant), *sugars, fiber, sodium, fat, protein, carbohydrates.*
[g] Predictors: (constant), *sugars, fiber, sodium, fat, protein, carbohydrates, calories.*
[h] Predictors: (constant), *sugars, fiber, sodium, fat, protein, carbohydrates, calories, vitamins.*
[i] Predictors: (constant), *sugars, fiber, sodium, fat, protein, carbohydrates, calories, vitamins, potassium.*

TABLE 3.16 ANOVA Tables for the First Four Models Selected by the Forward Selection Procedure[a]

Model		Sum of Squares	df	Mean Square	F	Significance
1	Regression	8,701.675	1	8,701.675	103.672	0.000[b]
	Residual	6,295.113	75	83.935		
	Total	14,996.788	76			
2	Regression	12,117.782	2	6,058.891	155.734	0.000[c]
	Residual	2,879.006	74	38.905		
	Total	14,996.788	76			
3	Regression	13,487.911	3	4,495.970	217.517	0.000[d]
	Residual	1,508.877	73	20.670		
	Total	14,996.788	76			
4	Regression	14,421.759	4	3,605.440	451.441	0.000[e]
	Residual	575.030	72	7.987		
	Total	14,996.788	76			

[a] Dependent variable: *nutritional rating.*
[b] Predictors: (constant), *sugars.*
[c] Predictors: (constant), *sugars, fiber.*
[d] Predictors: (constant), *sugars, fiber, sodium.*
[e] Predictors: (constant), *sugars, fiber, sodium, fat.*

From Table 3.16 we have $\mathrm{MSE}_{sugars,\,fiber} = 38.905$, giving us

$$F(fiber|sugars) = \frac{\mathrm{SS}_{fiber\,|\,sugars}}{\mathrm{MSE}_{sugars,\,fiber}} = \frac{3416.107}{38.905} = 87.8$$

With a sample size of 77 and $p = 2$ parameters in the model, this test statistic follows an $F_{1,\,n-p-2} = F_{1,\,73}$-distribution. The p-value for this test statistic is approximately zero, thereby rejecting the null hypothesis that fiber should not be included after sugars.

Backward Elimination Procedure Applied to the *Cereals* Data Set

In the backward elimination procedure, we begin with all of the variables in the model. The partial F-statistic is then calculated for each variable in the model. Examples of these would be $F(weight|sugars, fiber, \ldots, cups)$ and $F(cups|sugars, fiber, \ldots, weight)$. The variable with the smallest partial F-statistic, $F_{\min}$, is examined, which in this case is *weight*. If $F_{\min}$ is not significant, which is the case here, the variable is dropped from the model. On the next pass, the variable with the smallest partial F-statistic is *cups*, which again is not significant. Thus, *cups* is also omitted from the model. On the third pass, the variable with the smallest partial F-statistic is the *shelf 2* indicator variable. However, the p-value associated with this $F_{\min}$ is not large enough to warrant noninclusion in the model according to the inclusion criteria (more on this in a bit). Therefore, the procedure terminates, and reports

TABLE 3.17 Model Summaries from the Backward Elimination Procedure

Model	R	R^2	Adjusted R^2	Std. Error of the Estimate
1	0.999[a]	0.999	0.999	0.51098
2	0.999[b]	0.999	0.999	0.50813
3	0.999[c]	0.999	0.999	0.51091

[a] Predictors: (constant), *shelf 2, fat, sodium, weight, cups, protein, vitamins, carbohydrates, fiber, sugars, calories, potassium.*
[b] Predictors: (constant), *shelf 2, fat, sodium, cups, protein, vitamins, carbohydrates, fiber, sugars, calories, potassium.*
[c] Predictors: (constant), *shelf 2, fat, sodium, protein, vitamins, carbohydrates, fiber, sugars, calories, potassium.*

the following model:

$$y = \beta_0 + \beta_1(sugars) + \beta_2(fiber) + \beta_3(sodium) + \beta_4(fat)$$
$$+ \beta_5(protein) + \beta_6(carbohydrates) + \beta_7(calories)$$
$$+ \beta_8(vitamins) + \beta_9(potassium) + \beta_{10}(shelf 2)\, \varepsilon$$

Denote this model as model B. Note that the forward selection and backward elimination methods disagree on the preferred model, with the variable *shelf 2* included here but not included by the forward selection procedure. We shall investigate why this occurs below.

Table 3.17 shows the summaries for the models as the unhelpful variables were eliminated. Note that as variables were dropped, there is no change R^2_{adj}, at least to three decimal places, while the evidence from the standard error of the estimate is inconclusive. The results in Table 3.18 may be used to calculate the partial F-statistics. Table 3.18 contains the ANOVA tables for the models generated by the backward elimination procedure. Model 1 represents the model with all the predictors in the

TABLE 3.18 ANOVA Tables for the Models Selected by the Backward Elimination Procedure[a]

Model		Sum of Squares	df	Mean Square	F	Significance
1	Regression	14,980.078	12	1,248.340	4,781.082	0.000[b]
	Residual	16.710	64	0.261		
	Total	14,996.788	76			
2	Regression	14,980.005	11	1,361.819	5,274.321	0.000[c]
	Residual	16.783	65	0.258		
	Total	14,996.788	76			
3	Regression	14,979.560	10	1,497.956	5,738.554	0.000[d]
	Residual	17.228	66	0.261		
	Total	14,996.788	76			

[a] Dependent variable: *rating.*
[b] Predictors: (constant), *shelf 2, fat, sodium, weight, cups, protein, vitamins, carbohydrates, fiber, sugars, calories, potassium.*
[c] Predictors: (constant), *shelf 2, fat, sodium, cups, protein, vitamins, carbohydrates, fiber, sugars, calories, potassium.*
[d] Predictors: (constant), *shelf 2, fat, sodium, protein, vitamins, carbohydrates, fiber, sugars, calories, potassium.*

model. Model 2 represents the model with all the predictors except *weight*. We have

$$SS_{weight\,|\,all\ other\ variables} = SS_{all\ variables} - SS_{all\ variables\ except\ weight}$$
$$= 14,980.078 - 14,980.005$$
$$= 0.073$$

Then, using the information from Table 3.18, the test statistic for the partial *F*-test is the following:

$$F(weight|\text{all other variables}) = \frac{SS_{weight|all\ other\ variables}}{MSE_{all\ variables}} = \frac{0.073}{0.261} = 0.280$$

This value of 0.280 lies at about the 40th percentile of the $F_{1,\,n-p-2} = F_{1,\,72}$ distribution, giving us a *p*-value for this hypothesis test of 0.60. Therefore, the null hypothesis that weight should not be included in the model, given all the other variables, is not rejected, and the variable *weight* is thereby eliminated from the model.

Stepwise Selection Procedure Applied to the *Cereals* Data Set

The stepwise selection procedure is a modification of the forward selection procedure, where the algorithm checks at each step whether all variables currently in the model are still significant. In this example, each variable that had been entered remained significant when the other variables were also entered. Thus, for this example, the results were the same as for the forward selection procedure (model A) with the same model summaries, as shown in Table 3.15.

Best Subsets Procedure Applied to the *Cereals* Data Set

Table 3.19 provides the results from Minitab's application of the best subsets procedure on the *cereals* data set. The predictor variable names are given on the upper right, formatted vertically. Each horizontal line in the table represents a separate model, with the "X"'s shown under the predictors included in a particular model. Thus, the first model has only *sugars*; the second model has only *calories*; the third model has only *fiber*; the fourth model has both *sugars* and *fiber*; and so on. Four model selection criteria are reported for each model: R^2, R^2_{adj}, Mallows' C_p, and s.

MALLOWS' C_P STATISTIC

We now discuss the C_p statistic, developed by Mallows [7]. The C_p statistic takes the form

$$C_p = \frac{SSE_p}{MSE_{full}} - [n - 2\,(p+1)]$$

where *p* represents the number of predictors in the current (working) model, SSE_p the error sum of squares of the model with *p* predictors, and MSE_{full} the mean-squared error of the full model, that is, the model with all predictors entered. For a model that fits well, it can be shown [2] that $E\left(C_p\right) = p + 1$. Thus, we would expect the

TABLE 3.19 Best Subsets Results for the *Cereals* Data Set[a]

Vars	R-Sq	R-Sq(adj)	Mallows C-p	S	Calories	Protein	Fat	Sodium	Fiber	Carbos	Sugars	Potass	Vitamins	Cups	Weight	Shelf 2
1	58.0	57.5	24037.0	9.1616							X					
1	47.5	46.8	30067.7	10.244					X							
1	33.3	32.5	38211.7	11.545				X								
2	80.8	80.3	10955.5	6.2374	X						X					
2	73.8	73.1	14972.0	7.2854							X	X				
2	70.9	70.1	16623.1	7.6748	X				X							
3	89.9	89.5	5709.9	4.5464				X	X		X					
3	86.6	86.0	7635.1	5.2493			X		X		X					
3	84.7	84.0	8732.7	5.6108	X				X		X					
4	96.2	96.0	2135.3	2.8260			X	X	X		X					
4	92.7	92.3	4102.0	3.8882		X	X	X				X				
4	91.7	91.2	4718.5	4.1658				X	X	X	X					
5	97.5	97.3	1368.2	2.2958	X	X			X	X	X					
5	97.0	96.8	1641.9	2.5054	X		X	X	X		X					

Vars	R-Sq	R-Sq(adj)	C-p	S	1	2	3	4	5	6	7	8	9	10	11	12	13
5	96.7	96.4	1848.6	2.6528					X	X	X	X		X			
6	98.4	98.3	848.7	1.8441					X	X	X	X	X	X			
6	98.2	98.1	943.5	1.9376				X	X	X	X	X		X			
6	98.2	98.0	995.7	1.9872			X		X	X	X	X		X			
7	99.0	98.9	511.7	1.4722			X	X	X	X	X	X	X	X			
7	99.0	98.9	517.0	1.4789				X	X	X	X	X	X	X		X	
7	98.9	98.8	575.9	1.5525			X	X	X	X	X	X	X	X			
8	99.5	99.5	209.2	1.0148			X	X	X	X	X	X	X	X	X		
8	99.4	99.3	307.0	1.1855		X	X	X	X	X	X	X	X	X			
8	99.4	99.3	309.6	1.1896			X	X	X	X	X	X	X	X	X		
9	99.9	99.9	13.0	0.52216		X	X	X	X	X	X	X	X	X	X		
9	99.6	99.5	195.4	0.99173		X	X	X	X	X	X	X	X	X	X		
9	99.6	99.5	200.9	1.0026		X	X	X	X	X	X	X	X	X	X		
10	**99.9**	**99.9**	**11.0**	**0.51091**	**X**	**X**	**X**	**X**	**X**	**X**	**X**	**X**	**X**	**X**	**X**		
10	99.9	99.9	13.9	0.52198	X	X	X	X	X	X	X	X	X	X	X	X	
10	99.9	99.9	14.9	0.52575	X	X	X	X	X	X	X	X	X	X	X		X
11	99.9	99.9	11.3	0.50813	X	X	X	X	X	X	X	X	X	X	X	X	
11	99.9	99.9	12.8	0.51403	X	X	X	X	X	X	X	X	X	X	X	X	X
11	99.9	99.9	15.7	0.52549	X	X	X	X	X	X	X	X	X	X	X	X	X
12	99.9	99.9	13.0	0.51098	X	X	X	X	X	X	X	X	X	X	X	X	X

[a] Best model in boldface type.

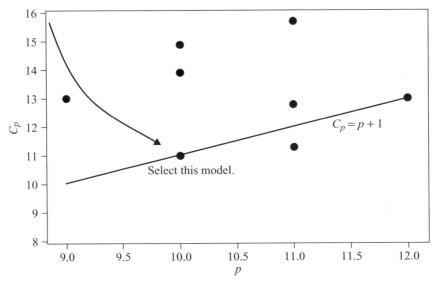

Figure 3.12   A plot of Mallows' C_p against the number of predictors, p, can help select the best model.

value of C_p for a well-fitting model to take a value not far from $p + 1$. On the other hand, models that show a considerable lack of fit will take values of C_p above (and sometimes far above) $p + 1$. The full model, with all variables entered, always has $C_p = p + 1$ but is often not the best model.

It is useful to plot the value of C_p against the number of predictors, p. Figure 3.12 shows such a plot for the *cereals* data set regression. To increase granularity, only those models where the value of C_p is near p are shown in the plot. One heuristic for choosing the best model is to select the model where the value of C_p first approaches or crosses the line $C_p = p + 1$ as p increases.

Consider Figure 3.12. No points are plotted for $p < 9$ since the C_p values were too far away from $C_p = p + 1$ to be helpful. However, the general trend for the values of C_p is to fall as p increases, as can be seen from Table 3.19. As we reach $p = 9$, we have $C_p = 13$, which is not too far away from the line $C_p = p + 1$; thus, we may wish to bear this model in mind as a possible candidate model.

Finally, when we reach $p = 10$, we have for one of the models, $C_p = 11$, which is exactly on the line $C_p = p + 1$. Therefore, the C_p heuristic would be to select this model as the current best model. This model, shown in bold in Table 3.19, is as follows:

$$y = \beta_0 + \beta_1(sugars) + \beta_2(fiber) + \beta_3(sodium) + \beta_4(fat)$$
$$+ \beta_5(protein) + \beta_6(carbohydrates) + \beta_7(calories)$$
$$+ \beta_8(vitamins) + \beta_9(potassium) + \beta_{10}(shelf\,2) + \varepsilon$$

This is of course model B the model recommended to us by the backward elimination method. The other model, with $p = 9$ and $C_p = 13$, is the model recommended to us by the forward selection and stepwise selection method models, A:

$$y = \beta_0 + \beta_1(sugars) + \beta_2(fiber) + \beta_3(sodium) + \beta_4(fat)$$
$$+ \beta_5(protein) + \beta_6(carbohydrates) + \beta_7(calories) + \beta_8(vitamins)$$
$$+ \beta_9(potassium) + \varepsilon$$

VARIABLE SELECTION CRITERIA

Thus, we have two candidate models vying for designation as the best model, with each model chosen by two model selection procedures. The only difference between the models is the inclusion of the *shelf 2* indicator variable. Let us take a moment to examine why the forward selection method did not include this variable, whereas the backward elimination method did.

So far, we have blindly applied the variable selection procedures, using the default selection criteria given by the algorithms. In many cases, these default values work quite nicely, but the analyst should always be aware of the thresholds being applied to omit or retain variables in the variable selection process. Figure 3.13 shows the dialog box for setting the entry/removal thresholds for the Clementine software, with the default values shown. Variables will be added to the model only if the associated *p*-value for the partial *F*-test is smaller than the entry value specified in this dialog box, and removed only if the *p*-value is larger than the removal value specified.

If analysts wish to be more parsimonious, a lower entry threshold may be specified, which will make it more difficult for variables of borderline significance to be entered into the model. Similarly, a lower removal threshold will make it easier to omit variables of borderline significance. On the other hand, if the analyst wishes to be more inclusive, higher levels for the entry and removal thresholds may be specified. Clearly, however, the entry threshold value must be less than the removal value.

So what is the significance of the *shelf 2* indicator variable given that the other variables in Table 3.15 are in the model? Table 3.20 shows that the *p*-value for the *t*-test for the *shelf 2* variable is 0.05. Earlier we learned how the *t*-test and the (appropriate) *F*-test were equivalent. Thus, it would follow that the *p*-value for the sequential *F*-test for inclusion of *shelf 2* is 0.05.

We can verify this *p*-value using the sequential *F*-test directly, as follows. From Table 3.21 we have the regression sum of squares for the full model (including *shelf 2* but ignoring *cups* and *weight*) equal to 14,979.560. Also from Table 3.21 we have

Figure 3.13 Setting the entry/removal thresholds in Clementine.

TABLE 3.20 *Shelf 2* Indicator Variable Has a Significance of 0.05, as Shown by the *t*-Test

```
The regression equation is
Rating = 54.3 - 0.230 Calories + 3.25 Protein - 1.67 Fat - 0.0552 Sodium
         + 3.47 Fiber + 1.16 Carbos - 0.708 Sugars - 0.0330 Potassium
         - 0.0496 Vitamins + 0.314 shelf 2
```

Predictor	Coef	SE Coef	T	P	VIF
Constant	54.2968	0.4488	120.99	0.000	
Calories	- 0.229610	0.007845	- 29.27	0.000	6.8
Protein	3.24665	0.08582	37.83	0.000	2.6
Fat	- 1.66844	0.09650	- 17.29	0.000	2.7
Sodium	- 0.0552464	0.0008142	- 67.86	0.000	1.4
Fiber	3.46905	0.07165	48.41	0.000	8.5
Carbos	1.16030	0.03127	37.11	0.000	5.1
Sugars	- 0.70776	0.03343	- 21.17	0.000	6.4
Potassium	- 0.032982	0.002416	- 13.65	0.000	8.6
Vitamins	- 0.049640	0.002940	- 16.88	0.000	1.3
shelf 2	**0.3140**	**0.1573**	**2.00**	**0.050**	**1.4**

```
S = 0.510915 R-Sq = 99.9% R-Sq(adj) = 99.9%
```

Analysis of Variance

Source	DF	SS	MS	F	P
Regression	10	14979.6	1498.0	5738.55	0.000
Residual Error	66	17.2	0.3		
Total	76	14996.8			

the regression sum of squares from the reduced model (not including *shelf 2*) given as 14,978.521. Thus, we have

$$SS_{shelf\ 2\ |\ all\ other\ variables} = SS_{all\ variables} - SS_{all\ variables\ except\ shelf\ 2}$$
$$= 14,979.560 - 14,978.521$$
$$= 1.039$$

From Table 3.21 we have $MSE_{all\ variables} = 0.261$. Hence,

$$F(shelf\ 2|all\ other\ variables) = \frac{SS_{shelf\ 2|all\ other\ variables}}{MSE_{all\ variables}} = \frac{1.039}{0.261} = 3.9808$$

TABLE 3.21 Regression ANOVA Tables Without and with *Shelf 2*

Model		Sum of Squares	df	Mean Square	F	Significance
With	Regression	14,978.521	9	1,664.280	6,104.043	0.000
Shelf 2	Residual	18.268	67	0.273		
	Total	14,996.788	76			
Without	Regression	14,979.560	10	1,497.956	5,738.554	0.000
Shelf 2	Residual	17.228	66	0.261		
	Total	14,996.788	76			

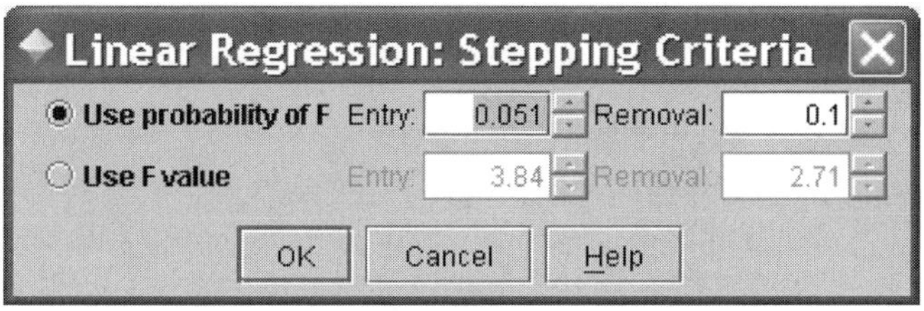

Figure 3.14 Adjusting the entry threshold for the forward selection algorithm.

This value of 3.9808 for the sequential F-statistic lies at the 95th percentile of the $F_{1,n-p-2} = F_{1,65}$-distribution, thereby verifying our p-value of 0.05 for the inclusion of the *shelf 2* indicator variable in the model.

Now recall that 0.05 happens to be the default entry threshold for both the forward selection and stepwise selection procedures. Thus, if we adjust the entry threshold level just a touch upward (say, to 0.051), we would expect *shelf 2* to be included in the final models from both of these procedures. Figure 3.14 shows the dialog box for adjusting the entry threshold level for Clementine's forward selection algorithm, with the level moved up slightly to 0.051. Finally, Table 3.22 shows the model summary results from the forward selection algorithm using the adjusted entry threshold value of 0.051. Note that, as expected, *shelf 2* is now included, as the last variable to be entered into the model. Otherwise, Table 3.22 is exactly the same as Table 3.15, the forward selection results using the default threshold value.

TABLE 3.22   Model Summary Results for the Forward Selection Procedure, After Adjusting the Entry Threshold Upward Slightly and with Inclusion of *Shelf 2*

Model	R	R^2	Adjusted R^2	Std. Error of the Estimate
1	0.762[a]	0.580	0.575	9.16160
2	0.899[b]	0.808	0.803	6.23743
3	0.948[c]	0.899	0.895	4.54638
4	0.981[d]	0.962	0.960	2.82604
5	0.985[e]	0.970	0.968	2.50543
6	0.987[f]	0.975	0.973	2.31269
7	0.995[g]	0.990	0.989	1.47893
8	0.998[h]	0.995	0.995	1.01477
9	0.999[i]	0.999	0.999	0.52216
10	0.999[j]	0.999	0.999	0.51091

[a] Predictors: (constant), *sugars.*
[b] Predictors: (constant), *sugars, fiber.*
[c] Predictors: (constant), *sugars, fiber, sodium.*
[d] Predictors: (constant), *sugars, fiber, sodium, fat.*
[e] Predictors: (constant), *sugars, fiber, sodium, fat, protein.*
[f] Predictors: (constant), *sugars, fiber, sodium, fat, protein, carbohydrates.*
[g] Predictors: (constant), *sugars, fiber, sodium, fat, protein, carbohydrates, calories.*
[h] Predictors: (constant), *sugars, fiber, sodium, fat, protein, carbohydrates, calories, vitamins.*
[i] Predictors: (constant), *sugars, fiber, sodium, fat, protein, carbohydrates, calories, vitamins, potassium.*
[j] Predictors: (constant), *sugars, fiber, sodium, fat, protein, carbohydrates, calories, vitamins, potassium, shelf 2.*

At this point, all four of our variable selection algorithms point to the same model as the best model. We now designate model B, as our *working model*:

$$y = \beta_0 + \beta_1(sugars) + \beta_2(fiber) + \beta_3(sodium) + \beta_4(fat)$$
$$+ \beta_5(protein) + \beta_6(carbohydrates) + \beta_7(calories)$$
$$+ \beta_8(vitamins) + \beta_9(potassium) + \beta_{10}(shelf2) + \varepsilon$$

Let us simply reiterate that one need not report only one model as a final model. Two or three models may be carried forward, and input sought from managers about which model may be most ameliorative of the business or research problem. However, it is often convenient to have one "working model" selected, because of the complexity of model building in the multivariate environment. Note, however, that the variable selection criteria for choosing the "best" model do not account for the multicollinearity that still exists among the predictors. Alert readers will have seen from Table 3.20 that the variance inflation factors for four or five variables are rather high, and will need some attention.

But first we need to address a problem that our working model has with a set of outliers. Figure 3.15 is a plot of the standardized residuals versus the fitted values for the current working model. Note the set of four outliers in the lower section of the plot. These are all cereals whose nutritional rating is lower than expected given their of predictor variable levels. These cereals are:

- *Record 46*: Raisin Nut Bran
- *Record 52*: Apple Cinnamon Cheerios
- *Record 55*: Honey Nut Cheerios
- *Record 56*: Oatmeal Raisin Crisp

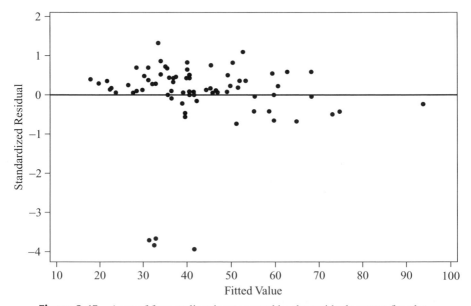

Figure 3.15 A set of four outliers is uncovered by the residuals versus fits plot.

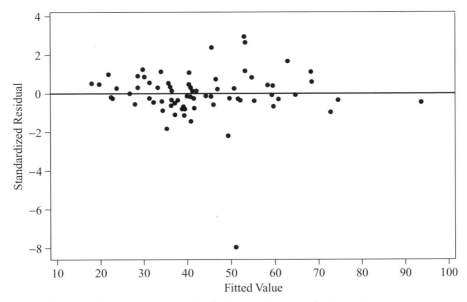

Figure 3.16   After setting aside the four outliers, one further outlier pops up.

It is not clear why the nutritional rating for these cereals is unexpectedly low. Perhaps these cereals contain certain other ingredients, not listed among our variables, which lower their nutritional value. Regardless of the reason, these cereals are obstructing the efficacy of the overall regression model for the bulk of the cereals in the data set, and will therefore be set aside.

However, after omitting these four cereals, one further extreme outlier appears in the data set, as shown in the plot of the standardized residuals versus the fitted values in Figure 3.16. This cereal is Quaker Oatmeal, with the remarkable standardized residual of -7.87, meaning that its actual nutritional rating is 7.87 residual standard errors below its expected rating, given its predictor values. We therefore also omit this cereal from the analysis and plunge ahead with the remaining 72 cereals.

Finally, Figure 3.17 shows that after omitting this fifth outlier, we obtain a healthy plot of the standardized residuals versus fitted values. No clear patterns are evident in this plot, which would indicate violation of the regression assumptions of constant variance or independence. Also, the normal probability plot in Figure 3.18 supports the normality assumption. Therefore, apart from the multicollinearity, which we still need to address, we have reason to be quite happy with our model for estimating nutritional rating. The regression results for this model are provided in Table 3.23. Some of these results, such as the reported value of 100% for R^2 and R^2_{adj}, are quite extraordinary. But a closer inspection of the results shows that these reportedly perfect 100% results are probably just due to rounding.

Note from Table 3.23 that both SSE and MSE are reported to equal zero; this is consistent with the perfect values for R^2 and R^2_{adj}. However, the standard error of the estimate, s, is reported to differ (however slightly) from zero. We know that $s = \sqrt{MSE}$; thus, it is likely that the zero and 100% results shown in Table 3.23 are

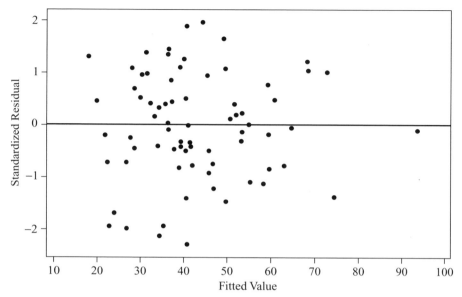

Figure 3.17 Finally, after omitting the fifth outlier, we obtain a healthy residuals versus fitted values plot.

due simply to rounding. This is verified by the SPSS regression printout shown in Table 3.24, which provides more precise results.

This is just another example of how computer output can sometimes be misleading, which therefore requires that the data analyst understand the mechanisms and workings of the statistical models. Table 3.23 tells us that our model, in some

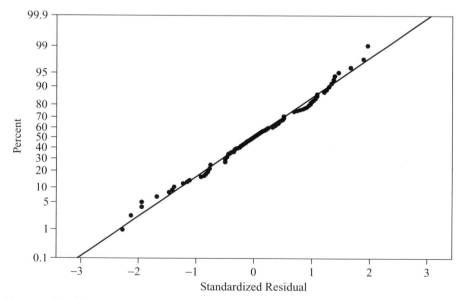

Figure 3.18 The normality assumption is supported by the normal probability plot for the remaining 72 cereals.

TABLE 3.23 Regression Results for Working Model B[a]

```
The regression equation is
Rating = 54.9 - 0.223 Calories + 3.27 Protein - 1.69 Fat - 0.0545 Sodium
       + 3.44 Fiber + 1.09 Carbos - 0.725 Sugars - 0.0340 Potassium
       - 0.0512 Vitamins - 0.000002 shelf 2
```

Predictor	Coef	SE Coef	T	P	VIF
Constant	54.9271	0.0000	2014113.85	0.000	
Calories	- 0.222724	0.000001	- 315293.55	0.000	17.2
Protein	3.27317	0.00001	639653.95	0.000	2.7
Fat	- 1.69140	0.00001	- 226909.09	0.000	5.0
Sodium	- 0.0544927	0.0000000	- 1176223.46	0.000	1.3
Fiber	3.44348	0.00000	818194.24	0.000	9.3
Carbos	1.09245	0.00000	330481.84	0.000	14.6
Sugars	- 0.724893	0.000003	- 232998.09	0.000	16.7
Potassium	- 0.0339934	0.0000001	- 245597.05	0.000	9.0
Vitamins	- 0.0512122	0.0000002	- 309676.00	0.000	1.2
shelf 2	- 0.00000193	0.00000908	- 0.21	0.832	1.5

```
S = 0.0000285908  R-Sq = 100.0%  R-Sq(adj) = 100.0%
```

Analysis of Variance

Source	DF	SS	MS	F	P
Regression	10	14450.7	1445.1	1.76781E+12	0.000
Residual Error	61	0.0	0.0		
Total	71	14450.7			

[a] Have we reached perfection? No, the 100% R^2 and R^2_{adj} are just due to rounding.

ways, is perfect. The data analyst knows better. From Table 3.24, we can find the actual value for R^2 to be

$$R^2 = \frac{SSR}{SST} = \frac{14,450.67}{14,450.671} = 0.9999999308$$

which is nevertheless remarkably high. We also see from Table 3.23 that the indicator variable *shelf 2* is no longer significant. Perhaps *shelf 2* was associated somehow with the cereals that have been omitted. We therefore omit this variable from the model, and adopt as our new working model, model A:

$$y = \beta_0 + \beta_1(sugars) + \beta_2(fiber) + \beta_3(sodium)$$
$$+ \beta_4(fat) + \beta_5(protein) + \beta_6(carbohydrates)$$
$$+ \beta_7(calories) + \beta_8(vitamins) + \beta_9(potassium) + \varepsilon$$

TABLE 3.24 More Precise Regression Results (Almost Perfect)

	Sum of Squares	df	Mean Square	F	Significance
Regression	14,450.670	10	1,445.067	98,000,000	0.000[a]
Residual	0.0008957	61	0.00001468		
Total	14,450.671	71			

[a] Predictors: (constant), shelf 2, fat, sodium, fiber, vitamins, sugars, protein, carbohydrates, potassium, calories; dependent variable: rating.

TABLE 3.25 Results of Regression After Omitting the *Shelf 2* Indicator Variable[a]

Model		Sum of Squares	df	Mean Square	F	Significance
1	Regression	14,450.670	9	1,605.630	100,000,000	0.000[b]
	Residual	0.0009636	62	0.00001554		
	Total	14,450.671	71			

		Unstandardized Coefficients		Standardized Coefficients,			Collinearity Statistics	
Model		B	Std. Error	β	t	Significance	Tolerance	VIF
1	(Constant)	54.924	0.004		15,122.123	0.000		
	Calories	−0.223	0.000	−0.311	−2,287.163	0.000	0.058	17.205
	Protein	3.274	0.001	0.250	4,639.159	0.000	0.372	2.692
	Fat	−1.691	0.001	−0.120	−1,645.658	0.000	0.202	4.953
	Sodium	−0.054	0.000	−0.320	−8,537.817	0.000	0.764	1.310
	Fiber	3.444	0.001	0.594	5,930.641	0.000	0.107	9.333
	Carbohydrates	1.093	0.000	0.301	2,399.500	0.000	0.069	14.585
	Sugars	−0.725	0.000	−0.226	−1,701.926	0.000	0.061	16.445
	Potassium	−0.034	0.000	−0.175	−1,802.578	0.000	0.114	8.774
	Vitamins	−0.051	0.000	−0.082	−2,263.919	0.000	0.818	1.222

[a] Dependent variable: rating.
[b] Predictors: *(constant), vitamins, fat, fiber, sugars, sodium, protein, carbohydrates, potassium, calories.*

Table 3.25 provides the results from the model A multiple regression. The regression diagnostics (not shown) are acceptable and similar to those of model B above.

USING THE PRINCIPAL COMPONENTS AS PREDICTORS

However, it is time that we tackled the problem of multicollinearity indicated by the large variance inflation factors for several of the predictors. (But first, we should acknowledge that this *cereals* data set is dissimilar in one respect from most data mining data sets that you will encounter in the real world. The nutritional rating may in fact represent a nearly deterministic function of the various predictors. This is what is keeping the standard errors of the coefficients so small, even in the presence of multicollinearity. What is happening here is that we are closing in on the actual values used in the government formula to assign nutritional rating to breakfast cereals.) To do this, we turn to the dimension reduction methodology we learned in Chapter 1: *principal components analysis* (PCA).

First, the predictors from model A are all standardized using z-scores. Then the correlation structure of the standardized is examined, as shown in Table 3.26. The principal components analysis will then use this correlation structure of the standardized variables to identify a certain number of independent components. Nine variables were entered, but we seek to find a fewer number of orthogonal components. How many components, then, should be extracted?

TABLE 3.26 Correlation Matrix, on Which the Principal Components Are Based

	Calories	Protein	Fat	Sodium	Fiber	Carbohydrates	Sugar	Potassium	Vitamins
cal-z	1.000	0.026	0.509	0.299	−0.290	0.271	0.565	−0.068	0.268
prot-z	0.026	1.000	0.185	−0.002	0.516	−0.018	−0.302	0.561	0.050
fat-z	0.509	0.185	1.000	0.019	0.020	−0.277	0.289	0.189	−0.008
sodium-z	0.299	−0.002	0.019	1.000	−0.061	0.320	0.047	−0.025	0.347
fiber-z	−0.290	0.516	0.020	−0.061	1.000	−0.397	−0.133	0.907	−0.030
carbs-z	0.271	−0.018	−0.277	0.320	−0.397	1.000	−0.461	−0.381	0.217
sugars-z	0.565	−0.302	0.289	0.047	−0.133	−0.461	1.000	0.026	0.105
potas-z	−0.068	0.561	0.189	−0.025	0.907	−0.381	0.026	1.000	0.026
vitamin-z	0.268	0.050	−0.008	0.347	−0.030	0.217	0.105	0.026	1.000

1. *Eigenvalue criterion.* According to this criterion, only components with eigenvalues of at least 1.0 should be extracted. Table 3.27 shows three such components, with a fourth component being very close to 1.0, with a 0.997 eigenvalue. Thus, this criterion would suggest either three or four components.

2. *Proportion of variance explained criterion.* There is no concrete threshold for this criterion. We would, however, like to account for as much of the variability as possible while retaining a relatively small number of components. Table 3.27 shows us that 82% of the variability is accounted for by the first four components, and 89% is accounted for by the first five components. Thus, this criterion would suggest perhaps four or five components.

3. *Minimum communality criterion.* This criterion recommends that enough components should be extracted so that the communality (proportion of variance of a particular variable that is shared by the other variables) for each of these variables in the model exceeds a certain threshold, such as 50%. Table 3.28 shows that the communalities for each of the variables is greater than 60% four components are extracted, but the communality for *vitamin-z* is below 50% when only

TABLE 3.27 Eigenvalues and Proportion of Variance Explained by the Nine Components

Component	Initital Eigenvalues		
	Total	% of Variance	Cumulative %
1	2.634	29.269	29.269
2	2.074	23.041	52.310
3	1.689	18.766	71.077
4	0.997	11.073	82.149
5	0.653	7.253	89.402
6	0.518	5.752	95.154
7	0.352	3.916	99.070
8	0.065	0.717	99.787
9	0.019	0.213	100.000

TABLE 3.28 Communalities When Extracting Three and Four Components[a]

	Extracting Three Components		Extracting Four Components	
	Initial	Extraction	Initial	Extraction
cal-z	1.000	0.835	1.000	0.893
prot-z	1.000	0.653	1.000	0.802
fat-z	1.000	0.550	1.000	0.796
sodium-z	1.000	0.524	1.000	0.614
fiber-z	1.000	0.881	1.000	0.921
carbs-z	1.000	0.815	1.000	0.885
sugars-z	1.000	0.803	1.000	0.910
potas-z	1.000	0.894	1.000	0.909
vitamn-z	1.000	0.442	1.000	0.665

[a]Extraction method: principal component analysis.

three components are extracted. Thus, this criterion may suggest extracting four components.

4. *Scree plot criterion.* The scree plot in Figure 3.19 may be viewed as beginning to flatten out between the fourth and fifth component numbers. Thus, this criterion may suggest retaining four components.

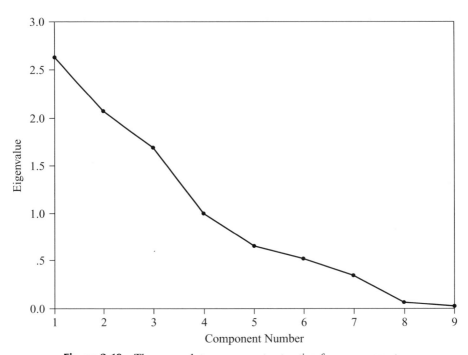

Figure 3.19 The scree plot may suggest extracting four components.

TABLE 3.29   Rotated Component Matrix for Four Components[a]

	Component			
	1	2	3	4
cal-z		0.830		
prot-z	0.735			−0.442
fat-z		0.853		
sodium-z			0.770	
fiber-z	0.936			
carbs-z				−0.762
sugars-z		0.407		0.834
potas-z	0.939			
vitamn-z			0.812	

[a] Extraction method: principal component analysis; rotation method: varimax with Kaiser normalization; rotation converged in seven iterations.

Taking all four criteria into account, we therefore decide to extract four components. Using *varimax* rotation, we obtain the rotated component matrix shown in Table 3.29, where for clarity, coefficients smaller than 0.4 in absolute value have been surpressed. Thumbnail profiles of these components may be given as follows:

$$Principal\ component\ 1 = 0.939\ potassium + 0.936\ fiber + 0.735\ protein$$

As we saw earlier, *fiber* and *potassium* are highly correlated, and the inclusion of *protein* in this component shows that *protein* shares in this correlation, as can be seen from Table 3.26. When it comes time to perform regression using these principal components, we would expect that this component will have a positive regression coefficient, since these ingredients are normally viewed as nutritious.

$$Principal\ component\ 2 = 0.853\ fat + 0.830\ calories + 0.407\ sugars$$

Table 3.26 shows that *fat* and *sugars* is each correlated with *calories*, which perhaps should come as no surprise. The correlation between *fat* and *sugars* is milder but still enough for the algorithm to assign them to the same component. We would expect that the relationship between nutritional rating and *principal component 2* shall be negative; that is, as *fat/calories/sugars* increases, the nutritional rating is expected to decrease.

$$Principal\ component\ 3 = 0.812\ vitamins + 0.770\ sodium$$

We would assume that having more vitamins is a good thing, but that having more sodium may be a bad thing for a cereal to have. Thus, it is difficult for a nonnutritionist to predict what the relationship between this component and nutritional rating will be.

$$Principal\ component\ 4 = 0.834\ sugars − 0.762\ carbohydrates − 0.442\ protein$$

Here we have a contrasting component, which opposes *sugars* to *carbohydrates* and *protein*. Since *sugars* has a positive coefficient and *protein* a negative coefficient, we might expect this component to have a negative relationship with nutritional rating.

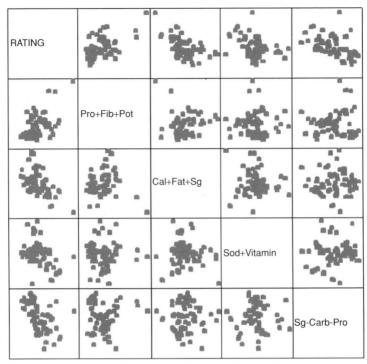

Figure 3.20 Matrix plot of nutritional rating with the four principal components.

Now that the principal components have been extracted, we may finally proceed with the regression of nutritional rating on the principal components. A matrix plot of nutritional rating and the four principal components is provided in Figure 3.20. The first column of scatter plots shows the relationships between nutritional rating and each of the four principal components. As expected, the relationship with the first principal component, *potassium + fiber + protein*, is positive. Also as expected, the relationship with the second principal component, *fat + calories + sugars*, is negative, as is that with the fourth principal component, *sugars − carbohydrates − protein*. Further, the relationship with the third principal component, *vitamins + sodium*, is also negative, perhaps because of the detrimental effects of too much sodium in the diet.

The regression results are provided in Table 3.30. $R^2_{\text{adj}} = 0.951$, meaning that these four principal components together account for over 95% of the variability in the nutritional rating. The dimension of the prediction space has been reduced from nine variables to four components. However, this reduction comes with a small cost of about 5% of unaccounted variability. Note that the variance inflation factors for each of the principal components is exactly 1.00, which is the minimum. This is because the principal components are independent, and thus have correlation zero with each other, as shown in Table 3.31. Since the components are completely uncorrelated, there is no danger whatsoever of multicollinearity. As the matrix plot indicated, the regression coefficient (7.664) for the first principal component is positive, while the other three coefficients are negative.

TABLE 3.30   Results for Model 1 of Regression of Nutritional Rating on the Four Principal Components[a]

R	R^2	Adjusted R^2	Std. Error of the Estimate
0.977^b	0.954	0.951	3.1435987

	Sum of Squares	df	Mean Square	F	Significance
Regression	13,788.563	4	3,447.141	348.823	0.000^b
Residual	662.108	67	9.882		
Total	14,450.671	71			

	Unstandardized Coefficient		Standardized Coefficient,			Collinearity Statistics	
	B	Std. Error	β	t	Significance	Tolerance	VIF
Principal Component							
(*constant*)	43.107	0.370		116.355	0.000		
Principal component 1	7.664	0.373	0.537	20.544	0.000	1.000	1.000
Principal component 2	−7.521	0.373	−0.527	−20.159	0.000	1.000	1.000
Principal component 3	−5.221	0.373	−0.366	−13.996	0.000	1.000	1.000
Principal component 4	−7.186	0.373	−0.504	−19.261	0.000	1.000	1.000

[a] Dependent variable: *rating*.
[b] Predictors: (constant), *Principal component 1, Principal component 2, Principal component 3, Principal component 4.*

SUMMARY

A *multiple regression model* uses a linear surface such as a plane or hyperplane, to approximate the relationship between a continuous response (target) variable and a set of predictor variables. In general, for a multiple regression with m predictor variables, we would interpret coefficient b_i as follows: The estimated change in the response variable for a unit increase in variable x_i is b_i when all other variables are held constant. When building models, if a new variable is useful, s will decrease; but if the new variable is not useful for predicting the target variable, s may in fact increase. This type of behavior makes s, the standard error of the estimate, a more attractive indicator than R^2 of whether a new variable should be added to the model, since R^2 always increases when a new variable is added, regardless of its usefulness.

TABLE 3.31   Pearson Correlations[a]

	Principal component 1	Principal component 2	Principal component 3	Principal component 4
Principal component 1	1.000	0.000	0.000	0.000
Principal component 2	0.000	1.000	0.000	0.000
Principal component 3	0.000	0.000	1.000	0.000
Principal component 4	0.000	0.000	0.000	1.000

[a] The Principal components are independent, and thus have zero correlation with each other.

The multiple regression model is a straightforward extension of the simple linear regression model, with analogous assumptions about the error term. We examined five inferential methods in this chapter: (1) the t-test for the relationship between the response variable y and a particular predictor variable x_i, in the presence of the other predictor variables, $x_{(i)}$, where $x_{(i)} = x_1, x_2, \ldots, x_{i-1}, x_{i+1}, \ldots, x_m$ denotes the set of all predictors not including x_i; (2) the F-test for the significance of the regression as a whole; (3) the confidence interval, β_i, for the slope of the ith predictor variable; (4) the confidence interval for the mean of the response variable y given a set of particular values for the predictor variables $x_1, x_2, \ldots, x_m$; and (5) the prediction interval for a random value of the response variable y given a set of particular values for the predictor variables $x_1, x_2, \ldots, x_m$.

One may apply a separate t-test for each predictor $x_1, x_2,$ or x_3, examining whether a linear relationship exists between the target variable y and that particular predictor. On the other hand, the F-test considers the linear relationship between the target variable y and the *set of predictors* (e.g., $\{x_1, x_2, x_3\}$) taken as a whole. Categorical predictor variables may also be used as inputs to regression models, through the use of indicator variables (dummy variables). For use in regression, a categorical variable with k categories must be transformed into a set of $k - 1$ indicator variables. An *indicator variable*, also known as a *dummy variable*, is a binary 0/1 variable, which takes the value 1 if the observation belongs to the given category, and takes the value 0 otherwise. These indicator variables define a set of parallel (hyper-) planes. The vertical distance between these parallel planes, as measured by the coefficient for the indicator variable, represents the estimated effect of the particular indicator variable on the target variable with respect to the reference category.

In the interests of parsimony, we should find some way to penalize the R^2 measure for models that include predictors that are not useful. Fortunately, such a penalized form for R^2 does exist, and is known as the *adjusted R^2*. If R^2_{adj} is much less than R^2, this is an indication that at least one variable in the model may be extraneous, and the analyst should consider omitting that variable from the model. When one is building models in multiple regression, one should use R^2_{adj} and s rather than the raw R^2.

The *sequential sums of squares* partitions the SSR into the unique portions of the SSR that are explained by the particular predictors given any earlier predictors. Thus, the values of the sequential sums of squares depends on the *order* in which the variables are entered into the model.

Multicollinearity is a condition where some of the predictor variables are correlated with each other. Multicollinearity leads to instability in the solution space, possibly leading to incoherent results. The high variability associated with the estimates means that different samples may produce coefficient estimates with widely different values. *Variance inflation factors* may be used to detect the presence of multicollinearity. Depending on the task confronting the analyst, multicollinearity may not in fact present a fatal defect. Multicollinearity does not degrade the accuracy of the response predicted. However, the data miner must therefore strictly limit the use of a multicollinear model to estimation and prediction of the target variable. Interpretation of the model would not be appropriate, since the individual coefficients may not make sense in the presence of multicollinearity.

To assist the data analyst in determining which variables should be included in a multiple regression model, several different *variable selection methods* have been developed, including (1)forward selection, (2) backward elimination, (3) stepwise selection, and (4) best subsets. In forward selection, the model starts with no variables in it, and the variable with the highest sequential F-statistic is entered at each step. For the backward elimination procedure, the model begins with all of the variables in it, and the variable with the smallest partial F-statistic is removed. The stepwise procedure modifies the forward selection procedure so that variables that have been entered into the model in earlier steps may still be withdrawn if they later turn out to be nonsignificant. In the best subsets procedure, the software reports the best k models containing 1, 2, ..., p predictor and reports the values for R^2, R^2_{adj}, Mallows' C_p. One heuristic for choosing the best model is to select the model where the value of C_p first approaches or crosses the line $C_p = p + 1$ as p increases.

REFERENCES

1. Cereals data set, in Data and Story Library, http://lib.stat.cmu.edu/DASL/. Also available at the book series Web site.‘
2. Norman Draper and Harry Smith, *Applied Regression Analysis*, Wiley, New York, 1998.
3. David S. Moore and George P. McCabe, *Introduction to the Practice of Statistics*, 5th ed., W. H. Freeman, New York 2005.
4. J. Neter, W. Wasserman, and M. H. Kutner, *Applied Linear Statistical Models*, 2nd ed., Richard D. Irwin, Homewood, IL, 1985.
5. Neil A. Weiss, *Introductory Statistics*, 5th ed., Addison-Wesley, Reading, MA, 2002.
6. David G. Kleinbaum, Lawrence L. Kupper, and Keith E. Muller, *Applied Regression Analysis and Other Multivariable Methods*, 2nd ed., Brooks/Cole, Monterey, CA, 1998.
7. C. L. Mallows, Some comments on C_p, *Technometrics*, Vol. 15, pp. 661–675, 1973.

EXERCISES

Clarifying the Concepts

3.1. Determine whether the following statements are true or false. If a statement is false, explain why and suggest how one might alter the statement to make it true.

(a) If we would like to approximate the relationship between a response and two continuous predictors, we would need a plane.

(b) In linear regression, although the response variable is typically continuous, it may be categorical as well.

(c) In general, for a multiple regression with m predictor variables, we would interpret, coefficient b_i as follows: The estimated change in the response variable for a unit increase in variable x_i is b_i.

(d) In multiple regression, the residual is represented by the vertical distance between the data point and the regression plane or hyperplane.

(e) Whenever a new predictor variable is added to the model, the value of R^2 always goes up.

(f) The alternative hypothesis in the F-test for the overall regression asserts that the regression coefficients all differ from zero.

(g) The standard error of the estimate is a valid measure of the usefulness of the regression, without reference to an inferential model (i.e., the assumptions need not be relevant).

(h) If we were to use only the categorical variables as predictors, we would have to use *analysis of variance* and could not use linear regression.

(i) For use in regression, a categorical variable with k categories must be transformed into a set of k indicator variables.

(j) The first sequential sum of squares is exactly the value for SSR from the simple linear regression of the response on the first predictor.

(k) The variance inflation factor has a minimum of zero, but no upper limit.

(l) A variable that has been entered into the model early in the forward selection process will remain significant once other variables have been entered into the model.

(m) The variable selection criteria for choosing the best model account for the multi-collinearity among the predictors.

(n) The variance inflation factors for principal components using varimax rotation always equal 1.0.

3.2. Clearly explain why s and R^2_{adj} are preferable to R^2 as measures for model building.

3.3. Explain the difference between the t-test and the F-test for assessing the significance of the predictors.

3.4. Construct indicator variables for the categorical variable *class*, which takes four values: freshman, sophomore, junior, and senior.

3.5. When using indicator variables, explain the meaning and interpretation of the indicator variable coefficients, graphically and numerically.

3.6. Discuss the concept of the level of significance (α). At what value should it be set? Who should decide the value of α? What if the observed p-value is close to α? Describe a situation where a particular p-value will lead to two different conclusions given two different values for α.

3.7. Explain what it means when R^2_{adj} is much less than R^2.

3.8. Explain the difference between the sequential sums of squares and the partial sums of squares. For which procedures do we need these statistics?

3.9. Explain some of the drawbacks of a set of predictors with high multicollinearity.

3.10. Which statistics report the presence of multicollinearity in a set of predictors? Explain, using the formula, how this statistic works. Also explain the effect that large and small values of this statistic will have on the standard error of the coefficient.

3.11. Compare and contrast the effects that multicollinearity has on the point and intervals estimates of the response versus the values of the predictor coefficients.

3.12. Describe the differences and similarities among the forward selection procedure, the backward elimination procedure, and the stepwise procedure.

3.13. Describe how the best subsets procedure works. Why not always use the best subsets procedure?

3.14. Describe the behavior of Mallows' C_p statistic, including the heuristic for choosing the best model.

3.15. Suppose that we wished to limit the number of predictors in the regression model to a lesser number than those obtained using the default settings in the variable selection criteria. How should we alter each of the selection criteria? Now suppose that we wished to increase the number of predictors? How then should we alter each of the selection criteria?

3.16. Explain the circumstances under which the value for R^2 would reach 100%. Now explain how the p-value for any test statistic could reach zero.

Working with the Data

3.17. Consider the multiple regression output for model 1 from SPSS in Table E 3.17 using the *nutrition* data set on the book series Web site. Answer the following questions.

(a) What is the response? What are the predictors?

(b) What is the conclusion regarding the significance of the overall regression? How do you know? Does this mean that all the predictors are important? Explain.

(c) What is the typical error in prediction? (*Hint*: This may take a bit of digging.)

(d) How many foods are included in the sample?

(e) How are we to interpret the value for b_0, the coefficient for the constant term? Is this coefficient significantly different from zero? Explain how this makes sense.

(f) Which of the predictors probably does not belong in the model? Explain how you know this. What might be your next step after viewing these results?

TABLE E3.17[a]

	Sum of Squares	df	Mean Square	F	Significance
Regression	282,629,126.8	6	47,104,854.46	132,263.1	0.000[b]
Residual	339,762.5	954	356.145		
Total	282,968,889.3	960			

	Unstandardized Coefficient		Standardized Coefficient,			Collinearity Statistics	
	B	Std. Error	β	t	Significance	Tolerance	VIF
(Constant)	−0.323	0.768		−0.421	0.674		
Protein	4.274	0.088	0.080	48.330	0.000	0.463	2.160
Fat	8.769	0.023	0.535	375.923	0.000	0.621	1.611
Cholesterol	0.006	0.007	0.001	0.897	0.370	0.535	1.868
Carbohydrates	3.858	0.013	0.558	293.754	0.000	0.349	2.864
Iron	−1.584	0.304	−0.009	−5.187	0.000	0.404	2.475
Sodium	0.005	0.001	0.006	4.032	0.000	0.557	1.796

[a] Dependent variable : *calories*.
[b] Predictors: (constant), *sodium, cholestrol, iron, fat, protein, carbohydrates*.

(g) Suppose that we omit cholesterol from the model and rerun the regression. Explain what will happen to the value of R^2.

(h) Which predictor is negatively associated with the response? Explain how you know this.

(i) Discuss the presence of multicollinearity. Evaluate the strength of evidence for the presence of multicollinearity. Based on this, should we turn to principal components analysis?

(j) Clearly and completely express the interpretation for the coefficient for *sodium*.

(k) Suppose that a certain food was predicted to have 60 calories fewer than it actually has, based on its content of the predictor variables. Would this be considered unusual? Explain specifically how you would determine this.

3.18. To follow up, next consider the multiple regression output for model 1 from SPSS in Table E3.18. Three predictor variables have been added: *saturated fat, monounsaturated fat*, and *polyunsaturated fat*. Discuss the presence of multicollinearity. Evaluate the strength of evidence for the presence of multicollinearity. Based on this, should we turn to principal components analysis?

TABLE E3.18[a]

	Unstandardized Coefficient		Standardized Coefficient,			Collinearity Statistics	
	B	Std. Error	β	t	Significance	Tolerance	VIF
(Constant)	−0.158	0.772		−0.205	0.838		
Protein	4.278	0.088	0.080	48.359	0.000	0.457	2.191
Fat	9.576	1.061	0.585	9.023	0.000	0.000	3379.867
Cholesterol	0.01539	0.008	0.003	1.977	0.048	0.420	2.382
Carbohydrates	3.860	0.014	0.558	285.669	0.000	0.325	3.073
Iron	−1.672	0.314	−0.010	−5.328	0.000	0.377	2.649
Sodium	0.005183	0.001	0.006	3.992	0.000	0.555	1.803
Saturated fat	−1.011	1.143	−0.020	−0.884	0.377	0.002	412.066
Monounsaturated Fat	−0.974	1.106	−0.025	−0.881	0.379	0.002	660.375
Polyunsaturated Fat	−0.600	1.111	−0.013	−0.541	0.589	0.002	448.447

[a] Dependent variable : *calories*.

3.19. Consider the multiple regression output for model 1 from SPSS in Table E3.19, using the *New York* data set on the book series Web site. The data set contains demographic information about a set of towns in New York State. The response *male-fem* is the number of males in the town for every 100 females. The predictors are the percentage under the age of 18, the percentage between 18 and 64, and the percentage over 64 living in the town (all expressed in percents, such as 57.0), along with the town's total population. Answer the following questions.

(a) Note that the variable *pct-064* was excluded. Explain why this variable was excluded automatically from the analysis by the software. (*Hint*: Consider the analogous case of using too many indicator variables to define a particular categorical variable.)

TABLE E3.19[a]

	Sum of Squares	df	Mean Square	F	Significance
Regression	10,00298.8	3	33,432.919	44.213	0.000[b]
Residual	59,4361.3	786	756.185		
Total	69,4660.1	789			

	Unstandardized Coefficient		Standardized Coefficient,			Collinearity Statistics	
	B	Std. Error	β	t	Significance	Tolerance	VIF
(Constant)	−63.790	16.855		−3.785	0.000		
tot-pop	−0.00000190	0.000	−0.017	−0.506	0.613	1.000	1.000
pct-U18	0.660	0.249	0.105	2.657	0.008	0.700	1.428
pc-18-64	2.250	0.208	0.427	10.830	0.000	0.700	1.428

[a] Dependent variable : *Male-Fem.*
[b] Predictors: (constant), *pc-18-64, tot-pop, pct-U18.*
[c] Predictors omitted: *pct-064.*

(b) What is the conclusion regarding the significance of the overall regression?

(c) What is the typical error in prediction?

(d) How many towns are included in the sample?

(e) Which of the predictors probably does not belong in the model? Explain how you know this. What might be your next step after viewing these results?

(f) Suppose that we omit *tot-pop* from the model and rerun the regression. Explain what will happen to the value of R^2.

(g) Discuss the presence of multicollinearity. Evaluate the strength of evidence for the presence of multicollinearity. Based on this, should we turn to principal components analysis?

(h) Clearly and completely express the interpretation for the coefficient for *pct-U18*. Discuss whether this makes sense.

Hands-on Analysis

3.20. In the chapter it was surmised that the reason the *shelf 2* indicator variable was no longer important was that perhaps it was somehow associated with the cereals that had been omitted because they were outliers. Investigate whether this was indeed the case.

3.21. Open the *nutrition* data set on the book series Web site.

(a) Build the best multiple regression model you can for the purposes of predicting calories, using all the other variables as the predictors. Don't worry about whether or not the predictor coefficients are stable.

(i) Compare and contrast the results from the forward selection, backward elimination, and stepwise variable selection procedures.

(ii) Apply the best subsets procedure, and compare against the previous methods.

(iii) (*Extra credit*) Write a script that will perform all possible regressions. Did the variable selection algorithms find the best regression?

(b) Build the best multiple regression model you can for the purposes both of predicting the response and of profiling the predictors' individual relationship with the response. Make sure that you account for multicollinearity.

3.22. Open the *New York* data set at the book series Web site. Build the best multiple regression model you can for the purposes of predicting the response, using the gender ratio as the response and all the other variables as the predictors.

(a) Compare and contrast the results from the forward selection, backward elimination, and stepwise variable selection procedures.

(b) Apply the best subsets procedure, and compare against the previous methods.

(c) Perform all possible regressions. Did the variable selection algorithms find the best regression?

3.23. Open the *crash* data set at the book series Web site. Build the best multiple regression model you can for the purposes of predicting head injury severity, using all the other variables as the predictors.

(a) Determine which variables must be made into indicator variables.

(b) Determine which variables might be superfluous.

(c) Build two parallel models, one where we account for multicollinearity and another where we do not. For which purposes may each of these models be used?

3.24. Continuing with the *crash* data set, combine the four injury measurement variables into a single variable, defending your choice of combination function. Build the best multiple regression model you can for the purposes of predicting injury severity, using all the other variables as the predictors. Build two parallel models, one where we account for multicollinearity and another where we do not. For which purposes may each of these models be used?

CHAPTER **4**

LOGISTIC REGRESSION

Linear regression is used to approximate the relationship between a continuous response variable and a set of predictor variables. However, the response variable is often categorical rather than continuous. For such cases, linear regression is not appropriate, but the analyst can turn to an analogous method, logistic regression, which is similar to linear regression in many ways. *Logistic regression* refers to methods for describing the relationship between a categorical response variable and a set of predictor variables. In this chapter we explore the use of logistic regression for binary or dichotomous variables; those interested in using logistic regression for response variables with more than two categories may refer to Hosmer and Lemeshow [1]. To motivate logistic regression, and to illustrate its similarities to linear regression, consider the following example.

Data Mining Methods and Models By Daniel T. Larose
Copyright © 2006 John Wiley & Sons, Inc.

SIMPLE EXAMPLE OF LOGISTIC REGRESSION

Suppose that medical researchers are interested in exploring the relationship between patient *age* (x) and the presence (1) or absence (0) of a particular *disease* (y). The data collected from 20 patients are shown in Table 4.1, and a plot of the data are shown in Figure 4.1. The plot shows the least-squares regression line (dashed straight line) and the logistic regression line (solid curved line), along with the estimation error for patient 11 ($age = 50, disease = 0$) for both lines. Note that the least-squares regression line is linear, which means that linear regression assumes that the relationship between the predictor and the response is linear. Contrast this with the logistic regression line, which is nonlinear, meaning that logistic regression assumes that the relationship between the predictor and the response is nonlinear. The scatter plot makes plain the discontinuity in the response variable; scatter plots that look like this should alert the analyst not to apply linear regression.

Consider the prediction errors for patient 11. The distance between the data point for patient 11 ($x = 50$, $y = 0$) and the linear regression line is indicated by the dashed vertical line, and the distance between the data point and logistic regression line is shown by the solid vertical line. Clearly, the distance is greater for the linear regression line, which means that linear regression does a poorer job of estimating the presence of disease than logistic regression does for patient 11. Similarly, this observation is also true for most of the other patients.

Where does the logistic regression line come from? Consider the *conditional mean of Y given X = x*, denoted as $E(Y|x)$. This is the expected value of the response variable for a given value of the predictor. Recall that in linear regression, the response variable is considered to be a random variable defined as $Y = \beta_0 + \beta_1 x + \varepsilon$. Now, since the error termε has mean zero, we obtain $E(Y|x) = \beta_0 + \beta_1 x$ for linear regression, with possible values extending over the entire real number line.

For simplicity, denote the conditional mean $E(Y|x)$ as $\pi(x)$. Then the conditional mean for logistic regression takes on a different form from that of linear

TABLE 4.1 Age of 20 Patients, with Indicator of Disease

Patient ID	Age, x	Disease, y	Patient, ID	Age, x	Disease, y
1	25	0	11	50	0
2	29	0	12	59	1
3	30	0	13	60	0
4	31	0	14	62	0
5	32	0	15	68	1
6	41	0	16	72	0
7	41	0	17	79	1
8	42	0	18	80	0
9	44	1	19	81	1
10	49	1	20	84	1

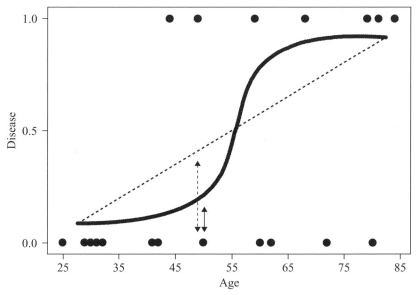

Figure 4.1   Plot of *disease* versus age, with least-squares and logistic regression lines.

regression. Specifically,

$$\pi(x) = \frac{e^{\beta_0+\beta_1 x}}{1 + e^{\beta_0+\beta_1 x}} \tag{4.1}$$

Curves of the form of equation (4.1) are called *sigmoidal* because they are S-shaped and therefore nonlinear. Statisticians have chosen the logistic distribution to model dichotomous data because of its flexibility and interpretability. The minimum for $\pi(x)$ is obtained at $\lim_{a\to-\infty} e^a/(1 + e^a) = 0$, and the maximum for $\pi(x)$ is obtained at $\lim_{a\to\infty} e^a/(1 + e) = 1$. Thus, $\pi(x)$ is of a form that may be interpreted as a probability, with $0 \le \pi(x) \le 1$. That is, $\pi(x)$ may be interpreted as the probability that the positive outcome (e.g., disease) is present for records with $X = x$, and $1 - \pi(x)$ may be interpreted as the probability that the positive outcome is absent for such records.

Linear regression models assume that $Y = \beta_0 + \beta_1 x + \varepsilon$, where the error term ε is normally distributed with mean zero and constant variance. The model assumption for logistic regression is different. Since the response is dichotomous, the errors can take only one of two possible forms: If $Y = 1$ (e.g., disease is present), which occurs with probability $\pi(x)$ (the probability that the response is positive), $\varepsilon = 1 - \pi(x)$, the vertical distance between the data point $Y = 1$ and the curve

$$\pi(x) = \frac{e^{\beta_0 + \beta_1 x}}{1 + e^{\beta_0 + \beta_1 x}}$$

directly below it, for $X = x$. On the other hand, if $Y = 0$ (e.g., disease is absent), which occurs with probability $1 - \pi(x)$ (the probability that the response is negative), $\varepsilon = 0 - \pi(x) = -\pi(x)$, the vertical distance between the data point $Y = 0$ and the curve $\pi(x)$ directly above it, for $X = x$. Thus, the variance of ε is $\pi(x)[1 - \pi(x)]$, which is the variance for a binomial distribution, and the response variable in logistic regression $Y = \pi(x) + \varepsilon$ is assumed to follow a binomial distribution with probability of success $\pi(x)$.

A useful transformation for logistic regression is the *logit transformation*, as follows:

$$g(x) = \ln \frac{\pi(x)}{1 - \pi(x)} = \beta_0 + \beta_1 x$$

The logit transformation $g(x)$ exhibits several attractive properties of the linear regression model, such as its linearity, its continuity, and its range from negative to positive infinity.

MAXIMUM LIKELIHOOD ESTIMATION

One of the most attractive properties of linear regression is that closed-form solutions for the optimal values of the regression coefficients may be obtained, courtesy of the least-squares method. Unfortunately, no such closed-form solution exists for estimating logistic regression coefficients. Thus, we must turn to *maximum likelihood estimation*, which finds estimates of the parameters for which the likelihood of observing the data is maximized.

The *likelihood function* $l(\beta|x)$ is a function of the parameters $\beta = \beta_0, \beta_1, \ldots, \beta_m$ which expresses the probability of the observed data, x. By finding the values of $\beta = \beta_0, \beta_1, \ldots, \beta_m$ that maximize $l(\beta|x)$, we thereby uncover the *maximum likelihood estimators*, the parameter values most favored by the observed data. The probability of a positive response given the data is $\pi(x) = P(Y = 1|x)$, and the probability of a negative response given the data is given by $1 - \pi(x) = P(Y = 0|x)$. Then, observations where the response is positive ($X_i = x_i, Y_i = 1$) will contribute probability $\pi(x)$ to the likelihood, while observations where the response is negative ($X_i = x_i, Y_i = 0$) will contribute probability $1 - \pi(x)$ to the likelihood. Thus, since $Y_i = 0$ or 1, the contribution to the likelihood of the ith observation may be expressed as $[\pi(x_i)]^{y_i} [1 - \pi(x_i)]^{1-y_i}$. The assumption that the observations are independent allows us to express the likelihood function $l(\beta|x)$ as the product of the individual terms:

$$l(\beta|x) = \prod_{i=1}^{n} [\pi(x_i)]^{y_i} [1 - \pi(x_i)]^{1-y_i}$$

The log likelihood $L(\beta|x) = \ln [l(\beta|x)]$ is computationally more tractable:

$$L(\beta|x) = \ln [l(\beta|x)] = \sum_{i=1}^{n} \{y_i \ln [\pi(x_i)] + (1 - y_i) \ln [1 - \pi(x_i)]\} \qquad (4.2)$$

The maximum likelihood estimators may be found by differentiating $L(\beta|x)$ with respect to each parameter and setting the resulting forms equal to zero. Unfortunately, unlike linear regression, closed-form solutions for these differentiations are not available. Therefore, other methods must be applied, such as iterative weighted least squares (see McCullagh and Nelder [2]).

INTERPRETING LOGISTIC REGRESSION OUTPUT

Let's examine the results of the logistic regression of *disease* on *age*, shown in Table 4.2. The coefficients, that is, the maximum likelihood estimates of the unknown parameters β_0 and β_1, are given as $b_0 = -4.372$ and $b_1 = 0.06696$. Thus,

$$\pi(x) = \frac{e^{\beta_0 + \beta_1 x}}{1 + e^{\beta_0 + \beta_1 x}}$$

is estimated as

$$\hat{\pi}(x) = \frac{e^{\hat{g}(x)}}{1 + e^{\hat{g}(x)}} = \frac{e^{-4.372 + 0.06696\,(age)}}{1 + e^{-4.372 + 0.06696\,(age)}}$$

with the estimated logit

$$\hat{g}(x) = -4.372 + 0.06696(age)$$

These equations may then be used to estimate the probability that the disease is present in a particular patient given the patient's age. For example, for a 50-year-old patient, we have

$$\hat{g}(x) = -4.372 + 0.06696(50) = -1.024$$

and

$$\hat{\pi}(x) = \frac{e^{\hat{g}(x)}}{1 + e^{\hat{g}(x)}} = \frac{e^{-1.024}}{1 + e^{-1.024}} = 0.26$$

Thus, the estimated probability that a 50-year-old patient has the disease is 26%, and the estimated probability that the disease is not present is $100\% - 26\% = 74\%$. On the other hand, for a 72-year-old patient, we have

$$\hat{g}(x) = -4.372 + 0.06696(72) = -0.449$$

and

$$\hat{\pi}(x) = \frac{e^{\hat{g}(x)}}{1 + e^{\hat{g}(x)}} = \frac{e^{-0.449}}{1 + e^{-0.449}} = 0.61$$

The estimated probability that a 72-year-old patient has the disease is 61%, and the estimated probability that the disease is not present is 39%.

TABLE 4.2   Results of Logistic Regression of *Disease* on *Age*

Logistic Regression Table

					Odds	95% CI	
Predictor	Coef	StDev	Z	P	Ratio	Lower	Upper
Constant	-4.372	1.966	-2.22	0.026			
Age	0.06696	0.03223	2.08	0.038	1.07	1.00	1.14

Log-Likelihood = -10.101
Test that all slopes are zero: G = 5.696, DF = 1, P-Value = 0.017

INFERENCE: ARE THE PREDICTORS SIGNIFICANT?

Recall from simple linear regression that the regression model was considered significant if MSR was large compared to MSE. The mean-squared regression (MSR) is a measure of the improvement in estimating the response when we include, rather than ignoring, the predictor. If the predictor variable is helpful for estimating the value of the response variable, MSR will be large, the test statistic $F = \text{MSR/MSE}$ will also be large, and the linear regression model will be considered significant. Significance of the coefficients in logistic regression is determined analogously. Essentially, we examine whether the model that includes a particular predictor provides a substantially better fit to the response variable than that of a model that does not include this predictor.

Define the *saturated model* to be the model that contains as many parameters as data points, such as a simple linear regression model with only two data points. Clearly, the saturated model predicts the response variable perfectly, and there is no prediction error. We may then look upon the *observed* values for the response variable to be the values predicted from the saturated model. To compare the values predicted by our fitted model (with fewer parameters than data points) to the values predicted by the saturated model, we use the *deviance* [2], as defined here:

$$\text{deviance } D = -2 \ln \left[\frac{\text{likelihood of the fitted model}}{\text{likelihood of the saturated model}} \right]$$

Here we have a ratio of two likelihoods, so that the resulting hypothesis test is called a *likelihood ratio test*. To generate a measure whose distribution is known, we must take $-2 \ln$ [likelihood ratio]. Denote the estimate of $\pi(x_i)$ from the fitted model to be $\hat{\pi}_i$. Then for the logistic regression case, and using equation (4.2), we have deviance

$$D = -2 \ln \sum_{i=1}^{n} \left[y_i \ln \frac{\hat{\pi}_i}{y_i} + (1 - y_i) \ln \frac{1 - \hat{\pi}_i}{1 - y_i} \right]$$

The deviance represents the error left over in the model after the predictors have been accounted for. As such, it is analogous to the sum of squares error in linear regression.

The procedure for determining whether a particular predictor is significant is to find the deviance of the model without the predictor and subtract the deviance of the model with the predictor thus:

$$G = \text{deviance (model without predictor)} - \text{deviance (model with predictor)}$$

$$= -2 \ln \left[\frac{\text{likelihood without predictor}}{\text{likelihood with predictor}} \right]$$

Let $n_1 = \sum y_i$ and $n_0 = \sum (1 - y_i)$. Then, for the case of a single predictor only, we have

$$G = 2 \left\{ \sum_{i=1}^{n} [y_i \ln [\hat{\pi}_i] + (1 - y_i) \ln [1 - \hat{\pi}_i]] - [n_1 \ln(n_1) + n_0 \ln(n_0) - n \ln(n)] \right\}$$

For the *disease* example, note from Table 4.2 that the log likelihood is given as -10.101. Then

$$G = 2\{-10.101 - [7\ln(7) + 13\ln(13) - 20\ln(20)]\} = 5.696$$

as indicated in Table 4.2.

The test statistic G follows a chi-square distribution with 1 degree of freedom (i.e., $\chi^2_{\nu=1}$), assuming that the null hypothesis is true that $\beta_1 = 0$. The resulting p-value for this hypothesis test is therefore $P(\chi^2_1) > G_{observed} = P(\chi^2_1) > 5.696 = 0.017$, as shown in Table 4.2. This fairly small p-value indicates that there is evidence that *age* is useful in predicting the presence of *disease*.

Another hypothesis test used to determine whether a particular predictor is significant is the *Wald test* (e.g., Rao [3]). Under the null hypothesis that $\beta_1 = 0$, the ratio

$$Z_{\text{Wald}} = \frac{b_1}{\text{SE}(b_1)}$$

follows a standard normal distribution, where SE refers to the standard error of the coefficient as estimated from the data and reported by the software. Table 4.2 provides the coefficient estimate and the standard error as follows: $b_1 = 0.06696$, and $\text{SE}(b_1) = 0.03223$, giving us

$$Z_{\text{Wald}} = \frac{0.06696}{0.03223} = 2.08$$

as reported under z for the coefficient *age* in Table 4.2. The p-value is then reported as $P(|z| > 2.08) = 0.038$. This p-value is also fairly small, although not as small as the likelihood ratio test, and therefore concurs in the significance of *age* for predicting *disease*.

We may construct $100(1 - \alpha)\%$ confidence intervals for the logistic regression coefficients as follows:

$$b_0 \pm z \cdot \text{SE}(b_0)$$
$$b_1 \pm z \cdot \text{SE}(b_1)$$

where z represents the z-critical value associated with $100(1 - \alpha)\%$ confidence. In our example, a 95% confidence interval for the slope β_1 could be found thus:

$$b_1 \pm z \cdot \text{SE}(b_1) = 0.06696 \pm (1.96)(0.03223)$$
$$= 0.06696 \pm 0.06317$$
$$= (0.00379, \ 0.13013)$$

Since zero is not included in this interval, we can conclude with 95% confidence that $\beta_1 \neq 0$ and that therefore the variable *age* is significant. The results above may be extended from the simple (one predictor) logistic regression model to the multiple (many predictors) logistic regression model. See Hosmer and Lemeshow [1, Chap. 2] for details.

INTERPRETING A LOGISTIC REGRESSION MODEL

Recall from simple linear regression that the slope coefficient β_1 was interpreted as the change in the response variable for every unit increase in the predictor. The slope coefficient β_1 is interpreted analogously in logistic regression, but through the logit function. That is, the slope coefficient β_1 may be interpreted as the change in the value of the logit for a unit increase in the value of the predictor. In other words,

$$\beta_1 = g(x + 1) - g(x)$$

In this section we discuss the interpretation of β_1 in simple logistic regression for three cases: (1) a dichotomous predictor, (2) a polychotomous predictor, and (3) a continuous predictor.

To facilitate our interpretation, we need to consider the concept of *odds*. Odds may be defined as the probability that an event occurs divided by the probability that the event does not occur. For example, earlier we found that the estimated probability that a 72-year-old patient has the disease is 61%, and the estimated probability that the 72-year-old patient does not have the disease is 39%. Thus, the odds of a 72-year-old patient having the disease is odds $= 0.61/0.39 = 1.56$. We also found that the estimated probabilities of a 50-year-old patient having or not having the disease are 26% and 74%, respectively, providing odds for the 50-year-old patient to be odds $= 0.26/0.74 = 0.35$.

Note that when the event is more likely than not to occur, odds > 1; when the event is less likely than not to occur, odds < 1; and when the event is just as likely as not to occur, odds $= 1$. Note also that the concept of odds differs from the concept of probability, since probability ranges from zero to 1, and odds can range from zero to infinity. Odds indicate how much more likely it is that an event occurred compared to its not occurring.

In binary logistic regression with a dichotomous predictor, the odds that the response variable occurred ($y = 1$) for records with $x = 1$ can be denoted as

$$\frac{\pi(1)}{1 - \pi(1)} = \frac{e^{\beta_0 + \beta_1}/(1 + e^{\beta_0 + \beta_1})}{1/(1 + e^{\beta_0 + \beta_1})} = e^{\beta_0 + \beta_1}$$

Correspondingly, the odds that the response variable occurred for records with $x = 0$ can be denoted as

$$\frac{\pi(0)}{1 - \pi(0)} = \frac{e^{\beta_0}/(1 + e^{\beta_0})}{1/(1 + e^{\beta_0})} = e^{\beta_0}$$

We also need to discuss the *odds ratio* (OR), defined as the odds that the response variable occurred for records with $x = 1$ divided by the odds that the response variable occurred for records with $x = 0$. That is,

$$\begin{aligned}
\text{OR} &= \frac{\pi(1)/[1 - \pi(1)]}{\pi(0)/[1 - \pi(0)]} \\
&= \frac{e^{\beta_0 + \beta_1}}{e^{\beta_0}} \\
&= e^{\beta_1}
\end{aligned} \tag{4.3}$$

The odds ratio has come into widespread use in the research community because of this simply expressed relationship between the odds ratio and the slope coefficient.

For example, if a clinical trial reports that the odds ratio for endometrial cancer among ever-users and never-users of estrogen replacement therapy is 5.0, this may be interpreted as meaning that ever-users of estrogen replacement therapy are five times more likely to develop endometrial cancer than are never-users.

The odds ratio is sometimes used to estimate the *relative risk*, defined as the probability that the response occurs for $x = 1$ divided by the probability that the response occurs for $x = 0$. That is,

$$\text{relative risk} = \frac{\pi(1)}{\pi(0)}$$

For the odds ratio to be an accurate estimate of the relative risk, we must have $[1 - \pi(0)]/[1 - \pi(1)] \approx 1$, which we obtain when the probability that the response occurs is small for both $x = 1$ and $x = 0$.

Interpreting a Model for a Dichotomous Predictor

Recall the *churn* data set [4], where we were interested in predicting whether a customer would leave the company's service (churn) based on a set of predictor variables. For this simple logistic regression example, assume that the only predictor available is *VoiceMail Plan*, a flag variable indicating membership in the plan. The cross-tabulation of *churn* by VoiceMail Plan membership is shown in Table 4.3.

The likelihood function is then given by

$$l(\beta|x) = [\pi(0)]^{403} \times [1 - \pi(0)]^{2008} \times [\pi(1)]^{80} \times [1 - \pi(1)]^{842}$$

Note that we may use the entries from Table 4.3 to construct the odds and the odds ratio directly.

- Odds of those with VoiceMail Plan churning $= \pi(1)/[1 - \pi(1)] = 80/842 = 0.0950$
- Odds of those without VoiceMail Plan churning $= \pi(0)/[1 - \pi(0)] = 403/2008 = 0.2007$

and

$$\text{OR} = \frac{\pi(1)/[1 - \pi(1)]}{\pi(0)/[1 - \pi(0)]} = \frac{80/842}{403/2008} = 0.47$$

That is, those who have the VoiceMail Plan are only 47% as likely to churn as are those without the VoiceMail Plan. Note that the odds ratio can also be calculated as

TABLE 4.3   Cross-Tabulation of *Churn* by Membership in the VoiceMail Plan

	VoiceMail = No, $x = 0$	VoiceMail = Yes, $x = 1$	Total
Churn = false, $y = 0$	2008	842	2850
Churn = true, $y = 1$	403	80	483
Total	2411	922	3333

TABLE 4.4   Results of Logistic Regression of Churn on the VoiceMail Plan

```
Logistic Regression Table

                                                 Odds      95% CI
Predictor       Coef     SE Coef       Z       P Ratio  Lower  Upper
Constant    -1.60596  0.0545839  -29.42  0.000
VMail       -0.747795  0.129101    -5.79  0.000  0.47   0.37   0.61

Log-Likelihood = -1360.165
Test that all slopes are zero: G = 37.964, DF = 1, P-Value = 0.000
```

the following cross-product:

$$OR = \frac{\pi(1)\,[1 - \pi(0)]}{\pi(0)\,[1 - \pi(1)]} = \frac{80(2008)}{403(842)} = 0.47$$

The logistic regression can then be performed in Minitab, with the results shown in Table 4.4. First, note that the odds ratio reported by Minitab equals 0.47, the same value that we found using the cell counts directly. Next, equation (4.3) tells us that odds ratio $= e^{\beta_1}$. We verify this by noting that $b_1 = -0.747795$, so that $e^{b_1} = 0.47$.

Here we have $b_0 = -1.60596$ and $b_1 = -0.747795$. So the probability of churning for a customer belonging ($x = 1$) or not belonging ($x = 0$) to the VoiceMail Plan is estimated as

$$\hat{\pi}(x) = \frac{e^{\hat{g}(x)}}{1 + e^{\hat{g}(x)}} = \frac{e^{-1.60596 + -0.747795x}}{1 + e^{-1.60596 + -0.747795x}}$$

with the estimated logit

$$\hat{g}(x) = -1.60596 - 0.747795x$$

For a customer belonging to the plan, we estimate his or her probability of churning:

$$\hat{g}(x) = -1.60596 - (0.747795)(1) = -2.3538$$

Membership in VoiceMail Plan protects against churn. (Courtesy: Chantal Larose.)

and

$$\hat{\pi}(x) = \frac{e^{\hat{g}(x)}}{1 + e^{\hat{g}(x)}} = \frac{e^{-2.3538}}{1 + e^{-2.3538}} = 0.0868$$

So the estimated probability that a customer who belongs to the VoiceMail Plan will churn is only 8.68%, which is less than the overall proportion of churners in the data set, 14.5%, indicating that belonging to the VoiceMail Plan protects against churn. Also, this probability could have been found directly from Table 4.3:

$$P(churn|VoiceMail\ Plan) = \frac{80}{922} = 0.0868$$

For a customer not belonging to the VoiceMail Plan, we estimate the probability of churning:

$$\hat{g}(x) = -1.60596 - (0.747795)(0) = -1.60596$$

and

$$\hat{\pi}(x) = \frac{e^{\hat{g}(x)}}{1 + e^{\hat{g}(x)}} = \frac{e^{-1.60596}}{1 + e^{-1.60596}} = 0.16715$$

This probability is slightly higher than the overall proportion of churners in the data set, 14.5%, indicating that not belonging to the VoiceMail Plan may be slightly indicative of churning. This probability could also have been found directly from Table 4.3:

$$P(churn|\overline{VoiceMail\ Plan}) = \frac{403}{2411} = 0.16715$$

Next, we apply the Wald test for the significance of the parameter for the VoiceMail Plan. We have $b_1 = -0.747795$ and $SE(b_1) = 0.129101$, giving us

$$Z_{Wald} = \frac{-0.747795}{0.129101} = -5.79$$

as reported under z for the coefficient *VoiceMail Plan* in Table 4.4. The p-value is $P(|z| > 5.79) \cong 0.000$, which is strongly significant. There is strong evidence that the *VoiceMail Plan* variable is useful for predicting churn.

A $100(1 - \alpha)\%$ confidence interval for the odds ratio may be found thus:

$$\exp\left[b_1 \pm z \cdot \hat{SE}(b_1)\right]$$

where $\exp[a]$ represents e^a. Thus, here we have a 95% confidence interval for the odds ratio given by

$$\exp\left[b_1 \pm z \cdot \hat{SE}(b_1)\right] = \exp\left[-0.747795 \pm (1.96)(0.129101)\right]$$
$$= (e^{-1.0008}, e^{-0.4948})$$
$$= (0.37, 0.61)$$

as reported in Table 4.4. Thus, we are 95% confident that the odds ratio for churning among VoiceMail Plan members and nonmembers lies between 0.37 and 0.61. Since the interval does not include $e^0 = 1$, the relationship is significant with 95% confidence.

We can use the cell entries to estimate the standard error of the coefficients directly, as follows (result from Bishop et al. [5]). The standard error for the logistic

TABLE 4.5 Reference Cell Encoding for the *Customer Service Calls* Indicator Variables

	CSC-Med	CSC-Hi
Low (0 or 1 calls)	0	0
Medium (2 or 3 calls)	1	0
High ($\geq$ 4 calls)	0	1

regression coefficient b_1 for *VoiceMail Plan* is estimated as follows:

$$\hat{SE}(b_1) = \sqrt{\frac{1}{403} + \frac{1}{2008} + \frac{1}{80} + \frac{1}{842}} = 0.129101$$

In this *churn* example, the voice mail members were coded as 1 and the nonmembers coded as 0. This is an example of *reference cell coding*, where the reference cell refers to the category coded as zero. Odds ratios are then calculated as the comparison of the members *relative to* the nonmembers or with reference to the nonmembers.

In general, for variables coded as a and b rather than 0 and 1, we have

$$\ln[\text{OR}(a, b)] = \hat{g}(x = a) - \hat{g}(x = b)$$
$$= (b_0 + b_1 a) - (b_0 + b_1 b)$$
$$= b_1(a - b) \qquad (4.4)$$

So an estimate of the odds ratio in this case is given by $\exp[b_1(a - b)]$ which becomes e^{b_1} when $a = 1$ and $b = 0$.

Interpreting a Model for a Polychotomous Predictor

For the *churn* data set [4], suppose that we categorize the *customer service calls* variable into a new variable, *CSC*, as follows:

- *Zero or one customer service calls: CSC = Low*
- *Two or three customer service calls: CSC = Medium*
- *Four or more customer service calls: CSC = High*

Then *CSC* is a trichotomous predictor. How will logistic regression handle this? First, the analyst will need to code the data set using indicator (dummy) variables and reference cell coding. Suppose that we choose *CSC = Low* to be our reference cell. Then we assign the indicator variable values to two new indicator variables, *CSC-Med* and *CSC-Hi*, given in Table 4.5. Each record will have assigned to it a value of zero or 1 for each of *CSC-Med* and *CSC-Hi*. For example, a customer with 1 customer service call will have values *CSC-Med = 0* and *CSC-Hi = 0*, a customer with 3 customer service calls will have *CSC-Med = 1* and *CSC-Hi = 0*, and a customer with 7 customer service calls will have *CSC-Med = 0* and *CSC-Hi = 1*.

Table 4.6 shows a cross-tabulation of *churn* by *CSC*. Using *CSC = Low* as the reference class, we can calculate the odds ratios using the cross-products

TABLE 4.6 Cross-Tabulation of *Churn* by *CSC*

	$CSC = Low$	$CSC = Medium$	$CSC = High$	Total
Churn = false, $y = 0$	1664	1057	129	2850
Churn = true, $y = 1$	214	131	138	483
Total	1878	1188	267	3333

as follows:

- For *CSC = Medium*:

$$\text{OR} = \frac{131(1664)}{214(1057)} = 0.963687 \approx 0.96$$

- For *CSC = High*:

$$\text{OR} = \frac{138(1664)}{214(129)} = 8.31819 \approx 8.32$$

The logistic regression is then performed in Minitab with the results shown in Table 4.7.

Note that the odds ratio reported by Minitab are the same that we found using the cell counts directly. We verify the odds ratios given in Table 4.7, using equation (4.3):

- *For CSC-Med*: $\hat{\text{OR}} = e^{b_1} = e^{-0.0369891} = 0.96$
- *For CSC-Hi*: $\hat{\text{OR}} = e^{b_2} = e^{2.11844} = 8.32$

Here we have $b_0 = -2.051$, $b_1 = -0.0369891$, and $b_2 = 2.11844$. So the probability of churning is estimated as

$$\hat{\pi}(x) = \frac{e^{\hat{g}(x)}}{1 + e^{\hat{g}(x)}} = \frac{e^{-2.051 - 0.0369891(CSC\text{-}Med) + 2.11844(CSC\text{-}Hi)}}{1 + e^{-2.051 - 0.0369891(CSC\text{-}Med) + 2.11844(CSC\text{-}Hi)}}$$

with the estimated logit:

$$\hat{g}(x) = -2.051 - 0.0369891(CSC\text{-}Med) + 2.11844(CSC\text{-}Hi)$$

TABLE 4.7 Results of Logistic Regression of *Churn* on *CSC*

```
Logistic Regression Table

                                                Odds       95% CI
Predictor        Coef    SE Coef      Z      P  Ratio  Lower  Upper
Constant     -2.05100  0.0726213  -28.24  0.000
CSC-Med      -0.0369891  0.117701   -0.31  0.753  0.96   0.77   1.21
CSC-Hi        2.11844  0.142380   14.88  0.000  8.32   6.29  11.00

Log-Likelihood = -1263.368
Test that all slopes are zero: G = 231.557, DF = 2, P-Value = 0.000
```

For a customer with low customer service calls, we estimate his or her probability of churning:

$$\hat{g}(x) = -2.051 - 0.0369891(0) + 2.11844(0) = -2.051$$

and

$$\hat{\pi}(x) = \frac{e^{\hat{g}(x)}}{1 + e^{\hat{g}(x)}} = \frac{e^{-2.051}}{1 + e^{-2.051}} = 0.114$$

So the estimated probability that a customer with low numbers of customer service calls will churn is 11.4%, which is less than the overall proportion of churners in the data set, 14.5%, indicating that such customers churn somewhat less frequently than the overall group. Also, this probability could have been found directly from Table 4.6:

$$P(churn|CSC = Low) = \frac{214}{1878} = 0.114$$

For a customer with medium customer service calls, the probability of churn is estimated as

$$\hat{g}(x) = -2.051 - 0.0369891(1) + 2.11844(0) = -2.088$$

and

$$\hat{\pi}(x) = \frac{e^{\hat{g}(x)}}{1 + e^{\hat{g}(x)}} = \frac{e^{-2.088}}{1 + e^{-2.088}} = 0.110$$

The estimated probability that a customer with medium numbers of customer service calls will churn is 11.0%, which is about the same as that for customers with low numbers of customer service calls. The analyst may consider collapsing the distinction between *CSC-Med* and *CSC-Low*. This probability could have been found directly from Table 4.6:

$$P(churn|CSC = Medium) = \frac{131}{1188} = 0.110$$

For a customer with high customer service calls, the probability of churn is estimated as

$$\hat{g}(x) = -2.051 - 0.0369891(0) + 2.11844(1) = 0.06744$$

and

$$\hat{\pi}(x) = \frac{e^{\hat{g}(x)}}{1 + e^{\hat{g}(x)}} = \frac{e^{0.06744}}{1 + e^{0.06744}} = 0.5169$$

Thus, customers with high levels of customer service calls have a much higher estimated probability of churn, over 51%, which is more than triple the overall churn rate. Clearly, the company needs to flag customers who make 4 or more customer service calls and intervene with them before they attrit. This probability could also have been found directly from Table 4.6:

$$P(churn|CSC = High) = \frac{138}{267} = 0.5169$$

Applying the Wald test for the significance of the *CSC-Med* parameter, we have $b_1 = -0.0369891$ and $SE(b_1) = 0.117701$, giving us

$$Z_{Wald} = \frac{-0.0369891}{0.117701} = -0.31426$$

as reported under z for the coefficient *CSC-Med* in Table 4.7. The p-value is $P(|z| > 0.31426) = 0.753$, which is not significant. There is no evidence that the *CSC-Med* versus *CSC-Low* distinction is useful for predicting churn. For the *CSC-Hi* parameter, we have $b_1 = 2.11844$ and $SE(b_1) = 0.142380$, giving us

$$Z_{\text{Wald}} = \frac{2.11844}{0.142380} = 14.88$$

as shown for the coefficient *CSC-Hi* in Table 4.7. The p-value, $P(|z| > 14.88) \cong 0.000$, indicates that there is strong evidence that the distinction *CSC-Hi* versus *CSC-Low* is useful for predicting churn.

Examining Table 4.7, note that the odds ratios for both *CSC = Medium* and *CSC = High* are equal to those we calculated using the cell counts directly. Also note that the logistic regression coefficients for the indicator variables are equal to the natural log of their respective odds ratios:

$$b_{CSC\text{-}Med} = \ln(0.96) \approx \ln(0.963687) = -0.0369891$$
$$b_{CSC\text{-}High} = \ln(8.32) \approx \ln(8.31819) = 2.11844$$

For example, the natural log of the odds ratio of *CSC-Hi* to *CSC-Low* can be derived using equation (4.4) as follows:

$$\begin{aligned} \ln[OR(High, Low)] &= \hat{g}(High) - \hat{g}(Low) \\ &= [b_0 + b_1(CSC\text{-}Med = 0) + b_2(CSC\text{-}Hi = 1)] \\ &\quad - [b_0 + b_1(CSC\text{-}Med = 0) + b_2(CSC\text{-}Hi = 0)] \\ &= b_2 = 2.11844 \end{aligned}$$

Similarly, the natural log of the odds ratio of *CSC-Medium* to *CSC-Low* is given by

$$\begin{aligned} \ln[OR(Medium, Low)] &= \hat{g}(Medium) - \hat{g}(Low) \\ &= [b_0 + b_1(CSC\text{-}Med = 1) + b_2(CSC\text{-}Hi = 0)] \\ &\quad - [b_0 + b_1(CSC\text{-}Med = 0) + b_2(CSC\text{-}Hi = 0)] \\ &= b_1 = -0.0369891 \end{aligned}$$

Just as for the dichotomous case, we may use the cell entries to estimate the standard error of the coefficients directly. For example, the standard error for the logistic regression coefficient b_1 for *CSC-Med* is estimated as follows:

$$\hat{SE}(b_1) = \sqrt{\frac{1}{131} + \frac{1}{1664} + \frac{1}{214} + \frac{1}{1057}} = 0.117701$$

Also similar to the dichotomous case, we may calculate $100(1 - \alpha)\%$ confidence intervals for the odds ratios, for the ith predictor, as follows:

$$\exp\left[b_i \pm z \cdot \hat{SE}(b_i)\right]$$

For example, a 95% confidence interval for the odds ratio between *CSC-Hi* and *CSC-Low* is given by:

$$\begin{aligned} \exp\left[b_2 \pm z \cdot \hat{SE}(b_2)\right] &= \exp\left[2.11844 \pm (1.96)(0.142380)\right] \\ &= (e^{1.8394}, \ e^{2.3975}) \\ &= (6.29, \ 11.0) \end{aligned}$$

as reported in Table 4.7. We are 95% confident that the odds ratio for churning for customers with high customer service calls compared to customers with low customer service calls lies between 6.29 and 11.0. Since the interval does not include $e^0 = 1$, the relationship is significant with 95% confidence.

However, consider the 95% confidence interval for the odds ratio between *CSC-Med* and *CSC-Low*:

$$\exp\left[b_1 \pm z \cdot \hat{SE}(b_1)\right] = \exp\left[-0.0369891 \pm (1.96)(0.117701)\right]$$
$$= (e^{-0.2677}, \ e^{0.1937})$$
$$= (0.77, \ 1.21)$$

as reported in Table 4.7. We are 95% confident that the odds ratio for churning for customers with medium customer service calls compared to customers with low customer service calls lies between 0.77 and 1.21. Since this interval does include $e^0 = 1$, the relationship is not significant with 95% confidence. Depending on other modeling factors, the analyst may consider collapsing *CSC-Med* and *CSC-Low* into a single category.

Interpreting a Model for a Continuous Predictor

Our first example of predicting the presence of disease based on age was an instance of using a continuous predictor in logistic regression. Here we present another example, based on the *churn* data set [4]. Suppose that we are interested in predicting churn based on a single continuous variable, *day minutes*. We first examine an individual value plot of the day minute usage among churners and nonchurners, provided in Figure 4.2. The plot seems to indicate that churners have slightly higher mean day minute usage than nonchurners, meaning that heavier usage may be a predictor of churn. We verify this using the descriptive statistics given in Table 4.8. The mean and

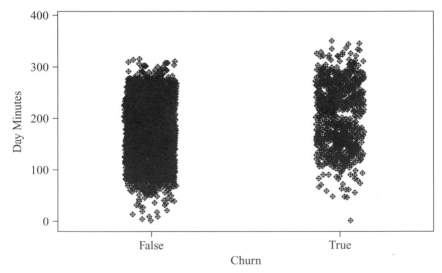

Figure 4.2   Churners have slightly higher mean *day minutes* usage.

TABLE 4.8   Descriptive Statistics for *Day Minutes* by *Churn*

Churn	N	Mean	St. Dev.	Min.	Q_1	Median	Q_3	Max.
False	2850	175.18	50.18	0.00	142.75	177.20	210.30	315.60
True	483	206.91	69.00	0.00	153.10	217.60	266.00	350.80

five-number-summary for the *churn = true* customers indicates higher day minute usage than for the *churn = false* customers, supporting the observation from Figure 4.2.

Is this difference significant? A two-sample *t*-test is carried out, the null hypothesis being that there is no difference in true mean day minute usage between churners and nonchurners. The results are shown in Table 4.9. The resulting *t*-statistic is −9.68, with a *p*-value rounding to zero, representing strong significance. That is, the null hypothesis that there is no difference in true mean day minute usage between churners and nonchurners is strongly rejected.

A word of caution is in order here about carrying out inference in data mining problems, or indeed in any problem where the sample size is very large. Most statistical tests become very sensitive at very large sample sizes, rejecting the null hypothesis for tiny effects. The analyst needs to understand that just because the effect is found to be statistically significant because of the huge sample size, it doesn't necessarily follow that the effect is of practical significance. The analyst should keep in mind the constraints and desiderata of the business or research problem, seek confluence of results from a variety of models, and always retain a clear eye for the interpretability of the model and the applicability of the model to the original problem.

Note that the *t*-test does not give us an idea of how an increase in *day minutes* affects the odds that a customer will churn. Neither does the *t*-test provide a method for finding the probability that a particular customer will churn, based on the customer's day minutes usage. To learn this, we must turn to logistic regression, which we now carry out, with the results given in Table 4.10.

First, we verify the relationship between the odds ratio for *day minutes* and its coefficient. $\hat{OR} = e^{b_1} = e^{0.0112717} = 1.011335 \cong 1.01$, as shown in Table 4.10. We discuss interpreting this value a bit later. In this example we have $b_0 = -3.92929$ and $b_1 = 0.0112717$. Thus, the probability of churning $\pi(x) = e^{\beta_0 + \beta_1 x}/(1 + e^{\beta_0 + \beta_1 x})$ for

TABLE 4.9   Results of a Two-Sample *t*-Test for *Day Minutes* by *Churn*

```
Two-sample T for Day Mins

Churn     N   Mean   StDev   SE Mean
False  2850  175.2    50.2      0.94
True    483  206.9    69.0       3.1

Difference = mu (False) - mu (True)
Estimate for difference: -31.7383
95% CI for difference:   (-38.1752, -25.3015)
T-Test of difference = 0 (vs not =): T-Value = -9.68
                               P-value = 0.000 DF = 571
```

TABLE 4.10 **Results of Logistic Regression of** *Churn* **on** *Day Minutes*

```
Logistic Regression Table


                                                    Odds      95% CI
Predictor        Coef     SE Coef      Z       P    Ratio  Lower  Upper
Constant      -3.92929   0.202822  -19.37  0.000
Day Mins      0.0112717  0.0009750   11.56  0.000   1.01   1.01   1.01


Log-Likelihood = -1307.129
Test that all slopes are zero: G = 144.035, DF = 1, P-Value = 0.000
```

a customer with a given number of day minutes is estimated as

$$\hat{\pi}(x) = \frac{e^{\hat{g}(x)}}{1 + e^{\hat{g}(x)}} = \frac{e^{-3.92929 + 0.0112717(day\,mins)}}{1 + e^{-3.92929 + 0.0112717(day\,mins)}}$$

with the estimated logit

$$\hat{g}(x) = -3.92929 + 0.0112717(day\,mins)$$

For a customer with 100 day minutes, we can estimate his or her probability of churning:

$$\hat{g}(x) = -3.92929 + 0.0112717(100) = -2.80212$$

and

$$\hat{\pi}(x) = \frac{e^{\hat{g}(x)}}{1 + e^{\hat{g}(x)}} = \frac{e^{-2.80212}}{1 + e^{-2.80212}} = 0.0572$$

Thus, the estimated probability that a customer with 100 day minutes will churn is less than 6%. This is less than the overall proportion of churners in the data set, 14.5%, indicating that low day minutes somehow protects against churn. However, for a customer with 300 day minutes, we have

$$\hat{g}(x) = -3.92929 + 0.0112717(300) = -0.54778$$

and

$$\hat{\pi}(x) = \frac{e^{\hat{g}(x)}}{1 + e^{\hat{g}(x)}} = \frac{e^{-0.54778}}{1 + e^{-0.54778}} = 0.3664$$

The estimated probability that a customer with 300 day minutes will churn is over 36%, which is more than twice the overall proportion of churners in the data set, indicating that heavy-use customers have a higher propensity to churn.

The deviance difference G for this example is given by

$$G = \text{deviance (model without predictor)} - \text{deviance (model with predictor)}$$

$$= -2\ln\frac{\text{likelihood without predictor}}{\text{likelihood with predictor}}$$

$$= 2\left\{\sum_{i=1}^{n}[y_i \ln[\hat{\pi}_i] + (1 - y_i)\ln[1 - \hat{\pi}_i]] - [n_1 \ln(n_1) + n_0 \ln(n_0) - n \ln(n)]\right\}$$

$$= 2\{-1307.129 - [483 \ln(483) + 2850 \ln(2850) - 3333 \ln(3333)]\} = 144.035$$

as indicated in Table 4.10. The p-value for the chi-square test for G, under the assumption that the null hypothesis is true ($\beta_1 = 0$), is given by $P(\chi_1^2) > G_{observed} = P(\chi_1^2) > 144.035 \cong 0.000$, as shown in Table 4.10. Thus, the logistic regression concludes that there is strong evidence that *day minutes* is useful in predicting *churn*.

Applying the Wald test for the significance of the *day minutes* parameter, we have $b_1 = 0.0112717$ and $SE(b_1) = 0.0009750$, giving us

$$Z_{Wald} = \frac{0.0112717}{0.0009750} = 11.56$$

as shown in Table 4.10. The associated p-value of $P(|z| > 11.56) \cong 0.000$, using $\alpha = 0.05$, indicates strong evidence for the usefulness of the *day minutes* variable for predicting churn.

Examining Table 4.10, note that the coefficient for *day minutes* is equal to the natural log of its odds ratio:

$$b_{CSC\text{-}Med} = \ln(1.01) \approx \ln(1.011335) = 0.0112717$$
$$b_{day\,mins} = \ln(1.01) \approx \ln(1.011335) = 0.0112717$$

Also, this coefficient may be derived, similar to equation (4.4), as follows:

$$\begin{aligned} \ln\left[OR\,(day\,minutes)\right] = \hat{g}(x+1) - \hat{g}(x) &= [b_0 + b_1(x+1)] \\ &\quad - [b_0 + b_1(x)] \\ &= b_1 = 0.0112717 \end{aligned} \tag{4.5}$$

This derivation provides us with the interpretation of the value for b_1. That is, b_1 *represents the estimated change in the log odds ratio for a unit increase in the predictor.* In this example, $b_1 = 0.0112717$, which means that for every additional day minute that the customer uses, the log odds ratio for churning increases by 0.0112717.

The value for the odds ratio we found above, $\widehat{OR} = e^{b_1} = e^{0.0112717} = 1.011335 \cong 1.01$, may be interpreted as the odds of a customer with $x + 1$ minutes churning compared to a customer with x minutes churning. For example, a customer with 201 minutes is about 1.01 times as likely to churn as a customer with 200 minutes. This unit-increase interpretation may be of limited usefulness, since the analyst may prefer to interpret the results using a different scale, such as 10 minutes or 60 minutes, or even (conceivably) 1 second. We therefore generalize the interpretation of the logistic regression coefficient as follows:

INTERPRETING THE LOGISTIC REGRESSION COEFFICIENT FOR A CONTINUOUS PREDICTOR

For a constant c, the quantity cb_1 represents the estimated change in the log odds ratio, for an increase of c units in the predictor.

This result can be seen to follow from the substitution of $\hat{g}(x + c) - \hat{g}(x)$ for $\hat{g}(x + 1) - \hat{g}(x)$ in equation (4.5):

$$\begin{aligned} \hat{g}(x+c) - \hat{g}(x) &= [b_0 + b_1(x+c)] - [b_0 + b_1(x)] \\ &= cb_1 \end{aligned}$$

For example, let $c = 60$, so that we are interested in the change in the log odds ratio for an increase in 60 day minutes in cell phone usage. This increase would be estimated as $cb_1 = 60(0.0112717) = 0.676302$. Consider a customer A, who had 60 more day minutes than customer B. Then we would estimate the odds ratio for customer A to churn compared to customer B to be $e^{0.676302} = 1.97$. That is, an increase of 60 day minutes nearly doubles the odds that a customer will churn.

Similar to the categorical predictor case, we may calculate $100(1 - \alpha)\%$ confidence intervals for the odds ratios as follows:

$$\exp\left[b_i \pm z \cdot \hat{SE}(b_i)\right]$$

For example, a 95% confidence interval for the odds ratio for *day minutes* is given by

$$\begin{aligned}
\exp\left[b_1 \pm z \cdot \hat{SE}(b_1)\right] &= \exp\left[0.0112717 \pm (1.96)(0.0009750)\right] \\
&= (e^{0.0093607}, e^{0.0131827}) \\
&= (1.0094, 1.0133) \\
&\cong (1.01, 1.01)
\end{aligned}$$

as reported in Table 4.10. We are 95% confident that the odds ratio for churning for customers with 1 additional day minute lies between 1.0094 and 1.0133. Since the interval does not include $e^0 = 1$, the relationship is significant with 95% confidence.

Confidence intervals may also be found for the odds ratio for the ith predictor when there is a change in c units in the predictor, as follows:

$$\exp\left[cb_i \pm zc \cdot \hat{SE}(b_i)\right]$$

For example, earlier we estimated the increase in the odds ratio when the day minutes increased by $c = 60$ minutes to be 1.97. The 99% confidence interval associated with this estimate is given by

$$\begin{aligned}
\exp\left[cb_i \pm zc \cdot \hat{SE}(b_i)\right] &= \exp\left[60(0.0112717) \pm 2.576\,(60)(0.0009750)\right] \\
&= \exp\left[0.6763 \pm 0.1507\right] \\
&= (1.69, 2.29)
\end{aligned}$$

So we are 99% confident that an increase of 60 day minutes will increase the odds ratio of churning by a factor between 1.69 and 2.29.

ASSUMPTION OF LINEARITY

Now, if the logit is not linear in the continuous variables, there may be problems with the application of estimates and confidence intervals for the odds ratio. The reason is that the estimated odds ratio is constant across the range of the predictor. For example, the estimated odds ratio of 1.01 is the same for every unit increase of *day minutes*, whether it is the 23rd minute or the 323rd minute. The same is true of the estimated odds ratio for the increase of 60 day minutes; the estimated odds ratio of 1.97 is the same whether we are referring to the 0–60-minute time frame or the 55–115-minute time frame, and so on.

Such an assumption of constant odds ratio is not always warranted. For example, suppose that we performed a logistic regression of *churn* on *customer service*

TABLE 4.11   Questionable Results of Logistic Regression of *Churn* on *Customer Service Calls*

```
Logistic Regression Table


                                                 Odds    95% CI
Predictor            Coef    SE Coef        Z       P Ratio Lower Upper
Constant         -2.49016  0.0863180  -28.85  0.000
CustServ Calls    0.396169  0.0345617   11.46  0.000  1.49  1.39  1.59


Log-Likelihood = -1313.618
Test that all slopes are zero: G = 131.058, DF = 1, P-Value = 0.000
```

calls, which takes the values 0 to 9. The results are shown in Table 4.11. The estimated odds ratio of 1.49 indicates that the odds ratio for churning increases by this amount for every additional customer service call that is made. We would therefore expect that a plot of *customer service calls* with a *churn* overlay would form a fairly regular steplike pattern. However, consider Figure 4.3, which shows a normalized histogram of *customer service calls* with a *churn* overlay. (The normalization makes each rectangle the same length, thereby increasing the contrast at the expense of information about bin size.) Darker portions indicate the proportion of customers who churn.

Note that we do not encounter a gradual step-down pattern as we proceed left to right. Instead, there is a single rather dramatic discontinuity at four customer service calls. This is the pattern we uncovered earlier when we performed binning on *customer service calls* and found that those with three or fewer calls had a much different propensity to churn than did customers with four or more. Specifically, the

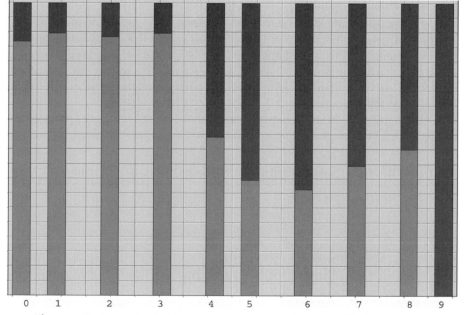

Figure 4.3   Normalized histogram of *customer service calls* with *churn* overlay.

TABLE 4.12 *Customer Service Calls* by *Churn*, with Estimated Odds Ratios

	Customer Service Calls									
	0	1	2	3	4	5	6	7	8	9
Churn = false	605	1059	672	385	90	26	8	4	1	0
Churn = true	92	122	87	44	76	40	14	5	1	2
Odds ratio		0.76	1.12	0.88	7.39	1.82	1.14	0.71	0.8	Undefined

results in Table 4.11 assert that, for example, moving from zero to one customer service calls increases the odds ratio by a factor of 1.49. This is not the case, as fewer customers with one call churn than do those with zero calls.

For example, Table 4.12 shows the counts of customers churning and not churning for the 10 values of *customer service calls*, along with the estimated odds ratio for the one additional customer service call. For example, the estimated odds ratio for moving from zero to one call is 0.76, which means that churning is less likely for those making one call than it is for those making none. The discontinuity at the fourth call is represented by the odds ratio of 7.39, meaning that a customer making his or her fourth call is more than seven times as likely to churn as a customer who has made three calls.

Note that the odds ratio of 1.49 which results from an inappropriate application of logistic regression is nowhere reflected in the actual data. If the analyst wishes to include *customer service calls* in the analysis (and it should be included), certain accommodations to nonlinearity must be made, such as the use of indicator variables (see the polychotomous example) or the use of higher-order terms (e.g., $x^2, x^3, \ldots$). Note the undefined odds ratio for column 9, which contains a zero cell. We discuss the zero-cell problem below.

For another example of the problem of nonlinearity, we turn to the *adult* data set [6], which was extracted from data provided by the U.S. Census Bureau. The task is to find the set of demographic characteristics that can best predict whether or not a person has an income of over \$50,000 per year. We restrict our attention to the derived variable, *capnet*, which equals the capital gains amount minus the capital losses, expressed in dollars.

The naive application of logistic regression of *income* on *capnet* provides the results shown in Table 4.13. The odds ratio for the *capnet* variable is reported as

TABLE 4.13 Results of Questionable Logistic Regression of Income on *Capnet*

```
Logistic Regression Table

                                                 Odds      95% CI
Predictor        Coef     SE Coef       Z      P  Ratio  Lower  Upper
Constant     -1.32926   0.0159903  -83.13  0.000
capnet       0.0002561  0.0000079   32.58  0.000   1.00   1.00   1.00

Log-Likelihood = -12727.406
Test that all slopes are zero: G = 2062.242, DF = 1, P-Value = 0.000
```

TABLE 4.14 *Income* Level Counts for Categories of *Capnet*

Income	*Capnet* Category							
	Loss		None		Gain < $3000		Gain ≥ $3000	
≤$50,000	574	49.7%	17,635	81.0%	370	100%	437	25.6%
>$50,000	582	50.3%	4,133	19.0%	0	0%	1269	74.4%
Total	1156		21,768		370		1706	

1.00, with both endpoints of the confidence interval also reported as 1.00. Do we conclude from this that *capnet* is not significant? If so, how do we resolve the apparent contradiction with the strongly significant z-test p-value of approximately zero?

Actually, of course, there is no contradiction. The problem lies in the fact that the odds ratio results are reported only to two decimal places. More detailed 95% confidence intervals are provided here:

$$\text{CI}(\text{OR}_{\text{capnet}}) = \exp[b_1 \pm z \cdot \hat{\text{SE}}(b_1)]$$
$$= \exp[0.0002561 \pm (1.96)(0.0000079)]$$
$$= (e^{0.0002406}, e^{0.0002716})$$
$$= (1.000241, 1.000272)$$

Thus, the 95% confidence interval for the *capnet* variable does not include the null value of $e^0 = 1$, indicating that this variable is in fact significant. Why is such precision needed? Because *capnet* is measured in dollars. One additional dollar in capital gains, for example, would presumably not increase the probability of a high income very dramatically—hence, the tiny but significant odds ratio.

However, nearly 87% of the records have zero *capnet* (neither capital gains nor capital losses). What effect would this have on the linearity assumption? Table 4.14 provides the income-level counts for a possible categorization of the *capnet* variable. Note that high income is associated with either *capnet* loss or *capnet* gain ≥ $3000, while low income is associated with *capnet* none or *capnet* gain < $3000. Such relationships are incompatible with the assumption of linearity. We would therefore like to rerun the logistic regression analysis, this time using the *capnet* categorization shown in Table 4.14.

ZERO-CELL PROBLEM

Unfortunately, we are now faced with a new problem, the presence of zero-count cells in the cross-classification table. There are no records of people in the data set with *income* greater than $50,000 and *capnet* gain less than $3000. Zero cells play havoc with the logistic regression solution, causing instability in the analysis and leading to possibly unreliable results. Rather than omitting the *gain* < $3000 category, we may try to collapse the categories or redefine them somehow to find some records for the zero cell. In this example we try to redefine the class limits for the two *capnet* gains categories, which will have the added benefit of finding a better balance of records

TABLE 4.15 *Income* Level Counts for Categories of *Capnet*: New Categorization

Income	Loss		None		Gain < $5000		Gain ≥ $5000	
≤ $50,000	574	49.7%	17,635	81.0%	685	83.0%	122	9.8%
> $50,000	582	50.3%	4,133	19.0%	140	17.0%	1129	90.2%
Total	1156		21,768		825		1251	

in these categories. The new class boundaries and cross-classification are shown in Table 4.15. The logistic regression of *income* on the newly categorized *capnet* has results that are shown in Table 4.16.

The reference category is zero *capnet*. The category gain < $5000 is not significant, since its proportions of high and low income are quite similar to those of zero *capnet*, as shown in Table 4.15. The categories of loss and gain ≥ $5000 are both significant, but at different orders of magnitude. People with a capital loss are 4.33 times as likely to have high income than are zero *capnet* persons, while people showing a *capnet* gain of at least $5000 are nearly 40 times more likely to have high income than is the reference category. The variability among these results reinforces the assertion that the relationship between *income* and *capnet* is nonlinear and that naive insertion of the *capnet* variable into a logistic regression would be faulty.

For a person showing a capnet loss, we can estimate his or her probability of having an income above $50,000. First the logit:

$$\hat{g}(x) = -1.45088 + 1.46472(1) = 0.01384$$

with probability

$$\hat{\pi}(x) = \frac{e^{\hat{g}(x)}}{1 + e^{\hat{g}(x)}} = \frac{e^{0.01384}}{1 + e^{0.01384}} = 0.5035$$

So the probability that a person with a capnet loss has an income above $50,000 is about 50 : 50. Also, we can estimate the probability that a person showing a capnet

TABLE 4.16 Results of Logistic Regression of *Income* on Categorized *Capnet*

```
Logistic Regression Table

                                               Odds     95% CI
Predictor           Coef    SE Coef      Z     P Ratio Lower Upper
Constant         -1.45088 0.0172818 -83.95 0.000
capnet-cat
  gain < $5,000  -0.136894 0.0943471  -1.45 0.147  0.87  0.72  1.05
  gain >= $5,000  3.67595 0.0968562  37.95 0.000 39.49 32.66 47.74
  loss            1.46472 0.0613110  23.89 0.000  4.33  3.84  4.88

Log-Likelihood = -12156.651
Test that all slopes are zero: G = 3203.753, DF = 3, P-Value = 0.000
```

gain of at least $5000 will have an income above $50,000. The logit is

$$\hat{g}(x) = -1.45088 + 3.67595(1) = 2.22507$$

and the probability is

$$\hat{\pi}(x) = \frac{e^{\hat{g}(x)}}{1 + e^{\hat{g}(x)}} = \frac{e^{2.22507}}{1 + e^{2.22507}} = 0.9025$$

Note that these probabilities are the same as could be found using the cell counts in Table 4.15; similarly for a person with a capnet gain of under $5000. However, this category was found not to be significant. What, then, should be our estimate of the probability that a person with a small capnet gain will have high income?

Should we use the estimate provided by the cell counts and the logistic regression (probability = 17%), even though it was found not to be significant? The answer is no, not for formal estimation. To use nonsignificant variables for estimation increases the chances that the estimation will not be generalizable. That is, the generalizability (and hence, usefulness) of the estimation will be reduced.

Now, under certain circumstances, such as a cross-validated (see our discussion on validating the logistic regression, below) analysis, where all subsamples concur that the variable is nearly significant, the analyst may annotate the estimation with a note that there may be some evidence for using this variable in the estimation. However, in general, retain for estimation and prediction purposes only those variables that are significant. Thus, in this case, we would estimate the probability that a person with a small capnet gain will have high income as follows:

$$\hat{g}(x) = -1.45088$$

with probability:

$$\hat{\pi}(x) = \frac{e^{\hat{g}(x)}}{1 + e^{\hat{g}(x)}} = \frac{e^{-1.45088}}{1 + e^{-1.45088}} = 0.1899$$

which is the same as the probability that a person with zero capnet will have a high income.

MULTIPLE LOGISTIC REGRESSION

Thus far, we have examined logistic regression using only one variable at a time. However, very few data mining data sets are restricted to one variable! We therefore turn to multiple logistic regression, in which more than one predictor variable is used to classify the binary response variable. Returning to the *churn* data set [4], we examine whether a relationship exists between *churn* and the following set of predictors.

- *International Plan*, a flag variable
- *VoiceMail Plan*, a flag variable
- *CSC-Hi*, a flag variable indicating whether or not a customer had a high (≥ 4) level of customer services calls
- *Account length*, continuous

TABLE 4.17 **Results of Multiple Logistic Regression of *Churn* on Several Variables**

```
Logistic Regression Table


                                                    Odds      95% CI
Predictor              Coef    SE Coef      Z      P Ratio Lower Upper
Constant            -8.15980  0.536092 -15.22 0.000
Account Length  0.0008006 0.0014408   0.56 0.578  1.00  1.00  1.00
Day Mins        0.0134755 0.0011192  12.04 0.000  1.01  1.01  1.02
Eve Mins        0.0073029 0.0011695   6.24 0.000  1.01  1.01  1.01
Night Mins      0.0042378 0.0011474   3.69 0.000  1.00  1.00  1.01
Intl Mins       0.0853508 0.0210217   4.06 0.000  1.09  1.05  1.13
Int-l Plan
  yes            2.03287   0.146894  13.84 0.000  7.64  5.73 10.18
VMail Plan
  yes           -1.04435   0.150087  -6.96 0.000  0.35  0.26  0.47
CSC-Hi
  1              2.67683   0.159224  16.81 0.000 14.54 10.64 19.86


Log-Likelihood = -1036.038
Test that all slopes are zero: G = 686.218, DF = 8, P-Value = 0.000
```

- *Day minutes*, continuous
- *Evening minutes*, continuous
- *Night minutes*, continuous
- *International minutes*, continuous

The results are provided in Table 4.17. First, note that the overall regression is significant, as shown by the p-value of approximately zero for the G-statistic. Therefore, the overall model is useful for classifying *churn*. However, not all variables contained in the model need necessarily be useful. Examine the p-values for the (Wald) z-statistics for each of the predictors. All p-values are small except one, indicating that there is evidence that each predictor belongs in the model, except *account length*, the standardized customer account length. The Wald z-statistic for account length is 0.56, with a large p-value of 0.578, indicating that this variable is not useful for classifying *churn*. Further, the 95% confidence interval for the odds ratio includes 1.0, reinforcing the conclusion that *account length* does not belong in the model. Therefore, we now omit *account length* from the model and proceed to run the logistic regression again with the remaining variables. The results are shown in Table 4.18.

Comparing Table 4.18 to Table 4.17, we see that the omission of *account length* has barely affected the remaining analysis. All remaining variables are considered significant and retained in the model. The positive coefficients indicate predictors for which an increase in the value of the predictor is associated with an increase in the probability of churning. Similarly, negative coefficients indicate predictors associated with reducing the probability of churn. Unit increases for each of the *minutes* variables are associated with an increase in the probability of churn, as well as membership in the International Plan and customers with high levels of customer service calls. Only membership in the VoiceMail Plan reduces the probability of churn.

TABLE 4.18   Results of Multiple Logistic Regression After Omitting *Account Length*

```
Logistic Regression Table
```

					Odds	95% CI	
Predictor	Coef	SE Coef	Z	P	Ratio	Lower	Upper
Constant	-8.07374	0.512446	-15.76	0.000			
Day Mins	0.0134735	0.0011190	12.04	0.000	1.01	1.01	1.02
Eve Mins	0.0072939	0.0011694	6.24	0.000	1.01	1.01	1.01
Night Mins	0.0042223	0.0011470	3.68	0.000	1.00	1.00	1.01
Intl Mins	0.0853509	0.0210212	4.06	0.000	1.09	1.05	1.13
Int-l Plan							
yes	2.03548	0.146822	13.86	0.000	7.66	5.74	10.21
VMail Plan							
yes	-1.04356	0.150064	-6.95	0.000	0.35	0.26	0.47
CSC-Hi							
1	2.67697	0.159151	16.82	0.000	14.54	10.64	19.86

```
Log-Likelihood =-1036.192
Test that all slopes are zero: G = 685.910, DF = 7, P-Value = 0.000
```

Table 4.18 provides the estimated logit:

$$\hat{g}(x) = -8.07374 + 0.0134735(DayMins) + 0.0072939(EveMins)$$
$$+ 0.0042223(NightMins) + 0.0853509(IntlMins)$$
$$+ 2.03548(Int\text{-}l\ Plan = Yes) - 1.04356(VMail\ Plan = Yes)$$
$$+ 2.67697(CSC\text{-}Hi = 1)$$

where *Intl Plan = Yes*, *VMail Plan = Yes*, and *CSC-Hi = 1* represent indicator (dummy) variables. Then, using

$$\hat{\pi}(x) = \frac{e^{\hat{g}(x)}}{1 + e^{\hat{g}(x)}}$$

we may estimate the probability that a particular customer will churn given various values for the predictor variables. We estimate the probability of churn for the following customers:

1. *A low-usage customer belonging to no plans with few calls to customer service.* This customer has 100 minutes for each of day, evening and night minutes, and no international minutes. The logit

$$\hat{g}(x) = -8.07374 + 0.0134735(100) + 0.0072939(100)$$
$$+ 0.0042223(100) + 0.0853509(0)$$
$$+ 2.03548(0) - 1.04356(0) + 2.67697(0)$$
$$= -5.57477$$

The probability that customer 1 will churn is therefore

$$\hat{\pi}(x) = \frac{e^{\hat{g}(x)}}{1 + e^{\hat{g}(x)}} = \frac{e^{-5.57477}}{1 + e^{-5.57477}} = 0.003778$$

That is, a customer with low usage, belonging to no plans, and making few customer service calls has less than a 1% chance of churning.

2. *A moderate-usage customer belonging to no plans with few calls to customer service.* This customer has 180 day minutes, 200 evening and night minutes, and 10 international minutes, each number near the average for the category. Here is the logit:

$$\hat{g}(x) = -8.07374 + 0.0134735(180) + 0.0072939(200)$$
$$+0.0042223(200) + 0.0853509(10)$$
$$+2.03548(0) - 1.04356(0) + 2.67697(0)$$
$$= -2.491761$$

The probability that customer 2 will churn is

$$\hat{\pi}(x) = \frac{e^{\hat{g}(x)}}{1 + e^{\hat{g}(x)}} = \frac{e^{-2.491761}}{1 + e^{-2.491761}} = 0.076435$$

A customer with moderate usage, belonging to no plans, and making few customer service calls still has less than an 8% probability of churning.

3. *A high-usage customer belonging to the International Plan but not the VoiceMail Plan, with many calls to customer service.* This customer has 300 day, evening, and night minutes, and 20 international minutes. The logit is

$$\hat{g}(x) = -8.07374 + 0.0134735(300) + 0.0072939(300)$$
$$+0.0042223(300) + 0.0853509(20)$$
$$+2.03548(1) - 1.04356(0) + 2.67697(1)$$
$$= 5.842638$$

Thus, the probability that customer 3 will churn is

$$\hat{\pi}(x) = \frac{e^{\hat{g}(x)}}{1 + e^{\hat{g}(x)}} = \frac{e^{5.842638}}{1 + e^{5.842638}} = 0.997107$$

High-usage customers, belonging to the International Plan but not the Voice-Mail Plan, with many calls to customer service, have an astonishing 99.71% probability of churning. The company needs to deploy interventions for these types of customers as soon as possible, to avoid the loss of these customers to other carriers.

4. *A high-usage customer belonging to the VoiceMail Plan but not the International Plan, with few calls to customer service.* This customer also has 300 day, evening, and night minutes, and 20 international minutes. The logit is

$$\hat{g}(x) = -8.07374 + 0.0134735(300) + 0.0072939(300)$$
$$+ 0.0042223(300) + 0.0853509(20)$$
$$+ 2.03548(0) - 1.04356(1) + 2.67697(0)$$
$$= 0.086628$$

Hence, the probability that customer 4 will churn is

$$\hat{\pi}(x) = \frac{e^{\hat{g}(x)}}{1 + e^{\hat{g}(x)}} = \frac{e^{0.086628}}{1 + e^{0.086628}} = 0.5216$$

This type of customer has over a 50% probability of churning, which is more than three times the 14.5% overall churn rate.

For data that are missing one or more indicator variable values, it would not be appropriate simply to ignore these missing variables when making an estimation. For example, suppose that for customer 4, we had no information regarding membership in the VoiceMail Plan. If we then ignored the VoiceMail Plan variable when forming the estimate, we would get the following logit:

$$\hat{g}(x) = -8.07374 + 0.0134735(300) + 0.0072939(300)$$
$$+0.0042223(300) + 0.0853509(20)$$
$$+2.03548(0) + 2.67697(0)$$
$$= 1.130188$$

Note that this is the same value for $\hat{g}(x)$ that we would obtain for a customer who was known not to be a member of the VoiceMail plan. To estimate the probability of a customer whose VoiceMail plan membership was unknown using this logit would be incorrect. This logit would, instead, provide the probability of a customer who did not have the VoiceMail plan but was otherwise similar to customer 4, as follows:

$$\hat{\pi}(x) = \frac{e^{\hat{g}(x)}}{1 + e^{\hat{g}(x)}} = \frac{e^{1.130188}}{1 + e^{1.130188}} = 0.7559$$

Such a customer would have a churn probability of about 76%.

INTRODUCING HIGHER-ORDER TERMS TO HANDLE NONLINEARITY

We illustrate how to check the assumption of linearity in multiple logistic regression by returning to the *adult* data set [6]. For this example, we shall use only the following variables:

- *Age*
- *Education-num*
- *Hours-per-week*
- *Capnet* (= capital gain – capital loss)
- *Marital-status*
- *Sex*
- *Income* (the target variable, binary, either ≤$50,000 or >$50,000)

The three "married" categories in *marital-status* in the raw data were collapsed into a single "married" category. A normalized histogram of *age* with an overlay

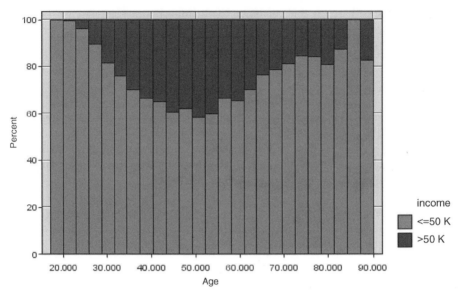

Figure 4.4   Normalized histogram of *age* with *income* overlay shows a quadratic relationship.

of the target variable *income* is shown in Figure 4.4. The darker bands indicate the proportion of high incomes. Clearly, this proportion increases until about age 52, after which it begins to drop again. This behavior is nonlinear and should not be naively modeled as linear in the logistic regression. Suppose, for example, that we went ahead and performed a logistic regression of *income* on the singleton predictor *age*. The results are shown in Table 4.19.

Table 4.19 shows that the predictor *age* is significant, with an estimated odds ratio of 1.04. Recall that the interpretation of this odds ratio is as follows: that the odds of having high income for someone of age $x + 1$ is 1.04 times higher than for someone of age x. Now consider this interpretation in light of Figure 4.4. The odds ratio of 1.04 is clearly inappropriate for the subset of subjects older than 50 or so. This is because the logistic regression assumes linearity, whereas the actual relationship is quadratic (nonlinear.) There are a couple of approaches we could take to alleviate this problem. First, we could use indicator variables as we did earlier. Here, we use an indicator variable *age 33–65*, where all records falling in this range are coded as 1 and all other records are coded as 0. This coding was used because the higher incomes were found to fall within this range in the histogram. The resulting logistic regression is shown in Table 4.20. The odds ratio is 5.01, indicating that persons between 33 and

TABLE 4.19   Results of a Naive Application of Logistic Regression of *Income* on *Age*

```
Logistic Regression Table

                                                Odds      95% CI
Predictor       Coef     SE Coef       Z       P  Ratio  Lower  Upper
Constant     -2.72401  0.0486021  -56.05  0.000
age           0.0388221  0.0010994   35.31  0.000   1.04   1.04   1.04
```

TABLE 4.20 Results of Logistic Regression of *Income* on *Age 33–65*

```
Logistic Regression Table

                                              Odds      95% CI
Predictor        Coef     SE Coef       Z      P  Ratio Lower  Upper
Constant      -2.26542  0.0336811  -67.26  0.000
age 33 - 65    1.61103  0.0379170   42.49  0.000  5.01  4.65   5.39
```

65 years of age are about five times more likely to have high income than persons outside this age range.

An alternative modeling method would be to model the quadratic behavior of the relationship directly, by introducing an age^2 (age-squared) variable. The logistic regression results are shown in Table 4.21. The odds ratio for the age variable has increased from the value of 1.04 determined previously, to 1.42. For the age^2 term, the odds ratio and the endpoints of the confidence interval are reported as 1.00, but this is only due to rounding. We use the fact that $OR = e^{b_2}$ to find the more accurate estimate of the odds ratio as $OR = e^{b_2} = e^{-0.0034504} = 0.99656$. Also, the 95% confidence interval is given by

$$CI(OR) = \exp\left[b_2 \pm z \cdot \hat{SE}(b_2) \right]$$
$$= \exp\left[-0.0034504 \pm (1.96)(0.0000992) \right]$$
$$= (e^{-0.003645}, e^{-0.003256})$$
$$= (0.9964, 0.9967)$$

which concurs with the p-value regarding the significance of the term.

The age^2 term acts as a kind of penalty function, reducing the probability of high income for records with high age. We examine the behavior of the age and age^2 terms working together by estimating the probability that each of the following people will have incomes greater than \$50,000: (1) a 30-year-old person, (2) a 50-year-old person, and (3) a 70-year-old person. We have the estimated logit:

$$\hat{g}(x) = -9.08016 + 0.347807(age) - 0.0034504(age^2)$$

which has the following values for our three persons:

(1) $\hat{g}(x) = -9.08016 + 0.347807(age) - 0.0034504(age^2) = -1.75131$
(2) $\hat{g}(x) = -9.08016 + 0.347807(age) - 0.0034504(age^2) = -0.31581$
(3) $\hat{g}(x) = -9.08016 + 0.347807(age) - 0.0034504(age^2) = -1.64063$

TABLE 4.21 Results of Introducing a Quadratic Term *Age²* to Model the Nonlinearity of *Age*

```
Logistic Regression Table

                                                  Odds      95% CI
Predictor          Coef      SE Coef       Z      P  Ratio Lower  Upper
Constant        -9.08016   0.194526  -46.68  0.000
age              0.347807  0.0089465   38.88  0.000  1.42  1.39   1.44
age-squared     -0.0034504 0.0000992  -34.77  0.000  1.00  1.00   1.00
```

Note that the logit is greatest for the 50-year-old, which models the behavior seen in Figure 4.4. Then the estimated probability of having an income greater than $50,000 is then found for our three people:

$$\hat{\pi}(x) = \frac{e^{\hat{g}(x)}}{1 + e^{\hat{g}(x)}}$$

$$\begin{cases} (1) = \dfrac{e^{-1.75131}}{1 + e^{-1.75131}} = 0.1479 \\[2mm] (2) = \dfrac{e^{-0.31581}}{1 + e^{-0.31581}} = 0.4217 \\[2mm] (3) = \dfrac{e^{-1.64063}}{1 + e^{-1.64063}} = 0.1624 \end{cases}$$

The probabilities that the 30-year-old, 50-year-old, and 70-year-old have an income greater than $50,000 are 14.79%, 42.17%, and 16.24%, respectively. This is compared to the overall proportion of the 25,000 records in the training set that have income greater than $50,000, which is 5984/25,000 = 23.94%.

One benefit of using the quadratic term (together with the original *age* variable) rather than the indicator variable is that the quadratic term is continuous and can presumably provide tighter estimates for a variety of ages. For example, the indicator variable *age 33–65* categorizes all records into two classes, so that a 20-year-old is binned together with a 32-year-old, and the model (all other factors held constant) generates the same probability of high income for the 20-year-old as for the 32-year-old. The quadratic term, however, will provide a higher probability of high income for the 32-year-old than for the 20-year-old (see the exercises).

Next, we turn to the *education-num* variable, which indicates the number of years of education the subject has had. The relationship between *income* and *education-num* is shown in Figure 4.5. The pattern shown in Figure 4.5 is also quadratic, although perhaps not as manifestly so as in Figure 4.4. As education increases, the proportion of subjects having high income also increases, but not at a linear rate. Until grade 8 or so, the proportion increases slowly, and then more quickly as education level increases. Therefore, modeling the relationship between income and education level as strictly linear would be an error; we again need to introduce a quadratic term.

Note that for *age*, the coefficient of the quadratic term age^2 was negative, representing a downward influence for very high ages. For *education-num*, however, the proportion of high incomes is highest for the highest levels of income, so that we would expect a positive coefficient for the quadratic term $education^2$. The results of a logistic regression run on *education-num* and $education^2$ are shown in Table 4.22. As expected, the coefficient for $education^2$ is positive. However, note that the variable *education-num* is not significant, since it has a large p-value and the confidence interval contains 1.0. We therefore omit *education-num* from the analysis and perform a logistic regression of income on $education^2$ alone, with the results shown in Table 4.23. Here the $education^2$ term is significant, and we have OR $= e^{b_1} = e^{0.0167617} = 1.0169$,

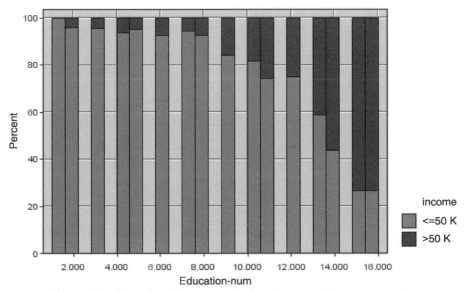

Figure 4.5 Normalized histogram of *education-num* with *income* overlay.

with the 95% confidence interval given by

$$\text{CI(OR)} = \exp\left[b_1 \pm z \cdot \hat{\text{SE}}(b_1)\right]$$
$$= \exp\left[0.0167617 \pm (1.96)(0.0003193)\right]$$
$$= (e^{0.01614},\ e^{0.01739})$$
$$= (1.01627,\quad 1.01754)$$

We estimate the probability that persons with the following years of education will have incomes greater than \$50,000: (1) 12 years of education, and (2) 16 years of education. The estimated logit:

$$\hat{g}(x) = -3.1328 + 0.0167617(education^2)$$

has the following values:

$$(1)\ \hat{g}(x) = -3.1328 + 0.0167617\,(12^2) = -0.719115$$
$$(2)\ \hat{g}(x) = -3.1328 + 0.0167617\,(16^2) = 1.1582$$

TABLE 4.22 **Results of Logistic Regression of *Income* on *Education-Num* and *Education*²**

```
Logistic Regression Table
```

Predictor	Coef	SE Coef	Z	P	Odds Ratio	95% CI Lower	Upper
Constant	-3.10217	0.235336	-13.18	0.000			
education-num	-0.0058715	0.0443558	-0.13	0.895	0.99	0.91	1.08
educ-squared	0.0170305	0.0020557	8.28	0.000	1.02	1.01	1.02

TABLE 4.23 **Results of Logistic Regression of *Income* on *Education*² Alone**

```
Logistic Regression Table
```

Predictor	Coef	SE Coef	Z	P	Odds Ratio	95% CI Lower	Upper
Constant	-3.13280	0.0431422	-72.62	0.000			
educ-squared	0.0167617	0.0003193	52.50	0.000	1.02	1.02	1.02

Then we can find the estimated probability of having an income greater than $50,000 as

$$\hat{\pi}(x) = \frac{e^{\hat{g}(x)}}{1 + e^{\hat{g}(x)}}$$

$$\begin{cases} (1) = \dfrac{e^{-0.719115}}{1 + e^{-0.719115}} = 0.3276 \\[2ex] (2) = \dfrac{e^{1.1582}}{1 + e^{1.1582}} = 0.7610 \end{cases}$$

The probabilities that people with 12 and 16 years of education will have an income greater than $50,000 are 32.76% and 76.10%, respectively. Evidently, for this population, it pays to stay in school.

Finally, we examine the variable *hours-per-week*, which represents the number of hours worked per week for the subject. The normalized histogram is shown in Figure 4.6. In this figure we certainly find nonlinearity. A quadratic term would seem indicated by the records up to 50 hours per week. However, at about 50 hours per week, the pattern changes, so that the overall curvature is that of a backward S-curve. Such a pattern is indicative of the need for a *cubic* term, where the cube of the original variable is introduced. We therefore do so here, introducing *hours*³ and performing

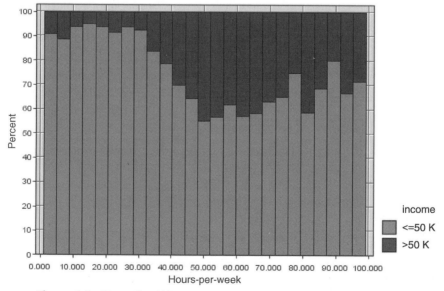

Figure 4.6 Normalized histogram of *hours-per-week* with *income* overlay.

TABLE 4.24 Results of Logistic Regression of *Income* on *Hours-per-Week*, *Hours^2*, and *Hours^3*

```
Logistic Regression Table


                                                 Odds     95% CI
Predictor            Coef    SE Coef      Z      P Ratio Lower Upper
Constant          -3.04582  0.232238  -13.12 0.000
hours-per-week    -0.0226237 0.0155537  -1.45 0.146  0.98  0.95  1.01
hours squared      0.0026616 0.0003438   7.74 0.000  1.00  1.00  1.00
hours cubed       -0.0000244 0.0000024 -10.14 0.000  1.00  1.00  1.00
```

the logistic regression of *income* on *hours-per-week*, *hours^2*, and *hours^3*, with the results shown in Table 4.24. Note that the original variable, *hours-per-week*, is no longer significant. We therefore rerun the analysis, including only *hours^2* and *hours^3*, with the results shown in Table 4.25. The *hours^2* and *hours^3* terms are both significant. Analysis and interpretation of these results are left to the exercises.

Putting all the previous results from this section together, we construct a logistic regression model for predicting *income* based on the following variables:

- *Age*
- *Age^2*
- *Education^2*
- *Hours^2*

- *Hours^3*
- *Capnet-cat*
- *Marital-status*
- *Sex*

The results, provided in Table 4.26, are analyzed and interpreted in the exercises.

VALIDATING THE LOGISTIC REGRESSION MODEL

Hosmer and Lebeshow [1] provide details for assessing the fit of a logistic regression model, including goodness-of-fit statistics and model diagnostics. Here, however, we investigate validation of the logistic regression model through the traditional method of a hold-out sample.

The training data set of 25,000 records was partitioned randomly into two data sets, training set A, of 12,450 records, and training set B, of 12,550 records. Training set A has 2953 records (23.72%) with income greater than $50,000; training set B has

TABLE 4.25 Results of Logistic Regression of *Income* on *Hours^2* and *Hours^3*

```
Logistic Regression Table


                                                Odds     95% CI
Predictor            Coef    SE Coef      Z     P Ratio Lower Upper
Constant          -3.37144  0.0708973  -47.55 0.000
hours squared      0.0021793 0.0000780   27.96 0.000  1.00  1.00  1.00
hours cubed       -0.0000212 0.0000009  -22.64 0.000  1.00  1.00  1.00
```

TABLE 4.26   Results of Multiple Logistic Regression of *Income*

```
Logistic Regression Table
```

					Odds	95% CI	
Predictor	Coef	SE Coef	Z	P	Ratio	Lower	Upper
Constant	-11.5508	0.282276	-40.92	0.000			
age	0.235060	0.0115234	20.40	0.000	1.26	1.24	1.29
age-squared	-0.0023038	0.0001253	-18.38	0.000	1.00	1.00	1.00
educ-squared	0.0163723	0.0004017	40.76	0.000	1.02	1.02	1.02
hours squared	0.0012647	0.0000888	14.25	0.000	1.00	1.00	1.00
hours cubed	-0.0000127	0.0000010	-12.35	0.000	1.00	1.00	1.00
capnet-cat							
gain < $5,000	-0.189060	0.109220	-1.73	0.083	0.83	0.67	1.03
gain >= $5,000	3.46054	0.114327	30.27	0.000	31.83	25.44	39.83
loss	1.15582	0.0793780	14.56	0.000	3.18	2.72	3.71
marital-status							
Married	2.15226	0.0749850	28.70	0.000	8.60	7.43	9.97
Never-married	-0.124760	0.0931762	-1.34	0.181	0.88	0.74	1.06
Separated	-0.0212868	0.175555	-0.12	0.903	0.98	0.69	1.38
Widowed	0.372877	0.169419	2.20	0.028	1.45	1.04	2.02
sex							
Male	0.209341	0.0554578	3.77	0.000	1.23	1.11	1.37

```
Log-Likelihood = -8238.566
Test that all slopes are zero: G = 11039.923, DF = 13, P-Value = 0.000
```

3031 records (24.15%) such records. Therefore, we cannot expect that the parameter estimates and odds ratios for the two data sets will be exactly the same.

Indicator variables are provided for *marital status* and *sex*. The reference categories (where all indicators equal zero) are *divorced* and *female*, respectively. The logistic regression results for training sets A and B are provided in Tables 4.27 and 4.28, respectively. Note that for both data sets, all parameters are significant (as shown by the *Wald-z p*-values) except the *separated* and *widowed* indicator variables for *marital status*. Overall, the coefficient values are fairly close to each other, except those with high variability, such as *male* and *separated*.

The estimated logit for training sets A and B are

$$\hat{g}_A(x) = -9.06305 + 0.0278994(age) + 0.374356(education\text{-}num)$$
$$+ 2.02743(married) - 0.489140(never\text{-}married)$$
$$- 0.369533(separated) - 0.0760889(widowed) + 0.166622(male)$$
$$+ 0.0309548(hours\text{-}per\text{-}week) + 0.0002292(capnet)$$

$$\hat{g}_B(x) = -8.85216 + 0.0224645(age) + 0.368721(education\text{-}num)$$
$$+ 2.02076(married) - 0.587585(never\text{-}married)$$
$$- 0.094394(separated) - 0.181349(widowed) + 0.311218(male)$$
$$+ 0.0316433(hours\text{-}per\text{-}week) + 0.0002455(capnet)$$

TABLE 4.27   Results of Logistic Regression for Training Set A

```
Logistic Regression Table


                                                  Odds    95% CI
Predictor            Coef    SE Coef      Z      P Ratio Lower Upper
Constant          -9.06305  0.232199 -39.03 0.000
age                0.0278994 0.0023420  11.91 0.000  1.03  1.02  1.03
education-num      0.374356  0.0120668  31.02 0.000  1.45  1.42  1.49
marital-status
  Married           2.02743  0.103258   19.63 0.000  7.59  6.20  9.30
  Never-married    -0.489140 0.127005   -3.85 0.000  0.61  0.48  0.79
  Separated        -0.369533 0.278258   -1.33 0.184  0.69  0.40  1.19
  Widowed          -0.0760889 0.233292  -0.33 0.744  0.93  0.59  1.46
sex
  Male              0.166622 0.0757310   2.20 0.028  1.18  1.02  1.37
hours-per-week     0.0309548 0.0023358  13.25 0.000  1.03  1.03  1.04
capnet             0.0002292 0.0000127  17.98 0.000  1.00  1.00  1.00


Log-Likelihood = -4358.063
Test that all slopes are zero: G = 4924.536, DF = 9, P-Value = 0.000
```

For each of these logits, we will estimate the probability that each of the following types of people have incomes over $50,000: (1) a 50-year-old married male with 20 years of education working 40 hours per week with a capnet of $500, (2) a 50-year-old married male with 16 years of education working 40 hours per week with no capital gains or losses, and (3) a 35-year-old divorced female with 12 years of education working 30 hours per week with no capital gains or losses.

1. For the 50-year-old married male with 20 years of education working 40 hours per week with a capnet of $500, we have the following logits for training sets A and B:

$$\hat{g}_A(x) = -9.06305 + 0.0278994(50) + 0.374356(20)$$
$$+2.02743(1) - 0.489140(0)$$
$$-0.369533(0) - 0.0760889(0) + 0.166622(1)$$
$$+0.0309548(40) + 0.0002292(500)$$
$$= 3.365884$$

$$\hat{g}_B(x) = -8.85216 + 0.0224645(50) + 0.368721(20)$$
$$+2.02076(1) - 0.587585(0)$$
$$-0.094394(0) - 0.181349(0) + 0.311218(1)$$
$$+0.0316433(40) + 0.0002455(500)$$
$$= 3.365945$$

TABLE 4.28 Results of Logistic Regression for Training Set B

```
Logistic Regression Table
```

Predictor	Coef	SE Coef	Z	P	Odds Ratio	95% CI Lower	Upper
Constant	-8.85216	0.230298	-38.44	0.000			
age	0.0224645	0.0023381	9.61	0.000	1.02	1.02	1.03
education-num	0.368721	0.0121961	30.23	0.000	1.45	1.41	1.48
marital-status							
Married	2.02076	0.100676	20.07	0.000	7.54	6.19	9.19
Never-married	-0.587585	0.126032	-4.66	0.000	0.56	0.43	0.71
Separated	0.0943940	0.222559	0.42	0.671	1.10	0.71	1.70
Widowed	-0.181349	0.246958	-0.73	0.463	0.83	0.51	1.35
sex							
Male	0.311218	0.0745234	4.18	0.000	1.37	1.18	1.58
hours-per-week	0.0316433	0.0023875	13.25	0.000	1.03	1.03	1.04
capnet	0.0002455	0.0000135	18.16	0.000	1.00	1.00	1.00

```
Log-Likelihood = -4401.957
Test that all slopes are zero: G = 5071.837, DF = 9, P-Value = 0.000
```

Thus, the estimated probability that this type of person will have an income exceeding $50,000 is, for each data set,

$$\hat{\pi}_A(x) = \frac{e^{\hat{g}(x)}}{1 + e^{\hat{g}(x)}} = \frac{e^{3.365884}}{1 + e^{3.365884}} = 0.966621$$

$$\hat{\pi}_B(x) = \frac{e^{\hat{g}(x)}}{1 + e^{\hat{g}(x)}} = \frac{e^{3.365945}}{1 + e^{3.365945}} = 0.966623$$

That is, the estimated probability that a 50-year-old married male with 20 years of education working 40 hours per week with a capnet of $500 will have an income exceeding $50,000 is 96.66%, as reported by both data sets, with a difference of only 0.000002 between them. If sound, the similarity of these estimated probabilities shows strong evidence for validation of the logistic regression. Unfortunately, these estimates are not sound, since they represent extrapolation on the education variable, whose maximum value in this data set is only 16 years. Therefore, these estimates should not be used in general and should certainly not be used for model validation.

2. For the 50-year-old married male with 16 years of education working 40 hours per week with a capnet of $500, the logits look like this:

$$\begin{aligned}
\hat{g}_A(x) = {}& -9.06305 + 0.0278994\,(50) + 0.374356\,(16) \\
& + 2.02743\,(1) - 0.489140\,(0) \\
& - 0.369533\,(0) - 0.0760889\,(0) + 0.166622\,(1) \\
& + 0.0309548\,(40) + 0.0002292\,(500) \\
= {}& 1.86846
\end{aligned}$$

$$\hat{g}_B(x) = -8.85216 + 0.0224645\,(50) + 0.368721\,(16)$$
$$+2.02076\,(1) - 0.587585\,(0)$$
$$-0.094394\,(0) - 0.181349\,(0) + 0.311218\,(1)$$
$$+0.0316433\,(40) + 0.0002455\,(500)$$
$$= 1.891061$$

The estimated probability that a 50-year-old married male with 16 years of education working 40 hours per week with a capnet of $500 will have an income exceeding $50,000 is therefore, for each data set,

$$\hat{\pi}_A(x) = \frac{e^{\hat{g}(x)}}{1 + e^{\hat{g}(x)}} = \frac{e^{1.86846}}{1 + e^{1.86846}} = 0.8663$$

$$\hat{\pi}_B(x) = \frac{e^{\hat{g}(x)}}{1 + e^{\hat{g}(x)}} = \frac{e^{1.891061}}{1 + e^{1.891061}} = 0.8689$$

That is, the estimated probability that such a person will have an income greater than $50,000 is reported by models based on both data sets to be about 87%. There is a difference of only 0.0026 between the point estimates, which may be considered small, although of course what constitutes small depends on the particular research problem, and other factors.

3. For the 35-year-old divorced female with 12 years of education working 30 hours per week with no capital gains or losses, we have the following logits:

$$\hat{g}_A(x) = -9.06305 + 0.0278994\,(35) + 0.374356\,(12)$$
$$+2.02743\,(0) - 0.489140\,(0)$$
$$-0.369533\,(0) - 0.0760889\,(0) + 0.166622\,(0)$$
$$+0.0309548\,(30) + 0.0002292\,(0)$$
$$= -2.66566$$

$$\hat{g}_B(x) = -8.85216 + 0.0224645\,(35) + 0.368721\,(12)$$
$$+2.02076\,(0) - 0.587585\,(0)$$
$$-0.094394\,(0) - 0.181349\,(0) + 0.311218\,(0)$$
$$+0.0316433\,(30) + 0.0002455\,(0)$$
$$= -2.69195$$

Therefore, for each data set, the estimated probability that this type of person will have an income exceeding $50,000 is

$$\hat{\pi}_A(x) = \frac{e^{\hat{g}(x)}}{1 + e^{\hat{g}(x)}} = \frac{e^{-2.66566}}{1 + e^{-2.66566}} = 0.06503$$

$$\hat{\pi}_B(x) = \frac{e^{\hat{g}(x)}}{1 + e^{\hat{g}(x)}} = \frac{e^{-2.69195}}{1 + e^{-2.69195}} = 0.06345$$

That is, the estimated probability that a 35-year-old divorced female with 12 years of education working 30 hours per week with no capital gains or losses will have an income greater than $50,000 is reported by models based on both data sets to be between 6.3 and 6.5%. There is a difference of only 0.00158 between the point estimates, which is slightly better (i.e., smaller) than the estimate for the 50-year-old male.

WEKA: HANDS-ON ANALYSIS USING LOGISTIC REGRESSION

In this exercise a logistic regression model is built using WEKA's Logistic class. A modified version of the *cereals* data set [7] is used as input, where the RATING field is discretized by mapping records with values greater than 42 to "High," while those less than or equal to 42 become "Low." This way, our model is used to classify a cereal as having either a "High" or "Low" nutritional rating. Our data set consists of the three numeric predictor fields: *PROTEIN*, *SODIUM*, and *FIBER*.

The data set is split into separate training and test files. The training file *cereals-train.arff* consists of 24 instances and is used to train our logistic regression model. The file is balanced 50–50, with half the instances taking on class value "High" while the other half have the value "Low." The mean values for the predictor fields *PROTEIN*, *SODIUM*, and *FIBER* are 2.667, 146.875, and 2.458, respectively. The complete training file is shown in Table 4.29.

Our training and test files are both represented in ARFF format, which is WEKA's standard method of representing the instances and attributes found in data sets. The keyword *relation* indicates the name for the file, which is followed by a block defining each *attribute* in the data set. Notice that the three predictor fields are defined as type *numeric*, whereas the target variable *RATING* is categorical. The *data* section lists each instance, which corresponds to a specific cereal. For example, the first line in the data section describes a cereal having *PROTEIN* = 3, *SODIUM* = 200, *FIBER* = 3.0, and *RATING* = High.

Let's load the training file and build the Logistic model:

1. Open the WEKA Explorer panel.
2. On the Preprocess tab, press Open file and specify the path to the training file, *cereals-train.arff*.

The WEKA Explorer panel displays several characteristics of the training file, as shown in Figure 4.7. The three predictor attributes and class variable are shown on the Attributes pane (left). Statistics for *PROTEIN*, including range (1–4), mean (2.667), and standard deviation (0.868), are shown on the Selected attribute pane (right). The Status bar at the bottom of the panel tells us that WEKA loaded the file successfully.

1. Select the Classify Tab.
2. Under Classifier, press the Choose button.
3. Select Classifiers → Functions → Logistic from the navigation hierarchy.
4. In our modeling experiment we have separate training and test sets; therefore, under Test options, choose the Use the training set option.
5. Click Start to build the model.

WEKA creates the logistic regression model and reports results in the Classifier output window. Although the results (not shown) indicate that the classification accuracy of the model, as measured against the training set, is 75% (18/24), we are interested in using the model to classify the unseen data found in the test set. The odds

TABLE 4.29   ARFF Trainning File *cereals-trains.arff*

```
@relation cereals-train.arff

@attribute PROTEIN numeric
@attribute SODIUM  numeric
@attribute FIBER   numeric
@attribute RATING {High,Low}

@data
3,200,3.000000,High
3,230,3.000000,High
3,200,3.000000,High
3,0,4.000000,High
4,150,2.000000,High
3,0,3.000000,High
4,260,9.000000,High
3,140,3.000000,High
2,0,3.000000,High
2,0,2.000000,High
3,80,1.000000,High
2,200,4.000000,High
2,180,1.500000,Low
4,150,3.000000,Low
2,140,2.000000,Low
4,95,3.000000,Low
1,220,0.000000,Low
2,180,0.000000,Low
3,140,4.000000,Low
3,170,2.000000,Low
2,200,1.000000,Low
3,250,1.500000,Low
2,200,1.000000,Low
1,140,0.000000,Low
```

ratios and values for the regression coefficients $\beta_0, \beta_1, \beta_2$, and β_3 are also reported by the model as shown in Table 4.30. We'll revisit these values shortly, but first let's evaluate our model against the test set.

1. Under Test options, choose Supplied test set. Click Set.
2. Specify the path to the test file, *cereals-test.arff.*
3. Click the More options button.
4. Check the Output text predictions on the test set option. Click OK.
5. Under Result list, right-click the Logistic model from the list. Choose Re-evaluate model on the current test set.

Again, the results appear in the Classifier output window; however, now the output shows that the Logistic regression model has classified 62.5% (5/8) of the instances

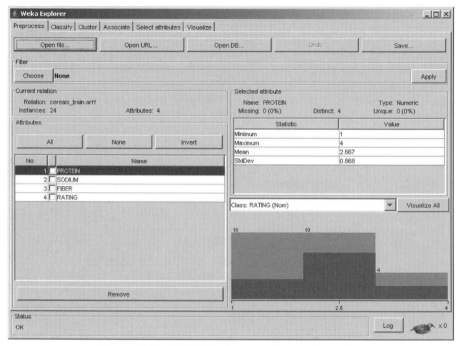

Figure 4.7 WEKA Explorer panel: preprocess tab.

in the test set correctly. In addition, the model now reports the actual predictions and probabilities by which it classified each instance, as shown in Table 4.31. For example, the first instance is incorrectly predicted (classified) to be "Low" with probability 0.567. The plus (+) symbol in the error column indicates this classification is incorrect according to the maximum (*0.567) probability. Let's compute the estimated logit $\hat{g}(x)$ for this instance according to the coefficients found in Table 4.30. However, we first examine the test file *cereals-test.arff* and determine that the first record contains the attribute-value pairs *PROTEIN* = 4, *SODIUM* = 135, *FIBER* = 2.0,

TABLE 4.30 Logistic Regression Coefficients

Variable	Coeff.
1	−0.0423
2	−0.0107
3	0.9476
Intercept	−0.5478
Odds Ratios...	
Variable	O.R.
1	0.9586
2	0.9893
3	2.5795

and *RATING* = High. Therefore, the estimated logit equals

$$\hat{g}(x) = -0.5478 - 0.0423(4) - 0.0107(135) + 0.9476(2) = -0.2663$$

It follows that

$$\hat{\pi}(x) = \frac{e^{-0.2663}}{1 + e^{-0.2663}} = 0.43382$$

Therefore, the estimated probability equals about 43.4% that a cereal with 4 grams of protein, 135 milligrams of sodium, and 2 grams of fiber is of high nutritional value. Note that WEKA reports this same probability (except for slight rounding variations) for the first instance in Table 4.31. It follows that the model estimates a probability equal to $1 - \hat{\pi}(x) = 56.6\%$ that this cereal has a low nutritional rating. Therefore, based on the higher probability, the model incorrectly classified the record as "Low."

Table 4.31 also shows reports the odds ratios for the three continuous predictors. For example, the odds ratio for *PROTEIN* is $\hat{OR} = e^{b_1} = e^{-0.0423} = 0.9586$. This is interpreted as the odds of a cereal with $x + 1$ grams of protein being of high nutritional value compared to a cereal with x grams of protein being highly nutritious.

SUMMARY

Linear regression is used to approximate the relationship between a continuous response variable and a set of predictor variables. *Logistic regression*, on the other hand, refers to methods for describing the relationship between a *categorical* response variable and a set of predictor variables.

Logistic regression assumes that the relationship between the predictor and the response is nonlinear. In linear regression, the response variable is considered to be a random variable $Y = \beta_0 + \beta_1 x + \varepsilon$ with conditional mean $\pi(x) = E(Y|x) = \beta_0 + \beta_1 x$. The conditional mean for logistic regression takes on a different form from that of linear regression. Specifically,

$$\pi(x) = \frac{e^{\beta_0 + \beta_1 x}}{1 + e^{\beta_0 + \beta_1 x}}$$

Curves of this form are called *sigmoidal* because they are S-shaped and therefore nonlinear. The minimum for $\pi(x)$ is obtained at $\lim_{a \to -\infty} [e^a/(1 + e^a)] = 0$, and

TABLE 4.31 Logistic Regression Test Set Predictions

```
=== Predictions on test set ===

inst#,  actual,  predicted,  error,  probability distribution
    1   1:High     2:Low        +           0.433       *0.567
    2   1:High     2:Low        +           0.357       *0.643
    3   1:High     1:High                  *0.586        0.414
    4   1:High     1:High                  *0.578        0.422
    5   2:Low      2:Low                    0.431       *0.569
    6   2:Low      2:Low                    0.075       *0.925
    7   2:Low      2:Low                    0.251       *0.749
    8   2:Low      1:High       +          *0.86         0.14
```

the maximum for $\pi(x)$ is obtained at $\lim_{a \to \infty}[e^a/(1 + e^a)] = 1$. Thus, $\pi(x)$ may be interpreted as the probability that the positive outcome is present for records with $X = x$, and $1 - \pi(x)$ may be interpreted as the probability that the positive outcome is absent for such records. The variance of ε is $\pi(x)[1 - \pi(x)]$, which is the variance for a binomial distribution, and the response variable in logistic regression $Y = \pi(x) + \varepsilon$ is assumed to follow a binomial distribution with probability of success $\pi(x)$. The *logit transformation* is as follows:

$$g(x) = \ln \frac{\pi(x)}{1 - \pi(x)} = \beta_0 + \beta_1 x$$

No closed-form solution exists for estimating logistic regression coefficients. Thus, we must turn to *maximum likelihood estimation*, which finds estimates of the parameters for which the likelihood of observing the observed data is maximized.

A *saturated model* is a model that which contains as many parameters as data points and so predicts the response variable perfectly with no prediction error. We may then look upon the *observed* values of the response variable to be the values predicted by the saturated model. To compare the values predicted by our fitted model (with fewer parameters than data points) to the values predicted by the saturated model, we use

$$\text{deviance} = -2\ln\left[\frac{\text{likelihood of the fitted model}}{\text{likelihood of the saturated model}}\right]$$

The resulting hypothesis test is called a *likelihood ratio test*.

The deviance represents the error left over in the model, after the predictors have been accounted for. As such, it is analogous to the sum of squares error in linear regression. To determine whether a particular predictor is significant, find the deviance of the model without the predictor, and subtract the deviance of the model with the predictor, thus:

$$G = deviance(\text{model without predictor}) - deviance(\text{model with predictor})$$
$$= -2\ln\left[\frac{\text{likelihood without predictor}}{\text{likelihood with predictor}}\right]$$

The test statistic G follows a chi-square distribution with 1 degree of freedom (i.e., $\chi^2_{\nu=1}$), assuming that the null hypothesis is true that $\beta_1 = 0$.

Odds may be defined as the probability that an event occurs divided by the probability that the event does not occur. The *odds ratio* (OR) is defined as the odds that the response variable occurred for records with $x = 1$ divided by the odds that the response variable occurred for records with $x = 0$. Conveniently, odds ratio $= e^{\beta_1}$. The odds ratio is sometimes used to estimate the *relative risk*, defined as the probability that the response occurs for $x = 1$ divided by the probability that the response occurs for $x = 0$.

The slope coefficient β_1 may be interpreted as the change in the value of the logit for a unit increase in the value of the predictor, $\beta_1 = g(x + 1) - g(x)$. The coefficient b_1 represents the estimated change in the log odds ratio for a unit increase in the predictor. In general, for a constant c, the quantity cb_1 represents the estimated change in the log odds ratio for an increase of c units in the predictor.

Zero cells play havoc with the logistic regression solution, causing instability in the analysis and leading to possibly unreliable results. Rather than omitting the categories with zero cells, we may try to collapse the categories or redefine them somehow, in order to find some records for the zero cells. The logistic regression results should always be validated using either the model diagnostics and goodness-of-fit statistics shown in Hosmer and Lemeshow [1], or the traditional data mining cross-validation methods.

REFERENCES

1. D. W. Hosmer and S. Lemeshow, *Applied Logistic Regression*, 2nd ed., Wiley, New York, 2000.
2. P. McCullagh and J. A. Nelder, *Generalized Linear Models*, 2nd ed., Chapman & Hall, London, 1989.
3. C. R. Rao, *Linear Statistical Inference and Its Application*, 2nd ed., Wiley, New York, 1973.
4. Churn data set, in C. L. Blake and C. J. Merz, UCI Repository of Machine Learning Databases, http://www.ics.uci.edu/~mlearn/MLRepository.html, University of California, Department of Information and Computer Science, Irvine, CA, 1998. Also available at the book series Web site.
5. Y. M. M. Bishop, S. E. Feinberg, and P. Holland, *Discrete Multivariate Analysis: Theory and Practice*, MIT Press, Cambridge, MA, 1975.
6. Adult data set, in C. L. Blake and C. J. Merz, UCI Repository of Machine Learning Databases, http://www.ics.uci.edu/~mlearn/MLRepository.html. University of California, Department of Information and Computer Science, Irvine, CA, 1998. *Adult* data set compiled by Ron Kohavi. Also available at the book series Web site.
7. Cereals data set, in Data and Story Library, http://lib.stat.cmu.edu/DASL/. Also available at the book series Web site.
8. Breast cancer data set, compiled by Dr. William H. Wohlberg, University of Wisconsin Hospitals, Madison, WI; cited in O. L. Mangasarian and W. H. Wohlberg, Cancer diagnosis via linear programming, *SIAM News*, Vol. 23, No. 5, September 1990.
9. German data set, compiled by Professor Dr. Hans Hofmann, University of Hamburg, Germany. Available from the "Datasets from UCI" site, hosted by Silicon Graphics, Inc. at http://www.sgi.com/tech/mlc/db/. Also available at the book series Web site.

EXERCISES

Clarifying the Concepts

4.1. Determine whether the following statements are true or false. If a statement is false, explain why and suggest how one might alter the statement to make it true.

(a) Logistic regression refers to methods for describing the relationship between a categorical response variable and a set of categorical predictor variables.

(b) Logistic regression assumes that the relationship between the predictor and the response is nonlinear.

(c) $\pi(x)$ may be interpreted as a probability.

(d) Logistic regression models assume that the error term ε is normally distributed with mean zero and constant variance.

(e) In logistic regression, closed-form solutions for the optimal values of the regression coefficients may be obtained.

(f) The saturated model predicts the response variable perfectly.

(g) The deviance represents the total variability in the response.

(h) Encoding a trichotomous predictor requires only two indicator variables.

(i) The t-test provides a method for finding the response probabilities.

(j) The interpretation of the logistic regression coefficient for a continuous predictor may be extended from the usual unit increase to an increase of any arbitrary amount.

(k) The estimated odds ratio is constant across the range of the predictor.

4.2. By hand, derive the logit result $g(x) = \beta_0 + \beta_1 x$.

4.3. Explain what is meant by maximum likelihood estimation and describe maximum likelihood estimators.

4.4. Explain clearly how the slope coefficient β_1 and its estimate b_1 may be interpreted in logistic regression. Provide at least two examples, using both a categorical and a continuous predictor.

4.5. What are odds? What is the difference between odds and probability?

4.6. What is the definition of the odds ratio? What is the relationship between the odds ratio and the slope coefficient β_1? For what quantity is the odds ratio sometimes used as an estimate?

4.7. Describe how we determine the statistical significance of the odds ratio using a confidence interval.

4.8. If the difference between a particular indicator variable and the reference category is not significant, what should the analyst consider doing?

4.9. Discuss the role of statistical inference with respect to the huge sample sizes prevalent in data mining.

4.10. Discuss the assumption that the odds ratio is constant across the range of the predictor, with respect to various types of relationships between the predictor and the response. Provide modeling options for when this assumption may not be reflected in the data.

4.11. Discuss the use of predictors that turn out to be nonsignificant in estimating response. When might this be appropriate, if at all? Why would this not be appropriate in general?

4.12. For data that are missing one or more indicator variable values, explain why it would not be appropriate simply to ignore these missing variables when making an estimation. Provide options for the data analyst in this case.

Working with the Data

4.13. The logistic regression output shown in Table E4.13 refers to the *breast cancer* data set [8]. Ten numeric predictors are used to predict the class malignant breast cancer tumor (class = 1) as opposed to benign tumor (class = 0).

(a) What is the value of the deviance difference? Is the overall logistic regression significant? How can you tell? What does it mean to say that the overall logistic regression is significant?

(b) Without reference to inferential significance, express the form of the logit.

(c) Which variables do not appear to be significant predictors of breast tumor class? How can you tell?

(d) Discuss whether the variables you cited in Part (c) should be used in predicting the class of tumor with an new, unseen data set.

(e) Discuss how you should handle variables with p-values around $0.05, 0.10,$ or 0.15.

(f) Explain what will happen to the deviance difference if we rerun the model dropping the nonsignificant variables. Work by analogy with the linear regression case.

TABLE E4.13

Logistic Regression Table

Predictor	Coef	SE Coef	Z	P	Odds Ratio
Constant	-10.1039	1.17490	-8.60	0.000	
Clump Thickness	0.535014	0.142018	3.77	0.000	1.71
Cell Size Uniformity	-0.0062797	0.209079	-0.03	0.976	0.99
Cell Shape Uniformity	0.322706	0.230602	1.40	0.162	1.38
Marginal Adhesion	0.330637	0.123451	2.68	0.007	1.39
Single Epithelial Cell Size	0.0966354	0.156593	0.62	0.537	1.10
Bare Nuclei	0.383025	0.0938437	4.08	0.000	1.47
Bland Chromatin	0.447188	0.171383	2.61	0.009	1.56
Normal Nucleoli	0.213031	0.112874	1.89	0.059	1.24
Mitoses	0.534836	0.328777	1.63	0.104	1.71

Log-Likelihood = -51.444
Test that all slopes are zero: G = 781.462, DF = 9, P-Value = 0.000

4.14. Next, the logistic regression for the *breast cancer* data set was run again, this time dropping the *cell size uniformity* and *single epithelial cell size* variables but retaining all the others. The logistic regression output shown in Table E4.14 contains the results.

(a) Explain why the deviance difference fell, but only by a small amount.

(b) Did you drop *cell shape uniformity* in Exercise 4.13? Are you surprised that the variable is now a significant predictor? Discuss the importance of retaining variables of borderline significance in the early stages of model building.

(c) Assume that our level of significance is 0.11. Express the logit using all significant variables.

(d) Find the probability that a tumor is malignant given the following:

  (i) The values for all predictors are at the minimum (1).

  (ii) The values for all predictors are at a moderate level (5).

  (iii) The values for all predictors are at the maximum (10).

(e) Calculate the 95% confidence intervals for the following predictor coefficients:

  (i) *Clump thickness*

  (ii) *Mitoses*

    Comment as to the evidence provided by the confidence interval regarding the significance of the mitoses coefficient.

TABLE E4.14

```
Logistic Regression Table
```

Predictor	Coef	SE Coef	Z	P	Odds Ratio	95% CI Lower	Upper
Constant	-9.98278	1.12607	-8.87	0.000			
Clump Thickness	0.534002	0.140788	3.79	0.000	1.71	1.29	2.25
Cell Shape Uniformity	0.345286	0.171640	2.01	0.044	1.41	1.01	1.98
Marginal Adhesion	0.342491	0.119217	2.87	0.004	1.41	1.11	1.78
Bare Nuclei	0.388296	0.0935616	4.15	0.000	1.47	1.23	1.77
Bland Chromatin	0.461943	0.168195	2.75	0.006	1.59	1.14	2.21
Normal Nucleoli	0.226055	0.110970	2.04	0.042	1.25	1.01	1.56
Mitoses	0.531192	0.324454	1.64	0.102	1.70	0.90	3.21

```
Log-Likelihood = -51.633
Test that all slopes are zero: G = 781.083, DF = 7, P-Value = 0.000
```

(f) Clearly interpret the value of the coefficients for the following predictors:

(i) *Bland chromatin*

(ii) *Normal nucleoli*

Hands-on Analysis

4.15. Open the *adult* data set, which is provided at the book series Web site. Construct the logistic regression model developed in the text with the age^2 term and the indicator variable *age 33–65*.

(a) Verify that using the quadratic term provides a higher estimate of the probability of high income for a 32-year-old than a 20-year-old.

(b) Analyze and interpret the results from Table 4.25.

(i) Find the form of the logit estimated.

(ii) Find the probability of high income for someone working 30, 40, 50, and 60 hours per week.

(iii) Construct and interpret a 95% confidence interval for each coefficient.

(c) Consider the results from Table 4.26. Construct the logistic regression model that produced these results.

(i) For indicator categories that are not significant, collapse the categories with the reference category. (How are you handling the category with the 0.083 *p*-value?)

(ii) Rerun the logistic regression with these collapsed categories.

(d) Based on your results from rerunning the logistic regression:

(i) Find the estimated logit.

(ii) Construct and interpret 95% confidence intervals for the coefficients for *age*, *sex-male*, and *educ-squared*. Verify that these predictors belong in the model.

(iii) Find the probability of high income for (1) a 20-year-old single female with 12 years of education working 20 hours per week with no capital gains or losses, and (2) a 50-year-old married male with 16 years of education working 40 hours per week with capital gains of $6000.

4.16. Open the *German* data set [9], which is provided on the book series Web site. The data set consists of 20 predictors, both continuous and categorical, and a single response variable, indicating whether the individual record represents a good or a bad credit risk. The predictors are as follows, with amounts in deutsche marks (DM):

- Status of existing checking account
- Duration in months
- Credit history
- Loan purpose
- Credit amount
- Savings account/bonds
- Presently employed since
- Payment as percentage of disposable income
- Personal status and gender
- Other debtors/guarantors
- Present residence since
- Property
- Age
- Other installment plans
- Housing
- Number of existing credits at this bank
- Job
- Number of people being liable to provide maintenance for
- Telephone
- Foreign worker

More information is available about this data set from the book series Web site. Construct the best logistic regression model you can, using as many of the methods we learned in this chapter as possible. Provide strong interpretive support for your model, including explanations of derived variables, indicator variables, and so on.

4.17. Open the *breast cancer* data set [8]. For each significant predictor, investigate, whether the linearity assumption is warranted. If not, ameliorate the situation using the methods discussed in this chapter.

4.18. Recall the WEKA Logistic example for classifying cereals as either high or low. Compute the probability that the fourth instance from the test set is classified either high or low. Does your probability match that produced by WEKA?

CHAPTER 5

NAIVE BAYES ESTIMATION AND BAYESIAN NETWORKS

BAYESIAN APPROACH

MAXIMUM A POSTERIORI CLASSIFICATION

NAIVE BAYES CLASSIFICATION

WEKA: HANDS-ON ANALYSIS USING NAIVE BAYES

BAYESIAN BELIEF NETWORKS

WEKA: HANDS-ON ANALYSIS USING BAYES NET

BAYESIAN APPROACH

In the field of statistics, there are two main approaches to probability. The usual way that probability is taught, as in most typical introductory statistics courses, represents the *frequentist* or *classical approach*. In the frequentist approach to probability, the population parameters are fixed constants whose values are unknown. These probabilities are defined to be the relative frequencies of the various categories, where the experiment is repeated an indefinitely large number of times. For example, if we toss a fair coin 10 times, it may not be very unusual to observe 80% heads; but if we toss the fair coin 10 trillion times, we can be fairly certain that the proportion of heads will be near 50%. It is this long-run behavior that defines probability for the frequentist approach.

However, there are situations for which the classical definition of probability is unclear. For example, what is the probability that terrorists will strike New York City with a dirty bomb? Since such an occurrence has never occurred, it is difficult to conceive what the long-run behavior of this gruesome experiment might be. In the frequentist approach to probability, the parameters are fixed, and the randomness lies in the data, which are viewed as a random sample from a given distribution with unknown but fixed parameters.

Data Mining Methods and Models By Daniel T. Larose
Copyright © 2006 John Wiley & Sons, Inc.

Figure 5.1 The Reverend Thomas Bayes
(1702–1761).

The *Bayesian approach* to probability turns these assumptions around. In Bayesian statistics, the parameters are considered to be random variables, and the data are considered to be known. The parameters are regarded as coming from a distribution of possible values, and Bayesians look to the observed data to provide information on likely parameter values.

Let θ represent the parameters of the unknown distribution. Bayesian analysis requires elicitation of a prior distribution for θ, called the *prior distribution, $p(\theta)$*. This prior distribution can model extant expert knowledge, if any, regarding the distribution of θ. For example, churn[1] modeling experts may be aware that a customer exceeding a certain threshold number of calls to customer service may indicate a likelihood to churn. This knowledge can be distilled into prior assumptions about the distribution of customer service calls, including its mean and standard deviation. If expert knowledge regarding the prior distribution is not available, Bayesian analysts may posit a *noninformative prior*, which assigns equal probability to all values of the parameter. For example, the prior probability of both churners and nonchurners could be set at 0.5 using a noninformative prior. (Note that if this assumption does not seem reasonable, you must be applying your expert knowledge about churn modeling!) Regardless, because the field of data mining often encounters huge data sets, the prior distribution should be dominated by the overwhelming amount of information to be found in the observed data.

Once the data have been observed, prior information about the distribution of θ can be *updated*, by factoring in the information about θ contained in the observed data. This modification leads to the *posterior distribution, $p(\theta|\mathbf{X})$*, where $\mathbf{X}$ represents the entire array of data. This updating of our knowledge about θ from prior distribution to posterior distribution was first performed by the Reverend Thomas Bayes (Figure 5.1), in his *Essay Towards Solving a Problem in the Doctrine of Chances* [1], published posthumously in 1763.

---

[1] *Churn* represents customers leaving one company in favor of another company's products or services.

The posterior distribution is found as follows:

$$p(\theta|\mathbf{X}) = \frac{p(\mathbf{X}|\theta)p(\theta)}{p(\mathbf{X})}$$

where $p(\mathbf{X}|\theta)$ represents the likelihood function, $p(\theta)$ the prior distribution, and $p(\mathbf{X})$ a normalizing factor called the *marginal distribution* of the data. Since the posterior is a distribution rather than a single value, we can conceivably examine any possible statistic of this distribution that we are interested in, such as the first quartile or the mean absolute deviation. However, it is common to choose the posterior mode, the value of θ that maximizes $p(\theta|\mathbf{X})$, for an estimate, in which case we call this estimation method the *maximum a posteriori* (MAP) *method*. For noninformative priors, the MAP estimate and the frequentist maximum likelihood estimate often coincide, since the data dominate the prior. The likelihood function $p(\mathbf{X}|\theta)$ derives from the assumption that the observations are independently and identically distributed according to a particular distribution $f(X|\theta)$, so that $p(\mathbf{X}|\theta) = \prod_{i=1}^{n} f(X_i|\theta)$.

The normalizing factor $p(\mathbf{X})$ is essentially a constant, for a given data set and model, so that we may express the posterior distribution like this: $p(\theta|\mathbf{X}) \propto p(\mathbf{X}|\theta)p(\theta)$. That is, given the data, the posterior distribution of θ is proportional to the product of the likelihood and the prior. Thus, when we have a great deal of information coming from the likelihood, as we do in most data mining applications, the likelihood will overwhelm the prior.

Criticism of the Bayesian framework has focused primarily on two potential drawbacks. First, elicitation of a prior distribution may be subjective. That is, two different subject matter experts may provide two different prior distributions, which will presumably percolate through to result in two different posterior distributions. The solution to this problem is (1) to select noninformative priors if the choice of priors is controversial, and (2) to apply lots of data so that the relative importance of the prior is diminished. Failing this, model selection can be performed on the two different posterior distributions, using model adequacy and efficacy criteria, resulting in the choice of the better model. Is reporting more than one model a bad thing?

The second criticism has been that Bayesian computation has been intractable in data mining terms for most interesting problems where the approach suffered from scalability issues. The curse of dimensionality hits Bayesian analysis rather hard, since the normalizing factor requires integrating (or summing) over all possible values of the parameter vector, which may be computationally infeasible when applied directly. However, the introduction of Markov chain Monte Carlo (MCMC) methods such as Gibbs sampling and the Metropolis algorithm has greatly expanded the range of problems and dimensions that Bayesian analysis can handle.

MAXIMUM A POSTERIORI CLASSIFICATION

How do we find the MAP estimate of θ? Well, we need the value of θ that will maximize $p(\theta|\mathbf{X})$; this value is expressed as $\theta_{\text{MAP}} = \arg\max_{\theta} p(\theta|\mathbf{X})$ since it is the argument (value) that maximizes $p(\theta|\mathbf{X})$ over all θ. Then, using the formula for the posterior distribution, we have, since $p(\mathbf{X})$ has no θ term,

$$\theta_{\text{MAP}} = \arg\max_{\theta} p(\theta|\mathbf{X}) = \arg\max_{\theta} \frac{p(\mathbf{X}|\theta)p(\theta)}{p(\mathbf{X})} = \arg\max_{\theta} p(\mathbf{X}|\theta)p(\theta) \qquad (5.1)$$

The Bayesian MAP classification is optimal; that is, it achieves the minimum error rate for all possible classifiers [2, p. 174]. Next, we apply these formulas to a subset of the *churn* data set [3], specifically so that we may find the maximum a posteriori estimate of churn for this subset.

First, however, let us step back for a moment and derive Bayes' theorem for simple events. Let A and B be events in a sample space. Then the *conditional probability* $P(A|B)$ is defined as

$$P(A|B) = \frac{P(A \cap B)}{P(B)} = \frac{\text{number of outcomes in both A and B}}{\text{number of outcomes in B}}$$

Also, $P(B|A) = P(A \cap B)/P(A)$. Now, reexpressing the intersection, we have $P(A \cap B) = P(B|A)P(A)$, and substituting, we obtain

$$P(A|B) = \frac{P(B|A)P(A)}{P(B)} \qquad (5.2)$$

which is Bayes' theorem for simple events.

We shall restrict our example to only two categorical predictor variables, *International Plan* and *VoiceMail Plan*, and the categorical target variable, *churn*. The business problem is to classify new records as either churners or nonchurners based on the associations of churn with the two predictor variables learned in the training set. Now, how are we to think about this churn classification problem (see Larose [4]) in the Bayesian terms addressed above? First, we let the parameter vector θ represent the dichotomous variable *churn*, taking on the two values *true* and *false*. For clarity, we denote θ as C for *churn*. The 3333×2 matrix $\mathbf{X}$ consists of the 3333 records in the data set, each with two fields, specifying either *yes* or *no* for the two predictor variables.

Thus, equation (5.1) can be reexpressed as

$$\theta_{\text{MAP}} = C_{\text{MAP}} = \arg\max_{C} p(I \cap V|C)p(C) \qquad (5.3)$$

where I represents the *International Plan* and V represents the *VoiceMail Plan*. Denote:

- I to mean *International Plan* $= yes$
- $\overline{I}$ to mean *International Plan* $= no$
- V to mean *VoiceMail Plan* $= yes$
- $\overline{V}$ to mean *VoiceMail Plan* $= no$
- C to mean *churn* $= true$
- $\overline{C}$ to mean *churn* $= false$

TABLE 5.1   Marginal and Conditional Probabilities for the *Churn* Data Set

	Count	Count	Probability
International Plan	No 3010	Yes 323	$P(I) = \dfrac{323}{323 + 3010} = 0.0969$
VoiceMail Plan	No 2411	Yes 922	$P(V) = \dfrac{922}{922 + 2411} = 0.2766$
Churn	False 2850	True 483	$P(C) = \dfrac{483}{483 + 2850} = 0.1449$
International Plan given *churn = false*	No 2664	Yes 186	$P(I|\overline{C}) = \dfrac{186}{186 + 2664} = 0.0653$
VoiceMail Plan given *churn = false*	No 2008	Yes 842	$P(V|\overline{C}) = \dfrac{842}{842 + 2008} = 0.2954$
International Plan given *churn = true*	No 346	Yes 137	$P(I|C) = \dfrac{137}{137 + 346} = 0.2836$
VoiceMail Plan given *churn = true*	No 403	Yes 80	$P(V|C) = \dfrac{80}{80 + 403} = 0.1656$

For example, for a new record containing $(I \cap V)$, we seek to calculate the following probabilities using equation (5.3). For customers who churn (churners):

$$P(\textit{International Plan} = \textit{yes, VoiceMail Plan} = \textit{yes}|\textit{churn} = \textit{true})P(\textit{churn} = \textit{true})$$
$$= P(I \cap V|C)P(C)$$

For customers who do not churn (nonchurners):

$$P(\textit{International Plan} = \textit{yes, VoiceMail Plan} = \textit{yes}|\textit{churn} = \textit{false})P(\textit{churn} = \textit{false})$$
$$= P(I \cap V|\overline{C})P(\overline{C})$$

We then determine which value for *churn* produces the larger probability and select it as C_{MAP}, the MAP estimate of *churn*.

   We begin by finding a series of marginal and conditional probabilities (Table 5.1), all of which we shall use as we build toward our MAP estimates. Also, since we may examine the entire training data set of 3333 records, we may calculate the posterior probabilities directly, as given in Table 5.2.

TABLE 5.2   Posterior Probabilities for the *Churn* Training Data Set

	Count	Count	Probability
Churn = true, given *International Plan = yes*	False 186	True 137	$P(C|I) = \dfrac{137}{(137 + 186)} = 0.4241$
Churn = true, given *VoiceMail Plan =* yes	False 842	True 80	$P(C|V) = \dfrac{80}{(80 + 842)} = 0.0868$

TABLE 5.3   Complement Probabilities for the *Churn* Training Data Set

$P(\overline{I}) = 1 - P(I) = 1 - 0.0969 = 0.9031$	$P(\overline{V}) = 1 - 0.2766 = 0.7234$
$P(\overline{C}) = 1 - 0.1449 = 0.8551$	$P(\overline{I}|\overline{C}) = 1 - 0.0653 = 0.9347$
$P(\overline{V}|\overline{C}) = 1 - 0.2954 = 0.7046$	$P(\overline{I}|C) = 1 - 0.2836 = 0.7164$
$P(\overline{V}|C) = 1 - 0.1656 = 0.8344$	$P(\overline{C}|I) = 1 - 0.4241 = 0.5759$
$P(\overline{C}|V) = 1 - 0.0868 = 0.9132$	

Note that using the probabilities given in Tables 5.1 and 5.2, we can easily find the complement of these probabilities by subtracting from 1. For completeness, we present these complement probabilities in Table 5.3. Let us verify Bayes' theorem for this data set using the probabilities in Table 5.1.

$$P(C|V) = \frac{P(V|C)P(C)}{P(V)} = \frac{0.1656(0.1449)}{0.2766} = 0.0868$$

which is the value for this posterior probability given in Table 5.2.

We are still not in a position to calculate the MAP estimate of *churn*. We must first find *joint conditional probabilities* of the form $P(I, V|C)$. Clementine's matrix node was used to provide the information about these joint conditional probabilities found in Table 5.4 by counting the records for which the respective joint conditions held. Now we can find the MAP estimate of *churn* for the four combinations of *International Plan* and *VoiceMail Plan* membership, using equation (5.3):

$$\theta_{\text{MAP}} = C_{\text{MAP}} = \arg\max_{C} p(I, V|C)p(C)$$

Suppose that we have a new record, where the customer belongs to the *International Plan* and *VoiceMail Plan*. Do we expect that this new customer will churn, or not? That is, what will be the maximum a posteriori estimate of *churn* for this new customer? We apply equation (5.3) for each of the *churn* or *nonchurn* cases and select the classification that provides the larger value.

TABLE 5.4   Joint Conditional Probabilities for the *Churn* Training Data Set

		Churn				*Churn*	
		False	*True*			*False*	*True*
$I \cap V$	No	2794	447	$I \cap V$	No	2720	382
	Yes	56	36		Yes	130	101
$p(I \cap V|C) = 36/(36 + 447) = 0.0745$				$p(I \cap \overline{V}|C) = 101/(101 + 382) = 0.2091$			
$p(I \cap V|\overline{C}) = 56/(56 + 2794) = 0.0196$				$p(I \cap \overline{V}|\overline{C}) = 130/(130 + 2720) = 0.0456$			
$\overline{I} \cap V$	No	2064	439	$\overline{I} \cap \overline{V}$	No	972	181
	Yes	786	44		Yes	1878	302
$p(\overline{I} \cap V|C) = 44/(44 + 439) = 0.0911$				$p(\overline{I} \cap \overline{V}|C) = 302/(302 + 181) = 0.6253$			
$p(\overline{I} \cap V|\overline{C}) = 786/(786 + 2064) = 0.2758$				$p(\overline{I} \cap \overline{V}|\overline{C}) = 1878/(1878 + 972) = 0.6589$			

Here we have for churners:

$$P(International\ Plan = yes,\ VoiceMail\ Plan = yes|churn = true)P(churn = true)$$
$$= P(I \cap V|C)P(C) = 0.0745(0.1449) = 0.0108$$

and for nonchurners

$$P(International\ Plan = yes,\ VoiceMail\ Plan = yes|churn = false)P(churn = false)$$
$$= P(I \cap V|\overline{C})P(\overline{C}) = 0.0196(0.8551) = 0.0167$$
$$P(I \cap V|\overline{C})P(\overline{C}) = 0.0196(0.8551) = 0.0168$$

Since 0.0167 for *churn = false* is the maximum of the two cases, $\theta_{MAP} = C_{MAP}$, the maximum a posteriori estimate of *churn* for this new customer is *churn = false*. For customers belonging to both plans, this MAP estimate of *churn = false* becomes our prediction; that is, we would predict that they would not churn.

Suppose that a new customer belongs to the *International Plan* but not the *VoiceMail Plan*. Then

$$P(I \cap \overline{V}|C)P(C) = 0.2091(0.1449) = 0.0303$$

and

$$P(I \cap \overline{V}|\overline{C})P(\overline{C}) = 0.0456(0.8551) = 0.0390$$

So $\theta_{MAP} = C_{MAP}$ is *churn = false*.

What if a new customer belongs to the *VoiceMail Plan* but not the *International Plan*? Then

$$P(\overline{I} \cap V|C)P(C) = (0.0911)(0.1449) = 0.0132$$

and

$$P(\overline{I} \cap V|\overline{C})P(\overline{C}) = 0.2758(0.8551) = 0.2358$$

Here again $\theta_{MAP} = C_{MAP}$ is *churn = false*.

Finally, suppose that a new customer belongs to neither the *International Plan* nor the *VoiceMail Plan*. Then

$$P(\overline{I} \cap \overline{V}|C)P(C) = 0.6253(0.1449) = 0.0906$$

and

$$P(\overline{I} \cap \overline{V}|\overline{C})P(\overline{C}) = 0.6589(0.8551) = 0.5634$$

so that, yet again, $\theta_{MAP} = C_{MAP}$ is *churn = false*.

Posterior Odds Ratio

Therefore, the MAP estimate for *churn* is *false* for each combination of *International Plan* and *VoiceMail Plan* membership. This result does not appear to be very helpful, since we will predict the same outcome for all customers regardless of their membership in the plans. However, not each of the classifications has the same strength of evidence. Next, we consider the level of evidence in each case, as defined by the *posterior odds ratio*. The posterior odds ratio represents a measure of the strength of evidence in favor of a particular classification and is calculated as follows.

> **POSTERIOR ODDS RATIO**
>
> $$\frac{p(\theta_c|\mathbf{X})}{p(\overline{\theta}_c|\mathbf{X})} = \frac{p(\mathbf{X}|\theta_c)p(\theta_c)}{p(\mathbf{X}|\overline{\theta}_c)p(\overline{\theta}_c)}$$
>
> where θ_c represents a particular classification of the unknown target variable.

A posterior odds ratio of exactly 1.0 would mean that the evidence from the posterior distribution supports both classifications equally. That is, the combination of information from the data and the prior distributions does not favor one category over the other. A value greater than 1.0 indicates that the posterior distribution favors the positive classification, while a value less than 1.0 represents evidence against the positive classification (e.g., *churn = true*). The value of the posterior odds ratio may be interpreted as indicating roughly the proportion or ratio of evidence provided by the posterior distribution in favor of the positive classification against the negative classification.

In our example, the posterior odds ratio for a new customer who belongs to both plans is

$$\frac{P(I \cap V|C)P(C)}{P(I \cap V|\overline{C})P(\overline{C})} = \frac{0.0108}{0.0168} = 0.6467$$

This means that that there is 64.67% as much evidence from the posterior distribution in support of *churn = true* as there is in support of *churn = false* for this customer.

For a new customer who belongs to the *International Plan* only, the posterior odds ratio is

$$\frac{P(I \cap \overline{V}|C)P(C)}{P(I \cap \overline{V}|\overline{C})P(\overline{C})} = \frac{0.0303}{0.0390} = 0.7769$$

indicating that there is 77.69% as much evidence from the posterior distribution in support of *churn = true* as there is in support of *churn = false* for such a customer.

New customers who belong to the *VoiceMail Plan* only have a posterior odds ratio of

$$\frac{P(\overline{I} \cap V|C)P(C)}{P(\overline{I} \cap V|\overline{C})P(\overline{C})} = \frac{0.0132}{0.2358} = 0.0560$$

indicating that there is only 5.6% as much evidence from the posterior distribution in support of *churn = true* as there is in support of *churn = false* for these customers.

Finally, for customers who belong to neither plan, the posterior odds ratio is

$$\frac{P(\overline{I} \cap \overline{V}|C)P(C)}{P(\overline{I} \cap \overline{V}|\overline{C})P(\overline{C})} = \frac{0.0906}{0.5634} = 0.1608$$

indicating that there is only 16.08% as much evidence from the posterior distribution in support of *churn = true* as there is in support of *churn = false* for customers who belong to neither plan.

Thus, although the MAP classification is *churn = false* in each case, the "confidence" in the classification varies greatly, with the evidence for *churn = true* ranging from 5.6% up to 77.69% of the evidence for *churn = false*. For customers who belong to the International Plan, the evidence for churn is much stronger. In fact, note from the MAP calculations above that the joint conditional probabilities for customers belonging to the *International Plan* (with or without the *VoiceMail Plan*) favored *churn = true*, but were overwhelmed by the preponderance of nonchurners in the data set, 85.51% to 14.49%, so that the MAP classification turned out to be *churn = false*. Thus, the posterior odds ratio allows us to assess the strength of evidence for our MAP classifications, which is more helpful to the analyst than a simple up-or-down decision.

Balancing the Data

However, since the classification decision was influenced by the preponderance of nonchurners in the data set, we may consider what might happen if we balanced the data set. Some data mining algorithms operate best when the relative frequencies of classes in the target variable are not extreme. For example, in fraud investigation, such a small percentage of transactions are fraudulent that an algorithm could simply ignore such transactions, classify only *nonfraudulent* and be correct 99.99% of the time. Therefore, balanced sampling methods are used to reduce the disparity among the proportions of target classes appearing in the training data. For example, in the fraud example, a training data set could be constructed that would contain (1) all of the fraudulent transactions, and (2) only a small percentage, say 1%, of the nonfraudulent transactions. A *stratified sampling* technique could then be applied, first partitioning by fraudulence, then taking all of the fraudulent records and a random sample of 1% of the nonfraudulent records. A less desirable approach would be to increase the proportion of fraudulent transactions by "cloning" them, that is, simply padding the database with copies of existing fraudulent records. This amounts to manufacturing data and tends to magnify random attribute values. ("Gosh, do 30% of our fraudulent transactions really take place under a full moon?")

In our case we have 14.49% of the records representing churners, which may be considered somewhat uncommon, although one could argue otherwise. Nevertheless, let us balance the training data set so that we have approximately 25% of the records representing churners. This may be accomplished if we (1) accept all of the *churn = true* records, and (2) take a random sample of 50% of our *churn = false* records. Since the original data set had 483 churners and 2850 nonchurners, this balancing procedure would provide us with $483/(483 + 1425) = 25.3\%$ *churn = true* records, as desired. Two drawbacks of balancing the data are that (1) the balanced data set will not have exactly the same character as the original data set, and (2). it is a shame to waste all that data (e.g., discard 1425 *churn = false* records).

Because some predictor variables have a higher correlation with the target variable than do other predictor variables, the character of the balanced data will change.

For example, suppose that churners have higher levels of *day minutes* than those of nonchurners. Then, when we balance the data set, the overall mean of *day minutes* will increase, since we have eliminated so many nonchurner records. Here, the mean *day minutes* increased from 179.775 to 183.206 after balancing (not shown), since balancing eliminated half of the nonchurner records, which were associated with lower *day minutes. Such changes cannot be avoided when balancing data sets.* Thus, direct overall comparisons between the original and balanced data sets are futile, since changes in character are inevitable. However, apart from these unavoidable changes, and although the random sampling tends to protect against systematic deviations, data analysts should provide evidence that their balanced data sets do not otherwise differ systematically from the original data set. This can be accomplished by examining the graphics and summary statistics from the original and balanced data set, *partitioned on the categories of the target variable.* Of course, the churners records for both data sets are identical, so we may proceed to the evidence for the nonchurner records.

Figure 5.2 provides a comparison of the nonchurner records from the original data set and the balanced data set for the variables *day minutes* and *customer service calls.* Figure 5.3 provides the distributions of *International Plan* members and *Voice-Mail Plan* members for the original data set and the balanced data set. There appear to be no systematic deviations. If such deviations are uncovered, the balancing should be reapplied. Cross-validation measures can be applied if the analyst is concerned about these deviations. Multiple randomly selected balanced data sets can be formed and the results averaged, for example. Hence, using the balanced *churn* data set, we once again compute the MAP estimate for *churn* for our four types of customers. Our updated probability of churning is

$$P(C_{\text{bal}}) = \frac{483}{483 + 1425} = 0.2531$$

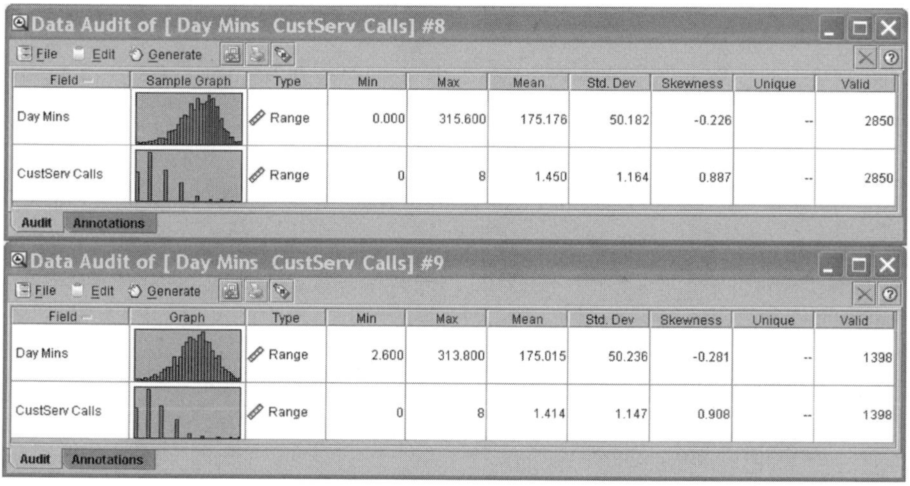

Figure 5.2 Graphical/statistical comparison of *day minutes* and *customer service calls* for nonchurners only. Original data set is on top.

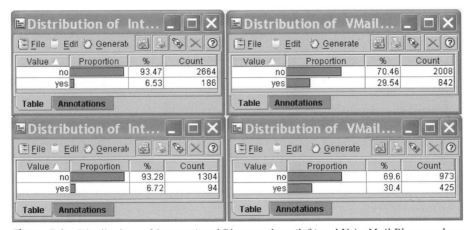

Figure 5.3 Distributions of *International Plan* members (left) and *VoiceMail Plan* members (right) for the original data set (top) and the balanced data set (bottom).

and for not churning is

$$P(\overline{C}_{\text{bal}}) = 1 - 0.2531 = 0.7469$$

For new customers who belong to the *International Plan* and *VoiceMail Plan*, we have

$$P(I \cap V | C_{\text{bal}})P(C_{\text{bal}}) = 0.0745(0.2531) = 0.0189$$

and

$$P(I \cap V | \overline{C}_{\text{bal}})P(\overline{C}_{\text{bal}}) = 0.0196(0.7469) = 0.0146$$

Thus, after balancing, C_{MAP}, the maximum a posteriori estimate of *churn* is *churn* = *true*, since 0.0189 is the greater value. Balancing has reversed the classification decision for this category of customers.

For customers who belong to the *International Plan* only, we have

$$P(I \cap \overline{V} | C_{\text{bal}})P(C_{\text{bal}}) = 0.2091(0.2531) = 0.0529$$

and

$$P(I \cap \overline{V} | \overline{C}_{\text{bal}})P(\overline{C}_{\text{bal}}) = 0.0456(0.7469) = 0.0341$$

The MAP estimate C_{MAP} is now *churn* = *true*, since 0.0529 is the greater value. Once again, balancing has reversed the original classification decision for this category of customers.

For new customers belonging only to the *VoiceMail Plan*, we have

$$P(\overline{I} \cap V | C_{\text{bal}})P(C_{\text{bal}}) = 0.0911(0.2531) = 0.0231$$

and

$$P(\overline{I} \cap V | \overline{C}_{\text{bal}})P(\overline{C}_{\text{val}}) = 0.2758(0.7469) = 0.2060$$

The MAP estimate has not changed from the original C_{MAP} : *churn* = *false* for members of the *VoiceMail Plan* only.

Finally, for new customers belonging to neither plan, we have

$$P(\overline{I} \cap \overline{V} | C_{bal}) P(C_{bal}) = 0.6253(0.2531) = 0.1583$$

and

$$P(\overline{I} \cap \overline{V} | \overline{C}_{bal}) P(\overline{C}_{bal}) = 0.6589(0.7469) = 0.4921$$

Again, the MAP estimate has not changed from the original C_{MAP} : *churn* = *false* for customers belonging to neither plan.

In the original data, MAP estimates were *churn* = *false* for all customers, a finding of limited actionability. Balancing the data set has provided different MAP estimates for different categories of new customers, providing executives with simple and actionable results. We may, of course, proceed to compute the posterior odds ratio for each of these classification decisions if we are interested in assessing the strength of evidence for the classifications. The reader is invited to do so in the exercises.

NAIVE BAYES CLASSIFICATION

For our simplified example using two dichotomous predictors and one dichotomous target variable, finding the MAP classification posed no computational difficulties. However, Hand et al. [5, p. 354] state that, in general, the number of probabilities that would need to be calculated to find the MAP classification would be on the order of k^m, where k is the number of classes for the target variable and m is the number of predictor variables. In our example, we had $k = 2$ classes in *churn* and $m = 2$ predictors, meaning that we had to find four probabilities to render a classification decision [e.g., $P(I \cap V | C)$, $P(C)$, $P(I \cap V | \overline{C})$, and $P(\overline{C})$].

On the other hand, suppose that we are trying to predict the marital status ($k = 5$: single, married, divorced, widowed, separated) of people based on a set of $m = 10$ demographic predictors. Then the number of probabilities to calculate would be $k^m = 5^{10} = 9,765,625$ probabilities. Note further that each of these 9,765,625 probabilities would need to be calculated based on relative frequencies of the appropriate cells in the 10-dimensional array. Using a minimum of 10 records per cell to estimate the relative frequencies, and on the unlikely assumption that the records are distributed uniformly across the array, the minimum requirement would be nearly 100 million records.

Thus, MAP classification is impractical to apply directly to any interesting real-world data mining scenarios. What, then, can be done? MAP classification requires that we find

$$\arg\max_{\theta} p(\mathbf{X}|\theta)p(\theta) = \arg\max_{\theta} p(X_1 = x_1, X_2 = x_2, \ldots, X_m = x_m | \theta)p(\theta)$$

The problem is not calculating $p(\theta)$, for which there is usually a small number of classes. Rather, the problem is the curse of dimensionality, that is, finding $p(X_1 = x_1, X_2 = x_2, \ldots, X_m = x_m | \theta)$ for all the possible combinations of the X-variables (the predictors). Here is where the search space explodes, so if there is a way to cut down on the search space for this problem, it is to be found right here.

Here is the key: Suppose we make the simplifying assumption that the predictor variables are conditionally independent given the target value (e.g., *churn = false*). Two events *A* and *B* are said to be *conditionally independent* if for a given event *C*, $p(A \cap B|C) = p(A|C)p(B|C)$. For example, conditional independence would state that for customers who churn, membership in one of the two plans (*I* or *V*) would not affect the probability of membership in the other plan. Similarly, the idea extends to customers who do not churn.

In general, the assumption of conditional independence may be expressed as follows:

$$p(X_1 = x_1, X_2 = x_2, \ldots, X_m = x_m|\theta) = \prod_{i=1}^{m} p(X_i = x_i|\theta)$$

The *naive Bayes classification* is therefore

$$\theta_{NB} = \arg\max_{\theta} \prod_{i=1}^{m} p(X_i = x_i|\theta)p(\theta)$$

When the conditional independence assumption is valid, the naive Bayes classification is the same as the MAP classification. Therefore, we investigate whether the assumption of conditional independence holds for our *churn* data set example, as shown in Table 5.5. In each case, note that the approximation for the nonchurners is several times closer than for the churners. This may indicate that the assumption of conditional independence assumption is best validated for nonrare categories, another argument in support of balancing when necessary.

We now proceed to calculate naive Bayes classifications for the *churn* data set. For a new customer belonging to both plans, we have for churners,

$$p(I|C)p(V|C)p(C) = 0.0470(0.1449) = 0.0068$$

and for nonchurners,

$$p(I|\overline{C})p(V|\overline{C})p(\overline{C}) = 0.0193(0.8551) = 0.0165$$

The naive Bayes classification for new customers who belong to both plans is therefore *churn = false* since 0.0165 is the larger of the two values. It turns out that just as for the MAP classifier, all four cases return a naive Bayes classification of *churn = false*. Also, after 25.31%/74.69% balancing, new customers who belong to the *International Plan* are classified by naive Bayes as churners, regardless of *VoiceMail Plan* membership, just as for the MAP classifier. These results are left to the exercises for verification.

When using naive Bayes classification, far fewer probabilities need to be estimated, just $k \cdot m$ probabilities rather than k^m for the MAP classifier: in other words, just the number of predictor variables times the number of distinct values of the target variable. In the marital status example, where we had $k = 5$ distinct marital statuses and $m = 10$ predictor variables, we would need to compute only $km = 5(10) = 50$ probabilities rather than the 9.7 million needed for the MAP classifier. At 10 records per cell, that would mean that only 500 records would be needed compared to the nearly

TABLE 5.5   Checking the Conditional Independence Assumption for the *Churn* Data Set

$(I \cap V)|C$	$(I \cap \overline{V})|C$
$p(I \cap V|C) = 0.0745$ $p(I|C)p(V|C)$ $\quad = 0.2836(0.1656) = 0.0470$ Difference $= |0.0745 - 0.0470| = 0.0275$	$p(I \cap \overline{V}|C) = 0.2091$ $p(I|C)p(\overline{V}|C)$ $\quad = 0.2836(0.8344) = 0.2366$ Difference $= |0.2091 - 0.2366| = 0.0275$
$(I \cap V)|\overline{C}$	$(I \cap \overline{V})|\overline{C}$
$p(I \cap V|\overline{C}) = 0.0196$ $p(I|\overline{C})p(V|\overline{C})$ $\quad = 0.0653(0.2954) = 0.0193$ Difference $= |0.0196 - 0.0193| = 0.0003$	$p(I \cap \overline{V}|\overline{C}) = 0.0456$ $p(I|\overline{C})p(V|\overline{C})$ $\quad = 0.0653(0.7046) = 0.0460$ $p(I|\overline{C})p(\overline{V}|\overline{C})$ $\quad = 0.0653(0.7046) = 0.0460$ Difference $= |0.0456 - 0.0460| = 0.0004$
$(\overline{I} \cap V)|C$	$(\overline{I} \cap \overline{V})|C$
$p(\overline{I} \cap V|C) = 0.0911$ $p(\overline{I}|C)p(V|C)$ $\quad = 0.7164(0.1656) = 0.1186$ Difference $= |0.0911 - 0.1186| = 0.0275$	$p(\overline{I} \cap \overline{V}|C) = 0.6253$ $p(\overline{I}|C)p(\overline{V}|C)$ $\quad = 0.7164(0.8344) = 0.5978$ Difference $= |0.6253 - 0.5978| = 0.0275$
$(\overline{I} \cap V)|\overline{C}$	$(\overline{I} \cap \overline{V})|\overline{C}$
$p(\overline{I} \cap V|\overline{C}) = 0.2758$ $p(\overline{I}|\overline{C})p(V|\overline{C})$ $\quad = 0.9347(0.2954) = 0.2761$ Difference $= |0.2758 - 0.2761| = 0.0003$	$p(\overline{I} \cap \overline{V}|\overline{C}) = 0.6589$ $p(\overline{I}|\overline{C})p(\overline{V}|\overline{C})$ $\quad = 0.9347(0.7046) = 0.6586$ Difference $= |0.6589 - 0.6586| = 0.0003$

100 million calculated earlier. Clearly, the conditional independence assumption, when valid, makes our life much easier. Further, since the naive Bayes classification is the same as the MAP classification when the conditional independence assumption is met, the naive Bayes classification is also optimal, in the sense of minimizing the error rate over all classifiers. In practice, however, departures from the conditional independence assumption tend to inhibit the optimality of the naive Bayes classifier.

Next, we examine the log of the posterior odds ratio, which can provide us with an intuitive measure of the amount that each variable contributes toward the classification decision. The posterior odds ratio takes the form

$$\frac{p(\theta_c|\mathbf{X})}{p(\overline{\theta}_c|\mathbf{X})} = \frac{p(\mathbf{X}|\theta_c)p(\theta_c)}{p(\mathbf{X}|\overline{\theta}_c)p(\overline{\theta}_c)} = \frac{p(X_1 = x_1, X_2 = x_2, \ldots, X_m = x_m|\theta)p(\theta_c)}{p(X_1 = x_1, X_2 = x_2, \ldots, X_m = x_m|\overline{\theta})p(\overline{\theta}_c)}$$

$$\overset{\text{conditional}}{\underset{\text{assumption}}{\text{independence}}} = \frac{\prod_{i=1}^{m} p(X_i = x_i|\theta)p(\theta_c)}{\prod_{i=1}^{m} p(X_i = x_i|\overline{\theta})p(\overline{\theta}_c)}$$

which is the form of the posterior odds ratio for naive Bayes.

Next, consider the log of the posterior odds ratio. Since the log of a product is the sum of the logs, we have

$$\log \frac{\prod_{i=1}^{m} p(X_i = x_i | \theta) p(\theta_c)}{\prod_{i=1}^{m} p(X_i = x_i | \overline{\theta}) p(\overline{\theta}_c)}$$

$$= \log \left(\prod_{i=1}^{m} p(X_i = x_i | \theta) \right) + \log p(\theta_c) - \log \left(\prod_{i=1}^{m} p(X_i = x_i | \overline{\theta}) \right) - \log p(\overline{\theta}_c)$$

$$= \log \frac{p(\theta_c)}{p(\overline{\theta}_c)} + \sum_{i=1}^{m} \log \frac{p(X_i = x_i | \theta)}{p(X_i = x_i | \overline{\theta})}$$

This form of the log posterior odds ratio is useful from an interpretive point of view, since each term,

$$\log \left(\frac{p(X_i = x_i | \theta)}{p(X_i = x_i | \overline{\theta})} \right)$$

relates to the additive contribution, either positive or negative, of each attribute. For example, consider the log posterior odds ratio for a new customer who belongs to both the International Plan and the VoiceMail Plan. Then for the International Plan we have

$$\log \frac{p(I|C)}{p(I|\overline{C})} = \log \frac{0.2836}{0.0653} = 0.6378$$

and for the VoiceMail Plan we have

$$\log \frac{p(V|C)}{p(V|\overline{C})} = \log \frac{0.1656}{0.2954} = -0.2514$$

Thus, we see that membership in the International Plan contributes in a positive way to the likelihood that a particular customer will churn, whereas membership in the VoiceMail Plan decreases the churn probability. These findings concur with our results from the earlier volume [4].

The conditional independence assumption should not be made blindly. Correlated predictors, for example, violate the assumption. For example, in classifying risk for credit default, total assets and annual income would probably be correlated. However, naive Bayes would, for each classification (default, no default), consider total assets and annual income to be independent and uncorrelated. Of course, careful data mining practice includes dealing with correlated variables at the EDA stage anyway, since the correlation can cause problems for several different data methods. Principal components analysis can be used to handle correlated variables. Another option is to construct a user-defined composite, a linear combination of a small set of highly correlated variables. (See Chapter 1 for more information on handling correlated variables.)

As we saw in Chapter 4, a cell with frequency zero can pose difficulties for the analysis. Now, for naive Bayes estimation, what if a particular cell (combination of attribution values) has zero frequency? For example, of the 483 customers who churned, 80 had the VoiceMail Plan, so that $p(V|C) = 80/483 = 0.1656$. However,

---

ADJUSTED PROBABILITY ESTIMATE FOR ZERO-FREQUENCY CELLS

$$\frac{n_c + n_{\text{equiv}}\,p}{n + n_{\text{equiv}}}$$

where n represents the total number of records for this target class, n_c the number of these n records that also have the attribute value of interest, p the prior estimate of the probability being estimated, and n_{equiv} is a constant representing the *equivalent sample size*.

---

suppose that none of the churners had the VoiceMail Plan. Then $p(V|C)$ would equal $0/483 = 0.0$. The real problem with this is that since the conditional independence assumption means that we take the product of the marginal probabilities, this zero value for $p(V|C)$ will percolate through and dominate the result.

Since the naive Bayes classification contains $\prod_{i=1}^{m} p(X_i = x_i|\theta)$, a single zero probability in this product will render the entire product to be zero, which will also make $\prod_{i=1}^{m} p(X_i = x_i|\theta)p(\theta)$ zero, thereby effectively eliminating this class (*churn = true*) from consideration for any future probability involving the VoiceMail Plan. To avoid this problem, we posit an additional number of "virtual" samples, which provides the following adjusted probability estimate for zero-frequency cells.

The constant n_{equiv}, the additional number of virtual samples used to find the adjusted probability, controls how heavily the adjustment is weighted. In the absence of other information, the prior probability estimate p may be assigned to be the noninformative uniform prior $p = 1/k$, where k is the number of classes for the target variable. Thus, n_{equiv} additional samples, distributed according to p, are contributed to the calculation of the probability. In our example we have $n = 483$, $n_c = 0$, and $p = 1/2$. We choose $n_{\text{equiv}} = 1$ to minimize the effect of the intervention. The adjusted probability estimate for the zero = probability cell for $p(V|C)$ is therefore:

$$\frac{n_c + n_{\text{equiv}}\,p}{n + n_{\text{equiv}}} = \frac{0 + 1(1/2)}{483 + 1} = 0.0010$$

Numeric Predictors

Bayesian classification can be extended from categorical to continuous predictor variables, provided that we know the relevant probability distribution. Suppose that, in addition to *International Plan* and *VoiceMail Plan*, we also had access to *total minutes*, the total number of minutes used by the cell-phone customer, along with evidence that the distribution of *total minutes* is normal for both churners and nonchurners. The mean *total minutes* for churners is $\mu_{\text{churn}} = 635$ minutes, with a standard deviation of $\sigma_{\text{churn}} = 111$ minutes. The mean *total minutes* for nonchurners is $\mu_{\text{nonchurn}} = 585$, with a standard deviation of $\sigma_{\text{nonchurn}} = 84$ minutes. Thus, we assume that the distribution of *total minutes* for churners is normal (635,111) and for nonchurners is normal (585,84).

Let T_{churn} represent the random variable *total minutes* for churners. Then

$$p(T_{\text{churn}} = t) \cong f_{T|C}$$

$$= \frac{1}{\sqrt{2\pi}\,\sigma_{\text{churn}}} \exp\left[\frac{-1}{2\sigma_{\text{churn}}^2}(T_{\text{churn}} - \mu_{\text{churn}})^2\right]$$

$$= \frac{1}{\sqrt{2\pi}\,(111)} \exp\left[\frac{-1}{2(111)^2}(T_{\text{churn}} - 635)^2\right]$$

with an analogous form for nonchurners. [Here $\exp(y)$ represents e^y. Also, $f_{T|C}(t)$ is substituted for $p(T = t|C)$ since for continuous random variables, $p(T = t) = 0, \forall t$.]

Next, suppose we are interested in classifying new customers who have 800 *total minutes* and belong to both plans, using naive Bayes classification. We have for churners,

$$p(I \cap V \cap T = 800|C)P(C) = P(I|C)P(V|C)f_{T|C}(800)P(C)$$
$$= 0.2836(0.1656)(0.001191)(0.1449) = 0.000008105$$

and for nonchurners,

$$p(I \cap V \cap T = 800|\overline{C})P(\overline{C}) = P(I|\overline{C})P(V|\overline{C})f_{T|\overline{C}}(800)P(\overline{C})$$
$$= 0.0653(0.2954)(0.0001795)(0.8551) = 0.000002961$$

Hence, the naive Bayes classification for new customers who have 800 *total minutes* and belong to both plans is *churn = true* by a posterior odds ratio of

$$\frac{0.000008105}{0.000002961} = 2.74$$

In other words, the additional information that the new customer had 800 *total minutes* was enough to *reverse the classification* from *churn = false* (previously, without *total minutes*) to *churn = true*. This is due to the somewhat heavier cell-phone usage of the churners group, with a higher mean *total minutes*.

Assumptions of normality should not be made without supporting evidence. Should we take Figure 5.4 as supporting evidence for the normality of our distributions? No. The histogram in Figure 5.4 represents the collection of all churners and nonchurners lumped together, not the individual distributions for each category that we would like to work with. Therefore, Figure 5.4 does not represent supporting evidence for our assumptions.

Consider Figure 5.5, a Minitab comparison dot plot of the two distributions. Immediately we can see that indeed there are many more nonchurner records than churners. We also note that the balancing point (the mean, indicated by the triangle) for churners is greater than for nonchurners, supporting the statistics above. Finally, we notice that the normality assumption for nonchurners looks quite solid, whereas the normality assumption for the churners looks a little shaky.

Normal probability plots are then constructed for the two distributions just described and shown in Figure 5.6. In a normal probability plot, there should be no systematic deviations from linearity; otherwise, the normality assumption is called into question. In Figure 5.6 the gray points represent *total minutes* for churners, and the black points represent *total minutes* for nonchurners. Note that the bulk of the

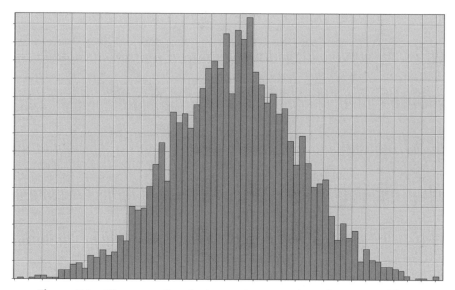

Figure 5.4   Histogram of *total minutes*, churners and nonchurners combined.

black points line up nearly perfectly on a straight line, indicating that the normality assumption is validated for nonchurners' *total minutes*. However, there does appear to be systematic curvature in the gray points, in a slight backward S-curve, indicating that the normality assumption for churners' *total minutes* is not validated. Since the assumption is not validated, all subsequent inference applying this assumption must be flagged as such for the enduser. For example, the naive Bayes classification of *churn = true* may or may not be valid, and the end user should be informed of this uncertainty.

Often, nonnormal distribution can be transformed to normality, using, for example, the Box–Cox transformation $T(y) = (y^{\lambda} - 1)/\lambda$. However, Figure 5.5 shows that *total minutes* for churners actually looks like a mixture of two normal distributions, which will prove resistant to monotonic transformations to normality. The mixture idea is intriguing and deserves further investigation. Data transformations were investigated more fully in Chapters 2 and 3.

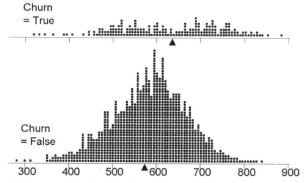

Figure 5.5   Comparison dot plot of *total minutes* for churners and nonchurners.

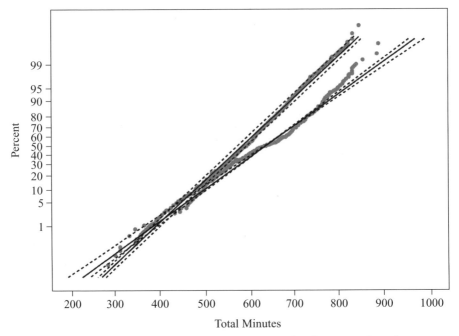

Figure 5.6 Normal probability plots of *total minutes* for churners and nonchurners.

Alternatively, one may dispense with the normality assumption altogether and choose to work directly with the observed empirical distribution of *total minutes* for churners and nonchurners. We are interested in comparing $p(T = 800)$ for each distribution; why not estimate this probability by estimating $p(798 \leq T \leq 802)$ directly for each distribution? It turns out that three of the churner customers had between 798 and 802 total minutes, compared to one for the nonchurner customers. So the probability estimates would be for the churners,

$$p(T = 800|C) \cong \frac{3}{483} = 0.006211$$

and for the nonchurners,

$$p(T = 800|\overline{C})\frac{1}{2850} = 0.0003509$$

Thus, to find the naive Bayes classification, for churners,

$$p(I \cap V \cap T = 800|C)P(C) = P(I|C)P(V|C)\hat{f}_{T|C}(800)P(C)$$
$$= 0.2836(0.1656)(0.006211)(0.1449) = 0.00004227$$

and for nonchurners,

$$p(I \cap V \cap T = 800|\overline{C})P(\overline{C}) = P(I|\overline{C})P(V|\overline{C})\hat{f}_{T|\overline{C}}(800)P(\overline{C})$$
$$= 0.0653(0.2954)(0.0003509)(0.8551)$$
$$= 0.000005788$$

[Here, $\hat{f}_{T|C}(800)$ represents our empirical estimate of $f_{T|C}(800)$.] Thus, once again, the naive Bayes classification for new customers who have 800 *total minutes* and belong to both plans is *churn* = *true*, this time by a posterior odds ratio of

$$\frac{0.00004227}{0.000005788} = 7.30$$

The evidence is even more solid in favor of a classification of *churn* = *true* for these customers, and we did not have to burden ourselves with an assumption about normality.

The empirical probability estimation method shown here should be verified over a range of margins of error. Above, we found the numbers of records within a margin of error of two records ($798 \leq T \leq 802$). The reader may verify that that there are eight churn records and three nonchurn records within 5 minutes of the desired 800 minutes, and that there are 15 churn records and five nonchurn records within 10 minutes of the desired 800 minutes. So the approximate $3:1$ ratio of churn records to nonchurn records in this area of the distribution seems fairly stable.

WEKA: HANDS-ON ANALYSIS USING NAIVE BAYES

In this exercise, WEKA's naive Bayes classifier is used to classify a small set of movie reviews as either positive (pos) or negative (neg). First, the text from 20 actual reviews is preprocessed to create a training file containing three Boolean attributes and a target variable. This file is used to train our naive Bayes model and contains a set of 20 individual review instances, where 10 reviews have the class value "pos" and the remaining 10 reviews take on the class value "neg." Similarly, a second file is created to test our model. In this case, *movies_test.arff* contains only four review instances, two of which are positive and two of which are negative.

During the preprocessing stage, the unigrams (specifically adjectives) are extracted from the reviews and a list of adjectives is derived. The three most frequently occurring adjectives are chosen from the list and form the set of attributes used by each review instance. Specifically, each instance is represented as a Boolean document vector of length three, where each attribute's value is either 1 or 0, corresponding to whether the review contains or does not contain the particular adjective, respectively. The ARFF-based training file *movies_train.arff* is shown in Table 5.6.

All attributes in the ARFF file are nominal and take on one of two values; inputs are either "0" or "1," and the target variable *CLASS* is either "pos" or "neg." The *data* section lists each instance, which corresponds to a specific movie review record. For example, the third line in the data section corresponds to a review where *more* = 1, *much* = 1, *other* = 0, and *CLASS* = neg.

Now, we load the training file and build the naive Bayes classification model.

1. Open the WEKA Explorer panel.
2. On the Preprocess tab, press Open file and specify the path to the training file, *movies_train.arff*.
3. Select the Classify Tab.
4. Under Classifier, press the Choose button.
5. Select Classifiers → Bayes → Naive Bayes from the navigation hierarchy.

TABLE 5.6   ARFF Movies Training File *movies_train.arff*

```
@relation movies_train.arff

@attribute more                        {0, 1}
@attribute much                        {0, 1}
@attribute other                       {0, 1}
@attribute CLASS                       {neg, pos}

@data
1, 0, 0, neg
1, 1, 0, neg
1, 1, 0, neg
0, 1, 1, neg
1, 1, 1, neg
1, 1, 0, neg
1, 0, 0, neg
1, 0, 1, neg
1, 1, 1, neg
1, 1, 1, neg
1, 1, 1, pos
1, 0, 1, pos
1, 1, 1, pos
1, 1, 1, pos
1, 0, 0, pos
1, 1, 0, pos
0, 1, 1, pos
1, 0, 1, pos
0, 0, 0, pos
1, 1, 1, pos
```

6. In our modeling experiment we have separate training and test sets; therefore, under Test options, choose the Use training set option.

7. Click Start to build the model.

WEKA creates the naive Bayes model and produces the results in the Classifier output window as shown in Figure 5.7. In general, the results indicate that the classification accuracy of the model, as measured against the training set, is 65% (13/20.)

Next, our model is evaluated against the unseen data found in the test set, *movies_test.arff*.

1. Under Test options, choose Supplied test set. Click Set.

2. Specify the path to the test file, *movies_test.arff*.

3. Under Result list, right-click the naive Bayes model from the list, and choose Re-evaluate model on the current test set.

Surprisingly, the Explorer panel shows that our naive Bayes model has classified all four movie reviews in the test set correctly. Although these results are encouraging from a real-world perspective, the training set lacks a sufficient number of both

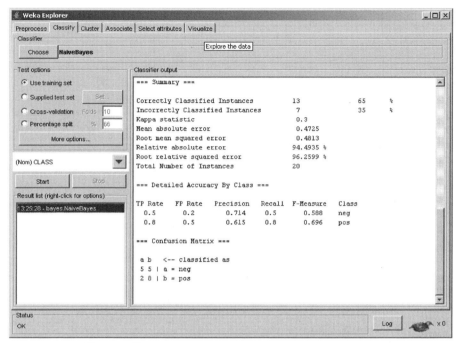

Figure 5.7   WEKA Explorer: naive Bayes training results.

attributes and examples to be considered practical in any real sense. We continue with the objective of becoming familiar with the naive Bayes classifier. Let's explore how naive Bayes arrived at the decision to classify the fourth record in the test set correctly. First, however, we examine the probabilities reported by the naive Bayes classifier.

1. Under Test options, press the More options button.

2. Select Output text predictions on the test set, and click OK.

3. Repeat the procedure to evaluate the model against the test set by right-clicking the naive Bayes model and then choosing Re-evaluate model on the current test set.

In addition to the classification results we just observed, the naive Bayes model now reports the actual probabilities it used to classify each review instance from the test set as either "pos" or "neg." For example, Table 5.7 shows that naive Bayes has classified the fourth instance from the test set as "pos" with a probability equal to 0.60. In Table 5.8, the conditional probabilities are calculated that correspond to the data found in *movies_train.arff*. For example, given that the review is negative, the conditional probability of the word *more* occurring is $p(more = 1|CLASS = neg) = 9/10$. In addition, we also know the prior probabilities of $p(CLASS = pos) = p(CLASS = neg) = 10/20 = 0.5$. These simply correspond with the fact that our training set is balanced 50–50.

Recall the method of adjusting the probability estimate to avoid zero-frequency cells, as described earlier in the chapter. In this particular case, naive Bayes produces an internal adjustment, where $n_{\text{equiv}} = 2$ and $p = 0.5$, to produce $(n_c + 1)/(n + 2)$.

TABLE 5.7 Naive Bayes Test Set Predictions

```
=== Predictions on test set ===

  inst#,     actual,  predicted,  error,  probability distribution
    1        1:neg      1:neg             *0.533        0.467
    2        1:neg      1:neg             *0.533        0.467
    3        2:pos      2:pos              0.444        *0.556
    4        2:pos      2:pos              0.4          *0.6
```

Therefore, we now calculate the probably of the fourth review from the test as set being either "pos" or "neg":

$$\prod_{i=1}^{3} p(X_i = x_i | CLASS = pos) p(CLASS = pos)$$

$$= \left(\frac{8+1}{10+2}\right)\left(\frac{4+1}{10+2}\right)\left(\frac{7+1}{10+2}\right)(0.5)$$

$$= \left(\frac{9}{12}\right)\left(\frac{5}{12}\right)\left(\frac{8}{12}\right)(0.5) \approx 0.1042$$

$$\prod_{i=1}^{3} p(X_i = x_i | CLASS = neg) p(CLASS = neg)$$

$$= \left(\frac{9+1}{10+2}\right)\left(\frac{3+1}{10+2}\right)\left(\frac{5+1}{10+2}\right)(0.5)$$

$$= \left(\frac{10}{12}\right)\left(\frac{4}{12}\right)\left(\frac{6}{12}\right)(0.5) \approx 0.0694$$

Finally, we normalize the probabilities and determine

$$p(pos) = \frac{0.1042}{0.1042 + 0.0694} \approx 0.6002$$

$$p(neg) = \frac{0.0694}{0.1042 + 0.0694} \approx 0.3998$$

Here, the review is classified as positive with a 0.60 probability. These results agree with those reported by WEKA in Table 5.7, which also classified the review as positive. In fact, our hand-calculated probabilities match those reported by WEKA. Although the data set used for this example is rather small, it demonstrates the use of the naive Bayes classifier in WEKA when using separate training and test files. More important, our general understanding of the algorithm has increased as a result of computing the probabilities that led to an actual classification by the model.

TABLE 5.8 Conditional Probabilities Derived from *movies_training.arff*

	More		Much		Other	
	1	0	1	0	1	0
neg	9/10	1/10	7/10	3/10	5/10	5/10
pos	8/10	2/10	6/10	4/10	7/10	3/10

BAYESIAN BELIEF NETWORKS

Naive Bayes classification assumes that the attributes are conditionally independent given the value of the target variable. This assumption may in fact be too strong for environments where dependence exists among the predictor variables. *Bayesian belief networks* (BBNs) are designed to allow joint conditional independencies to be defined among subsets of variables. BBNs, also called *Bayesian networks* or *Bayes nets*, take the form of a directed acyclic graph (DAG), where *directed* means that the arcs are traversed in one direction only, and *acyclic* means that no child node cycles back up to any progenitor.

An example of a Bayesian network in the form of a DAG is shown in Figure 5.8. The nodes represent variables, and the arcs represent the (directed) dependence among the variables. In general, node *A* is a *parent* or *immediate predecessor* of node *X*, and node *X* is a *descendant* of node *A*, if there exists a directed arc from node *A* to node *X*. The intrinsic relationship among the variables in a Bayesian network is as follows:

- Each variable in a Bayesian network is conditionally independent of its nondescendants in the network given its parents.

Thus, we have

$$p(X_1 = x_1, X_2 = x_2, \ldots, X_m = x_m) = \prod_{i=1}^{m} p(X_i = x_i | parents(X_i)) \qquad (5.4)$$

Note that the child node probability depends only on its parents.

Clothing Purchase Example

To introduce Bayesian networks, we shall use the clothing purchase example, illustrated by the Bayes net in Figure 5.8. Suppose that a clothes retailer operates two outlets, one in New York and one in Los Angeles, each producing sales throughout the four seasons. The retailer is interested in probabilities concerning three articles of clothing in particular: warm coats, business shirts, and Bermuda shorts. Questions of interest include the fabric weight of the article of clothing (light, medium, or heavy) and the color of the article (bright, neutral, or dark). To build a Bayesian network, there are two main considerations: (1) the dependence relationship among the variables of interest, and (2) the associated "local" probabilities.

The retailer has five variables: *season, location, clothing purchase, fabric weight*, and *color*. What is the dependence relationship among these variables? For example, does the season of the year depend on the color of the clothes purchased? Certainly not, since a customer's purchase of some bright clothing doesn't mean that spring is here, for example, although the customer may wish it so.

In fact, the season of the year does not depend on any of the other variables, so we place the node for the variable *season* at the top of the Bayes network, which indicates that it does not depend on the other variables. Similarly, *location* does not depend on the other variables, and is therefore placed at the top of the network. Since the fabric weight and the color of the clothing are not known until the article is purchased, the node for the variable *clothing purchase* is inserted next into the network, with arcs to each of the *fabric weight* and *color* nodes.

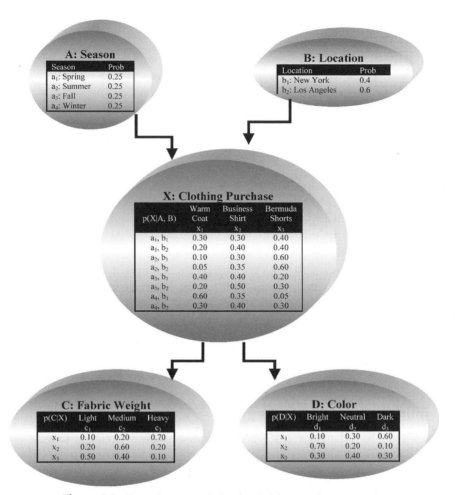

Figure 5.8 Bayesian network for the clothing purchase example.

The second consideration for constructing a Bayesian network is to specify all of the entries in the probability tables for each node. The probabilities in the *season* node table indicate that clothing sales for this retail establishment are uniform throughout the four seasons. The probabilities in the *location* node probability table show that 60% of sales are generated from their Los Angeles store and 40% from their New York store. Note that these two tables need not supply conditional probabilities, since the nodes are at the top of the network.

Assigning probabilities for *clothing purchase* requires that the dependence on the parent nodes be taken into account. Expert knowledge or relative frequencies (not shown) should be consulted. Note that the probabilities in each row of the table sum to 1. For example, the fourth row of the *clothing purchase* table shows the conditional probabilities of purchasing the articles of clothing from the Los Angeles store in the summer. The probabilities of purchasing a warm coat, a business shirt, and Bermuda shorts are 0.05, 0.35, and 0.60, respectively. The seventh row represents probabilities of purchasing articles of clothing from the New York store in

Bayes nets help determine purchase probabilities. (Courtesy: Chantal Larose).

winter. The probabilities of purchasing a warm coat, a business shirt, and Bermuda shorts are 0.60, 0.35, 0.05, respectively.

Given a particular item of clothing, the probabilities then need to be specified for *fabric weight* and *color*. A warm coat will have probabilities for being of light, medium, or heavy fabric, or 0.10, 0.20, and 0.70, respectively. A business shirt will have probabilities of having bright, neutral, or dark color of 0.70, 0.20, and 0.10, respectively. Note that the fabric weight or color depends only on the item of clothing purchased, not on the location or season. In other words, *color* is conditionally independent of *location* given the article of clothing purchased. This is one of the relationships of conditional independence to be found in this Bayesian network. Here are some others:

- *Color* is conditionally independent of *season* given clothing purchased.
- *Color* is conditionally independent of *fabric weight* given clothing purchased.
- *Fabric weight* is conditionally independent of *color* given clothing purchased.
- *Fabric weight* is conditionally independent of *location* given clothing purchased.
- *Fabric weight* is conditionally independent of *season* given clothing purchased.
- Note that we could say that *season* is conditionally independent of *location* given its parents. But since *season* has no parents in the Bayes net, this means that *season* and *location* are (unconditionally) independent.

Be careful when inserting arcs into the Bayesian network, since these represent strong assertions of conditional independence.

Using the Bayesian Network to Find Probabilities

Next, suppose we would like to find the probability that light-fabric neutral-colored Bermuda shorts were purchased in New York in the winter. Using equation (5.4), we may express what we seek as

$$p(A = a_4, B = b_2, C = c_1, D = d_2, X = x_3)$$
$$= p(A = a_4)p(B = b_2)p(X = x_3|A = a_4 \cap B = b_2)p(C = c_1|X = x_3)$$
$$\quad p(D = d_2|X = x_3)p(A = a_4, B = b_1, C = c_1, D = d_2, X = x_3)$$
$$= p(A = a_4)p(B = b_1)p(X = x_3|A = a_4 \cap B = b_1)p(C = c_1|X = x_3)$$
$$\quad p(D = d_2|X = x_3)$$
$$= p(season = winter)p(location = New\ York)$$
$$\quad \cdot p(clothing = shorts \mid season = winter\ \text{and}\ location = New\ York)$$
$$\quad \cdot p(fabric = light \mid clothing = shorts)p(color = neutral \mid clothing = shorts)$$
$$= 0.25(0.4)(0.05)(0.50)(0.40) = 0.001$$

Evidently, there is not much demand for light-fabric neutral-colored Bermuda shorts in New York in the winter.

Similarly, probabilities may be found in this way for any combinations of season, location, article of clothing, fabric weight, and color. Using the Bayesian network structure, we can also calculate prior probabilities for each node. For example, the prior probability of a warm coat is found as follows:

$$p(coat) = p(X = x_1)$$
$$= p(X = x_1|A = a_1 \cap B = b_1)p(A = a_1 \cap B = b_1)$$
$$\quad + p(X = x_1|A = a_1 \cap B = b_2)p(A = a_1 \cap B = b_2)$$
$$\quad + p(X = x_1|A = a_2 \cap B = b_1)p(A = a_2 \cap B = b_1)$$
$$\quad + p(X = x_1|A = a_2 \cap B = b_2)p(A = a_2 \cap B = b_2)$$
$$\quad + p(X = x_1|A = a_3 \cap B = b_1)p(A = a_3 \cap B = b_1)$$
$$\quad + p(X = x_1|A = a_3 \cap B = b_2)p(A = a_3 \cap B = b_2)$$
$$\quad + p(X = x_1|A = a_4 \cap B = b_1)p(A = a_4 \cap B = b_1)$$
$$\quad + p(X = x_1|A = a_4 \cap B = b_2)p(A = a_4 \cap B = b_2)$$
$$= (0.30)(0.10) + (0.20)(0.15) + (0.10)(0.10) + (0.05)(0.15)$$
$$\quad + (0.40)(0.10) + (0.20)(0.15) + (0.60)(0.10) + (0.30)(0.15)$$
$$= 0.2525$$

So the prior probability of purchasing a warm coat is 0.2525. Note that we used the information that *season* and *location* are independent, so that $p(A \cap B) = p(A)p(B)$. For example, the probability that a sale is made in the spring in New York is

$$p(A = a_1 \cap B = b_1) = p(A = a_1)p(B = b_1) = 0.25(0.4) = 0.10$$

Posterior probabilities may also be found. For example,

$$p(winter \mid coat) = \frac{p(coat)}{p(winter \cap coat)}$$

To find $p(winter \cap coat)$, we must first find $p(winter \cap New\ York \cap coat)$ and $p(winter \cap Los\ Angeles \cap coat)$. Using the conditional probability structure of the Bayesian network in Figure 5.8, we have

$$p(winter \cap New\ York \cap coat) = p(winter)p(New\ York)p(coat|winter \cap New\ York)$$
$$= 0.25(0.4)(0.6) = 0.06$$

$$p(winter \cap Los\ Angeles \cap coat)$$
$$= p(winter)p(Los\ Angeles)p(coat \mid winter \cap Los\ Angeles)$$
$$= 0.25(0.6)(0.3) = 0.045$$

So

$$p(winter \cap coat) = 0.06 + 0.045 = 0.105$$

Thus, we have

$$p(winter|coat) = \frac{p(coat)}{p(winter \cap coat)} = \frac{0.2525}{0.105} = 0.4158$$

Then the Bayes net could provide a classification decision using the highest posterior probability among $p(winter \mid coat)$, $p(spring \mid coat)$, $p(summer \mid coat)$, and $p(fall \mid coat)$ (*see the exercises*).

A Bayesian network represents the joint probability distribution for a given set of variables. What is a joint probability distribution? Let $X_1, X_2, \ldots, X_m$ represent a set of m random variables, with each random variable X_i defined on space S_{X_i}. For example, a normal random variable X is defined on space S_X, where S_X is the real number line. Then the joint space of $X_1, X_2, \ldots, X_m$ is defined as the cross-product $S_{X_1} \times S_{X_2} \times \cdots \times S_{X_m}$. That is, each joint observation consists of the vector of length m of observed field values $\langle x_1, x_2, \ldots, x_m \rangle$. The distribution of these observations over the joint space is called the *joint probability distribution*.

The Bayesian network represents the joint probability distribution by providing (1) a specified set of assumptions regarding the conditional independence of the variables, and (2) the probability tables for each variable given its direct predecessors. For each variable, information regarding both is provided. For a subset of variables $X_1, X_2, \ldots, X_m$, the joint probability may be found thus:

$$p(X_1 = x_1, X_2 = x_2, \ldots, X_m = x_m) = \prod_{i=1}^{m} p(X_i = x_i \mid parents\ (X_i))$$

where we define $parents(X_i)$ to be the set of immediate predecessors of X_i in the network. The probabilities $p(X_i = x_i \mid parents(X_i))$ and $p(X_i = x_i \mid parents(X_i))$ are the probabilities that have been specified in the probability table associated with the node for X_i.

How does learning take place in a Bayesian network? When the structure of the network is known and the field values have all been observed, learning in Bayesian nets is straightforward. The local (node-specific) probability tables are fully specified, and any joint, conditional, prior, or posterior probability desired may be calculated. However, when some of the field values are hidden or unknown, we need to turn to other methods, with the goal of filling in all the entries in the local probability distribution table. Russell et al. [6] suggest a gradient descent method for learning in Bayesian networks. In this paradigm, the unknown entries in the probability distribution tables are considered to be unknown weights, and gradient descent methods, analogous to the neural network learning case (e.g., Larose [4, Chap. 7] and Mitchell [2, Chap. 4]), can be applied to find the optimal set of weights (probability values) given the data.

Bayes' nets were originally designed to aid subject matter experts to specify the conditional independence structure among variables graphically. However, analysts may also attempt to discern the unknown structure of Bayes nets by studying the dependence and independence relationships among the variable values observed. Sprites et al. [7] and Ramoni and Sebastian [8] provide further information about learning both the content and structure of Bayesian networks.

WEKA: HANDS-ON ANALYSIS USING THE BAYES NET CLASSIFIER

Let's revisit the *movies* data set; however, this time, classification of the data is explored using WEKA's Bayes Net classifier. Similar to our last experiment, the 20 instances in *movies_train.arff* are used to train our model, whereas it is tested using the four reviews in *movies_test.arff*. Let's begin by loading the training file.

1. From the WEKA Explorer panel, press Open file.
2. Specify the path to the training file, *movies_train.arff*.
3. If successful, the Explorer panel looks similar to Figure 5.9 and indicates that the relation *movies_train.arff* consists of 20 instances with four attributes. It also shows, by default, that *CLASS* is specified as the class variable for the data set.
4. Select the Classify tab.

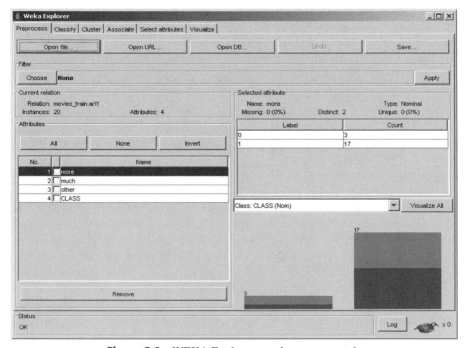

Figure 5.9 WEKA Explorer panel: preprocess tab.

TABLE 5.9   Bayes Net Test Set Predictions

```
=== Predictions on test set ===

inst#,   actual, predicted, error,   probability distribution
   1     1:neg      1:neg            *0.521         0.479
   2     1:neg      1:neg            *0.521         0.479
   3     2:pos      2:pos             0.423        *0.577
   4     2:pos      2:pos             0.389        *0.611
```

5. Under Classifier, press Choose.

6. Select Classifiers → Bayes → Bayes Net from the navigation hierarchy.

7. Under Test options, specify Supplied training set.

8. Click Start.

The results are reported in the Classifier output window. The classification accuracy for Bayes Net is 65% (13/20), which is identical to the results reported by naive Bayes. Again, let's evaluate our classification model using the data from *movies_test.arff*, with the goal of determining the probabilities by which Bayes Net classifies these instances.

1. Under Test options, choose Supplied test set. Press the Set button.

2. Press Open file and specify the location of the test file, *movies_test.arff*.

3. Under Test options, press the More options button.

4. Check the Output text predictions on the test set option. Click OK.

5. Under Result list, right-click the Bayes Net model from the list, and choose Re-evaluate model on the current test.

Now the predictions for each instance, including their associated probability, are reported in the Classifier output window. For example, Bayes Net correctly classified instance 3 as "pos," with probability 0.577, as shown in Table 5.9. Next, let's evaluate how Bayes Net made its classification decision for the third instance. First, recall the data set used to build our model, shown in Table 5.6. From here the prior probabilities for the attributes *more*, *much*, and *other* can be derived; for example, $p(more = 1) = 17/20$ and $p(more = 0) = 3/20$. In addition, to avoid zero-probability cells, Bayes Net uses a simple estimation method that adds 0.5 to each cell count. Using this information, the prior probability tables for the three parent nodes used in the network are shown in Table 5.10.

TABLE 5.10   Prior Probabilities Derived from *movies_training.arff*

More		Much		Other	
1	**0**	**1**	**0**	**1**	**0**
17.5/20	3.5/20	13.5/20	7.5/20	12.5/20	8.5/20

Now, according to the model built from the training set data, we calculate the probability of classifying the third record from the test set as *pos* using the formula

$$p(more = 0, much = 0, after = 0, CLASS = pos)$$
$$= p(more = 0)(much = 0)(after = 0)p(CLASS = pos \mid more = 0)$$
$$p(CLASS = pos \mid much = 0)p(CLASS = pos \mid after = 0)$$

As described above, Bayes Net also adds 0.5 to the conditional probability table cell counts to prevent zero-based probabilities from occurring. For example, the conditional probability $p(CLASS = pos \mid more = 0) = 2/10$ becomes $2.5/10$ using this internal adjustment. Therefore, given the values for *more*, *much*, and *other* found in the third instance, the probability of a positive classification is computed as follows:

$$p(more = 0, much = 0, after = 0, CLASS = pos)$$
$$= \left(\frac{3.5}{20}\right) \cdot \left(\frac{7.5}{20}\right) \cdot \left(\frac{8.5}{20}\right) \cdot \left(\frac{2.5}{10}\right) \cdot \left(\frac{4.5}{10}\right) \cdot \left(\frac{3.5}{10}\right)$$
$$= (0.175)(0.375)(0.425)(0.25)(0.45)(0.35) \approx 0.001098$$

Likewise, the probability of a negative classification is derived using a similar approach:

$$p(more = 0, much = 0, after = 0, CLASS = neg)$$
$$= \left(\frac{3.5}{20}\right) \cdot \left(\frac{7.5}{20}\right) \cdot \left(\frac{8.5}{20}\right) \cdot \left(\frac{1.5}{10}\right) \cdot \left(\frac{3.5}{10}\right) \cdot \left(\frac{5.5}{10}\right)$$
$$= (0.175)(0.375)(0.425)(0.15)(0.35)(0.55) \approx 0.000805$$

Our last step is to normalize the probabilities as follows:

$$p(pos) = \frac{0.001098}{0.001098 + 0.000805} \approx 0.57698$$
$$p(neg) = \frac{0.000805}{0.001098 + 0.000805} \approx 0.42302$$

Our calculations have determined that according to the Bayes Net model built from the training set, instance 3 is classified as positive with probability 0.577. Again, our hand-calculated probabilities agree with those produced by the WEKA model, as shown in Table 5.9. Clearly, our results indicate that "hand-computing" the probability values for a network of moderate size is a nontrivial task.

SUMMARY

In Bayesian statistics, the parameters are considered to be random variables, and the data are considered to be known. The parameters are regarded to come from a distribution of possible values, and Bayesians look to the observed data to provide information on likely parameter values. Let θ represent the parameters of the unknown distribution. Bayesian analysis requires elicitation of a prior distribution for θ, called the *prior distribution*, $p(\theta)$. In the field of data mining, huge data sets are often encountered; therefore, the prior distribution should be dominated by the overwhelming amount of information to be found in the observed data.

Once the data have been observed, prior information about the distribution of θ can be *updated* by factoring in the information about θ contained in the observed data. This modification leads to the *posterior distribution,* $p(\theta|\mathbf{X})$, where $\mathbf{X}$ represents the entire array of data. The posterior distribution of θ given the data is proportional to the product of the likelihood and the prior.

A common estimation method is to choose the posterior mode, the value of θ that maximizes $p(\theta|\mathbf{X})$ for an estimate, in which case we call this estimation method the *maximum a posteriori* (MAP) *method*. The Bayesian MAP classification is optimal; that is, it achieves the minimum error rate for all possible classifiers. The MAP classifier may be expressed as $\theta_{\mathrm{MAP}} = \arg\max_{\theta} p(\mathbf{X}|\theta)p(\theta)$. Bayes' theorem is given by

$$P(A|B) = \frac{P(B|A)P(A)}{P(B)}$$

where A and B are events.

The posterior odds ratio represents a measure of the strength of evidence in favor of a particular classification and is calculated as

$$\frac{p(\theta_c|\mathbf{X})}{p(\overline{\theta}_c|\mathbf{X})} = \frac{p(\mathbf{X}|\theta_c)p(\theta_c)}{p(\mathbf{X}|\overline{\theta}_c)p(\overline{\theta}_c)}$$

where θ_c represents a particular classification of the unknown target variable. A value greater than 1 indicates that the posterior distribution favors the positive classification; a value less than 1 represents evidence against the positive classification (e.g., *churn = true*). The value of the posterior odds ratio may be interpreted as indicating roughly the proportion of evidence provided by the posterior distribution in favor of the positive classification against the negative classification.

In general, the number of probabilities that would need to be calculated to find the MAP classification would be on the order of k^m, where k is the number of classes for the target variable and m is the number of predictor variables. However, we may make the simplifying assumption that the predictor variables are conditionally independent given the target value. Two events A and B are said to be *conditionally independent* if for a given event C, $p(A \cap B|C) = p(A|C)p(B|C)$.

Thus, the *naive Bayes classification* is

$$\theta_{NB} = \arg\max_{\theta} \prod_{i=1}^{m} p(X_i = x_i|\theta)p(\theta)$$

When the conditional independence assumption is valid, the naive Bayes classification is the same as the MAP classification. When using naive Bayes classification, far fewer probabilities need to be estimated, just km probabilities rather than k^m for the MAP classifier, in other words, just the number of predictor variables times the number of distinct values of the target variable. Bayesian classification can be extended from categorical to continuous predictor variables, provided that we know the relevant probability distribution.

Bayesian belief networks (BBNs) are designed to allow joint conditional independencies to be defined among subsets of variables. BBNs, also called *Bayesian networks* or *Bayes nets*, take the form of a directed acyclic graph (DAG), where *directed* means that the arcs are traversed in one direction only, and *acyclic* means that no child node cycles back up to any progenitor. The nodes represent variables, and the arcs represent the (directed) dependence among the variables.

In general, node A is a *parent* or *immediate predecessor* of node X, and node X is a *descendant* of node A, if there exists a directed arc from node A to node X. The intrinsic relationship among the variables in a Bayesian network is as follows: *Each variable in a Bayesian network is conditionally independent of its nondescendants in the network, given its parents.* The Bayesian network represents the joint probability distribution by providing that (1) a specified set of assumptions regarding the conditional independence of the variables, and (2) the probability tables for each variable, given its direct predecessors. For each variable, information regarding both (1) and (2) is provided.

REFERENCES

1. Thomas Bayes, Essay towards solving a problem in the doctrine of chances, *Philosophical Transactions of the Royal Society of London*, 1763.
2. Tom Mitchell, *Machine Learning*, WCB–McGraw-Hill, Boston, 1997.
3. Churn data set, in C. L. Blake, and C. J. Merz, UCI Repository of Machine Learning Databases, http://www.ics.uci.edu/~mlearn/MLRepository.html, University of California, Department of Information and Computer Science, Irvine, CA, 1998. Also available at the book series Web site.
4. Daniel Larose, *Discovering Knowledge in Data: An Introduction to Data Mining*, Wiley, Hoboken, NJ, 2005.
5. David Hand, Heiki Mannila, and Padhraic Smyth, *Principles of Data Mining*, MIT Press, Cambridge, MA, 2001.
6. Stuart Russell, John Binder, Daphne Koller, and Keiji Kanazawa, Local learning in probabilistic networks with hidden variables, in *Proceedings of the 14th International Joint Conference on Artificial Intelligence*, pp. 1146–1152, Morgan Kaufmann, San Francisco, CA, 1995.
7. Peter Sprites, Clark Glymour, and Richard Scheines, *Causation, Prediction, and Search*, Springer-Verlag, New York, 1993.
8. Marco Ramoni and Paola Sebastiani, Bayesian methods, in Michael Berthold and David J. Hand, ed., *Intelligent Data Analysis*, Springer-Verlag, Berlin, 1999.
9. Breast cancer data set, compiled by Dr. William H. Wohlberg, University of Wisconsin Hospitals, Madison, WI; cited in O. L. Mangasarian and W. H. Wohlberg, Cancer diagnosis via linear programming, *SIAM News*, Vol. 23, No. 5, September 1990.

EXERCISES

Clarifying the Concepts

5.1. Describe the differences between the frequentist and Bayesian approaches to probability.

5.2. Explain the difference between prior and posterior distributions.

5.3. In most data mining applications, why would we expect the maximum a posteriori estimate to be close to the maximum likelihood estimate?

5.4. Describe in plain English the maximum a posteriori classification.

5.5. Explain the interpretation of the posterior odds ratio. Why do we need it?

5.6. Describe what balancing is, and when and why it may be needed. Also describe two techniques for achieving a balanced data set, and explain why one method is preferred.

5.7. Explain why we cannot avoid altering, even slightly, the character of the data set when we apply balancing.

5.8. Explain why the MAP classification is impractical to apply directly for any interesting real-world data mining application.

5.9. What is conditional independence? Provide examples of events that are conditionally independent and of events that are not conditionally independent.

5.10. When is the naive Bayes classification the same as the MAP classification? In terms of optimality, what does this mean for the naive Bayes classifier?

5.11. Explain why the log posterior odds ratio is useful. Provide an example.

5.12. Using the concept of distribution, describe the process for using continuous predictors in Bayesian classification,

5.13. (*Extra credit*) Investigate the mixture idea for the continuous predictor mentioned in the text.

5.14. Discuss working with the empirical distribution. Describe how this can be used to estimate true probabilities.

5.15. Explain the difference in assumptions between naive Bayes classification and Bayesian networks.

5.16. Describe the intrinsic relationship among the variables in a Bayesian network.

5.17. What are the two main considerations when building a Bayesian network?

Working with the Data

5.18. Using the balanced data set, compute the posterior odds ratio for each of the combinations of International Plan and VoiceMail Plan membership.

5.19. Using 25.31%/74.69% balancing, calculate the naive Bayes classification for all four possible combinations of International Plan and VoiceMail Plan membership.

5.20. Verify the empirical distribution results referred to in the text of the numbers of records within the certain margins of error of 800 minutes for churners and nonchurners.

5.21. Find the naive Bayes classifier for the following customers:

   (a) Belongs to neither plan, with 400 day minutes

   (b) Belongs to the International Plan only, with 400 minutes

   (c) Belongs to both plans, with 400 minutes

   (d) Belongs to both plans, with zero minutes (comment)

   Use the empirical distribution where necessary.

5.22. Provide the MAP classification for *season* given that a warm coat was purchased, in the clothing purchase example in the Bayesian network section.

5.23. Revisit the WEKA naive Bayes example. Calculate the probability that the first instance in *movies_test.arff* is "pos" and "neg." Do your calculations agree with those reported by WEKA leading to a negative classification?

5.24. Compute the probabilities by which the Bayes Net model classifies the fourth instance from the test file *movies_test.arff*. Do your calculations result in a positive classification as reported by WEKA?

Hands-on Analysis

5.25. Open the *breast cancer* data set [9]. Ten numeric predictors are used to predict the class of malignant breast cancer tumor (class = 1) as opposed to benign tumor (class = 0).

   (a) Consider using only two predictors, *mitoses* and *clump thickness*, to predict tumor class. Categorize the values for *mitoses* as follows: Low = 1, High = 2 to 10. Categorize the values for *clump thickness* as follows: Low = 1 to 5, High = 6 to 10. Discard the original variables and use these categorized predictors.

   (b) Find the prior probabilities for each of the predictors and the target variable. Find the complement probabilities of each.

   (c) Find the conditional probabilities for each of the predictors given that the tumor is malignant. Then find the conditional probabilities for each of the predictors given that the tumor is benign.

   (d) Find the posterior probability that the tumor is malignant given that *mitoses* is **(i)** high, and **(ii)** low.

   (e) Find the posterior probability that the tumor is malignant given that *clump thickness* is **(i)** high, and **(ii)** low.

   (f) Construct the joint conditional probabilities, similar to Table 5.4.

   (g) Using your results from part (f), find the maximum a posteriori classification of tumor class for each of the following combinations:

   (i) *Mitoses* = low and *clump thickness* = low

   (ii) *Mitoses* = low and *clump thickness* = high

   (iii) *Mitoses* = high and *clump thickness* = low

   (iv) *Mitoses* = high and *clump thickness* = high

(h) For each of the combinations in part (g), find the posterior odds ratio.

(i) (*Optional*) Assess the validity of the conditional independence assumption using calculations similar to Table 5.5.

(j) Find the naive Bayes classifications for each of the combinations in part (g).

(k) For each of the predictors, find the log posterior odds ratio, and explain the contribution of this predictor to the probability of a malignant tumor.

CHAPTER 6

GENETIC ALGORITHMS

INTRODUCTION TO GENETIC ALGORITHMS

Genetic algorithms (GAs) attempt to mimic computationally the processes by which natural selection operates, and apply them to solve business and research problems. Developed by John Holland in the 1960s and 1970s [1] genetic algorithms provide a framework for studying the effects of such biologically inspired factors as mate selection, reproduction, mutation, and crossover of genetic information. In the natural world, the constraints and stresses of a particular environment force the different species (and different individuals within species) to compete to produce the fittest offspring. In the world of genetic algorithms, the fitness of various potential solutions are compared, and the fittest potential solutions evolve to produce ever more optimal solutions.

Not surprisingly, the field of genetic algorithms has borrowed heavily from genomic terminology. Each cell in our body contains the same set of *chromosomes*, strings of DNA that function as a blueprint for making one of us. Then each chromosome can be partitioned into *genes*, which are blocks of DNA designed to encode a particular trait, such as eye color. A particular instance of the gene (e.g., brown eyes) is an *allele*. Each gene is to be found at a particular *locus* on the chromosome. Recombination, or *crossover*, occurs during reproduction, where a new chromosome

---

Data Mining Methods and Models By Daniel T. Larose
Copyright © 2006 John Wiley & Sons, Inc.

is formed by combining the characteristics of both parents' chromosomes. *Mutation*, the altering of a single gene in a chromosome of the offspring, may occur randomly and relatively rarely. The offspring's *fitness* is then evaluated, either in terms of viability (living long enough to reproduce) or in the offspring's fertility.

In the field of genetic algorithms, a *chromosome* refers to one of the candidate solutions to the problem, a *gene* is a single bit or digit of the candidate solution, an *allele* is a particular instance of the bit or digit (e.g., 0 for binary-encoded solutions or the number 7 for real-valued solutions). Recall that binary numbers have base 2, so that the first "decimal" place represents "ones," the second represents "twos," the third represents "fours," the fourth represents "eights," and so on. So the binary string 10101010 represents

$$(1 \times 128) + (0 \times 64) + (1 \times 32) + (0 \times 16) + (1 \times 8) + (0 \times 4) + (1 \times 2)$$
$$+(0 \times 1) = 170$$

in decimal notation.

Three operators are used by genetic algorithms:

1. *Selection.* The selection operator refers to the method used for selecting which chromosomes will be reproducing. The fitness function evaluates each of the chromosomes (candidate solutions), and the fitter the chromosome, the more likely it will be selected to reproduce.

2. *Crossover.* The crossover operator performs recombination, creating two new offspring by randomly selecting a locus and exchanging subsequences to the left and right of that locus between two chromosomes chosen during selection. For example, in binary representation, two strings 11111111 and 00000000 could be crossed over at the sixth locus in each to generate the two new offspring 11111000 and 00000111.

3. *Mutation.* The mutation operator randomly changes the bits or digits at a particular locus in a chromosome: usually, however, with very small probability. For example, after crossover, the 11111000 child string could be mutated at locus two to become 10111000. Mutation introduces new information to the genetic pool and protects against converging too quickly to a local optimum.

Most genetic algorithms function by iteratively updating a collection of potential solutions called a *population*. Each member of the population is evaluated for fitness on each cycle. A new population then replaces the old population using the operators above, with the fittest members being chosen for reproduction or cloning. The fitness function $f(x)$ is a real-valued function operating on the chromosome (potential solution), not the gene, so that the x in $f(x)$ refers to the numeric value taken by the chromosome at the time of fitness evaluation.

BASIC FRAMEWORK OF A GENETIC ALGORITHM

The following introductory GA framework is adapted from Mitchell [2] in her interesting book *An Introduction to Genetic Algorithms*.

- *Step 0: Initialization.* Assume that the data are encoded in bit strings (1's and 0's). Specify a *crossover probability* or *crossover rate* p_c and a *mutation probability* or *mutation rate* p_m. Usually, p_c is chosen to be fairly high (e.g., 0.7), and p_m is chosen to be very low (e.g., 0.001).
- *Step 1:* The population is chosen, consisting of a set of n chromosomes each of length l.
- *Step 2:* The fitness $f(x)$ is calculated for each chromosome in the population.
- *Step 3:* Iterate through the following steps until n offspring have been generated.

  - *Step 3a: Selection.* Using the values from the fitness function $f(x)$ from step 2, assign a probability of selection to each chromosome, with higher fitness providing a higher probability of selection. The usual term for the way these probabilities are assigned is the *roulette wheel method*. For each chromosome x_i, find the proportion of this chromosome's fitness to the total fitness summed over all the chromosomes. That is, find $f(x_i)/\sum_i f(x_i)$ and assign this proportion to be the probability of selecting that chromosome for parenthood. (Each chromosome then has a proportional slice of the putative roulette wheel spun to choose the parents.) Then select a pair of chromosomes to be parents, based on these probabilities. Allow the same chromosome to have the potential to be selected to be a parent more than once. Allowing a chromosome to pair with itself will generate tree copies of that chromosome to the new generation. If the analyst is concerned about converging to a local optimum too quickly, perhaps such pairing should not be allowed.

  - *Step 3b: Crossover.* Select a randomly chosen locus (*crossover point*) for where to perform the crossover. Then, with probability p_c, perform crossover with the parents selected in step 3a, thereby forming two new offspring. If the crossover is not performed, clone two exact copies of the parents to be passed on to the new generation.

  - *Step 3c: Mutation.* With probability p_m, perform mutation on each of the two offspring at each locus point. The chromosomes then take their place in the new population. If n is odd, discard one new chromosome at random.

- *Step 4:* The new population of chromosomes replaces the current population.
- *Step 5:* Check whether termination criteria have been met. For example, is the change in mean fitness from generation to generation vanishingly small? If convergence is achieved, stop and report results; otherwise, go to step 2.

Each cycle through this algorithm is called a *generation*, with most GA applications taking from 50 to 500 generations to reach convergence. Mitchell [2] suggests that researchers try several different runs with different random number seeds, and report the model evaluation statistics (e.g., best overall fitness) averaged over several different runs.

SIMPLE EXAMPLE OF A GENETIC ALGORITHM AT WORK

Let's examine a simple example of a genetic algorithm at work. Suppose that our task is to find the maximum value of the normal distribution with mean $\mu = 16$ and standard deviation $\sigma = 4$ (Figure 6.1). That is, we would like to find the maximum value of

$$f(x) = \frac{1}{\sqrt{2\pi}\,\sigma} \exp\left[\frac{-1}{2\sigma^2}(X - \mu)^2\right] = \frac{1}{\sqrt{2\pi}\,(4)} \exp\left[\frac{-1}{2(4)^2}(X - 16)^2\right]$$

We allow X to take on only the values described by the first five binary digits, that is, 00000 through 11111, or 0 to 31 in decimal notation.

First Iteration

- *Step 0: Initialization.* We define the *crossover rate* to be $p_c = 0.75$ and the *mutation rate* to be $p_m = 0.002$.
- *Step 1:* Our population will be a set of four chromosomes chosen randomly from the set 00000 – 11111. So $n = 4$ and $l = 5$. These are *00100* (4), *01001* (9), *11011* (27), and *11111* (31).
- *Step 2:* The fitness $f(x)$ is calculated for each chromosome in the population (Table 6.1).
- *Step 3:* Iterate through the following steps until n offspring have been generated.
  - *Step 3a: Selection.* We have the sum of the fitness values equal to

$$\sum_i f(x_i) = 0.001108 + 0.021569 + 0.002273 + 0.000088$$
$$= 0.025038$$

    Then the probability that each of our chromosomes will be selected for parenthood is found by dividing their value for $f(x)$ by the sum 0.025038. These

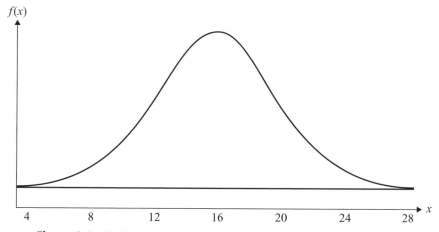

Figure 6.1   Finding the maximum value of the normal (**16, 4**) distribution.

TABLE 6.1 Fitness and Probability of Selection for Each Chromosome

Chromosome	Decimal Value	Fitness	Selection Probability
00100	4	0.001108	0.04425
01001	9	0.021569	0.86145
11011	27	0.002273	0.09078
11111	31	0.000088	0.00351

are also shown in Table 6.1. Clearly, chromosome *01001* gets a very large slice of the roulette wheel! The random selection process gets under way. Suppose that chromosome *01001* and *11011* are selected to be the first pair of parents, since these are the two chromosomes with the highest fitness.

○ *Step 3b: Crossover.* The locus is randomly chosen to be the second position. Suppose that the large crossover rate of p_c, 0.75, leads to crossover between *01001* and *11011* occurring at the second position. This is shown in Figure 6.2. Note that the strings are partitioned between the first and second bits. Each child chromosome receives one segment from each of the parents. The two chromosomes thus formed for the new generation are *01011* (11) and *11001* (25).

○ *Step 3c: Mutation.* Because of the low mutation rate, suppose that none of the genes for *01011* or *11001* are mutated. We now have two chromosomes in our new population. We need two more, so we cycle back to step 3a.

○ *Step 3a: Selection.* Suppose that this time, chromosomes *01001* (9) and *00100* (4) are selected by the roulette wheel method.

○ *Step 3b: Crossover.* However, this time suppose that crossover does not take place. Thus, clones of these chromosomes become members of the new generation, *01001* and *00100*. We now have $n = 4$ members in our new population.

• *Step 4.* The new population of chromosomes therefore replaces the current population.

• *Step 5.* We iterate back to step 2.

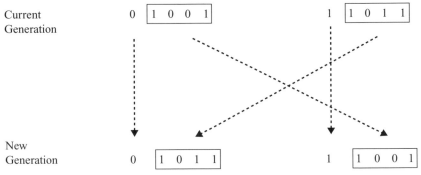

Figure 6.2 Performing crossover at locus two on the first two parents.

TABLE 6.2   Fitness and Probability of Selection for the Second Generation

Chromosome	Decimal Value	Fitness	Selection Probability
00100	4	0.001108	0.014527
01001	9	0.021569	0.282783
01011	11	0.045662	0.598657
11001	25	0.007935	0.104033

Second Iteration

- *Step 2:* The fitness $f(x)$ is calculated for each chromosome in the population (Table 6.2).

  ○ *Step 3a: Selection.* The sum of the fitness values for the second generation is $\sum_i f(x_i) = 0.076274$, which means that the average fitness among the chromosomes in the second generation is three times that of the first generation. The selection probabilities are calculated and shown in Table 6.2.

We ask you to continue this example in the exercises.

MODIFICATIONS AND ENHANCEMENTS: SELECTION

For the selection operator, the analyst should be careful to balance fitness with diversity. If fitness is favored over variability, a set of highly fit but suboptimal chromosomes will dominate the population, reducing the ability of the GA to find the global optimum. If diversity is favored over fitness, model convergence will be too slow. For example, in the first generation above, one particular gene *01001* (9) dominated the fitness measure, with over 86% of the selection probability. This is an example of *selection pressure*, and a potential example of the *crowding* phenomenon in genetic algorithms, where one particular chromosome that is much fitter than the others begins to reproduce, generating too many clones and similar copies of itself in future generations. By reducing the diversity of the population, crowding impairs the ability of the genetic algorithm to continue to explore new regions of the search space.

A variety of techniques are available to handle crowding. De Jong [3] suggested that new-generation chromosomes should replace the individual most similar to itself in the current generation. Goldberg and Richardson [4] posited a *fitness-sharing function*, where a particular chromosome's fitness was decreased by the presence of similar population members, where the more similarity, the greater the decrease. Thus, diversity was rewarded.

Changing the mating conditions can also be used to increase population diversity. Deb and Goldberg [5] showed that if mating can take place only between sufficiently similar chromosomes, distinct "mating groups" will have a propensity to form. These groups displayed low within-group variation and high between-group variation. On the other hand, Eshelman [6] and Eshelman and Schaffer [7] investigated the opposite strategy by not allowing matings between chromosomes that were sufficiently alike. The result was to maintain high variability within the population as a whole.

Sigma scaling, proposed by Forrest [8], maintains the selection pressure at a relatively constant rate by scaling a chromosome's fitness by the standard deviation of the fitnesses. If a single chromosome dominates at the beginning of the run, the variability in fitnesses will also be large, and scaling by the variability will reduce the dominance. Later in the run, when populations are typically more homogeneous, scaling by this smaller variability will allow the highly fit chromosomes to reproduce. The sigma-scaled fitness is as follows:

$$f_{\text{sigma scaled}}(x) = 1 + \frac{f(x) - \mu_f}{\sigma_f}$$

where μ_f and σ_f refer to the mean fitness and standard deviation of the fitnesses for the current generation.

Boltzmann selection varies the selection pressure, depending on how far along in the run the generation is. Early on, it may be better to allow lower selection pressure, allowing the less fit chromosomes to reproduce at rates similar to the fitter chromosomes, thereby maintaining a wider exploration of the search space. Later in the run, increasing the selection pressure will help the GA to converge more quickly to the optimal solution, hopefully the global optimum. In Boltzmann selection, a *temperature* parameter T is gradually reduced from high levels to low levels. A chromosome's adjusted fitness is then found as follows:

$$f_{\text{Boltzmann}}(x) = \frac{\exp(f(x)/T)}{\text{mean}[\exp(f(x)/T)]}$$

As the temperature falls, the difference in expected fitness increases between high-fit and low-fit chromosomes.

Elitism, developed by De Jong [3], refers to the selection condition requiring that the GAs retain a certain number of the fittest chromosomes from one generation to the next, protecting them against destruction through crossover, mutation, or inability to reproduce. Michell [2], Haupt and Haupt [9], and others report that elitism greatly improves GA performance.

Rank selection ranks the chromosomes according to fitness. Ranking avoids the selection pressure exerted by the proportional fitness method, but it also ignores the absolute differences among the chromosome fitnesses. Ranking does not take variability into account and provides a moderate adjusted fitness measure, since the probability of selection between chromosomes ranked k and $k + 1$ is the same regardless of the absolute differences in fitness.

Tournament ranking is computationally more efficient than rank selection while preserving the moderate selection pressure of rank selection. In tournament ranking, two chromosomes are chosen at random and with replacement from the population. Let c be a constant chosen by the user to be between zero and 1 (e.g., 0.67). A random number r, $0 \le r \le 1$, is drawn. If $r < c$, the fitter chromosome is selected for parenthood; otherwise, the less fit chromosome is selected.

MODIFICATIONS AND ENHANCEMENTS: CROSSOVER

Multipoint Crossover

The single-point crossover operator that we have outlined here suffers from what is known as *positional bias*. That is, the performance of the genetic algorithm depends, in part, on the order in which the variables occur in the chromosome. So genes in loci 1 and 2 will often be crossed over together, simply because of their proximity to each other, whereas genes in loci 1 and 7 will rarely cross over together. Now, if this positioning reflects natural relationships within the data and among the variables, this is not such a concern, but such a priori knowledge is relatively rare. The solution is to perform *multipoint crossover*, as follows. First, randomly select a set of crossover points, and split the parent chromosomes at those points. Then, to form the children, recombine the segments by alternating between the parents, as illustrated in Figure 6.3.

Uniform Crossover

Another alternative crossover operator is *uniform crossover*. In uniform crossover, the first child is generated as follows. Each gene is randomly assigned to be that of either one or the other parent, with 50% probability. The second child would then take the inverse of the first child. One advantage of uniform crossover is that the genes inherited are independent of position. Uniform crossover is illustrated in Figure 6.4. A modified version of uniform crossover would be to allow the probabilities to depend on the fitness of the respective parents.

Eiben and Smith [10] discuss the roles of crossover and mutation, and the cooperation and competition between them with respect to the search space. They describe crossover as *explorative*, discovering promising new regions in the search space by making a large jump to a region between the two parent areas. They describe mutation as *exploitative*, optimizing present information within an already discovered promising region, creating small random deviations and thereby not wandering far from the parents. Crossover and mutation complement each other, since only crossover can bring together information from both parents, and only mutation can introduce completely new information.

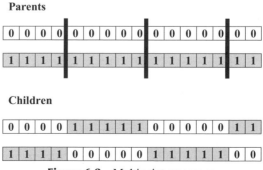

Figure 6.3   Multipoint crossover.

Children

Figure 6.4 Uniform crossover.

GENETIC ALGORITHMS FOR REAL-VALUED VARIABLES

The original framework for genetic algorithms was developed for binary-encoded data, since the operations of crossover and mutation worked naturally and well with such data. However, most datamining data come in the form of real numbers, often with many decimals' worth of precision. Some analysts have tried quantizing the real-valued (continuous) data into binary form. However, to reexpress the real-valued data in binary terms will necessarily result in a loss of information, due to the degradation in precision caused by rounding to the nearest binary digit. To combat this loss in precision, each binary chromosome would need to be made longer, adding digits that will inevitably impair the speed of the algorithm. Therefore, methods for applying GAs directly to real-valued data have been investigated. Eiben and Smith [10] suggest the following methods for performing the crossover operation.

Single Arithmetic Crossover

Let the parents be $\langle x_1, x_2, \ldots, x_n \rangle$ and $\langle y_1, y_2, \ldots, y_n \rangle$. Pick the kth gene at random. Then let the first child be of the form $\langle x_1, x_2, \ldots, \alpha y_k + (1 - \alpha)x_k, \ldots, x_n \rangle$ and the second child be of the form $\langle y_1, y_2, \ldots, \alpha x_k + (1 - \alpha)y_k, \ldots, y_n \rangle$, for $0 \leq \alpha \leq 1$. For example, let the parents be $\langle 0.5, 1.0, 1.5, 2.0 \rangle$ and $\langle 0.2, 0.7, 0.2, 0.7 \rangle$, let $\alpha = 0.4$, and select the third gene at random. Then, single arithmetic crossover would produce the first child to be $\langle 0.5, 1.0, (0.4)(0.2) + (0.6)(1.5), 2.0 \rangle = \langle 0.5, 1.0, 0.98, 2.0 \rangle$, and the second child to be $\langle 0.2, 0.7, (0.4)(1.5) + (0.6)(0.2), 0.7 \rangle = \langle 0.2, 0.7, 0.72, 0.7 \rangle$.

Simple Arithmetic Crossover

Let the parents be $\langle x_1, x_2, \ldots, x_n \rangle$ and $\langle y_1, y_2, \ldots, y_n \rangle$. Pick the kth gene at random, and mix values for all genes at this point and beyond. That is, let the first child be of the form $\langle x_1, x_2, \ldots, \alpha y_k + (1 - \alpha)x_k, \ldots, \alpha y_n + (1 - \alpha)x_n \rangle$, and the second child be of the form $\langle y_1, y_2, \ldots, \alpha x_k + (1 - \alpha)y_k, \ldots, \alpha x_n + (1 - \alpha)y_n \rangle$, for $0 \leq \alpha \leq 1$. For example, let the parents be $\langle 0.5, 1.0, 1.5, 2.0 \rangle$ and $\langle 0.2, 0.7, 0.2, 0.7 \rangle$, let $\alpha = 0.4$, and select the third gene at random. Then, simple arithmetic crossover would produce the first child to be

$$\langle 0.5, \ 1.0, \ (0.4)(0.2) + (0.6)(1.5), \ (0.4)(0.7) + (0.6)(2.0) \rangle$$
$$= \langle 0.5, \ 1.0, \ 0.98, \ 1.48 \rangle,$$

and the second child to be

$$\langle 0.2, \ 0.7, \ (0.4)(1.5) + (0.6)(0.2), \ (0.4)(2.0) + (0.6)(0.7) \rangle$$
$$= \langle 0.2, \ 0.7, \ 0.72, \ 1.22 \rangle.$$

Whole Arithmetic Crossover

Let the parents be $\langle x_1, x_2, \ldots, x_n \rangle$ and $\langle y_1, y_2, \ldots, y_n \rangle$. Perform the mixture above to the entire vector for each parent. The calculation of the child vectors is left as an exercise. Note that for each of these arithmetic crossover techniques, the affected genes represent intermediate points between the parents' values, with $\alpha = 0.5$ generating the mean of the parents' values.

Discrete Crossover

Here, each gene in the child chromosome is chosen with uniform probability to be the gene of one or the other of the parents' chromosomes. For example, let the parents be $\langle 0.5, \ 1.0, \ 1.5, \ 2.0 \rangle$ and $\langle 0.2, \ 0.7, \ 0.2, \ 0.7 \rangle$; one possible child could be $\langle 0.2, \ 0.7, \ 1.5, \ 0.7 \rangle$, with the third gene coming directly from the first parent and the others coming from the second parent.

Normally Distributed Mutation

To avoid converging too quickly toward a local optimum, a normally distributed "random shock" may be added to each variable. The distribution should be normal, with a mean of zero and a standard deviation of σ, which controls the amount of change (since most random shocks will lie within one σ of the original variable value). If the resulting mutated variable lies outside the allowable range, its value should be reset so that it lies within the range. If all variables are mutated, clearly $p_m = 1$ in this case. For example, suppose that the mutation distribution is $normal(\mu = 0, \sigma = 0.1)$, and that we wish to apply the mutation to the child chromosome from the discrete crossover example, $\langle 0.2, \ 0.7, \ 1.5, \ 0.7 \rangle$. Assume that the four random shocks generated from this distribution are 0.05, -0.17, -0.03, and 0.08. Then, the child chromosome becomes $\langle 0.2 + 0.05, \ 0.7 - 0.17, \ 1.5 - 0.03, \ 0.7 + 0.08 \rangle = \langle 0.25, \ 0.53, \ 1.47, \ 0.78 \rangle$.

USING GENETIC ALGORITHMS TO TRAIN A NEURAL NETWORK

A neural network consists of a *layered, feedforward, completely connected* network of artificial neurons, or *nodes*. Neural networks are used for classification or estimation. See Mitchell [11], Fausett [12], Haykin [13], Larose [14], or Reed and Marks [15]

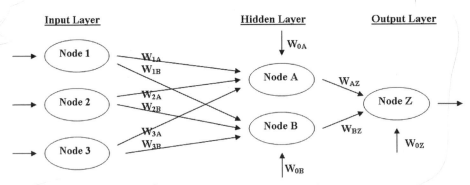

Figure 6.5 Simple neural network.

for details on neural network topology and operation. Figure 6.5 provides a basic diagram of a simple neural network. The *feedforward* nature of the network restricts the network to a single direction of flow and does not allow looping or cycling. The neural network is composed of two or more layers, although most networks consist of three layers: an *input layer*, a *hidden layer*, and an *output layer*. There may be more than one hidden layer, although most networks contain only one, which is sufficient for most purposes. The neural network is *connected completely*, meaning that every node in a given layer is connected to every node in the next layer, although not to other nodes in the same layer. Each connection between nodes has a weight (e.g., W_{1A}) associated with it. At initialization, these weights are randomly assigned to values between zero and 1.

How does the neural network learn? Neural networks represent a supervised learning method, requiring a large training set of complete records, including the target variable. As each observation from the training set is processed through the network, an output value is produced from the output node (assuming that we have only one output node). This output value is then compared to the actual value of the target variable for this training set observation, and the error (actual − output) is calculated. This prediction error is analogous to the residuals in regression models. To measure how well the output predictions are fitting the actual target values, most neural network models use the sum of squared errors:

$$\text{SSE} = \sum_{\text{records}} \sum_{\text{output nodes}} (\text{actual} - \text{output})^2$$

where the squared prediction errors are summed over all the output nodes and over all the records in the training set.

The problem is therefore to construct a set of model weights that will minimize this SSE. In this way, the weights are analogous to the parameters of a regression model. The "true" values for the weights that will minimize SSE are unknown, and our task is to estimate them given the data. However, due to the nonlinear nature of the sigmoid functions permeating the network, there exists no closed-form solution for minimizing SSE, as there exists for least-squares regression. Most neural network models therefore use *back-propagation*, a gradient-descent optimization method, to help find the set of weights that will minimize SSE. Back-propagation takes the prediction error (*actual − output*) for a particular record and percolates the error back through the network, assigning partitioned "responsibility" for the error to the various connections. The weights on these connections are then adjusted to decrease the error, using gradient descent.

However, since finding the best set of weights in a neural network is an optimization task, GAs are wonderfully suited to doing so. The drawbacks of back-propagation include the tendency to become stuck at local minima (since it follows a single route through the weight space) and the requirement to calculate derivative or gradient information for each weight. Also, Unnikrishnan et al. [16] state that improper selection of initial weights in back-propagation will delay convergence. Genetic algorithms, on the other hand, perform a global search, lessening the chances of becoming caught in a local minimum, although of course there can be no guarantees that the global minimum has been obtained. Also, GAs require no derivative or gradient information to be calculated. However, neural networks using GAs for training the weights run more slowly than traditional neural networks using back-propagation.

Genetic algorithms apply a much different search strategy than back-propagation. The gradient descent methodology in back-propagation moves from one solution vector to another vector that is quite similar. The genetic algorithm search methodology, however, can shift much more radically, generating a child chromosome that may be completely different than that of either parent. This behavior decreases the probability that GAs will become stuck in local optima.

Huang et al. [17] apply a neural network optimized with a genetic algorithm to forecast financial distress in life insurance companies. Unnikrishnan et al. [16] used genetic algorithms to optimize the weights in a neural network, which was used to model a three-dimensional ultrasonic positioning system. They represented the network weights in the form of chromosomes, similar to Table 6.3 for the chromosome for the neural network weights in Figure 6.5. However, their chromosome was 51 weights long, reflecting their 5–4–4–3 topology of five input nodes, four nodes in each of two hidden layers, and three output nodes. The authors cite the length of the chromosome as the reason the model was outperformed by both a back-propagation neural network and a traditional linear model.

Montana and Davis [18] provide an example of using genetic algorithms to optimize the weights in a neural network (adapted here from Mitchell [2]). Their research task was to classify "lofargrams" (underwater sonic spectrograms) as either *interesting* or *not interesting*. Their neural network had a 4–7–10–1 topology, giving a total of 126 weights in their chromosomes. The fitness function used was the usual neural network metric,

$$SSE = \sum_{records} \sum_{output\ nodes} (actual - output)^2$$

except that the weights being adjusted represented the genes in the chromosome.

TABLE 6.3 Chromosome Representing Weights from Neural Network in Figure 6.5

W_{1A}	W_{1B}	W_{2A}	W_{2B}	W_{3A}	W_{3B}	W_{0A}	W_{0B}	W_{AZ}	W_{BZ}	W_{0Z}

TABLE 6.4 **Neural Network Weights Indicating Results of Crossover**

	W_{1A}	W_{1B}	W_{2A}	W_{2B}	W_{3A}	W_{3B}	W_{0A}	W_{0B}	W_{AZ}	W_{BZ}	W_{0Z}
Parent 1	0.1	−0.2	0.7	−0.6	0.4	0.9	−0.1	0.3	−0.5	0.8	−0.2
Parent 2	0.2	−0.4	0.5	−0.5	0.3	0.7	−0.2	0.1	−0.6	0.9	−0.3
Child	0.1	−0.4	0.7	−0.5	0.4	0.7	−0.1	0.1	−0.6	0.9	−0.3

For the crossover operator, they used a modified discrete crossover. Here, for each noninput node in the child chromosome, a parent chromosome is selected at random, and the incoming links from the parent are copied to the child for that particular node. Thus, for each pair of parents, only one child is created. For the mutation operator, they used a random shock similar to the normal distribution mutation shown above. Because neural network weights are constrained to lie between −1 and 1, the resulting weights after application of the mutation must be checked so that they do not stray outside this range.

The modified discrete crossover is illustrated in Table 6.4 and Figure 6.6. In this example, the weights incoming to node *A* are supplied by parent 1, and the weights incoming to nodes *B* and *Z* are supplied by parent 2 (shaded). The random shock mutation is illustrated in Table 6.5 and Figure 6.7. In this example, the mutation was applied to the weights incoming to node *B* only for the child generated from the crossover operation. The new weights are not far from the old weights. Montana and Davis's GA-based neural network outperformed a back-propagation neural network despite a total of 126 weights in their chromosomes.

WEKA: HANDS-ON ANALYSIS USING GENETIC ALGORITHMS

This exercise explores the use of WEKA's Genetic Search class to optimize (choose) a subset of inputs used to classify patients as having either benign or malignant forms of breast cancer. The input file *breast-cancer.arff* used in our experiment is adapted from the Wisconsin Breast Cancer Database [19]. *Breast-cancer.arff* contains 683 instances after deleting 16 records containing one or more missing values. In addition, it contains nine numeric inputs ("sample code number" attribute deleted) and a target attribute *class* which takes on values 2 (benign) and 4 (malignant). Table 6.6 shows the ARFF header and first 10 instances from *breast-cancer.arff*:

Next, we load the input file and become familiar with the *class* distribution.

1. Open the WEKA Explorer panel.
2. From the Preprocess tab, press Open file and specify the path to the input file, *breast-cancer.arff*.
3. Under Attributes (lower left), select the *class* attribute from the list.

The WEKA Preprocess Tab displays the distribution for *class* and indicates that 65% (444/683) of the records have value 2 (benign), while the remaining 35% (239/683) have value 4 (malignant), as shown in Figure 6.8.

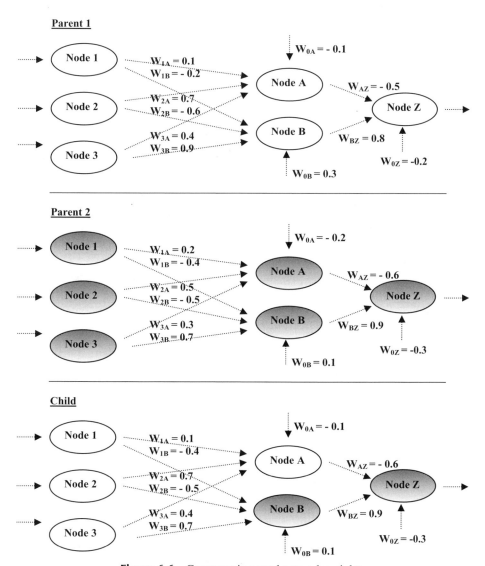

Figure 6.6   Crossover in neural network weights.

Next, let's establish a baseline and classify the records using naive Bayes with 10-fold cross validation, where *all* nine attributes are input to the classifier.

1. Select the Classify Tab.
2. Under Classifier, press the Choose button.
3. Select Classifiers → Bayes → Naive Bayes from the navigation hierarchy.
4. By default, under Test options, notice that WEKA specifies Cross-validation. We'll use this option for our experiment because we have a single data file.
5. Click Start.

TABLE 6.5   Weights Before and After Mutation

	W_{1A}	W_{1B}	W_{2A}	W_{2B}	W_{3A}	W_{3B}	W_{0A}	W_{0B}	W_{AZ}	W_{BZ}	W_{0Z}
Before	0.1	−0.4	0.7	−0.5	0.4	0.7	−0.1	0.1	−0.6	0.9	−0.3
Shock	None	−0.05	None	−0.07	None	0.02	None	None	None	None	None
After	0.1	−0.45	0.7	−0.57	0.4	0.72	−0.1	0.1	−0.6	0.9	−0.3

The results in the Classifier output window show that naive Bayes achieves a very impressive 96.34% (658/683) classification accuracy. This obviously leaves little room for improvement. Do you suppose that all nine attributes are equally important to the task of classification? Is there possibly a subset of the nine attributes, when selected as input to naive Bayes, which leads to improved classification accuracy?

Before determining the answers to these questions, let's review WEKA's approach to attribute selection. It's not unusual for real-word data sets to contain irrelevant, redundant, or noisy attributes, which ultimately contribute to degradation in classification accuracy. In contrast, removing nonrelevant attributes often leads to improved classification accuracy. WEKA's supervised attribute selection filter enables a combination of evaluation and search methods to be specified, where the objective is to determine a useful *subset* of attributes as input to a learning scheme.

Network before Mutation

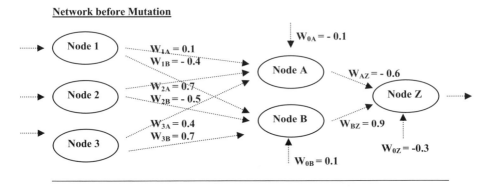

Network after Mutation of Weights Incoming to Node B

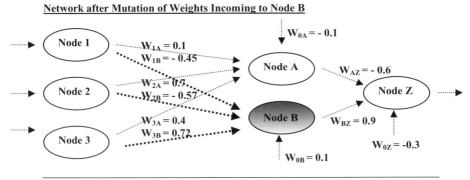

Figure 6.7   Mutation in neural network weights.

TABLE 6.6   Breast Cancer Input File *breast-cancer.arff*

```
@relation breast-cancer.arff

@attribute clump-thickness       numeric
@attribute uniform-cell-size     numeric
@attribute uniform-cell-shape    numeric
@attribute marg-adhesion         numeric
@attribute single-cell-size      numeric
@attribute bare-nuclei           numeric
@attribute bland-chromatin       numeric
@attribute normal-nucleoli       numeric
@attribute mitoses               numeric
@attribute class                 {2,4}

@data
5,1,1,1,2,1,3,1,1,2
5,4,4,5,7,10,3,2,1,2
3,1,1,1,2,2,3,1,1,2
6,8,8,1,3,4,3,7,1,2
4,1,1,3,2,1,3,1,1,2
8,10,10,8,7,10,9,7,1,4
1,1,1,1,2,10,3,1,1,2
2,1,2,1,2,1,3,1,1,2
2,1,1,1,2,1,1,1,5,2
4,2,1,1,2,1,2,1,1,2
. . .
```

WEKA contains a Genetic Search class with default options that include a population size of $n = 20$ chromosomes, crossover probability $p_c = 0.6$, and mutation probability $p_m = 0.033$. Figure 6.9 shows the default options available in the Genetic Search dialog. As specified, the Genetic Search algorithm creates an initial set of 20 chromosomes. An individual chromosome in the initial population may consist of the attribute subset

1	4	6	7	9

where each of the five *genes* represents an attribute index. For example, the first gene in our example chromosome is the attribute *clump-thickness*, as represented by its index position $= 1$. In our configuration the WrapperSubsetEval evaluation method serves as the fitness function $f(x)$ and calculates a fitness value for each chromosome.

WrapperSubsetEval evaluates each of the attribute subsets (chromosomes) according to a specified learning scheme. In the example below we'll specify naive Bayes. In this way, the usefulness of a chromosome is determined as a measure of the classification accuracy reported by naive Bayes. In other words, the chromosomes leading to higher classification accuracy are more relevant and receive a higher fitness score.

Now, let's apply WEKA's Genetic Search class to our attribute set. To accomplish this task, we first have to specify the evaluator and search options for attribute selection.

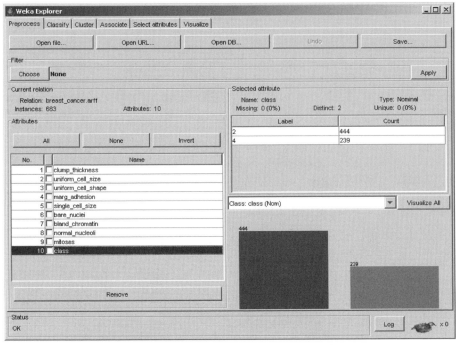

Figure 6.8 WEKA Explorer: *class* distribution.

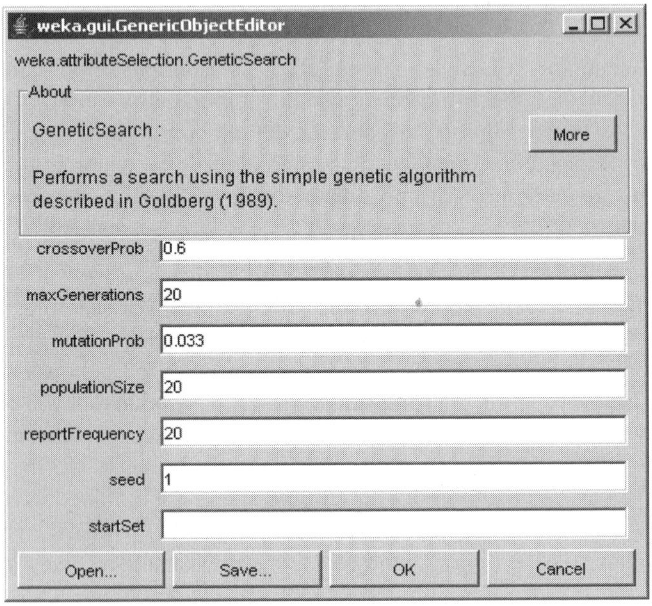

Figure 6.9 Genetic search dialog.

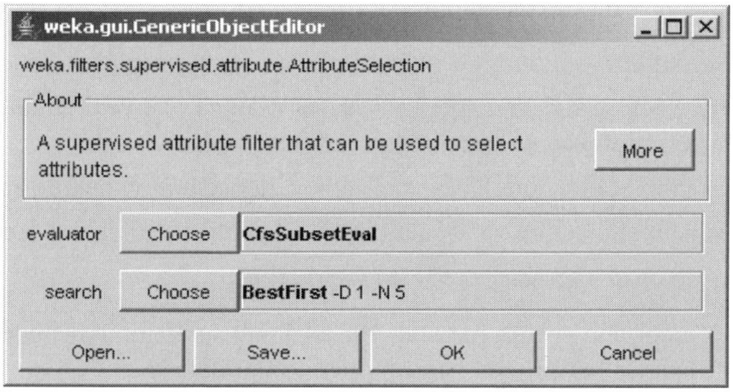

Figure 6.10   AttributeSelection dialog.

1. Select the Preprocess Tab.
2. Under Filter, press the Choose button.
3. Select Filters → Supervised → Attribute → AttributeSelection from the navigation hierarchy. As a result, the text "AttributeSelection . . ." is shown next to the Choose button.
4. Now, click on the text "AttributeSelection . . .".

The AttributeSelection dialog appears as shown in, Figure 6.10, where the default Evaluator and Search methods are displayed. Next, we'll override these default options by specifying new evaluator and search methods.

1. Next to evaluator, press the Choose button.
2. Select AttributeSelection → WrapperSubsetEval from the navigation hierarchy.
3. Click on the text "WrapperSubsetEval" next to the evaluator Choose button. The WrapperSubsetEval dialog appears as shown in Figure 6.11. By default, WEKA specifies the ZeroR classifier.

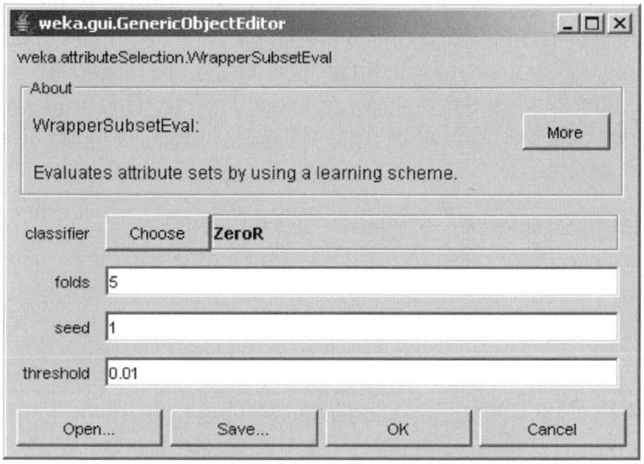

Figure 6.11   WrapperSubsetEval dialog.

4. Press the Choose button, next to classifier.

5. Select Classifiers → Bayes → Naive Bayes from the navigation hierarchy.

6. Click OK to close the WrapperSubsetEval dialog. The evaluation method for AttributeSelection is now specified.

7. On the AttributeSelection dialog, press the Choose button next to search.

8. Select AttributeSelection → GeneticSearch from the navigation hierarchy.

9. Press OK to close the AttributeSelection dialog.

The evaluator and search methods for attribute selection have been specified; however, our changes haven't yet been applied to our data set.

10. Press the Apply button on the right side of the Explorer panel.

After processing the command, WEKA displays updated results in the Explorer panel. In particular, under Attributes, notice the list now shows seven predictor attributes. That is, the two attributes *single-cell-size* and *mitoses* have been removed from the attribute list. Let's reclassify the records using naive Bayes with 10-fold cross-validation; however, this time *only* seven attributes are input to the classifier.

1. Select the Classify Tab.

2. Under Classifier, press the Choose button.

3. Select Classifiers → Bayes → Naive Bayes from the navigation hierarchy.

4. Cross-validation is specified.

5. Click Start.

Now, naive Bayes reports 96.78% (661/683) classification accuracy, which indicates that the second model outperforms the first model by almost 0.05% (96.78% versus 96.34%). That is, classification accuracy has increased where only seven of the nine attributes are specified as input. Although these results do not show a dramatic improvement in accuracy, this simple example has demonstrated how WEKA's Genetic Search algorithm can be included as part of an attribute selection approach.

Let's further examine the results reported by WEKA's Genetic Search method, where the characteristics of the candidate population are described. The following procedures should look similar to those performed above. This time, however, we're invoking the attribute selection filter from WEKA's Select attributes Tab, which provides detailed output.

1. Return to the Preprocess Tab on the Explorer panel.

2. Press the Undo button (top right). This removes the filter we applied to the data set earlier.

3. Select the Select attributes Tab from the Explorer panel.

4. Under Attribute Evaluator, press the Choose button.

5. Select AttributeSelection → WrapperSubsetEval from the navigation hierarchy.

6. Click on the text "WrapperSubsetEval ..." to open the WrapperSubsetEval dialog.

TABLE 6.7   Attributes Selected by the Attribute Selection Method

Selected attributes:	1,2,3,4,6,7,8 : 7
	clump-thickness
	uniform-cell-size
	uniform-cell-shape
	marg-adhesion
	bare-nuclei
	bland-chromatin
	normal-nucleoli

7. Press the Choose button next to the classifier.

8. Select Classifiers → Bayes → Naive Bayes from the navigation hierarchy. Now the evaluator is specified.

9. Under Search Method, press the Choose button.

10. Select AttributeSelection → GeneticSearch from the navigation hierarchy.

Now, the attribute selection evaluator and search methods are specified. By default, under Attribute Selection Mode, WEKA specifies Use full training set. Click the Start button to select the attributes. WEKA reports results in the Attribute selection output window and includes the attributes it selected, as shown in Table 6.7.

Not surprisingly, this is the same list of attributes that we derived earlier using the attribute selection method. In other words, notice that *single-cell-size* and *mitoses* are not included in the attribute subset. By default, the Genetic Search method specifies default options *report frequency* $= 20$ and *max generations* $= 20$, which cause WEKA to report population characteristics for the initial and final populations. For example, the initial population characteristics for the 20 chromosomes are shown in Table 6.8.

Here, each subset is a chromosome and *merit* is the fitness score reported by naive Bayes, which equals the corresponding classification error rate. For example, consider the chromosome $\{4, 6, 7, 9\}$ reported in Table 6.8 with merit 0.053; this value corresponds[1] to the classification error rate reported by naive Bayes using fivefold cross-validation when $\{4, 6, 7, 9\}$ are specified as input.

Also, each chromosome's scaled fitness is reported in the *scaled* column, where WEKA uses the *linear scaling* technique to scale the values. By definition, the raw fitness and scaled fitness values have the linear relationship $f' = af + b$, where f and f are the scaled and raw fitness values, respectively. The constants a and b are chosen where $f'_{avg} = f_{avg}$ and $f'_{max} = C_{mult} f'_{avg}$. The constant C_{mult} represents the expected number of copies of the fittest individual in the population, and for small populations is typically set[2] to a value in the range 1.2 to 2.0.

Therefore, by computing the average fitness values presented in Table 6.8 we obtain $f_{avg} = 0.055753$ and $f'_{avg} = 0.055755$, which agrees with the rule by which the constants a and b are chosen. Because the value for C_{mult} is not an option in WEKA, the fitness values from the last two rows from Table 6.8 are selected to solve the

---

[1] Actually, this value may differ slightly, due to the value for the WrapperSubsetEval *threshold* option.

[2] WEKA sets this value internally.

TABLE 6.8 Initial Population Characteristics Reported by a Genetic Search

Initial population merit	scaled	subset
0.053	0.05777	4 6 7 9
0.04978	0.06014	1 2 3 4 7 9
0.03807	0.06873	1 2 3 4 6 9
0.05564	0.05584	6 7 8
0.13177	0	8
0.03953	0.06765	2 3 5 6 7 8
0.0448	0.06379	2 6 7
0.09048	0.03028	5 8
0.07028	0.0451	2
0.04275	0.06529	1 6 8 9
0.04187	0.06593	3 4 5 6 7 8
0.04275	0.06529	2 4 6 7 8
0.08492	0.03436	4 5
0.0612	0.05176	2 4 7
0.03865	0.0683	1 2 4 6 7 9
0.03807	0.06873	1 3 4 6 9
0.04275	0.06529	3 6 7 8 9
0.05329	0.05756	2 4 8
0.05271	0.05799	1 4 7 8
0.04275	0.06529	3 6 7 8 9

simultaneously equations for a and b, according to the relationship $f' = a \cdot f + b$:

$$0.05799 = 0.05271a + b$$
$$0.06529 = 0.04275a + b$$

Subtracting the second equation from the first, we obtain

$$-0.0073 = 0.00996a$$
$$a = -\frac{0.0073}{0.00996} = -0.73293 \qquad b = 0.096623$$

We use the definition $f'_{max} = C_{mult} f_{avg}$ to determine

$$C_{mult} = \frac{f'_{max}}{f_{avg}} = \frac{0.06873}{0.055753} = 1.23$$

Finally, observe that the fifth row in Table 6.8 has $f' = 0$. The raw fitness value of 0.13177 corresponds to the largest classification error in the population produced by chromosome {8}, and as a result, f' is mapped to zero to avoid the possibility of producing negatively scaled fitnesses.

In this exercise we've analyzed a simple classification problem where Genetic Search was used to find an attribute subset that improved naive Bayes classification accuracy compared to using the full set of attributes. Although this problem has only nine attributes, there are still $2^9 - 1 = 511$ possible attribute subsets that can be input to a classifier. Imagine building a classification model from a set of 100 inputs. Here, there are $2^{100} - 1 = 1.27 \times 10^{30}$ possible attribute subsets from which to choose. In situations such as these, Genetic Search techniques may prove helpful in determining useful attribute subsets.

SUMMARY

Genetic algorithms (GAs), developed by John Holland in the 1960s and 1970s, attempt to mimic computationally the processes by which natural selection operates. Genetic algorithms provide a framework for studying the effects of such biologically inspired factors as mate selection, reproduction, mutation, and crossover of genetic information. Three operators are used by genetic algorithms: *selection*, *crossover*, and *mutation*. The selection operator refers to the method used for selecting which chromosomes will be reproducing. The fitness function evaluates each of the chromosomes (candidate solutions), and the fitter the chromosome, the more likely it will be selected to reproduce. The crossover operator performs recombination, creating two new offspring by randomly selecting a locus and exchanging subsequences to the left and right of that locus between two chromosomes chosen during selection. The mutation operator randomly changes the bits or digits at a particular locus in a chromosome, usually, however, with very low probability. Mutation introduces new information to the genetic pool and protects against converging too quickly to a local optimum.

Each member of the population of potential solutions is evaluated for fitness on each cycle. A new population then replaces the old population using the operators above, with the fittest members being chosen for reproduction or cloning. Fitness is measured using a fitness function $f(x)$, a real-valued function operating on the chromosome (potential solution). For the selection operator, the analyst should be careful to balance fitness with diversity. If fitness is favored over variability, a set of highly fit but suboptimal chromosomes will dominate the population, reducing the ability of the GA to find the global optimum. If diversity is favored over fitness, model convergence will be too slow.

Crowding occurs when one particular chromosome which is much fitter than the others begins to reproduce, generating too many clones and similar copies of itself in future generations. By reducing the diversity of the population, crowding impairs the ability of the genetic algorithm to continue to explore new regions of the search space. A variety of techniques are available to handle crowding.

Single-point crossover suffers from positional bias, in which the performance of the genetic algorithm depends in part on the order that the variables occur in the chromosome. Multipoint crossover or uniform crossover can be used to alleviate this.

The original framework for genetic algorithms was developed for binary-encoded data, since the operations of crossover and mutation worked naturally and well with such data. However, most data mining data come in the form of real numbers, often with many decimals worth of precision. Eiben and Smith [10] suggest the following methods for performing crossover and mutation on continuous data: single arithmetic crossover, simple arithmetic crossover, whole arithmetic crossover, discrete crossover, and normally distributed mutation.

Genetic algorithms are often used to perform optimization within a neural network, as an alternative to the usual back-propagation method. Genetic algorithms have less of a tendency to become stuck in local minima than do back-propagation methods.

REFERENCES

1. John Holland, *Adaptation in Natural and Artificial Systems*, University of Michigan Press, Ann Arbon, MI; 1975; 2nd ed., MIT Press, Cambridge, MA, 1992.
2. Melanie Mitchell, *An Introduction to Genetic Algorithms*, MIT Press, Cambridge, MA, 2002; first edition, 1996.
3. Kenneth De Jong, An analysis of the behavior of a class of genetic adaptive systems, Ph.D. dissertation, University of Michigan, Ann Arbor, MI, 1975.
4. David Goldberg and Jon Richardson, Genetic algorithms with sharing for multi-modal function optimization, in J. Greffenstette, ed., *Genetic Algorithms and Their Applications: Proceedings of the 2nd International Conference on Genetic Algorithms*, Lawrence Erlbaum Associates, Hillsdale, NJ, 1987.
5. Kalyanmoy Deb and David Goldberg. An investigation of niche and species formation in genetic function optimization, in J. Greffenstette, ed., *Proceedings of the 3rd International Conference on Genetic Algorithms*, Morgan Kaufmann, San Francisco, CA, 1989.
6. Larry Eschelman, The CHC adaptive search algorithm: how to have safe search when engaging in nontraditional genetic recombination, in G. Rawlins, ed., *Foundations of Genetic Algorithms*, Morgan Kaufmann, San Francisco, CA, 1991.
7. Larry Eshelman and J. David Schaffer, Preventing premature convergence in genetic algorithms by preventing incest, in R. Belew and L. Booker, eds., *Proceedings of the 4th International Conference on Genetic Algorithms*, Morgan Kaufmann, San Francisco, CA, 1991.
8. Stephanie Forrest, Scaling fitnesses in the genetic algorithm, in Documentation for PRISONERS DILEMMA and NORMS Programs That Use the Genetic Algorithm, unpublished manuscript, 1985.
9. Randy Haupt and Sue Ellen Haupt, *Practical Genetic Algorithms*, Wiley, New York, 1998.
10. A. E. Eiben and Jim Smith, *Introduction to Evolutionary Computing*, Springer-Verlag, Berlin, 2003.
11. Tom Mitchell, *Machine Learning*, WCB–McGraw-Hill, Boston, 1997.
12. Laurene Fausett, *Fundamentals of Neural Networks*, Prentice Hall, Englewood cliffs, NJ, 1994.
13. Simon Haykin, *Neural Networks: A Comprehensive Foundation*, Prentice Hall, Englewood cliffs, NJ, 1990.
14. Daniel Larose, *Discovering Knowledge in Data: An Introduction to Data Mining*, Wiley, Hoboken, NJ, 2005.
15. Russell D. Reed and Robert J. Marks II, *Neural Smithing: Supervised Learning in Feedforward Artificial Neural Networks*, MIT Press, Cambridge, MA, 1999.
16. Nishant Unnikrishnan, Ajay Mahajan, and Tsuchin Chu. Intelligent system modeling of a three-dimensional ultrasonic positioning system using neural networks and genetic algorithms, in *Proceedings of the Institution for Mechanical Engineers*, Vol. 217, Part I, *Journal of Systems and Control Engineering*, 2003.
17. Chin-Sheng Huang, Robert Dorsey, and Mary Ann Boose. Life insurer financial distress prediction: a neural network model, *Journal of Insurance Regulation*, Vol. 13, No. 2, Winter 1994.

18. David Montana and Lawrence Davis. Training feedforward networks using genetic algorithms, in *Proceedings of the International Joint Conference on Artificial Intelligence*, Morgan Kaufmann, San Francisco, CA, 1989.

19. Breast cancer dataset, compiled by Dr. William H. Wolberg, University of Wisconsin Hospitals, Madison, WI, obtained January 8, 1991.

EXERCISES

Clarifying the Concepts

6.1. Match each of the following genetic algorithm terms with its definition or description.

Term	Definition
(a) Selection	One of the candidate solutions to the problem.
(b) Generation	Scales the chromosome fitness by the standard deviation of the fitnesses, thereby maintaining selection pressure at a constant rate.
(c) Crowding	The operator that determines which chromosomes will reproduce.
(d) Crossover	Genes in neighboring loci will often be crossed together, affecting the performance of the genetic algorithm.
(e) Chromosome	The operator that introduces new information to the genetic pool to protect against premature convergence.
(f) Positional bias	A feedforward, completelyconnected, multilayer network.
(g) Uniform crossover	A cycle through the genetic algorithm.
(h) Mutation	One particularly fit chromosome generates too many clones and close copies of itself, thereby reducing population diversity.
(i) Sigma scaling	The selection condition requiring that the genetic algorithm retain a certain number of the fittest chromosomes from one generation to the next.
(j) Gene	The operator that performs recombination, creating two new offspring by combining the parents' genes in new ways.
(k) Elitism	Each gene is randomly assigned to be that of either one parent or the other, with 50% probability.
(l) Neural network	A single bit of the candidate solution.

6.2. Discuss why the selection operator should be careful to balance fitness with diversity. Describe the dangers of an overemphasis on each.

6.3. Compare the strengths and weakness of using back-propagation and genetic algorithms for optimization in neural networks.

Working with the Data

6.4 Continue the example in the text, where the fitness is determined by the normal $(16, 4)$ distribution. Proceed to the end of the third iteration. Suppress mutation, and perform crossover only once, on the second iteration at locus four.

6.5 Calculate the child vectors for the whole arithmetic crossover example in the text. Use the parents indicated in the section on simple arithmetic crossover, with $\alpha = 0.5$. Comment on your results.

Hands-on Analysis

6.6 (*Extra credit*) Write a computer program for a simple genetic algorithm. Implement the example discussed in the text using the normal $(16, 4)$ fitness function. Let the crossover rate be 0.6 and the mutation rate be 0.01. Start with the population of all integers 0 to 31. Generate 25 runs and measure the generation at which the optimal decision of $x = 16$ is encountered. If you have time, vary the crossover and mutation rates and compare the results.

6.7 Repeat the procedure using the *breast-cancer.arff* data set with WEKA by selecting an attribute subset using Genetic Search. This time, however, specify naive Bayes with *use kernel estimator = true* for both attribute selection and 10 fold cross validation. Now, contrast the classification results using the full set of attributes compared to the attribute subset selected using Genetic Search. Does classification accuracy improve?

CHAPTER 7

CASE STUDY: MODELING RESPONSE TO DIRECT MAIL MARKETING

CROSS-INDUSTRY STANDARD PROCESS FOR DATA MINING

BUSINESS UNDERSTANDING PHASE

DATA UNDERSTANDING AND DATA PREPARATION PHASES

MODELING AND EVALUATION PHASES

CROSS-INDUSTRY STANDARD PROCESS FOR DATA MINING

The case study in this chapter is carried out using the Cross-Industry Standard Process for Data Mining (CRISP–DM). According to CRISP–DM, a given data mining project has a life cycle consisting of six phases, as illustrated in Figure 7.1. Note that the phase sequence is *adaptive*. That is, the next phase in the sequence often depends on the outcomes associated with the preceding phase. The most significant dependencies between phases are indicated by the arrows. For example, suppose that we are in the modeling phase. Depending on the behavior and characteristics of the model, we may have to return to the data preparation phase for further refinement before moving forward to the model evaluation phase. The six phases are as follows:

1. *Business understanding phase*. The first phase in the CRISP–DM standard process may also be termed the *research understanding phase*.

    a. Enunciate the project objectives and requirements clearly in terms of the business or research unit as a whole.

    b. Translate these goals and restrictions into the formulation of a data mining problem definition.

    c. Prepare a preliminary strategy for achieving these objectives.

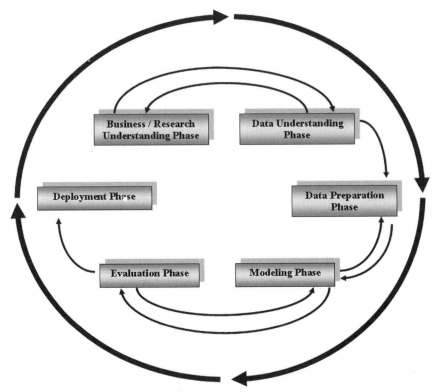

Figure 7.1 CRISP–DM is an iterative, adaptive process.

2. *Data understanding phase*
   a. Collect the data.
   b. Use exploratory data analysis to familiarize yourself with the data, and discover initial insights.
   c. Evaluate the quality of the data.
   d. If desired, select interesting subsets that may contain actionable patterns.

3. *Data preparation phase*
   a. This labor-intensive phase covers all aspects of preparing the final data set, which will be used for subsequent phases, from the initial, raw, dirty data.
   b. Select the cases and variables you want to analyze and that are appropriate for your analysis.
   c. Perform transformations on certain variables, if needed.
   d. Clean the raw data so that it is ready for the modeling tools.

4. *Modeling phase*
   a. Select and apply appropriate modeling techniques.
   b. Calibrate model settings to optimize results.
   c. Often, several different techniques may be applied for the same data mining problem.

    d. Loop back to the data preparation phase as required to bring the form of the data into line with the specific requirements of a particular data mining technique.

5. *Evaluation phase*

    a. The modeling phase has delivered one or more models. These models must be evaluated for quality and effectiveness before we deploy them for use in the field.

    b. Determine whether the model in fact achieves the objectives set for it in phase 1.

    c. Establish whether some important facet of the business or research problem has not been accounted for sufficiently.

    d. Finally, come to a decision regarding the use of the data mining results.

6. *Deployment phase*

    a. Model creation does not signify the completion of the project. Need to make use of created models according to business objectives.

    b. Example of a simple deployment: Generate a report.

    c. Example of a more complex deployment: Implement a parallel data mining process in another department.

    d. For businesses, the customer often carries out the deployment based on your model.

For more on CRISP–DM, see Chapman et al. [1], Larose [2], or www.crisp-dm .org.

BUSINESS UNDERSTANDING PHASE

Direct Mail Marketing Response Problem

In this detailed case study, our task is to predict which customers are most likely to respond to a direct mail marketing promotion. The *clothing-store* data set [3], located at the book series Web site, represents actual data provided by a clothing store chain in New England. Data were collected on 51 fields for 28,799 customers. More information about the data set is provided in the data understanding phase below.

    Our data mining task is a classification problem. We are to classify which customers will respond to a direct mail marketing promotion based on information collected about the customers. How does this problem fit into the business as a whole? Clearly, for the clothing store, the overriding objective is to increase profits. Therefore, the goal of our classification model should also be to increase profits. Model evaluative measures that assess the effect of the classification model on the business's bottom line will therefore be applied. In the following sections we examine this case study using Clementine 8.5 data mining software, available from SPSS, Inc.

Building the Cost/Benefit Table

Classification models are often evaluated on accuracy rates, error rates, false negative rates, and false positive rates. These measures can be applied to any classification problem. However, for a particular classification problem, these measures may not select the optimal model. The reason is that each classification problem carries with it a unique set of costs and benefits, which stem from the particular set of circumstances unique to that business or research problem.

The cost of a false positive (wrongly predicting positive response) may be low in certain environments but higher in other environments. For example, in direct marketing, a false positive may cost no more than a postcard, while in HIV testing, a false positive on the ELISA test will be more expensive, leading to second-level HIV testing. (On the other hand, of course, false negatives in HIV testing are very serious indeed, which is why the ELISA test allows a higher rate of false positives, to maintain the false negative rate as low as possible.)

In business problems, such as our direct mail marketing problem, company managers may require that model comparisons be made in terms of cost/benefit analysis. Recall from *Discovering Knowledge in Data: An Introduction to Data Mining* [2] that it is useful to construct a cost/benefit table when performing classification. This is done to provide model comparison in terms of anticipated profit or loss by associating a cost or benefit with each of the four possible combinations of correct and incorrect classifications.

Let us consider each of the four possible decision outcomes (true negative, true positive, false negative, and false positive) and assign reasonable costs to each decision outcome.

1. *True negative* (TN). The model predicted that this customer would not respond to the direct mail marketing promotion, so no postcard was mailed to him or her. In reality, this customer would not have responded to the promotion. Therefore, the correct decision was made. No costs were incurred, since no postcard was sent; no sales were made, and no prospective sales were lost.

2. *True positive* (TP). The model predicted that this customer would respond to the direct mail marketing promotion, so a promotion was mailed to him or her. In reality, this customer would indeed have responded to the promotion. Therefore, again the correct decision was made. The direct mailing cost, with materials, postage, and handling, is $2 per promotion unit mailed. However, this particular TP customer, upon receiving the postcard, would have come into the store to make purchases. The question then becomes: How much money would we reasonably expect the customer to spend, and how much of that amount spent could be considered profit? Table 7.1 shows the statistics associated with the average amount spent per visit for all 28,799 customers. The mean is $113.59, which we shall use as our estimate of the amount this customer will spend on the visit after receiving the promotion. (The median is another reasonable estimate, which we did not use in this example. By the way, why is the mean larger than the median? *Hint*: Check out the maximum: Imagine spending an average of $1919.88 per visit to a clothing store.) Assume that 25% of this $113.59, or $28.40, represents profit. Then the benefit associated with this customer is the profit expected from the visit, $28.40, minus the cost associated with the mailing, $2.00, that is, $26.40.

TABLE 7.1   Statistics Associated with the Average Amount Spent per Visit for All Customers

Count	28,799
Mean	113.588
Minimum	0.490
Maximum	1,919.880
Standard deviation	86.981
Median	92.000

3. *False negative* (FN). In most marketing problems, which decision error is worse, a false negative or a false positive? A false positive means that you contacted a nonresponsive customer, which is not very costly. But a false negative means that you failed to contact a customer who would have responded positively to the promotion. This error is much more expensive, and marketing classification modelers should endeavor to minimize the probability of making this type of error. What is the cost associated with making a false negative decision in this case? There is no cost of contact for this customer, since we did not contact him or her. But had this customer been in fact contacted, he or she would have responded, and spent money at the clothing store. The estimated amount is the same as above, $113.59, of which $28.40 would have been profit. Therefore, the lost profit associated with this customer is $28.40.

4. *False positive* (FP). False positives are much less serious for marketing models. Here, the cost associated with contacting a nonresponsive customer is the $2 for postage and handling. We can therefore see that in the context of this particular problem, a false negative is $28.40/2.00 = 14.2$ times as expensive as a false positive.

We may thus proceed to construct the cost/benefit table for this clothing store marketing promotion example, as shown in Table 7.2. Note that benefit is shown as

TABLE 7.2   Cost/Benefit Decision Summary for the Clothing Store Marketing Promotion Problem

Outcome	Classification	Actual Response	Cost	Rationale
True negative	Nonresponse	Nonresponse	$0	No contact, no lost profit
True positive	Response	Response	−$26.4	Estimated profit minus cost of mailing
False negative	Nonresponse	Response	$28.40	Lost profit
False positive	Response	Nonresponse	$2.00	Materials, postage, and handling cost

negative cost. The cost/benefit table in Table 7.2 will be the final arbitrator of which model we select as optimal for this problem, error rates notwithstanding.

DATA UNDERSTANDING AND DATA PREPARATION PHASES

Clothing Store Data Set

For this case study we meld together the data understanding and data preparation phases, since what we learn in each phase immediately affects our actions in the other phase. The *clothing-store* data set contains information about 28,799 customers in the following 51 fields:

- Customer ID: unique, encrypted customer identification
- Zip code
- Number of purchase visits
- Total net sales
- Average amount spent per visit
- Amount spent at each of four different franchises (four variables)
- Amount spent in the past month, the past three months, and the past six months
- Amount spent the same period last year
- Gross margin percentage
- Number of marketing promotions on file
- Number of days the customer has been on file
- Number of days between purchases
- Markdown percentage on customer purchases
- Number of different product classes purchased
- Number of coupons used by the customer
- Total number of individual items purchased by the customer
- Number of stores the customer shopped at
- Number of promotions mailed in the past year
- Number of promotions responded to in the past year
- Promotion response rate for the past year
- Product uniformity (low score = diverse spending patterns)
- Lifetime average time between visits
- Microvision lifestyle cluster type
- Percent of returns
- Flag: credit card user
- Flag: valid phone number on file
- Flag: Web shopper

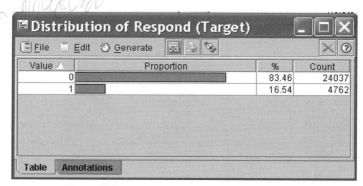

Figure 7.2 Most customers are nonresponders.

- 15 variables providing the percentages spent by the customer on specific classes of clothing, including sweaters, knit tops, knit dresses, blouses, jackets, career pants, casual pants, shirts, dresses, suits, outerwear, jewelry, fashion, legwear, and the collectibles line; also a variable showing the brand of choice (encrypted)

- Target variable: response to promotion

These data are based on a direct mail marketing campaign conducted last year. We use this information to develop classification models for this year's marketing campaign. In the data understanding phase, we become more familiar with the data set using exploratory data analysis (EDA) and graphical and descriptive statistical methods for learning about data. First, what is the proportion of responders to the direct mail marketing promotion? Figure 7.2 shows that only 4762 of the 28,799 customers, or 16.54%, responded to last year's marketing campaign (1 indicates response, 0 indicates nonresponse.) Since the proportion of responders is so small, we may decide to apply balancing to the data prior to modeling.

One of the variables, the Microvision lifestyle cluster type, contains the market segmentation category for each customer as defined by Claritas Demographics [4]. There are 50 segmentation categories, labeled 1 to 50; the distribution of the most prevalent 20 cluster types over the customer database is given in Figure 7.3.

The six most common lifestyle cluster types in our data set are:

1. *Cluster 10: Home Sweet Home*—families, medium-high income and education, managers/professionals, technical/sales

2. *Cluster 1: Upper Crust*—metropolitan families, very high income and education, homeowners, manager/professionals

3. *Cluster 4: Midlife Success*—families, very high education, high income, managers/professionals, technical/sales

4. *Cluster 16: Country Home Families*—large families, rural areas, medium education, medium income, precision/crafts

5. *Cluster 8: Movers and Shakers*—singles, couples, students, and recent graduates, high education and income, managers/professionals, technical/sales

6. *Cluster 15: Great Beginnings*—young, singles and couples, medium-high education, medium income, some renters, managers/professionals, technical/sales

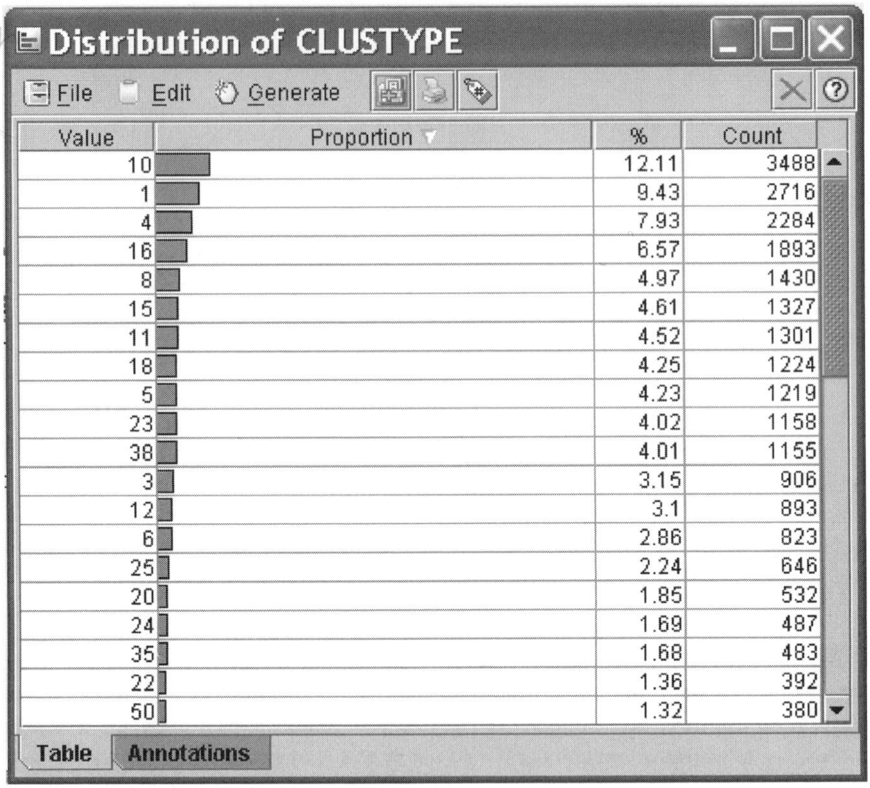

Value	Proportion ▼	%	Count
10		12.11	3488
1		9.43	2716
4		7.93	2284
16		6.57	1893
8		4.97	1430
15		4.61	1327
11		4.52	1301
18		4.25	1224
5		4.23	1219
23		4.02	1158
38		4.01	1155
3		3.15	906
12		3.1	893
6		2.86	823
25		2.24	646
20		1.85	532
24		1.69	487
35		1.68	483
22		1.36	392
50		1.32	380

Figure 7.3 The 20 most prevalent Microvision lifestyle cluster types.

Overall, the clothing store seems to attract a prosperous clientele with fairly high income and education. Cluster 1, *Upper Crust*, represents the wealthiest of the 50 cluster types and is the second most prevalent category among our customers.

Moving to other variables, we turn to the customer ID. Since this field is unique to every customer and is encrypted, it can contain no information that is helpful for our task of predicting which customers are most likely to respond to the direct mail marketing promotion. It is therefore omitted from further analysis.

The zip code can potentially contain information useful in this task. Although ostensibly numeric, zip codes actually represent a categorization of the client database by geographic locality. However, for the present problem, we set this field aside and concentrate on the remaining variables.

Transformations to Achieve Normality or Symmetry

Most of the numeric fields are right-skewed. For example, Figure 7.4 shows the distribution of *product uniformity*, a variable that takes large values for customers who purchase only a few different classes of clothes (e.g., blouses, legwear, pants) and

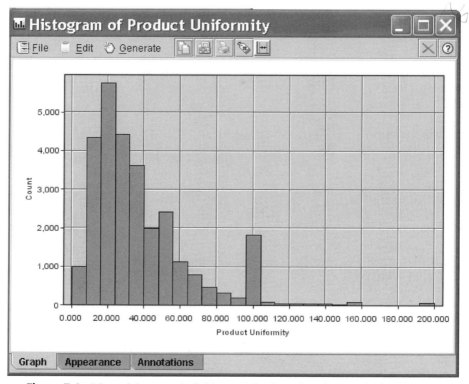

Figure 7.4 Most of the numeric fields are right-skewed, such as product uniformity.

small values for customers who purchase many different classes of clothes. Later we shall see that high product uniformity is associated with low probability of responding to the promotion. Figure 7.4 is right-skewed, with most customers having a relatively low product uniformity measure, while fewer customers have larger values. The customers with large values for product uniformity tend to buy only one or two classes of clothes.

Many data mining methods and models, such as principal components analysis and logistic regression, function best when the variables are normally distributed or, failing that, at least symmetric. Thus, we therefore apply transformations to all of the numerical variables that require it, to induce approximate normality or symmetry. The analyst may choose from the transformations indicated in Chapter 2, such as the *natural log transformation*, the *square root transformation*, a *Box–Cox transformation*, or a *power transformation* from the ladder of re-expressions. For our variables which contained only positive values, we applied the natural log transformation. However, for the variables that contained zero values as well as positive values, we applied the square root transformation, since $\ln(x)$ is undefined for $x = 0$.

Figure 7.5 shows the distribution of product uniformity after the natural log transformation. Although perfect normality is not obtained, the result is nevertheless much less skewed than the raw data distribution, allowing for smoother application of

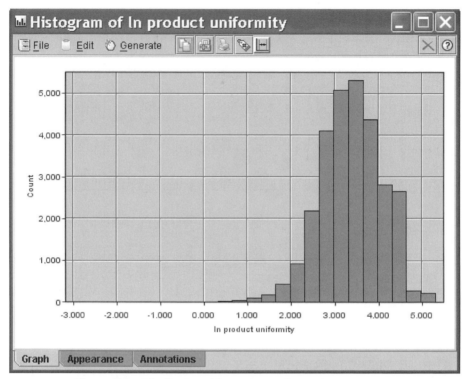

Figure 7.5 Distribution of *ln product uniformity* is less skewed.

several data mining methods and models. Recall that the data set includes 15 variables providing the percentages spent by the customer on specific classes of clothing, including sweaters, knit tops, knit dresses, blouses, and so on. Now, a small percentage (usually, <1%) of records contain percentage values that are negative. It is not clear how percentages can take negative values, or what the meaning of these negative values is, in the context of this problem. Communication with the database analyst or other domain specialist is in order. However, absent that option, we adjust these anomalous values upward to zero dollars. Another option would have been to take the absolute value of these negative amounts, on the assumption that the figures represent returns of earlier purchases.

Figure 7.6 shows the distribution, after adjustment, of the *percentage spent on blouses*. We see a spike at zero, along with the usual right-skewness, which calls for a transformation. The square root transformation is applied, with results shown in Figure 7.7. Note that the spike at zero remains, while the remainder of the data appear nicely symmetric. The dichotomous character of Figure 7.7 motivates us to derive a flag variable for all blouse purchasers. Figure 7.8 shows the distribution of this flag variable, with about 58% of customers having purchased a blouse at one time or another. Flag variables were also constructed for the other 14 clothing percentage variables.

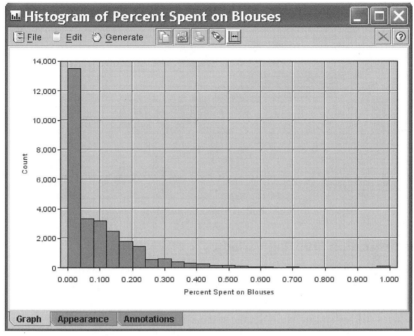

Figure 7.6   Distribution of *percentage spent on blouses*.

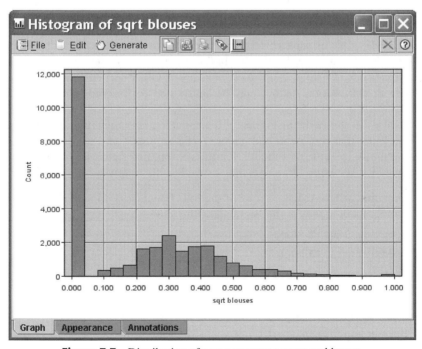

Figure 7.7   Distribution of *sqrt percentage spent on blouses*.

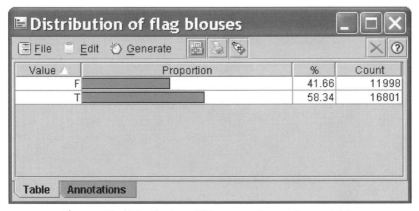

Figure 7.8 Distribution of *blouse purchasers flag variable*.

Standardization and Flag Variables

When there are large differences in variability among the numerical variables, the data analyst needs to apply standardization. The transformations already applied do help in part to reduce the difference in variability among the variables, but substantial differences still exist. For example, the standard deviation for the variable *sqrt spending in the last six months* is 10.02, while the standard deviation for the variable *sqrt # coupons used* is 0.735. To avoid the greater variability of the *sqrt spending in the last six months* variable overwhelming the *sqrt # coupons used* variable, the numeric fields should be normalized or standardized. Here, we choose to standardize the numeric fields, so that they all have a mean of zero and a standard deviation of 1. For each variable, this is done by subtracting the mean of the variable and dividing by the standard deviation, to arrive at the *z-score*. In this analysis, the resulting variable names are prefixed with a "*z*" (e.g., *z sqrt # coupons used*). Other normalization techniques, such as min-max normalization, may be substituted for *z*-score standardization if desired.

Figure 7.9 shows the histogram of the variable *z sqrt spending last one month*. Note the spike that represents the majority of customers who have not spent any money at the store in the past month. For this reason, flag (indicator) variables were constructed for *spending last one month*, as well as the following variables:

- Spending at the AM store (one of the four franchises), to indicate which customers spent money at this particular store
- Spending at the PS store
- Spending at the CC store
- Spending at the AX store
- Spending in the last three months
- Spending in the last six months
- Spending in the same period last year (SPLY)
- Returns, to indicate which customers have ever returned merchandise

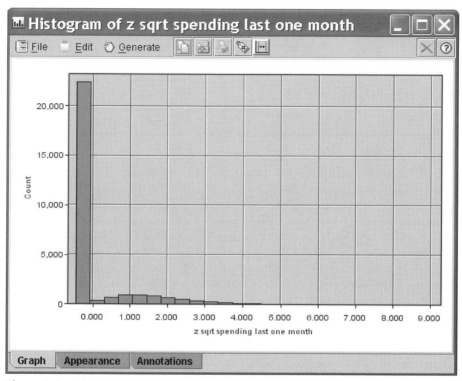

Figure 7.9 Histogram of *z sqrt spending last one month* motivates us to create a flag variable to indicate which customers spent money in the past month.

- Response rate, to indicate which customers have ever responded to a marketing promotion before
- Markdown, to indicate which customers have purchased merchandise that has been marked down

Deriving New Variables

The data preparation phase offers the data miner the opportunity to clarify relationships between variables and to derive new variables that may be useful for the analysis. For example, consider the following three variables: (1) amount spent (by customer) in the last month, (2) amount spent in the last three months, and (3) amount spent in the last six months. Clearly, the amount spent by the customer in the last month is also contained in the other two variables, the amount spent in the last three months and the last six months. Therefore, the amount spent in the last month is getting triple-counted. Now, the analyst may not wish for this most recent amount to be so heavily weighted. For example, in time-series models, the more recent measurements are the most heavily weighted. In this case, however, we prefer not to triple-count the most recent month and must therefore derive two new variables, as shown in Table 7.3.

TABLE 7.3 New Derived Spending Variables

Derived Variable	Formula
Amount spent in previous months 2 and 3	Amount spent in last three months – amount spent in last one month
Amount spent in previous months 4, 5, and 6	Amount spent in last six months – amount spent in last three months

By "amount spent in previous months 2 and 3" we mean the amount spent in the period 90 days to 30 days previous. We shall thus use the following three variables: (1) amount spent in the last month; (2) amount spent in previous months 2 and 3; and (3) amount spent in previous months 4, 5, and 6. We omit the following variables: amount spent in the last three months, and amount spent in the last six months.

Note that even with these derived variables, the most recent month's spending may still be considered to be weighted more heavily than any of the other months' spending. This is because the most recent month's spending has its own variable, while the previous two and three month's spending have to share a variable, as do the previous four, five, and 6 months spending.

The raw data set may have its own derived variables already defined. Consider the following variables: (1) number of purchase visits, (2) total net sales, and (3) average amount spent per visit. The *average amount spent per visit* represents the ratio

$$average = \frac{total\ net\ sales}{number\ of\ purchase\ visits}$$

Since the relationship among these variables is functionally defined, it may turn out that the derived variable is strongly correlated with the other variables. The analyst should check this. Figure 7.10 shows that there is only weak correlation between the derived variable *average* and either of the other variables. On the other hand, the correlation is strong between *total net sales* and *number of purchase visits*. This strong correlation bears watching; we return to this below. By the way, the correlation coefficients between the raw variables should be the same as the correlation coefficients obtained by the z-scores of those variables.

Exploring the Relationships Between the Predictors and the Response

We return to the correlation issue later, but first we would like to investigate the variable-by-variable association between the predictors and the target variable, *response to the marketing promotion*. Ideally, the analyst should examine graphs and statistics for every predictor variable, especially with respect to the relationship with the response. However, the huge data sets prevalent in most data mining applications make this a daunting task. Therefore, we would like to have some way to examine the most useful predictors in an exploratory framework.

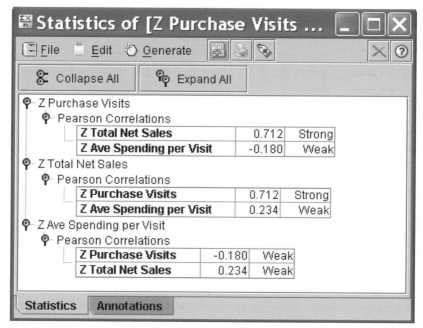

Figure 7.10 Check to make sure that the derived variable is not correlated with the original variables.

Of course, choosing the most useful variables is a modeling task, which lies downstream of our present phase, the EDA-flavored data understanding phase. However, a very rough tool for choosing some useful variables to examine at this early phase is correlation. That is, examine the correlation coefficients for each predictor with the response, and select for further examination those variables that have the largest absolute correlations, say, $|r| \geq 0.30$.

The data miner should, of course, be aware that this is simply a rough EDA tool, and linear correlation with a 0–1 response variable is not appropriate for inference or modeling at this stage. Nevertheless, this method can be useful for paring down the number of variables that would be helpful to examine at the EDA stage. Table 7.4 provides a list of the variables with the highest absolute correlation with the target variable, *response*.

We therefore examine the relationship between these selected predictors and the response variable. First, Figure 7.11 shows a histogram of *z ln lifetime average time between visits*, with an overlay of *response* (0 = no response to the promotion). It appears that records at the upper end of the distribution have lower response rates. To make the interpretation of overlay results more clearly, we turn to a normalized histogram, where each bin has the same height, shown in Figure 7.12.

Figure 7.12 makes it clear that the rate of response to the marketing promotion decreases as the lifetime average time between visits increases. This makes sense, since customers who visit the store more rarely will presumably be less likely to respond to the promotion. For the remaining variables from Table 7.4, we examine

TABLE 7.4 Variables with the Largest Absolute Correlation with the Target Variable, *Response*

Variable	Correlation Coefficient	Relationship
z ln lifetime ave time between visits	−0.431	Negative
z ln purchase visits	0.399	Positive
z ln # individual items purchased	0.368	Positive
z ln total net sales	0.336	Positive
z ln promotions responded in last year	0.333	Positive
z ln # different product classes	0.329	Positive
z ln # coupons used	0.322	Positive
z ln days between purchases	−0.321	Negative

the normalized histogram only, to save space. However, the analyst should not depend on the normalized histograms alone, since these do not display information about the differing densities in the distribution.

Figure 7.13 shows the normalized histograms for the following variables, *z ln purchase visits*, *z ln # individual items purchased*, *z ln total net sales*, and *z ln # different product classes*. All of the relationships show that as the variable increases,

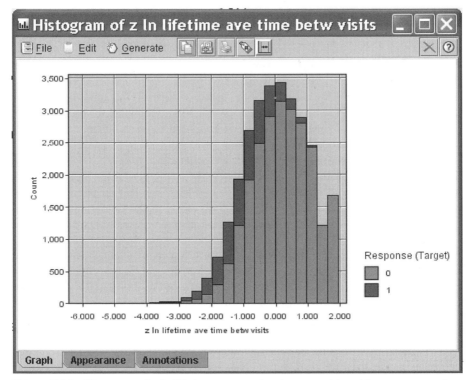

Figure 7.11 Histogram of *z ln lifetime average time between visits* with *response* overlay: may be difficult to interpret.

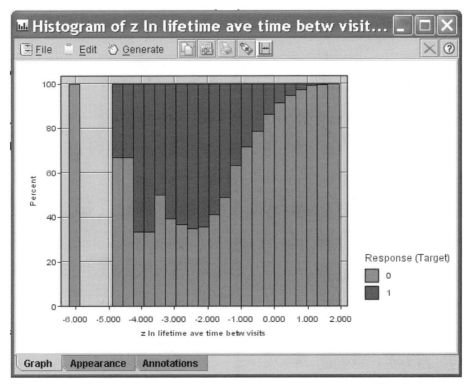

Figure 7.12 Normalized histogram of *z ln lifetime average time between visits* with *response* overlay: easier to discern a pattern.

the response rate increases as well. This is not surprising, since we might anticipate that customers who shop at our stores often, purchase many different items, spend a lot of money, and buy a lot of different types of clothes might be interested in responding to our marketing promotion.

Figure 7.14 shows the relationships between the response variable and the remaining three variables from Table 7.4, *z sqrt responded* (number of promotions responded to in the past year), *z sqrt # coupons used*, and *z ln days between purchases*. We see that the response rate increases as the number of promotions responded to increases, just as it does as the number of coupons used increases. However, the response rate decreases as the number of days between purchases increases. We might expect that the eight variables from Table 7.4 will turn out, in one form or another, to be among the best predictors of promotion response. This is investigated further in the modeling phase.

Next consider Figure 7.15, which shows the normalized version of Figure 7.7, the histogram of *sqrt percentage spent on blouses*, this time with an overlay of the *response* variable. Note from Figure 7.15 that apart from those who spend nothing on blouses (the leftmost bin), as the percentage spent on blouses increases, the response rate *decreases*. This behavior is not restricted to blouses, and is prevalent among all the clothing percentage variables (not shown). What this seems to indicate is that

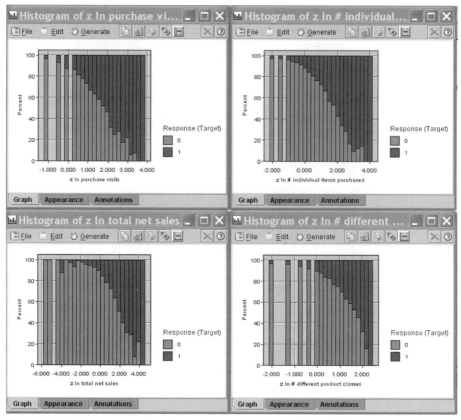

Figure 7.13   The response rate increases as the *z ln number of purchase visits, z ln number of individual items purchased, z ln total net sales*, and *z ln number of different product classes* increase.

customers who concentrate on a particular type of clothing, buying only one or two types of clothing (e.g., blouses), tend to have a lower response rate.

The raw data file contains a variable that measures product uniformity, and based on the behavior observed in Figure 7.15, we would expect the relationship between product uniformity and response to be negative. This is indeed the case, as shown by the normalized histogram in Figure 7.16. The highest response rate is shown by the customers with the lowest uniformity, that is, the highest diversity of purchasing habits, in other words, customers who purchase many different types of clothing.

Next, we turn to an examination of the relationship between the response and the many flag variables in the data set. Figure 7.17 provides a directed web graph of the relationship between the response (upper right) and the following indicator variables (counterclockwise from the response): credit card holder, spending months 4, 5, and 6, spending months 2 and 3, spending last one month, spending same period last year, returns, response rate, markdown, Web buyer, and valid phone number on file. Web graphs are exploratory tools for determining which categorical variables may be of interest for further study.

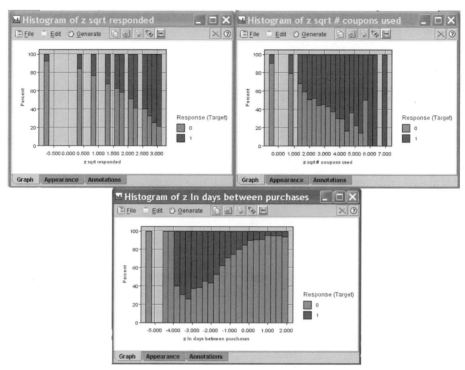

Figure 7.14 The response rate is positively related to the *z sqrt number of promotions responded to*, and the *z sqrt number of coupons used*, but negatively related to the *z ln number of days between purchases*.

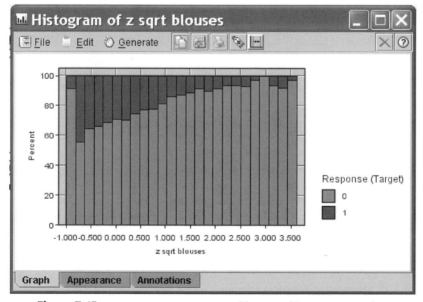

Figure 7.15 *z sqrt percentage spent on blouses*, with *response* overlay.

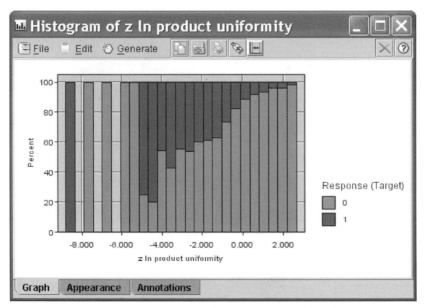

Figure 7.16 As customers concentrate on only one type of clothing, the response rate goes down.

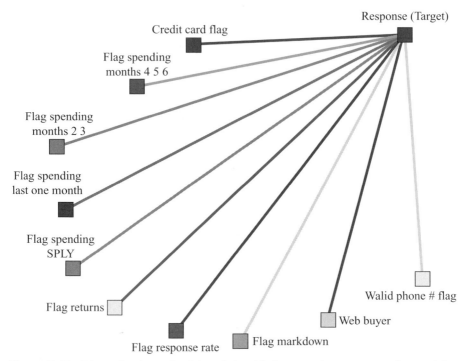

Figure 7.17 Directed web graph of the relationship between the *response* and several flag variables.

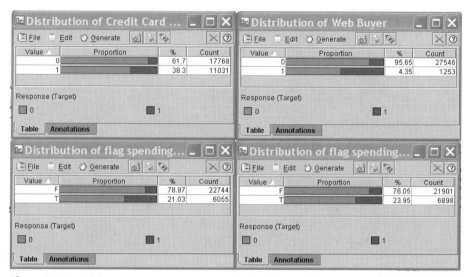

Figure 7.18   Higher response rates are associated with web buyers, credit card holders, customers who made a purchase within the past month (lower left), and customers who made a purchase in the same period last year (lower right).

In this graph, only the true values for the various flags are indicated. The darkness and solidity of the line connecting the flag variable with the response is a measure of the association of that variable with the response. In particular, these connections represent percentages of the *true* predictor flag values associated with the *true* value of the response. Therefore, more solid connections represent a greater association with responding to the promotion. Among the most solid connections in Figure 7.17 are the following: (1) Web buyer, (2) credit card holder, (3) spending last one month, and (4) spending same period last year. We therefore examine the normalized distribution of each of these indicator variables, with the *response* overlay, as shown in Figure 7.18. The counts (and percentages) shown in Figure 7.18 indicate the frequencies (and relative frequencies) of the predictor flag values and do not represent the proportions shown graphically. To examine these proportions, we turn to the set of results matrices (confusion matrices) in Figure 7.19.

Consider the highlighted cells in Figure 7.19, which indicate the proportions of customers who have responded to the promotion, conditioned on their flag values. Credit card holders are about three times as likely as non-credit card holders (28.066% versus 9.376%) to respond to the promotion. Web buyers (those who have made purchases via the company's Web shopping option) are also nearly three times as likely to respond compared to those who have not made a purchase via the Web (44.852% versus 15.247%). Customers who have made a purchase in the last month are nearly three times as likely to respond to the promotion (33.642% versus 11.981%). Finally, those who made a purchase in the same period last year are twice as likely to respond than those who did not make a purchase during the same period last year (27.312% versus 13.141%). We would therefore expect these flag variables to play some nontrivial role in the model-building phase downstream.

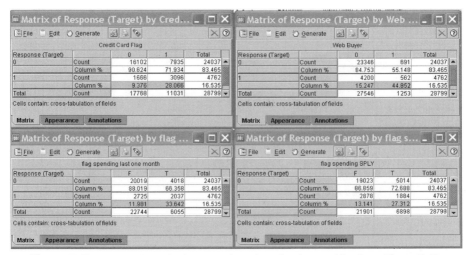

Figure 7.19 The statistics in these matrices describe the graphics from Figure 7.18.

Recall Figure 7.3, which showed the 20 most common Microvision lifestyle clusters. What is the relationship between these clusters and the probability of responding to the direct mail marketing promotion? Figure 7.20 shows the normalized distribution of the clusters, with response overlay. Somewhat surprisingly, there do not appear to be any substantial differences in response among the clusters. We return to this result later during the modeling phase.

Investigating the Correlation Structure Among the Predictors

Recall that depending on the objective of our analysis, we should be aware of the dangers of multicollinearity among the predictor variables. We therefore investigate the pairwise correlation coefficients among the predictors and note those correlations that are the strongest. Table 7.5 contains a listing of the pairwise correlations that are the strongest in absolute value among the predictors.

Figure 7.21 shows a scatter plot of *z ln total net sales* versus *z ln number of items purchased*, with a *response* overlay. The strong positive correlation is evident in that as the number of items purchased increases, the total net sales tends to increase.

TABLE 7.5 Strongest Absolute Pairwise Correlations Among the Predictors

Predictor	Predictor	Correlation
z ln purchase visits	*z ln # different product classes*	0.804
z ln purchase visits	*z ln # individual items purchased*	0.860
z ln # promotions on file	*z ln # promotions mailed in last year*	0.890
z ln total net sales	*z ln # different product classes*	0.859
z ln total net sales	*z ln # individual items purchased*	0.907
z ln days between purchase	*z ln lifetime ave time between visits*	0.847
z ln # different product classes	*z ln # individual Items purchased*	0.930

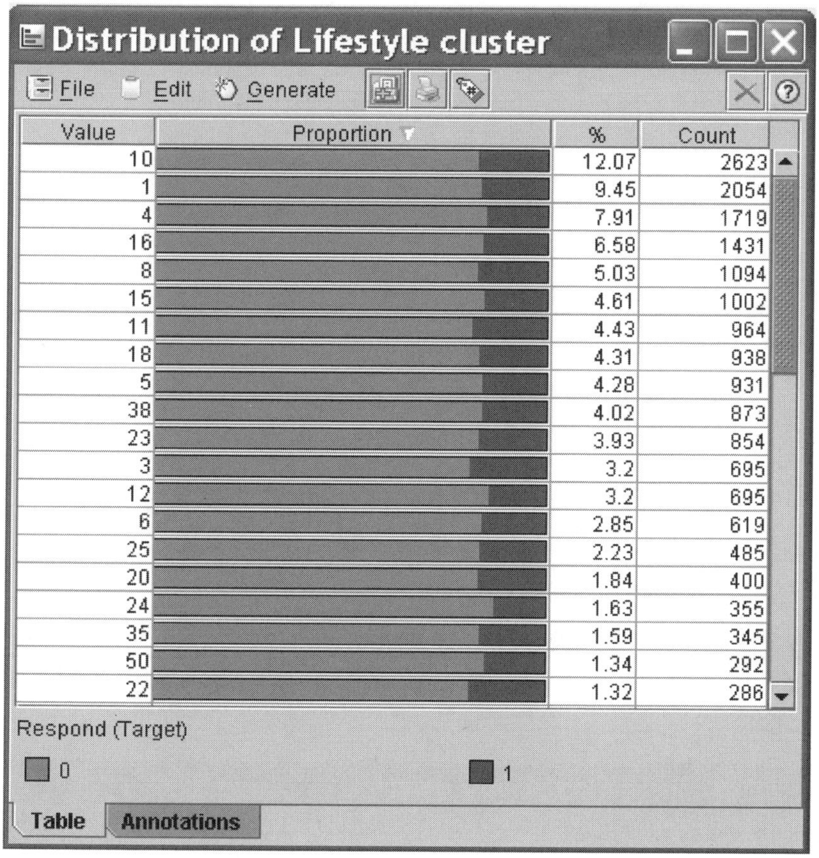

Value	Proportion	%	Count
10		12.07	2623
1		9.45	2054
4		7.91	1719
16		6.58	1431
8		5.03	1094
15		4.61	1002
11		4.43	964
18		4.31	938
5		4.28	931
38		4.02	873
23		3.93	854
3		3.2	695
12		3.2	695
6		2.85	619
25		2.23	485
20		1.84	400
24		1.63	355
35		1.59	345
50		1.34	292
22		1.32	286

Figure 7.20 There are no substantial differences in promotion response among the 20 most prevalent microvision lifestyle cluster types.

Of course, such a relationship makes sense, since purchasing more items would presumably tend to result in spending more money. Also, at the high end of both variables (the upper right), responders tend to outnumber nonresponders, while at the lower end (the lower left), the opposite is true.

For an example of a negative relationship, we may turn to Figure 7.22, the scatter plot of *z gross margin percentage* versus *z markdown*, with *response* overlay. The correlation between these variables is −0.772, so they did not make the list in Table 7.5. In the scatter plot, it is clear that as markdown increases, the gross margin percentage tends to decrease. Note that the markdown variable seems to have a floor, presumably associated with customers who never buy anything on sale. The relationship with response is less clear in this scatter plot than in Figure 7.21.

A convenient method for examining the relationship between categorical variables and *response* is a cross-tabulation, using a function of the response instead of raw cell counts. For example, suppose that we are interested in the relationship between response to the promotion and two types of customers: those who have purchased sweaters and those who have made a purchase within the last month. Figure 7.23

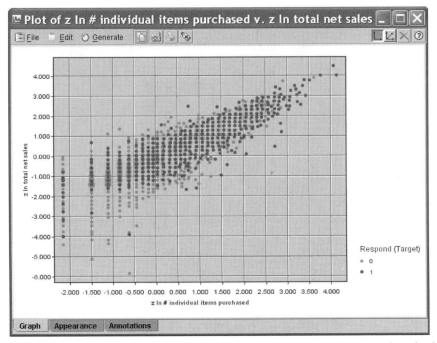

Figure 7.21 Scatter plot of *z ln total net sales* versus *z ln number of items purchased*, with *response* overlay.

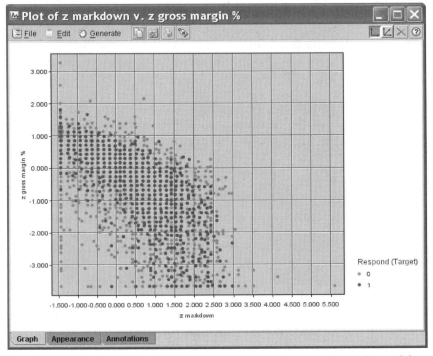

Figure 7.22 Negative relationship between *z gross margin percentage* and *z markdown*.

Figure 7.23   Cross-tabulation of spending within the last month versus sweater purchase, with cell values representing promotion response percentages.

contains such a cross-tabulation, with the cells representing the mean value of the target variable (response). Since the target represents a dichotomous variable, the means therefore represent proportions.

Thus, in the cross-tabulation, we see that customers who have neither bought sweaters nor made a purchase in the last month have only a 0.06 probability of responding to the direct-mail marketing promotion. On the other hand, customers who have both bought a sweater and made a purchase in the last month have a 0.357 probability of responding positively to the promotion. If a customer has a true flag value for exactly one of the two predictors, the *spending last one month* variable is slightly more indicative of promotion response than is the sweaters variable (0.194 versus 0.146 probability, respectively).

MODELING AND EVALUATION PHASES

Of course, exploratory data analysis is fun and can provide many useful insights. However, it is time now to move on to the formal modeling stage so that we may bring to bear on our promotion response problem the suite of data mining classification algorithms. An outline of our modeling strategy is as follows:

- Partition the data set into a training data set and a test data set.
- Provide a listing of the inputs to all models.
- Apply principal components analysis to address multicollinearity.
- Apply cluster analysis and briefly profile the resulting clusters.
- Balance the training data set to provide the algorithms with similar numbers of records for responders and nonresponders.
- Establish the baseline model performance in terms of expected profit per customer contacted, in order to calibrate the performance of candidate models.

- Apply the following classification algorithms to the training data set:
  - Classification and regression trees (CARTs)
  - C5.0 decision tree algorithm
  - Neural networks
  - Logistic regression
- Evaluate each of these models using the test data set.
- Apply misclassification costs in line with the cost–benefit table defined in the business understanding phase.
- Apply overbalancing as a surrogate for misclassification costs, and find the most efficacious overbalance mixture.
- Combine the predictions from the four classification models using model voting.
- Compare the performance of models that use principal components with models that do not use the components, and discuss the role of each type of model.

Because our strategy calls for applying many models that need to be evaluated and compared, we hence move fluidly back and forth between the modeling phase and the evaluation phase. First we partition the data set into a training data set and a test data set. Figure 7.24 shows one method of accomplishing this using Clementine 8.5. A new variable is defined, *training test*, which is distributed uniformly between zero and 1. The rectangle attached to the node indicates that the *data cache* has been set; this is necessary so that the same records will be assigned to each partition every time the process is run.

The data miner decides the proportional size of the training and test sets, with typical sizes ranging from 50% training/50% test, to 90% training/10% test. In this case study we choose a partition of approximately 75% training and 25% test. In Clementine this may be done by selecting those records whose *training test* value is at most 0.75 and outputting those records to a file, in this case called Case Study 1 Training Data Set. Similarly, the remaining records are output to the Case Study 1 Test Data Set.

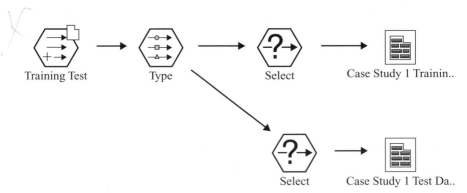

Figure 7.24 Partitioning the data set into a training data set and a test data set.

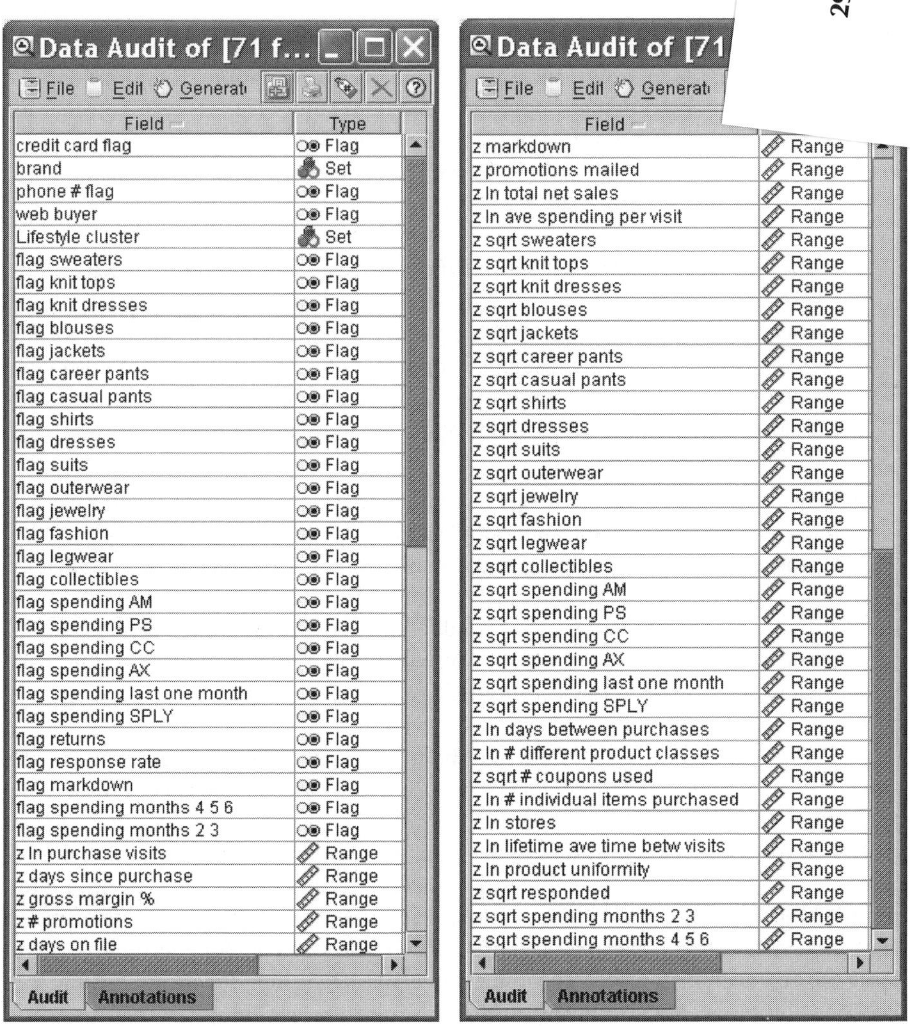

Figure 7.25 Input variables for classification models.

The analyst should always provide the client or end user with a comprehensive listing of the inputs to the models. These inputs should include derived variables, transformed variables, or raw variables, as well as principal components and cluster membership, where appropriate. Figure 7.25 contains a list of all the variables input to the classification models analyzed in this case study.

Note that all of the numeric (range) variables have been both transformed and standardized, that many flag variables have been derived, and that only two nonflag categorical variables remain, *brand*, and *lifestyle cluster*. In fact, only a handful of variables remain untouched by the data preparation phase, including the flag variables *Web buyer* and *credit card holder*. Later, when the principal components and clusters are developed, we shall indicate for which models these are to be used for input.

rincipal Components Analysis

Recall Table 7.5, which listed the strongest pairwise correlations found among the predictors. Bear in mind that strongly correlated predictors lead to multicollinearity, as discussed earlier. *Depending on the primary objective of the business or research problem*, the researcher may decide to substitute the principal components for a particular collection of correlated predictors.

- If the primary objective of the business or research problem pertains *solely* to estimation, prediction, or classification of the target variable, with no interest whatsoever in the characteristics of the predictors (e.g., customer profiling), substitution of the principal components for the collection of correlated predictors is not strictly required. As noted in Chapter 3, multicollinearity does not significantly affect point or interval estimates of the target variable.

- However, if the primary (or secondary) objective of the analysis is to assess or interpret the effect of the individual predictors on the response or to develop a profile of likely responders based on their predictor characteristics, substitution of the principal components for the collection of correlated predictors is strongly recommended. Although it does not degrade prediction accuracy, multicollinearity nevertheless plays havoc with the individual predictor coefficients, such as those used in linear or logistic regression.

Therefore, part of our strategy will be to report two types of best models, one (containing no principal components) for use solely in target prediction, and the other (containing principal components) for all other purposes, including customer profiling. We thus proceed to derive the principal components for the collection of correlated variables listed in Table 7.5 using the training data set. The minimum communality was 0.739, indicating that all seven variables share a healthy portion of the common variability. Varimax rotation is used, and two components are extracted, using the eigenvalue criterion. The eigenvalues for these components are 3.9 and 2.2. These two components account for a solid 87% of the variability among the seven variables in Table 7.5. The component loadings are given in Table 7.6. Here follow brief profiles of these components.

- *Principal component 1: purchasing habits.* This component consists of the most important customer general purchasing habits. Included here are the total number of items purchased, the number of different types of clothing purchased, the number of different times that customers came to the store to purchase something, and the total amount of money spent by the customer. All of these variables are positively correlated to each other. Conversely, the variable lifetime average time between visits is also included in this component, but it is negatively correlated to the others, since longer times between visits would presumably be negatively correlated with the other purchasing habits. We would expect that this component would be strongly indicative of response to the direct mail marketing promotion.

TABLE 7.6 Component Loadings for the Two Principal Components Extracted from the Training Data Set[a]

	Component	
	1	2
z ln # individual items purchased	0.915	
z ln # different product classes	0.887	
z ln purchase visits	0.858	
z ln lifetime ave time between visits	−0.858	
z ln total net sales	0.833	
z promotions mailed		0.944
z # promotions		0.932

[a] Extaction method: principal component analysis; rotation method: varimax with Kaiser normalization. Rotation converged in three iterations.

- *Principal component 2: promotion contacts.* This component consists solely of two variables, the number of promotions mailed in the past year, and the total number of marketing promotions on file. Note that there is no information in this component about the response of the customer to these promotion contacts. Thus, it is unclear whether this component will be associated with response to the promotion.

As mentioned in Chapter 1, the principal components extracted from the training data set should be validated by comparison with principal components extracted from the test data set. Table 7.7 contains the component loadings for the principal components extracted from the seven correlated variables in Table 7.5, this time using the test data set. Once again, two components are extracted using the eigenvalue criterion and varimax rotation. The eigenvalues for these components are again 3.9 and 2.2. This time, 87.2% of the variability is explained, compared to 87% earlier. A comparison of Tables 7.6 and 7.7 shows that the component loadings, although not identical, are nevertheless sufficiently similar to confirm that the extracted components are valid.

TABLE 7.7 Component Loadings for the Two Principal Components Extracted from the Test Data Set[a]

	Component	
	1	2
z ln # individual items purchased	0.908	
z ln # different product classes	0.878	
z ln lifetime ave time betw visits	−0.867	
z ln purchase visits	0.858	
z ln total net sales	0.828	
z promotions mailed		0.942
z # promotions		0.928

[a] Extaction method: principal component analysis; rotation method: varimax with Kaiser normalization. Rotation converged in three iterations.

̣is: BIRCH Clustering Algorithm

ister analysis. In *Discovering Knowledge in Data: An Introduction* ₀ ₁₂₁ we demonstrated hierarchical clustering, k-means clustering, and ...υnen clustering. For this case study, however, we shall apply the BIRCH clustering algorithm [5]. The BIRCH algorithm requires only one pass through the data set and therefore represents a scalable solution for very large data sets. The algorithm contains two main steps and hence is termed *two-step clustering* in Clementine. In the first step, the algorithm preclusters the records into a large number of small subclusters by constructing a cluster feature tree. In the second step, the algorithm then combines these subclusters into higher-level clusters, which represent the algorithm's clustering solution.

One benefit of Clementine's implementation of the algorithm is that unlike k-means and Kohonen clustering, the analyst need not prespecify the desired number of clusters. Thus, two-step clustering represents a desirable exploratory tool. For this case study, two-step clustering was applied with no prespecified desired number of clusters. The algorithm returned $k= 3$ clusters. The two main advantages of clustering are (1) exploratory cluster profiling, and (2) the use of the clusters as inputs to downstream classification models.

Figure 7.26 provides an excerpt from Clementine's cluster viewer. Across the top are the clusters, ordered by number of records per cluster, so that cluster 2 (8183 records) comes first, followed by cluster 3 (7891 records) and cluster 1 (5666 records). Down the left side are found variable names, in this case all of which are flags. In each row are found bar charts for that particular variable for each cluster. Since all the variables in Figure 7.26 are flags, the first bar in each bar chart represents 0 (false) and the second bar represents 1 (true).

Note that the bars representing 1 (i.e., a true value for the flag) for cluster 3 are consistently higher than those for clusters 1 or 2. In other words, for every variable listed in Figure 7.26, the proportion of true flag values for cluster 3 is greater than that for the other two clusters. For example, the proportion of customers in cluster 3 who spent money at the AX store is larger than the proportions for the other clusters, and similarly for the other variables in Figure 7.26.

Continuing our exploration of these clusters, Table 7.8 contains the mean values, by cluster, for a select group of numeric variables. Table 7.9 displays the proportion of true flag values, by cluster, for a select group of flag variables. Armed with the information in Figure 7.26, Tables 7.8 and 7.9, and similar information, we now proceed to construct profiles of each cluster.

- *Cluster 1: moderate-spending career shoppers*
  - ○ This cluster has the highest proportion of customers who have ever bought a suit.
  - ○ The proportion who have ever bought career pants is six times higher than cluster 2.
  - ○ The total net sales for this cluster is moderate, lying not far from the overall mean.

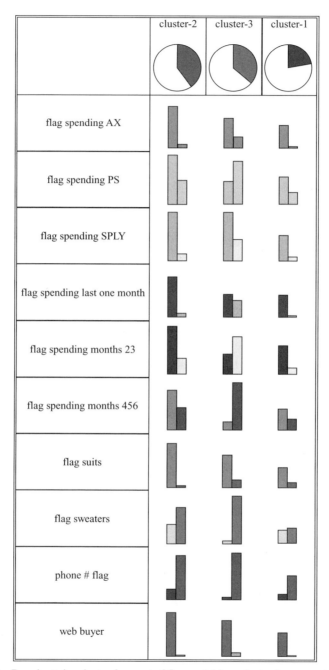

Figure 7.26   Bar charts by cluster for a set of flag variables: cluster 3 appears to be the most promising cluster.

TABLE 7.8 Mean Values by Cluster for a Select Group of Numeric Variables

	Cluster 1	Cluster 2	Cluster 3
z ln Purchase Visits	−0.575	−0.570	1.011
z ln Total Net Sales	−0.177	−0.804	0.971
z sqrt Spending Last One Month	−0.279	−0.314	0.523
z ln Lifetime Average Time Between Visits	0.455	0.484	−0.835
z ln Product Uniformity	0.493	0.447	−0.834
z sqrt # Promotion Responses in Past Year	−0.480	−0.573	0.950
z sqrt Spending on Sweaters	−0.486	0.261	0.116

  ○ Product uniformity is high, meaning that these shoppers tend to focus on particular types of clothing.
  ○ The overall shopping habits, however, do not indicate that these are the most loyal customers, since purchase visits and spending last month are low, whereas the time between visits is high. Also, this cluster has not tended to respond to promotions in the past year.

- *Cluster 2: low-spending casual shoppers*

  ○ This cluster has the lowest total net sales, with a mean nearly one standard deviation below the overall average.
  ○ Compared to cluster 1 (career clothes shoppers), this cluster tends to shop for more casual wear, having more than double the proportion of casual pants purchases and the highest overall amount spent on sweaters.
  ○ This cluster is not interested in suits, with only 0.1% ever had bought one.
  ○ This cluster is similar to cluster 1 in some respects, such as the low numbers of purchase visits, the low spending in the past month, the high product uniformity, the high time between visits, and the low response rate to past promotions.

- *Cluster 3: frequent, high-spending, responsive shoppers*

  ○ The mean purchase visits and the mean total net sales are each about one standard deviation above the overall average, meaning that this cluster represents frequent shoppers who tend to spend a lot.

TABLE 7.9 Proportion of True Values by Cluster for a Select Group of Flag Variables (%)

	Cluster 1	Cluster 2	Cluster 3
Credit card	27.6	16.7	68.6
Web buyer	1.9	1.2	8.9
Ever bought marked-down merchandise	77.6	81.7	99.8
Ever bought career pants	63.7	9.9	70.7
Ever responded to a promotion	26.2	19.4	88.2
Ever bought a suit	18.7	0.1	18.1
Ever bought casual pants	15.9	34.5	70.5

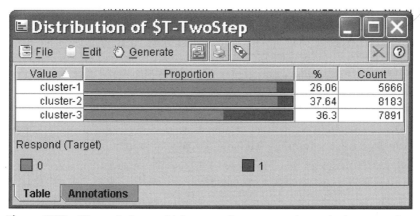

Figure 7.27   Cluster 3 shows a higher rate of response to the marketing promotion.

- ○ These shoppers have low product uniformity, meaning that they are not focusing on any particular type of clothing. For example, they buy both career pants and casual pants in about the same proportions.
- ○ These shoppers are responsive, since nearly 90% of them have responded to a marketing promotion in the past year.
- ○ A majority of these shoppers have a credit card on file, as opposed to the other two clusters.
- ○ This cluster buys online at a rate four times higher than either of the other clusters.

Based on the cluster profiles above, which cluster would you expect to be most responsive to the present direct mail marketing promotion? Clearly, we would expect cluster 3 to have a higher promotion response rate. Figure 7.27 shows the distribution of the clusters with a response overlay; indeed, cluster 3 is the most responsive. Figure 7.28 contains the cross-tabulation of cluster and target response.

Matrix of Respond (Target) by $T-TwoStep ...

File   Edit   Generate

$T-TwoStep 50%

Respond (Target)		cluster-1	cluster-2	cluster-3	Total
0	Count	5235	7605	5289	18129
	Column %	92.393	92.937	67.026	83.390
1	Count	431	578	2602	3611
	Column %	7.607	7.063	32.974	16.610
Total	Count	5666	8183	7891	21740
	Column %	100	100	100	100

Cells contain: cross-tabulation of fields

Matrix   Appearance   Annotations

Figure 7.28   Cross-tabulation of cluster (two-step) and response.

Note that the proportion of positive responders to the direct mail marketing promotion is more than four times larger for cluster 3 (32.974%) than for the other clusters (7.607% and 7.063%). Based on this result, we shall include cluster membership as an input to the downstream classification models, and we will not be surprised if cluster membership turns out to play some role in helping to classify potential responders correctly.

The classification models discussed below will contain the following inputs:

- *Model collection A* (includes principal components analysis: models appropriate for customer profiling, variable analysis, or prediction)
  - The 71 variables listed in Figure 7.25, *minus* the seven variables from Table 7.6 used to construct the principal components
  - The two principal components constructed using the variables in Table 7.6
  - The clusters uncovered by the BIRCH two-step algorithm
- *Model collection B* (PCA not included): models to be used for target prediction only)
  - The 71 variables listed in Figure 7.25
  - The clusters uncovered by the BIRCH two-step algorithm.

Balancing the Training Data Set

For classification models in which one of the target variable classes has much lower relative frequency than the other classes, balancing is recommended. For example, suppose that we are running a fraud classification model and our training data set consists of 100,000 transactions, only 1000 of which are fraudulent. Then our classification model could simply predict "nonfraudulent" for all transactions and achieve 99% classification accuracy. However, clearly this model is useless.

Instead, the analyst should balance the training data set so that the relative frequency of fraudulent transactions is increased. It is not recommended that current fraudulent records be cloned to achieve this balance, since this amounts to fabricating data. Rather, a sufficient number of nonfraudulent transactions should be set aside, thereby increasing the proportion of fraudulent transactions. For example, suppose that we wanted our 1000 fraudulent records to represent 25% of the balanced training data set rather than the 1% represented by these records in the raw training data set. That would mean that we could retain only 3000 nonfraudulent records. We would then need to discard from the analysis 96,000 of the 99,000 nonfraudulent records, using random selection. Of course, one always balks at discarding data, but in the data mining world, data are abundant. Also, in most practical applications, the imbalance is not as severe as this 99-to-1 fraud example, so that relatively fewer records need be omitted.

Another benefit of balancing the data is to provide the classification algorithms with a rich balance of records for each classification outcome, so that the algorithms have a chance to learn about all types of records, not just those with high target frequency. In our case study, the training data set contains 18,129 (83.4%) customers who have not responded to the direct mail marketing promotion and 3611 (16.6%)

customers who have responded. Although it is possible to proceed directly with the classification algorithms with this degree of imbalance, it is nevertheless recommended that balancing be applied so that the minority class contain at least 25% of the records, and perhaps at most 50%, depending on the specific problem.

In our case study, we apply balancing to achieve an approximate 50%–50% distribution for the response/nonresponse classes. To do this, we set the Clementine balance node to retain approximately 20% of the nonresponse records, randomly selected. The resulting balance is as follows: 3686 (50.5%) nonresponse records, and all of the 3611 response records (49.5%).

The test data set should never be balanced. The test data set represents new data that the models have not yet seen. Certainly, the real world will not balance tomorrow's data for our classification models; therefore, the test data set itself should not be balanced. Note that all model evaluation will take place using the test data set, so that the evaluative measures will all be applied to unbalanced (real-world-like) data. In other words, tables showing comparative measures of candidate models are obtained using the data found in the test set.

Establishing the Baseline Model Performance

How will we know when our models are performing well? Is 80% classification accuracy good enough? 90%? 95%? To be able to calibrate the performance of our candidate models, we need to establish benchmarks against which these models can be compared. These benchmarks often come in the form of baseline model performance for some simple models. Two of these simple models are (1) the "don't send a marketing promotion to anyone" model, and (2) the "send a marketing promotion to everyone" model.

Clearly, the company does not need to employ data miners to use either of these two models. Therefore, if after arduous analysis, the performance of the models reported by the data miner is lower than the performance of either of the baseline models above, the data miner better try again. In other words, the models reported by the data miner absolutely need to outperform these baseline models, hopefully by a margin large enough to justify the project.

Recall Table 7.2, the cost/benefit decision table for this case study. Applying those costs and benefits to these two baseline models, we obtain for the test data set (5908 negative responses and 1151 positive responses) the performance measures shown in Table 7.10. Which of these two baseline models performs better? A comparison of the overall error rates would lead one to prefer the "send to everyone" model. However, as we discussed earlier, data mining models need to take into account real-world considerations such as costs and benefits, so that traditional model performance measures such as false positive rate, false negative rate, and overall error rate are deemphasized. Instead, we deal directly with the bottom line: What effect would the deployment of this model have on the profitability of the company?

Here, the "don't send to anyone" model is costing the company an estimated $4.63 per customer in lost profits. Of the customers in this data set, 16.3% would have responded positively to the direct mail marketing promotion had they only been given the chance. Therefore, this model must be considered a complete failure and shall

TABLE 7.10 Performance Measures for Two Baseline Models

Model	TN Cost $0	TP Cost −$26.4	FN Cost $28.40	FP Cost $2.00	Overall Error Rate	Overall Cost
Don't send to anyone	5908	0	1151	0	16.3%	$32,688.40 ($4.63 per customer)
Send to everyone	0	1151	0	5908	83.7%	−$18,570.40 (−$2.63 per customer)

no longer be discussed. On the other hand, the "send to everyone" model is actually making money for the company, to the tune of an estimated $2.63 per customer. This "per customer" statistic embraces all customers in the test data set, including nonresponders. The 83.7% error rate is initially shocking until we take into account the low cost of the type of error involved. Therefore, it is this "send to everyone" model that we shall define as our baseline model, and the profit of $2.63 per customer is defined as the benchmark profit that any candidate model should outperform.

Model Collection A: Using the Principal Components

We begin modeling by applying our four main classification model algorithms to the data set using the principal components, and using 50%–50% balancing for the target field *response*. The results are provided in Table 7.11. Note that the percentages indicated in the FN and FP columns represent the false negative rate and the false positive rate, respectively. That is, FP percentage = FP/FP + TP and FN percentage = FN/FN + TN. The logistic regression model outperforms the other three, with a mean estimated profit of $1.68 per customer. However, clearly this is a moot point since none of these models come close to the minimum benchmark of $2.63 profit per customer established by the "send to everyone" model.

TABLE 7.11 Performance Results from Classification Models Using 50%–50% Balancing and Principal Components

Model	TN Cost $0	TP Cost −$26.40	FN Cost $28.40	FP Cost $2.00	Overall Error Rate	Overall Cost per Customer
Neural network	4694	672	479 9.3%	1214 64.4%	24.0%	−$0.24
CART	4348	829	322 6.9%	1560 65.3%	26.7%	−$1.36
C5.0	4465	782	369 7.6%	1443 64.9%	25.7%	−$1.03
Logistic regression	4293	872	279 6.1%	1615 64.9%	26.8%	−$1.68

Why are these models performing so poorly? The answer is that we have not applied misclassification costs. To develop candidate models that we will evaluate using a strictly defined cost–benefit matrix, we should seek to embed these costs within the models themselves. In Clementine 8.5, two classification algorithms are equipped with explicit mechanisms for defining asymmetric misclassification costs: C5.0 and CART. Therefore, our next step is to develop decision tree models using misclassification costs in C5.0 and CART. We proceed to define the cost of making a false negative decision to be 28.4 and the cost of making a false positive decision to be 2.0; there is no mechanism for defining the benefit of a true positive to be 26.4, so it is left as 1.0. It should be noted that using these values to define the misclassification costs is equivalent to setting the false negative cost to 14.2 and the false positive cost to 1.0.

Unfortunately, the application of these costs resulted in both the CART model and the C5.0 model classifying all customers as responders (not shown) (i.e., similar to the "send to everyone" model). Evidently, the combination of 50% balancing with these strong misclassification costs made it too expensive for either model to predict negatively. Therefore, the misclassification costs were reduced from the 14.2–1.0 ratio down to a 10.0–1.0 ratio, with the false negative cost equal to 10 and the false positive cost equal to 1. Again, this is equivalent to a false negative cost of 20 and a false positive cost of 2. The resulting performance measures are provided in Table 7.12. Suddenly, with the application of misclassification costs at the model-building stage, the overall profit per customer has jumped by more than a dollar. Both the CART model and the C5.0 model have now outperformed the baseline "send to everyone" model.

Let's take a closer look at these models. Figure 7.29 shows the results from the C5.0 model in Table 7.12. Note the highlighted node. For the 447 records in this node, only 20.8% of them are responders. Yet, as indicated by the "**1**" to the right of the arrow, the model is predicting that the customers in this node are responders. Why is this happening? Because the high false negative misclassification cost makes the model very wary of making negative predictions. This phenomenon helps to illustrate why the C5.0 model with 14.2–1 misclassification costs returned not a single negative prediction.

Also note from Figure 7.29 the dominant role played by the first principal component, *purchasing habits* (Table 7.6), denoted as $F\text{-}PCA\text{-}1$ in the decision tree.

TABLE 7.12 Performance Results from CART and C5.0 Classification Models Using 10–1 Misclassification Costs

Model	TN Cost $0	TP Cost −$26.40	FN Cost $28.40	FP Cost $2.00	Overall Error Rate	Overall Cost per Customer
CART	754	1147	4 0.5%	5154 81.8%	73.1%	−$2.81
C5.0	858	1143	8 0.9%	5050 81.5%	71.7%	−$2.81

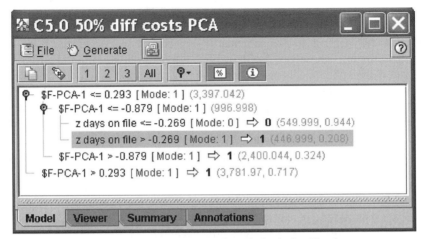

Figure 7.29   C5.0 decision tree using 10–1 misclassification costs.

This first principal component represents both the root node split and the secondary split, indicating that this component is easily the most important factor for predicting response.

We were able to apply misclassification costs for the CART and C5.0 models. But what about the algorithms that don't come with built-in misclassification cost options?

Overbalancing as a Surrogate for Misclassification Costs

Table 7.12 did not contain either a neural network model or a logistic regression model, since Clementine does not have an explicit method for applying misclassification costs for these algorithms. Nevertheless, there is an alternative method for achieving decision effects similar to those provided by the misclassification costs. This alternative method is *overbalancing*.

Table 7.13 contains the performance results for a series of neural network models run, using no principal components, for various levels of balancing. For the first model there is no balancing; for the second model the target variable is balanced 50%–50%; for the third model the target variable is overbalanced, about 65% responders and 35% nonresponders; for the fourth model the target variable is overbalanced, about 80% responders and 20% nonresponders; and for the fifth model the target variable is overbalanced, about 90% responders and 10% nonresponders. Note that the three models that have been overbalanced each outperform the baseline "send to everyone" model, even though none of these models applied misclassification costs directly. Thus, overbalancing, properly applied, may be used as a surrogate for misclassification costs.

The optimal performance by the neural network was obtained using the 80%–20% overbalancing ratio. Let's compare this performance against the other three algorithms using the same ratio. Table 7.14 shows the performance results for all four algorithms, using the 80%–20% overbalancing ratio.

TABLE 7.13   Performance Results from Neural Network Models for Various Levels of Balancing and Overbalancing

Model	TN Cost $0	TP Cost -$26.40	FN Cost $28.40	FP Cost $2.00	Overall Error Rate	Overall Cost per Customer
No balancing	5865	124	1027	43	15.2%	+$3.68
16.3%-83.7%			14.9%	25.7%		
Balancing	4694	672	479	1214	24.0%	-$0.24
50%-50%			9.3%	64.4%		
Overbalancing	1918	1092	59	3990	57.4%	-$2.72
65%-35%			3.0%	78.5%		
80%-20%	1032	1129	22	4876	69.4%	-$2.75
			2.1%	81.2%		
90%-10%	592	1141	10	5316	75.4%	-$2.72
			1.7%	82.3%		

The logistic regression model is the top performer in this group, though all four models outperform the baseline "send to everyone" model. A perusal of the output from the logistic regression model (not shown) shows that the logistic regression model deals with the inclusion of *lifestyle cluster* in the model by using 49 different indicator variables (representing the 50 different values for this single variable). This may be considered overparameterization of the model. If the field was of strong influence on the target response, we might consider keeping the field in the model, probably in binned form. However, because the different lifestyle clusters do not appear to be strongly associated with response or nonresponse, we should consider omitting the variable from the analysis. Retaining the variable to this point has led to an overparameterization of the neural network model; that is, the model has too many nodes for the amount of information represented by the variable. Therefore, we omit the variable and rerun the analysis from Table 7.13, with the results given in Table 7.15.

TABLE 7.14   Performance Results from the Four Algorithms Using the 80%-20% Overbalancing Ratio

Model	TN Cost $0	TP Cost -$26.40	FN Cost $28.40	FP Cost $2.00	Overall Error Rate	Overall Cost per Customer
Neural network	1032	1129	22	4876	69.4%	-$2.75
			2.1%	81.2%		
CART	1724	1111	40	4184	59.8%	-$2.81
			2.3%	79.0%		
C5.0	1195	1127	24	4713	67.1%	-$2.78
			2.0%	80.7%		
Logistic regression	2399	1098	53	3509	50.5%	-$2.90
			2.2%	76.2%		

TABLE 7.15 Performance Results from the Four Algorithms Using the 80%–20% Overbalancing Ratio After Omitting *Lifestyle Cluster*

Model	TN Cost $0	TP Cost −$26.40	FN Cost $28.40	FP Cost $2.00	Overall Error Rate	Overall Cost per Customer
Neural network	885	1132	19 2.1%	5023 81.6%	71.4%	−$2.73
CART	1724	1111	40 2.3%	4184 79.0%	59.8%	−$2.81
C5.0	1467	1116	35 2.3%	4441 79.9%	63.4%	−$2.77
Logistic regression	2389	1106	45 1.8%	3519 76.1%	50.5%	−$2.96

Note that the decision to discard the variable is made here in the modeling phase rather than the EDA phase. We should not discard variables in the EDA (data understanding) phase due simply to lack of apparent pairwise relationship with the response. One never knows what relationships exist in higher dimensions, and we should allow the models to decide which models should and should not be retained, as we have done here.

The exclusion of *lifestyle cluster* has improved the performance of the logistic regression model from $2.90 to an estimated $2.96 profit per customer. This $0.06 represents an improvement of 18% over the model that retained the variable, compared to the baseline model. Therefore, in this case, "less is more." On the other hand, the CART model is completely unaffected by the exclusion of *lifestyle cluster*, since the variable did not make it into the model to begin with. The performance of both the C5.0 model and the neural network model degraded slightly with the exclusion of the variable.

However, our best model so far remains the logistic regression model using 80%–20% balancing, no principal components, and excluding the *lifestyle cluster* field. Note that without the application of overbalancing as a surrogate for misclassification costs, we would not have had access to a helpful logistic regression model. This model provides an estimated profit per customer of $2.96, which represents a solid improvement of 45% over the models that applied misclassification costs ($2.81) directly as compared to the baseline benchmark of $2.63 [i.e., ($2.96 − $2.81)/($2.96 − $2.63) = 45%].

Combining Models: Voting

In Olympic figure skating, the champion skater is not decided by a single judge alone but by a panel of judges. The preferences of the individual judges are aggregated using some combination function, which then decides the winner. Data analysts may also be interested in combining classification models, so that the strengths and weaknesses of each model are smoothed out through combination with the other models.

One method of combining models is to use simple voting. For each record, each model supplies a prediction of either response (1) or nonresponse (0). We may then count the votes that each record obtains. For example, we are presently applying four classification algorithms to the promotion response problem. Hence, records may receive from 0 votes up to 4 votes predicting response. In this case, therefore, at the overall level, we may predict a positive response to the promotion based on any one of the following four criteria:

A. Mail a promotion only if all four models predict response.

B. Mail a promotion only if three or four models predict response.

C. Mail a promotion only if at least two models predict response.

D. Mail a promotion if any model predicts response.

Clearly, criterion A would tend to protect against false positives, since all four classification algorithms would have to agree on a positive prediction according to this criterion. Similarly, criterion D would tend to protect against false negatives, since only a single algorithm would need to predict a positive response. Each of these four criteria in effect defines a combination model whose performance may be evaluated, just as for any other model. Hence, Table 7.16 contains the performance results for each of these four combination models. The best combination model is the model defined by criterion B: *Mail a promotion only if three or four models predict response.* This criterion has an intuitive alternative representation: *Mail a promotion only if a majority of the models predict response.*

One disadvantage of using combination models is their lack of easy inter-pretability. We cannot simply point to a decision rule or p-value to explain why or

TABLE 7.16   Performance Results from Four Methods of Counting the Votes Using the 80%–20% Overbalancing Ratio After Omitting *Lifestyle Cluster*

Combination Model	TN Cost $0	TP Cost −$26.40	FN Cost $28.40	FP Cost $2.00	Overall Error Rate	Overall Cost per Customer
Mail a promotion only if all four models predict response	2772	1067	84 2.9%	3136 74.6%	45.6%	−$2.76
Mail a promotion only if three or four models predict response	1936	1115	36 1.8%	3972 78.1%	56.8%	−$2.90
Mail a promotion only if at least two models predict response	1207	1135	16 1.3%	4701 80.6%	66.8%	−$2.85
Mail a promotion if any model predicts response	550	1148	3 0.5%	5358 82.4%	75.9%	−$2.76

TABLE 7.17 Most Important Variables/Components and Their *p*-Values

Variable or Component	*p*-Value
Principal component 1: purchasing habits	0.000
Principal component 2: promotion contacts	0.000
z days on file	0.000
z ln average spending per visit	0.000
z ln days between purchases	0.000
z ln product uniformity	0.000
z sqrt spending CC	0.000
Web buyer flag	0.000
z sqrt knit dresses	0.001
z sqrt sweaters	0.001
z in stores	0.003
z sqrt career pants	0.004
z sqrt spending PS	0.005

why not a particular customer received a promotion. Recall that the most easily interpreted classification models are the decision trees, such as those produced by the CART or C5.0 algorithms. In our case, however, our best model was produced by logistic regression, which, for interpretability, lies midway between the decision trees and neural networks. Let us therefore take a closer look at this logistic regression model. Table 7.17 contains a list of the most important variables and components reported by the logistic regression model along with their *p*-values.

Much more modeling work could be done here; after all, most models are usually considered works in progress and few models are ever considered complete. Thus, in the interests of brevity, we move on to the other class of models that awaits us: the non-PCA models.

Model Collection B: Non-PCA Models

Finally, we examine the models that do not include the principal components. Instead, these models retain the set of correlated variables shown in Table 7.5, and thus should not be used for any purpose except prediction of the target variable, promotion response. On the other hand, since the set of correlated variables is highly predictive of the response, we would expect the non-PCA models to outperform the PCA models in terms of response prediction.

Our strategy in this section will mirror our work with the PCA models, with one special addition:

1. Apply CART and C5.0 models, using misclassification costs and 50% balancing.
2. Apply all four classification algorithms, using 80% overbalancing.
3. Combine the four classification algorithms, using voting.
4. Combine the four classification algorithms, using the *mean response probabilities.*

TABLE 7.18 Performance Results from CART and C5.0 Classification Models Using 14.2–1 Misclassification Costs

Model	TN Cost $0	TP Cost −$26.40	FN Cost $28.40	FP Cost $2.00	Overall Error Rate	Overall Cost per Customer
CART	1645	1140	11 0.7%	4263 78.9%	60.5%	−$3.01
C5.0	1562	1147	4 0.3%	4346 79.1%	61.6%	−$3.04

We begin by applying the decision trees algorithms, CART and C5.0, using 14.2–1 misclassification costs, and 50%–50% balancing. The results are provided in Table 7.18. Note that both models have already outperformed the best of the PCA models, with an estimated profit per customer of $3.04 and $3.01, compared to $2.96 for the logistic regression PCA model. Suppose, however, that we wished to enrich our pool of algorithms to include those without built-in misclassification costs. Then we can apply overbalancing as a surrogate for misclassification costs, just as we did for the PCA models. Table 7.19 contains the performance results from all four algorithms, using 80% overbalancing.

Note the wide disparity in model performance. Here, C5.0 is the winner, with a solid estimated profit of $3.15, representing the best overall prediction performance by a single model in this case study. The logistic regression model is not far behind, at $3.12. The neural network model, however, performs relatively poorly, at only $2.78. (It should be noted here that all neural network models run in this case study used Clementine's default settings and the *quick* option. Perhaps the neural network performance could be enhanced by tweaking the many settings and options available.)

Next, we combine the four models, first through the use of voting. Table 7.20 provides the performance metrics from the four methods of counting the votes,

TABLE 7.19 Performance Results from the Four Algorithms Using the 80%–20% Overbalancing Ratio

Model	TN Cost $0	TP Cost −$26.40	FN Cost $28.40	FP Cost $2.00	Overall Error Rate	Overall Cost per Customer
Neural network	1301	1123	28 2.1%	4607 80.4%	65.7%	−$2.78
CART	2780	1100	51 1.8%	3128 74.0%	45.0%	−$3.02
C5.0	2640	1121	30 1.1%	3268 74.5%	46.7%	−$3.15
Logistic regression	2853	1110	41 1.4%	3055 73.3%	43.9%	−$3.12

TABLE 7.20 Performance Results from Four Methods of Counting the Votes Using the 80%–20% Overbalancing Ratio for Non-PCA Models

Combination Model	TN Cost $0	TP Cost −$26.40	FN Cost $28.40	FP Cost $2.00	Overall Error Rate	Overall Cost per Customer
Mail a promotion only if all four models predict response	3307	1065	86 2.5%	2601 70.9%	38.1%	−$2.90
Mail a promotion only if three or four models predict response	2835	1111	40 1.4%	3073 73.4%	44.1%	−$3.12
Mail a promotion only if at least two models predict response	2357	1133	18 0.7%	3551 75.8%	50.6%	−$3.16
Mail a promotion if any model predicts response	1075	1145	6 0.6%	4833 80.8%	68.6%	−$2.89

where once again we use 80% overbalancing. The results from the combined models may be a bit surprising, since one combination method, mailing a promotion only if at least two models predict response, has outperformed all of the individual classification models, with a mean overall profit per customer of about $3.16. This represents the *synergy* of the combination model approach, where the combination of the models is in a sense greater than the sum of its parts. Here, the greatest profit is obtained when at least two models agree on sending a promotion to a potential recipient. The voting method of combining models has provided us with better results than we could have obtained from any of the individual models.

Combining Models Using the Mean Response Probabilities

Voting is not the only method for combining model results. The voting method represents, for each model, an up-or-down, black-and-white decision without regard for measuring the confidence in the decision. It would be nice if we could somehow combine the confidences that each model reports for its decisions, since such a method would allow finer tuning of the decision space.

Fortunately, such confidence measures are available in Clementine, with a bit of derivation. For each model's results Clementine reports not only the decision, but also a continuous field that is related to the confidence of the algorithm in its decision. When we use this continuous field, we derive a new variable that measures for each record the probability that this particular customer will respond positively to

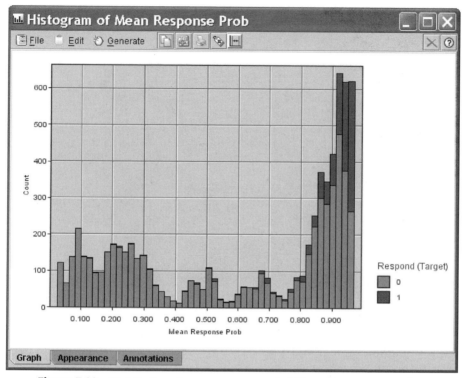

Figure 7.30 Distribution of *mean response probability*, with *response* overlay.

the promotion. This derivation is as follows:

If prediction = positive, then response probability = 0.5 + (confidence reported)/2
If prediction = negative, then response probability = 0.5 − (confidence reported)/2

For each model, the model response probabilities (MRPs) were calculated using this formula. Then the mean MRP was found by dividing the sum of the MRPs by 4. Figure 7.30 contains a histogram of the MRP with a promotion response overlay.

The multimodality of the distribution of MRP is due to the discontinuity of the transformation used in its derivation. To increase the contrast between responders and nonresponders, it is helpful to produce a normalized histogram with increased granularity, to enable finer tuning, obtained by increasing the number of bins. This normalized histogram is shown in Figure 7.31.

Next, based on this normalized histogram, the analyst may define bands that partition the data set according to various values of MRP. Recalling that the false negative error is 14.2 times worse than the false positive error, we should tend to set these partitions on the low side, so that fewer false negative decisions are made. For example, based on a perusal of Figure 7.31, we might be tempted to partition the records according to the criterion: MRP < 0.85 versus MRP ≥ 0.85, since it is near that value that the proportion of positive respondents begins to increase rapidly.

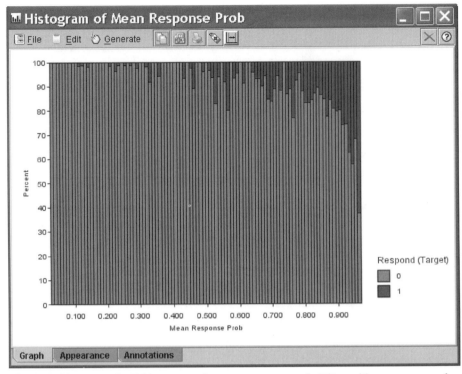

Figure 7.31 Normalized histogram of *mean response probability*, with *response* overlay showing finer granularity.

However, as shown in Table 7.21, the model based on such a partition is suboptimal since it allows so many false positives. As it turns out, the optimal partition is at or near 50% probability. In other words, suppose that we mail a promotion to a prospective customer under the following conditions:

- *Continuous combination model.* Mail a promotion only if the mean response probability reported by the four algorithms is at least 51%.

In other words, this continuous combination model will mail a promotion only if the mean probability of response reported by the four classification models is greater than half. This turns then out to be the optimal model uncovered by any of our methods in this case study, with an estimated profit per customer of $3.1744 (the extra decimal points help to discriminate small differences among the leading candidate models). Table 7.21 contains the performance metrics obtained by models defined by candidate partitions for various values of MRP. Note the minute differences in overall cost among several different candidate partitions. To avoid overfitting, the analyst may decide not to set in stone the winning partition value, but to retain the two or three leading candidates.

Thus, the continuous combination model defined on the partition at MRP = 0.51 is our overall best model for predicting response to the direct mail marketing

TABLE 7.21 Performance Metrics for Models Defined by Partitions for Various Values of MRP

Combination Model		TN Cost $0	TP Cost −$26.40	FN Cost $28.40	FP Cost $2.00	Overall Error Rate	Overall Cost per Customer
Partition :	MRP < 0.95 MRP ≥ 0.95	5648	353	798	260	15.0%	+$1.96
				12.4%	42.4%		
Partition :	MRP < 0.85 MRP ≥ 0.85	3810	994	157	2098	31.9%	−$2.49
				4.0%	67.8%		
Partition :	MRP < 0.65 MRP ≥ 0.65	2995	1104	47	2913	41.9%	−$3.11
				1.5%	72.5%		
Partition :	MRP < 0.54 MRP ≥ 0.54	2796	1113	38	3112	44.6%	−$3.13
				1.3%	73.7%		
Partition :	MRP < 0.52 MRP ≥ 0.52	2738	1121	30	3170	45.3%	−$3.1736
				1.1%	73.9%		
Partition :	MRP < 0.51 MRP ≥ 0.51	2686	1123	28	3222	46.0%	−$3.1744
				1.0%	74.2%		
Partition :	MRP < 0.50 MRP ≥ 0.50	2625	1125	26	3283	46.9%	−$3.1726
				1.0%	74.5%		
Partition :	MRP < 0.46 MRP ≥ 0.46	2493	1129	22	3415	48.7%	−$3.166
				0.9%	75.2%		
Partition :	MRP < 0.42 MRP ≥ 0.42	2369	1133	18	3539	50.4%	−$3.162
				0.8%	75.7%		

promotion. This model provides an estimated $3.1744 in profit to the company for every promotion mailed out. This is compared with the baseline performance, from the "send to everyone" model, of $2.63 per mailing. Thus, our model enhances the profitability of this direct mail marketing campaign by 20.7%, or 54.44 cents per customer. For example, if a mailing was to be made to 100,000 customers, the estimated increase in profits is $54,440. This increase in profits is due to the decrease in costs associated with mailing promotions to nonresponsive customers.

To illustrate, consider Figure 7.32, which presents a graph of the profits obtained by using the C5.0 model alone (not in combination). The darker line indicates the profits from the C5.0 model, after the records have been sorted, so that the most likely responders are first. The lighter line indicates the best possible model, which has perfect knowledge of who is and who isn't a responder. Note that the lighter line rises linearly to its maximum near the 16th percentile, since about 16% of the test data set records are positive responders; it then falls away linearly but more slowly as the costs of the remaining nonresponding 84% of the data set are incurred.

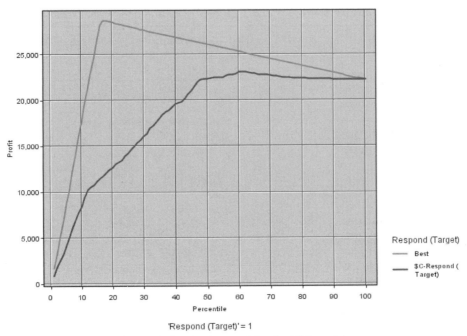

'Respond (Target)' = 1

Figure 7.32 Profits graph for the C5.0 model.

On the other hand, the C5.0 model profit curve reaches a plateau near the 50th percentile. That is, the profit curve is, in general, no higher at the 99th percentile than it is near the 50th percentile. *This phenomenon illustrates the futility of the "send to everyone" model, since the same level of profits can be obtained by contacting merely half the prospective customers as would be obtained by contacting them all.*

Since the profit graph is based on the records sorted as to likelihood of response, it is in a sense therefore related to the continuous combination model above, which also sorted the records by likelihood of response according to each of the four models. Note that there is a "change point" near the 50th percentile in both the profit graph and the continuous combination model.

SUMMARY

The case study in this chapter, Modeling Response to Direct Mail Marketing, was carried out using the Cross-Industry Standard Process for Data Mining (CRISP–DM). This process consists of six phases: (1) the business understanding phase, (2) the data understanding phase, (3) the data preparation phase, (4) the modeling phase, (5) the evaluation phase, and (6) the deployment phase.

In this case study, our task was to predict which customers were most likely to respond to a direct mail marketing promotion. The *clothing-store* data set [3], located at the book series Web site, represents actual data provided by a clothing store chain in New England. Data were collected on 51 fields for 28,799 customers. The objective of the classification model was to increase profits. A cost/benefit decision table was constructed, with false negatives penalized much more than false positives.

Most of the numeric fields were right-skewed and required a transformation to achieve normality or symmetry. After transformation, these numeric fields were standardized. Flag variables were derived for many of the clothing purchase variables. To flesh out the data set, new variables were derived based on other variables already in the data set.

EDA indicated that response to the marketing campaign was associated positively with the following variables, among others: *z ln purchase visits*, *z ln number of individual items purchase*, *z ln total net sales*, and *z ln promotions responded to in the last year*. *Response* was negatively correlated with *z ln lifetime average time between visits*. An interesting phenomenon uncovered at the EDA stage was the following: As customers concentrate on only one type of clothing purchase, the response rate goes down.

Strong pairwise associations were found among several predictors, with the strongest correlation between *z ln number of different product classes* and *z ln number of individual items purchased*.

The modeling and evaluation phases were combined and implemented using the following strategy:

- Partition the data set into a training data set and a test data set.
- Provide a listing of the inputs to all models.
- Apply principal components analysis to address multicollinearity.
- Apply cluster analysis and briefly profile the resulting clusters.
- Balance the training data set to provide the algorithms with similar numbers of records for responders and nonresponders.
- Establish the baseline model performance in terms of expected profit per customer contacted, in order to calibrate the performance of candidate models.
- Apply the following classification algorithms to the training data set:
  - Classification and regression trees (CARTs)
  - C5.0 decision tree algorithm
  - Neural networks
  - Logistic regression
- Evaluate each of these models using the test data set.
- Apply misclassification costs in line with the cost/benefit table defined in the business understanding phase.
- Apply overbalancing as a surrogate for misclassification costs, and find the most efficacious overbalance mixture.
- Combine the predictions from the four classification models using model voting.
- Compare the performance of models that use principal components with models that do not use the components, and discuss the role of each type of model.

Part of our strategy was to report two types of best models, one (containing no principal components) for use solely in target prediction, and the other (containing principal components) for all other purposes, including customer profiling. The subset of variables that were highly correlated with each other were shunted to a principal components analysis, which extracted two components from these seven correlated variables. *Principal component 1* represented purchasing habits and was expected to be highly indicative of promotion response.

Next, the BIRCH clustering algorithm was applied. Three clusters were uncovered: (1) moderate-spending career shoppers, (2) low-spending casual shoppers, and (3) frequent, high-spending, responsive shoppers. Cluster 3, as expected, had the highest promotion response rate.

Thus, the classification models contained the following inputs:

- *Model collection A* (included principal components analysis: models appropriate for customer profiling, variable analysis, or prediction

  ○ The 71 variables listed in Figure 7.25, *minus* the seven variables from Table 7.6 used to construct the principal components

  ○ The two principal components constructed using the variables in Table 7.6

  ○ The clusters uncovered by the BIRCH two-step algorithm

- *Model collection B* (PCA not included): models to be used for target prediction only

  ○ The 71 variables listed in Figure 7.25

  ○ The clusters uncovered by the BIRCH two-step algorithm

To be able to calibrate the performance of our candidate models, we established benchmark performance using two simple models:

- The "don't send a marketing promotion to anyone" model
- The "send a marketing promotion to everyone" model

Instead of using the overall error rate as the measure of model performance, the models were evaluated using the measure of overall cost derived from the cost–benefit decision table. The baseline overall cost for the "send a marketing promotion to everyone" model worked out to be –$2.63 per customer (i.e., negative cost = profit).

We began with the PCA models. Using 50% balancing and no misclassification costs, none of our classification models were able to outperform this baseline model. However, after applying 10–1 misclassification costs (available in Clementine only for the CART and C5.0 algorithms), both the CART and C5.0 algorithms outperformed the baseline model, with a mean cost of –$2.81 per customer. The most important predictor for these models was *principal component 1*, purchasing habits.

Overbalancing as a surrogate for misclassification costs was developed for those algorithms without the misclassification cost option. It was demonstrated that as the training data set becomes more overbalanced (fewer negative response records retained), the model performance improves, up to a certain point, when it again begins to degrade.

For this data set, the 80%–20% overbalancing ratio seemed optimal. The best classification model using this method was the logistic regression model, with a mean cost of –$2.90 per customer. This increased to –$2.96 per customer when the overparametrized variable *lifestyle cluster* was omitted.

Model voting was investigated. The best combination model mailed a promotion only if at least three of the four classification algorithms predicted positive response. However, the mean cost per customer for this combination model was only –$2.90 per customer. Thus, for the models including the principal components, the best model was the logistic regression model with 80%–20% overbalancing and a mean cost of –$2.96 per customer.

The best predictors using this model turned out to be the two principal components, purchasing habits and promotion contacts, along with the following variables: *z days on file*, *z ln average spending per visit*, *z ln days between purchases*, *z ln product uniformity*, *z sqrt spending CC*, *Web buyer*, *z sqrt knit dresses*, and *z sqrt sweaters*.

Next came the non-PCA models, which should be used for prediction of the response only, not for profiling. Because the original (correlated) variables are retained in the model, we expect the non-PCA models to outperform the PCA models with respect to overall cost per customer. This was immediately borne out in the results for the CART and C5.0 models using 50% balancing and 14.2–1 misclassification costs, which had mean costs per customer of –$3.01 and –$3.04, respectively. For the 80%–20% overbalancing ratio, C5.0 was the best model, with an overall mean cost of –$3.15 per customer, with logistic regression second with –$3.12 per customer.

Again, model combination using voting was applied. The best voting model mailed a promotion only if at least two models predicted positive response, for an overall mean cost of –$3.16 per customer. A second, continuous method for combining models was to work with the response probabilities reported by the software. The mean response probabilities were calculated, and partitions were assigned to optimize model performance. It was determined that the same level of profits obtained by the "send to everyone" model could also be obtained by contacting merely half of the prospective customers, as identified by this combination model.

As it turns out the optimal partition is at or near 50% probability. In other words, suppose that we mailed a promotion to a prospective customer under the following conditions: Mail a promotion only if the mean response probability reported by the four algorithms is at least 51%. In other words, this continuous combination model will mail a promotion only if the mean probability of response reported by the four classification models is greater than half. This turned out to be the optimal model uncovered by any of our methods in this case study, with an estimated profit per customer of $3.1744.

Compared with the baseline performance, from the "send to everyone" model, of $2.63 per mailing, this model enhances the profitability of this direct mail marketing campaign by 20.7%, or 54.44 cents per customer. For example, if a mailing was to be made to 100,000 customers, the estimated increase in profits is $54,440. This increase in profits is due to the decrease in costs associated with mailing promotions to nonresponsive customers.

REFERENCES

1. Peter Chapman, Julian Clinton, Randy Kerber, Thomas Khabaza, Thomas Reinart, Colin Shearer, and Rudiger Wirth, *CRISP-DM Step-by-Step Data Mining Guide*, http://www.crisp-dm.org/, 2000.
2. Daniel Larose, *Discovering Knowledge in Data: An Introduction to Data Mining*, Wiley, Hoboken, NJ, 2005.
3. Clothing store data set, compiled by Daniel Larose, 2005. Available at the book series Web site.
4. Claritas Demographics ®, http://www.tetrad.com/pcensus/usa/claritas.html.
5. Tian Zhang, Raghu Ramakrishnan, and Miron Livny, BIRCH: an effiecient data clustering method for very large databases, presented at Sigmod' 96, Montreal, Canada, 1996.

INDEX